TURNER TO CEZANNE

Essays by Colin B. Bailey, Paul Greenhalgh, and Oliver Fairclough
Catalogue entries by Bryony Dawkes and Bethany McIntyre
American Federation of Arts in association with Hudson Hills Press

CEZANNE

TURNER TO

Masterpieces from the Davies Collection
National Museum Wales

Oliver Fairclough and Bryony Dawkes

Gwendoline and Margaret Dav

progressive British collectors c
outstanding group of Impressi
paintings at a time when mode
ignored in Britain by both indiv

This catalogue is published in conjunction with *Turner to Cézanne: Masterpieces from the Davies Collection, National Museum Wales*, an exhibition organized by the American Federation of Arts and National Museum Wales.

The American Federation of Arts is a nonprofit institution that organizes art exhibitions for presentation in museums around the world, publishes exhibition catalogues, and develops education programs.

Guest Curator Oliver Fairclough
Publications Manager Michaelyn Mitchell
Managing Curator Lisa Small
Designer Studio Blue
Editor Stephanie Salomon

Note to the reader: Please note that not all works will be presented at all venues.

Front cover Joseph Mallord William Turner, *Morning after the Wreck*, ca. 1840 (cat. no. 51)
Back cover Paul Cézanne, *The François Zola Dam*, ca. 1877–78 (cat. no. 7)

Published in 2009 by the American Federation of Arts in association with Hudson Hills Press.
10 9 8 7 6 5 4 3 2 1

American Federation of Arts
305 East 47th Street, 10th Floor
New York, NY 10017
www.afaweb.org

Hudson Hills Press
3556 Main Street
Manchester, Vermont 05254
www.hudsonhills.com

Library of Congress
Cataloging-in-Publication Data

Fairclough, Oliver.
Turner to Cézanne : masterpieces from the Davies collection, National Museum Wales/by Oliver Fairclough and Bryony Dawkes; essays by Colin Bailey, Paul Greenhalgh, and Oliver Fairclough ; catalogue entries by Bryony Dawkes and Bethany McIntyre.
p. cm.
Catalog of an exhibition held at the Columbia Museum of Art, S.C. and four other institutions between Mar. 6, 2009 and Aug. 8, 2010.
Includes bibliographical references and index.

ISBN 978-1-885444-37-0 (pbk. : alk. paper) – ISBN 978-1-55595-299-0 (hardcover : alk. paper) 1. Painting, European – 19th century – Exhibitions. 2. Painting, European – 20th century – Exhibitions. 3. Davies, Gwendoline Elizabeth, ca. 1882–1951 – Art collections – Exhibitions. 4. Davies, Margaret Sidney, 1884–1963 – Art collections – Exhibitions. 5. Painting – Private collections – Wales –Cardiff – Exhibitions. 6. National Museum Wales – Exhibitions. I. Dawkes, Bryony. II. Bailey, Colin. III. Greenhalgh, Paul. IV. Columbia Museum of Art. V. Title.
ND457.F35 2009
759.94'074 – dc22
2008023408

were among the most
e day, assembling an
st and Post-Impressionist
French art was largely
als and institutions.

EXHIBITION ITINERARY

Columbia Museum of Art, South Carolina
March 6–June 7, 2009

Oklahoma City Museum of Art
June 25–September 20, 2009

Everson Museum of Art, Syracuse, New York
October 8, 2009–January 3, 2010

Corcoran Gallery of Art, Washington, D.C.
January 30–April 25, 2010

The Albuquerque Museum of Art & History
New Mexico
May 16–August 8, 2010

Printed in China

Contents

Foreword 8 Ackno
"The Great Joy of Collecting": M
Collection 12 Greenhalgh: Re
Art, Patronage, Optimism 22
Renoir's *La Parisienne* 30 Cat
Bibliography 170 Index 173

dgments 10 Fairclough:
ern French Art in the Davies
gnizing the Modern World:
iley: Looking Closely at
gue 38 Notes 162

Foreword

The gifts and bequests by Gwendoline and Margaret Davies have been fundamental to the character and identity of the National Museum of Wales. In 2007, Amgueddfa Cymru–National Museum Wales (the organization's modern name) marked its centenary. For the occasion, it celebrated the legacy of the Davies sisters through publications, a major exhibition, and events. *Turner to Cézanne: Masterpieces from the Davies Collection, National Museum Wales* builds on that celebration and offers a unique opportunity for audiences in the United States to appreciate the sisters' contribution to the cultural life of Wales.

Such was the level of care and insight that marked Gwendoline and Margaret's collecting that this exhibition is not simply the story of a collection. The sisters collected fine examples of works by the key figures in the development of French art and some of the British artists to whom the great figures of Impressionism were indebted. This exhibition can therefore act as a rich introduction to the evolution of modern art in Europe in the century from Turner to Cézanne.

One of the key findings of the new research undertaken for our 2007 exhibition *Industry to Impressionism* in Cardiff was a better understanding of the nature of the sisters' education in the visual arts. Previously, they had often been portrayed as immensely wealthy but rather sheltered young women who had responded to the promptings of an experienced art adviser. It is now evident that such a perception clouds a far more complex picture. The exhibition revealed the extent to which the sisters pursued their own inquiries into both historical and contemporary art. We now know they saw their task as combining civic duty with sharing the pleasure and reward they found in the arts and learning. Their outlook was to enable Wales, a country at the time without a cosmopolitan cultural center, to be connected to the wider European world.

Amgueddfa Cymru–National Museum Wales continues this ambition with its current project to expand and redesign its art galleries, which will be completed in 2012. They will, for the first time, tell a distinctive story of the visual arts in Wales set within an international context. Important works from before 1800 and after the mid-twentieth century will frame the Davies sisters' wonderful collections of nineteenth- and early twentieth-century art. Margaret Davies was particularly active in collecting British and Welsh contemporary art in the latter part of her life. Amgueddfa Cymru–National Museum Wales has continued to follow this example, creating the potential for vivid and distinctive displays of modern and contemporary art.

We hope this exhibition will give American audiences a fresh insight into the story of art from Turner to Cézanne. We also hope it will encourage those audiences to take a longer look at the richness of the arts in Wales and the many different dimensions of the arts in the United Kingdom that Amgueddfa Cymru–National Museum Wales is able to present.

Michael Houlihan Director General
Amgueddfa Cymru–National Museum Wales

Michael Tooby Director, Learning and Programs
Amgueddfa Cymru–National Museum Wales

Acknowledgments

In the early part of the twentieth century, two extraordinarily forward-thinking Welsh women, Gwendoline and Margaret Davies, amassed a collection of work by the most important names in the Realist, Naturalist, Impressionist, Aestheticist, Symbolist, Post-Impressionist, and Fauvist movements. The Davies sisters rank among the most important patrons in Europe at a key moment in the history of painting. Their remarkable collection was bequeathed to Amgueddfa Cymru–National Museum Wales, and we are delighted to have had the opportunity of collaborating with their staff on *Turner to Cézanne: Masterpieces from the Davies Collection, National Museum Wales.* This exhibition and the publication that accompanies it not only celebrate an outstanding collection but also effectively tell the story of European art from Turner to Cézanne.

The staff of the AFA deserves recognition for their wonderful work on behalf of the exhibition and publication. I wish to first recognize Lisa Small, Curator of Exhibitions, and Yvette Lee Crowley, former Curator of Exhibitions, for their contributions to the organization of this project. They had the invaluable help of Curatorial Assistants Theodore Walther and Brianne Jacobs. Michaelyn Mitchell, Director of Publications and Communications, coordinated all aspects of the production of this handsome and important catalogue, with the assistance of Amy Mazzariello, Publications/Communications Assistant, and Sarah Ingber, former Publications/Communications Coordinator. Kathleen Flynn, former Director of Exhibitions Department, provided invaluable oversight throughout the organization of the project. And Dottie Canady, Registrar, was responsible for preparing and touring the exhibition. I also want to acknowledge Suzanne Burke, Manager of Education; Cheryl Aldridge, Director of Development; and former staff members Susan Ross and Luis Croquer. Thomas Padon, former Deputy Director for Exhibitions and Programs, was instrumental in the development of the project and its early phases of organization.

At Amgueddfa Cymru–National Museum Wales, we wish to thank Oliver Fairclough, Keeper of Art at the museum and the guest curator of the exhibition; Bryony Dawkes, Curator of Partnership Projects, and Bethany McIntyre, Curator of Prints and Drawings, who wrote the entries; and Angela Gaffney, National Partnerships Manager, who managed the project with Michael Tooby, Director of Learning and Programs, who developed the exhibition idea with Thomas Padon. We also wish to thank Colin B. Bailey, Associate Director and Peter Jay Sharp Chief Curator, The Frick Collection; and Paul Greenhalgh, Director, Corcoran Gallery of Art, each of whom contributed essays to the publication.

We would like to acknowledge the superb work of Studio Blue in designing this catalogue, the careful editing that was done by Stephanie Salomon, and the support of our publishing partner, Hudson Hills Press.

Finally, we recognize the museums participating in the tour of this beautiful exhibition – the Columbia Museum of Art; the Oklahoma City Museum of Art; the Everson Museum of Art; the Corcoran Gallery of Art; and the Albuquerque Museum of Art & History. It has been a great pleasure to work with them, and we thank them for being such professional and enthusiastic partners.

Julia Brown Director, American Federation of Arts

This publication would have been impossible without the work on the Davies collection by past staff members at Amgueddfa Cymru–National Museum Wales: John Ingamells, former Director of the Wallace Collection, London; Peter Hughes; Mark Evans, Victoria and Albert Museum; and Ann Sumner, Director, Barber Institute of Fine Arts, University of Birmingham. The project also draws upon the research of many other scholars, notably Colin B. Bailey, Frances Fowle, John House, Madeleine Korn, Christopher Lloyd, Christopher Riopelle, and Anne Robbins. We are deeply grateful to Colin Bailey and Paul Greenhalgh who have contributed essays to this publication.

During 2006–07, when new research was conducted on Gwendoline and Margaret Davies for a major exhibition at Amgueddfa Cymru–National Museum Wales, many people were generous with time and information. First among these were the sisters' great-nephew, David, the present Lord Davies of Llandinam, and his wife Beryl. The sisters' niece Jean Cormack and their cousin Elizabeth Rowlands-Hughes shared personal memories of them. We are also grateful for information from Camilla Davies, Clive Edwards, Ottoline Mary Jones, Ian Parrott, Margaret Doreen Shieker, Thelma Watkin, and Gwyneth Williams. Robert Blayney, John Christopher, Jayne Davies, Mary Hackett, A.J. Heward Rees, Graham Richards, and Brian Taylor described their experience of the sisters and of their home, Gregynog. David Lewis was very generous with his own research on Gregynog. Thanks also go to Susan J. Davies; Lindsay Evans; Amanda Farr and her colleagues at Oriel Davies, Newtown; Andrew Green and his staff at Llyfrgell Genedlaethol Cymru–the National Library of Wales; Dorothy Harrop; Glyn Tegai Hughes, Susan Jones; Susan Morgan; Mary Oldham; Dafydd Rowlands-Hughes; Carolyn Stewart; and David Vickers. Professor Prys Morgan and Dr. Robert Meyrick also contributed essays to the publication, *Things of Beauty*, which accompanied that exhibition.

Oliver Fairclough, Keeper of Art, Amgueddfa Cymru–National Museum Wales, curated the present exhibition and contributed to this publication. The largest single contribution to the book, however, was made by Bryony Dawkes, Curator of Partnership Projects, who researched and wrote most of the catalogue entries. Others were compiled by Bethany McIntyre, Curator of Prints and Drawings. All three would like to acknowledge help from Louisa Briggs, Eveline Holsappel, David Jenkins, John Kenyon, Charlotte Topsfield, and Melanie Youngs. We are also grateful for the help provided by Rebecca Brumbill and Kevin Thomas from the Department of Photography.

At the museum, the exhibition management has been led by Angela Gaffney and Michael Tooby, and it has been coordinated by Tim Egan, Rebecca Ellison, Kate Lowry, Emily O'Reilly, and Clare Smith. The works have been prepared and packed by Keith Bowen, Hugh Chilcott, and Lee Jones.

Finally, our heartfelt thanks to friends at the American Federation of Arts who have, over a long gestation period, seen through this complex project: Cheryl Aldridge, Suzanne Burke, Dottie Canady, Luis Croquer, Yvette Lee Crowley, Kathleen Flynn, Sarah Ingber, Brianne Jacobs, Amy Mazzariello, Michaelyn Mitchell, Susan Ross, Lisa Small, and Theodore Walther.

Michael Houlihan Director General
Amgueddfa Cymru–National Museum Wales

Oliver Fairclough "The Great Joy of Collecting": Modern French Art in the Davies Collection

All the pictures in this exhibition were acquired by two sisters, Gwendoline Davies (1882–1951) and Margaret Davies (1884–1963), mostly between 1908 and 1922.[1] These are only part of a much larger collection of 260 works, which includes old master paintings, sculpture, and British twentieth-century pictures, later bequeathed to the National Museum of Wales in Cardiff.[2] Gwendoline (fig. 1) and Margaret Davies (fig. 2) were among the most progressive British collectors of the day, assembling an outstanding group of Impressionist and Post-Impressionist paintings[3] at a time when modern French art was largely ignored in Britain by both individuals and institutions.[4] The sisters never married, and both were earnest, shy, and ill at ease in society. In later life, when they devoted themselves to a bewildering range of good causes, they were sometimes seen as unworldly and rather sad figures. Their own journals and letters, especially those from the 1910s, when they were forming their collection, present a warmer picture of two young women who were both very ordinary and yet marked out by the extraordinary circumstances of their upbringing and great wealth.[5] These writings are quoted extensively in this essay. Two young, Sabbatarian, teetotal sisters from Montgomeryshire in rural Wales seem unlikely pioneers of modern art. Were their tastes therefore formed and their collecting driven by male dealers and advisers? Recent research suggests that, on the contrary, they had a quite sophisticated knowledge of both art history and modern European painting, that they were well traveled within Europe and beyond,[6] and that they had the determination and independence to make their own decisions. Commentators often have had little understanding of the milieu from which the sisters came – the Liberal Nonconformist, newly wealthy elite of Edwardian Wales. However, the political and social aspirations of this milieu influenced both the content and the purpose of their collection.[7]

At the age of twenty-five, Gwendoline and Margaret Davies each received a share of their family's fortune. They were by any standards extremely rich, and by 1913 they had spent over £110,000 on their art collection.[8] They owed their wealth to their millionaire grandfather, David Davies (1818–1890), the son of a poor tenant farmer, who worked his way up from the sawpits of his native Montgomeryshire to a seat in the House of Commons, making one of Victorian Britain's great industrial fortunes on his way from the deep mining of coal in the Rhondda Valley (fig. 3).[9] Davies stood out from other nouveau riche industrialists because of his Welshness and his devotion to Calvinistic Methodism, a fundamentalist branch of Nonconformism peculiar to Wales. From this, he drew a profound religious faith and a passionate belief in personal and social improvement through education.[10] Davies was the principal donor to the new University College of Wales at Aberystwyth, and a Liberal Party Member of Parliament from 1874 until 1886. As well as a great fortune, he bequeathed to his descendants a distinctive Welsh identity, a deep personal morality, and the beliefs that wealth is a sacred trust and that charity is an obligation before God.

Gwendoline and Margaret Davies were brought up with their brother, David (later first Lord Davies of Llandinam, 1880–1944), at Plas Dinam (fig. 4), a Victorian mansion in his native village bought

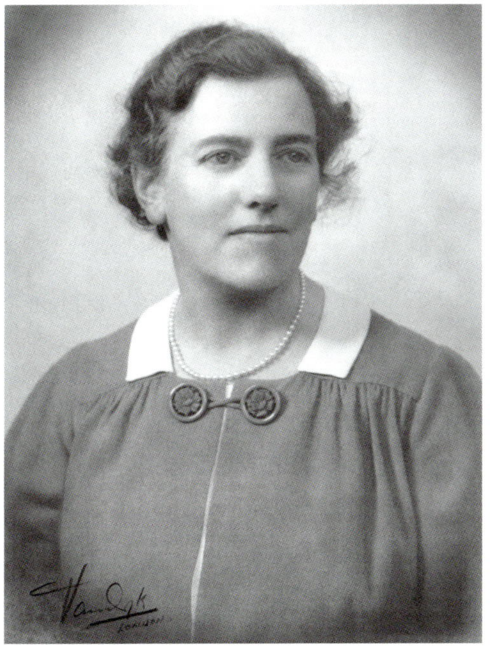

1

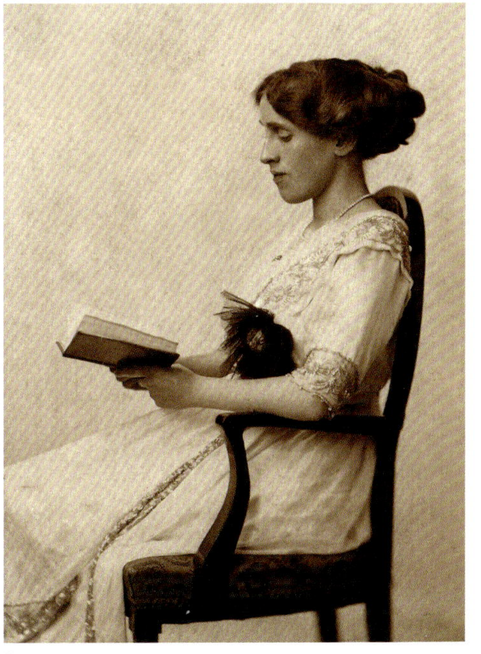

2

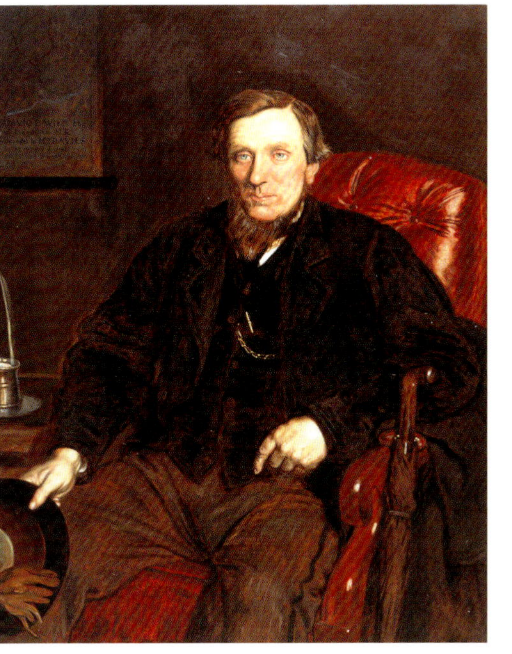

3

by their grandfather as a home for his only son. Their father, Edward Davies (1852–98), found responsibility for the family's massive industrial empire exhausting and died when he was only forty-five. He had married his first cousin, Mary Jones, who died in 1888, when their daughters (always known in the family as Gwen and Daisy) were just six and four years old. In 1892, he remarried, choosing his dead wife's younger sister.[11] Elizabeth (Mrs. Edward) Davies was a forceful and dominating stepmother until her death in 1942, but she was probably receptive to the sisters' interest in art, as she had bought a number of works herself, mostly minor, by Whistler, Burne-Jones, and others after her husband passed away.[12] The sisters were largely educated at Plas Dinam, though they briefly attended Highfield School, Hendon, near London.[13] A key figure in their lives was their governess, Jane Blaker (1869–1947), who arrived in 1895 and who remained in the family as their stepmother's companion after they were adults.[14] Her brother Hugh Blaker (fig. 5) was an artist (he had trained in Antwerp and Paris) and between 1905 and 1913 was curator of the Holburne Museum in Bath, later becoming an art dealer and critic.[15] He was also a passionate modernist and a friend and admirer of the Anglo-Irish dealer Sir Hugh Lane, who began his own collection of Impressionist paintings in 1905.[16] Blaker first met the sisters in 1908 and was soon buying for them at Christie's and introducing them to other London dealers. He is often seen as the sisters' Svengali. However, both were already interested in the visual arts and music. Margaret Davies had attended the Slade School of Fine Art in London.[17] She was a competent wood engraver, and she painted in oils throughout her life. Between

Figure 1 Gwendoline Davies (1882–1951), known as Gwen, the older, more determined and thoughtful sister and an accomplished musician. Private collection. Photograph Van Dyck, London, 1937

Figure 2 Margaret Davies (1884–1963), known as Daisy, the younger, more practical sister, was a painter and engraver. Private collection. Photograph ca. 1900

Figure 3 Ford Maddox Brown, *David Davies*, 1874. Oil on canvas, 44 ¾ x 35 in. Private collection, on loan to Amgueddfa Cymru–National Museum Wales (NMWA(L) 1521). This portrait of "Top Sawyer," the sisters' extraordinary entrepreneur grandfather, was commissioned by the directors of his Ocean Coal Company as a gift to his wife. It shows him at the height of his success, at age fifty-six. The Pre-Raphaelite artist Ford Maddox Brown painted few portraits. Suffering from gout early in 1874, he had trouble finishing this picture and its counterpart, a portrait of his wife.

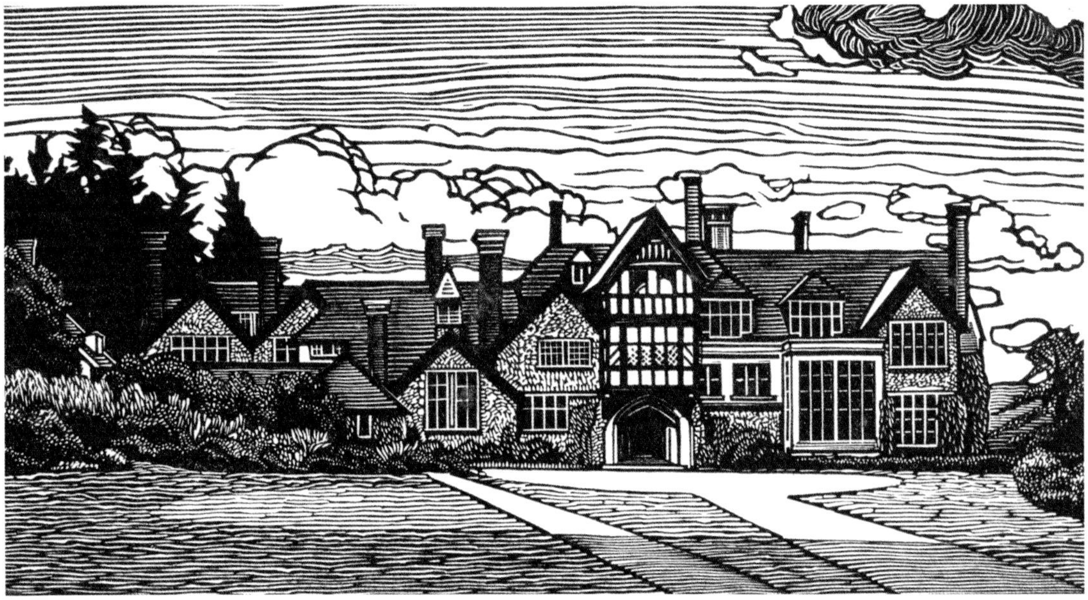

4

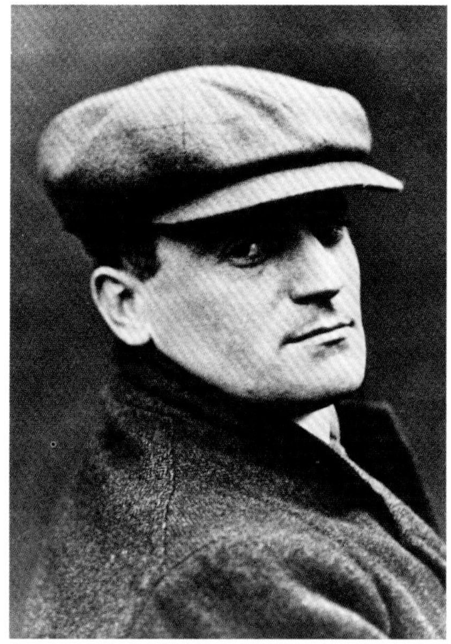

5

November 1907 and February 1908, she was in Dresden taking part in a course of lectures on the history of art from the Renaissance to the present, given by a Miss Watson, and visiting the city's galleries. Her notes survive and include comments on artists, and even on works, that were later to figure in the collection.[18] Gwendoline, too, made a systematic study of art history, and her papers include a table listing nearly one hundred Italian artists and the cities in which they worked, between the thirteenth and seventeenth centuries. She had first visited Italy in 1902, when Margaret was still at school, returning with her in 1908 and 1909.[19]

The sisters bought their first oil paintings in June 1908 – not the old masters they admired in Germany and Italy, but two landscapes by Camille Corot, *The Pond* (cat. no. 10), purchased by Gwendoline for £2,730, and *Fishermen Moored at a Bank* (fig. 6), sold to Margaret the following day by the Obach Gallery, London. Other works followed, and in November they bought two seascapes of the early 1840s by J.M.W. Turner, *The Morning after the Storm* and *The Storm* (cat. no. 54), from the London dealer Colnaghi for £14,860.[20] May 1909 saw Margaret buying from Blaker a painting by Anton Mauve and half a dozen oil sketches ascribed (wrongly) to John Constable, and Gwendoline acquiring two landscapes by David Cox and Jean-François Millet's *The Goose Girl at Gruchy* (cat. no. 30). It was already clear that theirs was to be a collection of recent, and primarily European, art. A few weeks earlier, on their way back from Italy, the sisters had stayed in Paris and made a visit to the Louvre, whereas Margaret wrote, "there is a very good collection by Corot" and "some very beautiful tiny gems by Millet of peasant life." Her taste was therefore still quite conservative and favored landscape painting of the mid-nineteenth century. When the sisters visited the Salon exhibition at the Grand Palais, Margaret commented that "one sees some very striking portraits, some pretty landscapes, some good groups and also many I do not care for, they are too impressionist to suit me." Another Paris exhibition at the Jardin des Tuileries of eighteenth-century portraits of women by French and English artists took her off in a quite different direction. She wrote enthusiastically about several of the works and on her return bought a portrait by George Romney (1734–1802) for £5,355.[21] In the Louvre, she had also admired the small historical genre pieces of Jean-Louis-Ernest Meissonier (cat. no. 27), then at the height of his popularity.[22] Other purchases in 1910 and 1911 display the same rather safe and conservative taste – works by Turner (cat. no. 48), Corot (cat. no. 11), Jozef Israels, Charles Bargue (cat. no. 1), and Whistler. The sisters responded to the serious, epic, and melancholy in Millet's scenes of peasant life; and three large unfinished pictures by this artist, among them, *Winter: The Faggot Gatherers* (cat. no. 31), now seem the most important of their early purchases. In 1912, Gwendoline bought Daumier's *The Night Walkers* (cat. no. 12), again from the gallery Wallis & Son, the first of nearly twenty oils and watercolors to be acquired over the next decade. This, too, was exceptional, as Daumier was then little known in Britain and had attracted few collectors.

As far as we know, the Davies sisters did not visit Roger Fry's now-celebrated exhibition *Manet and the Post-Impressionists* at the Grafton Galleries in November 1910, but by the summer of 1912, Impressionism,

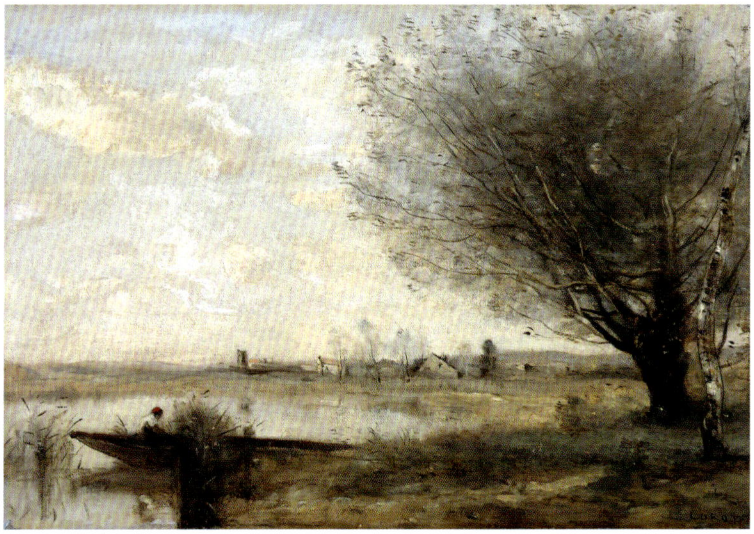

6

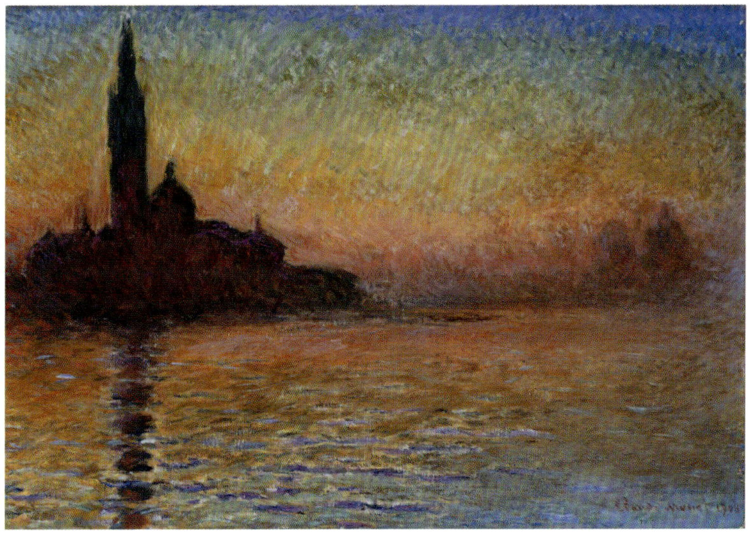

7

dismissed by Margaret in 1909, was beginning to attract their attention.[23] They made a return visit to Venice in April, and in Paris on the way home they almost certainly saw an exhibition of Monet's recent Venetian views at Bernheim-Jeune. In August, Hugh Blaker wrote from France:

> I will certainly keep my eyes open in Paris for anything good, and am delighted that you think of getting some examples of the Impressionists of 1870. Very few English collectors, except Hugh Lane, have bought them at all, although much of their best work is in America already. I expect you also know the work of Sisley, Pissarro and Renoir. These can still be got quite cheaply. Sisley, whose parents were English, was as good as any in my opinion, and Degas and Daumier are desirables of course.[24]

The attraction of Monet's Venetian paintings lay initially in their subject matter. The sisters loved the city, and in January 1912, Gwendoline had purchased Whistler's *Nocturne: Blue and Gold, St. Mark's Venice* (cat. no. 58) for £2,850. Blaker actually tried to dissuade them but was assured by Emile Bernheim that "there is not, nor will there ever be, another Venetian series by Monet. Two of the Venetian paintings, *Le Palais Dario* and *Le Palais Ducal*, remain with us: the others have been sold or have left for America whence they will not return as 15 percent import duty has been paid on them …"[25] The sisters had already bought three, *The Grand Canal, Venice,*[26] *San Giorgio Maggiore*, and *San Giorgio Maggiore by Twilight* (fig. 7). Also in October 1912, Gwendoline

Figure 4 Margaret Davies (1884–1963), *Plas Dinam*, ca. 1920. Woodcut. Private collection. Gwendoline and Margaret Davies were raised with their brother, David, at Plas Dinam, in the village of Llandinam in rural Montgomeryshire. The Victorian Gothic house was built by W. E. Nesfield in 1873–74. David Davies purchased the house as a home for his son, Edward, and his first wife, Mary Jones. It was here that the sisters initially hung their art collection before moving to Gregynog in 1924.

Figure 5 Hugh Blaker (1873–1936), the brother of the sisters' governess Jane, was an artist, critic, and collector who in 1905 became the curator of the Holburne Museum in Bath. He advised the sisters in their early days of collecting and influenced the way in which their taste developed. Amgueddfa Cymru–National Museum Wales. Photograph ca. 1906

Figure 6 Camille Corot, *Fishermen Moored at a Bank*, ca. 1865–70. Oil on canvas, 13 x 18 ⅜ in. Amgueddfa Cymru–National Museum Wales (NMWA 2444). This elegiac composition is one of numerous scenes of fishermen in boats, frequently moored near a willow tree. Corot described the gentle melancholy of such works: "Let us sit down by this pond still as a looking-glass. Nature has a weary look. Poor flowers! They know that the sylphs of evening are going to refresh them with dew." Margaret Davies purchased this painting in 1908.

Figure 7 Claude Monet, *San Giorgio Maggiore by Twilight*, 1908. Oil on canvas, 25 1⁄16 x 36 ⅜ in. Amgueddfa Cymru–National Museum Wales (NMWA 2485). One of the Venetian views bought by Gwendoline Davies from Bernheim-Jeune in October 1912. At the time, this vibrant work was the least regarded of the three acquired by the sisters.

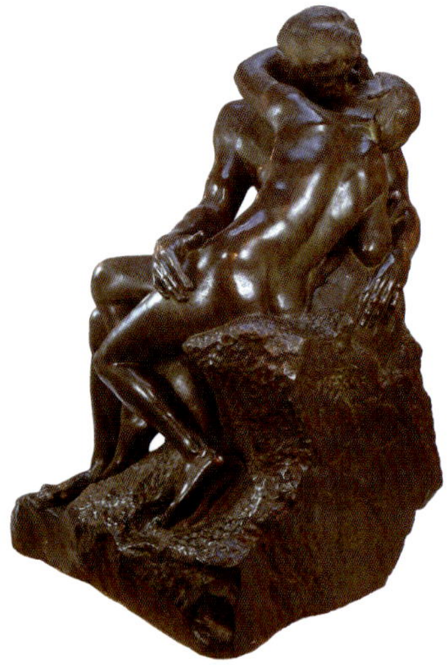

8

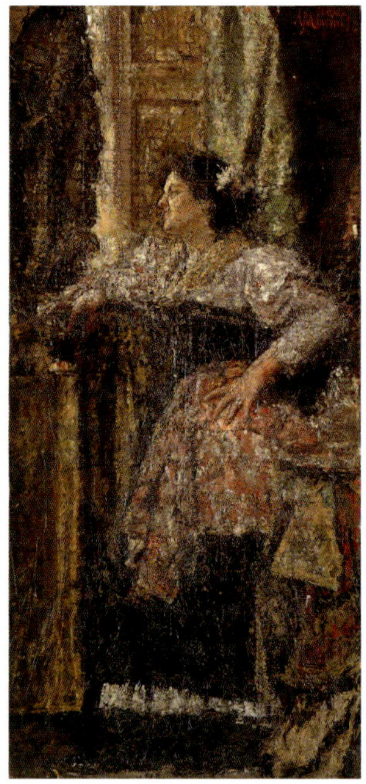

9

acquired a little oil sketch, *Effect of Snow at Petit-Montrouge* (cat. no. 24), now seen as Manet's first truly Impressionist work,[27] for a mere 6,000 francs (£240), and Boudin's *Venice, the Molo* (cat. no. 4), both from Durand-Ruel. These five works were relatively inexpensive, costing only some £4,420, but they took the collection in a radically new direction. During 1913 and in the opening months of 1914, the sisters consolidated their interest in Impressionism. They bought five more late works by Monet: a London view (cat. no. 33); *The Palazzo Dario* (cat. no. 35); and *Waterlilies* of 1905, 1906 (cat. no. 34), and 1908, as well as the great iconic painting most closely associated with them – Renoir's *La Parisienne* (see pp. 30–37 and cat. no. 39), bought by Gwendoline Davies in April 1913 for £5,000. However, the conversion to Impressionism was not total. The sisters continued to buy what they liked and what Blaker, and other advisers such as David Croal Thomson at Wallis & Son, and the artist Murray Urquhart, regarded as progressive. In addition to more Daumiers (cat. nos. 12, 13, and 14), Gwendoline acquired the first of several of Eugène Carrière's monochrome scenes of motherhood (cat. nos. 5 and 6). Between 1912 and 1914, the sisters bought six major works by Rodin (fig. 8)[28] and also acquired paintings by lesser known but then esteemed contemporaries – among them, Antonio Mancini (fig. 9), Adolphe Monticelli, and Matthijs Maris.[29]

Over a six-year period extending to the summer of 1914, Gwendoline and Margaret Davies had assembled one of the finest collections of European modern art in Britain. Except when traveling abroad, they continued to live quietly at Plas Dinam under the wing of their stepmother. Their lives were sheltered, privileged, and essentially private. In contrast, their older brother, David, was a busy public figure, serving as a Liberal Member of Parliament for Montgomeryshire beginning in 1906. He further developed his grandfather's industrial empire and was also a committed philanthropist. In 1911, he set up a charity to combat tuberculosis in Wales; by 1929, he had given away more than £250,000 in the promotion of public health, higher education, housing, temperance, the Calvinistic Methodist Church, and international peace. Gwendoline and Margaret remained close to their brother after he married in 1910. They also adopted a number of his good causes. They interested themselves in the University College of Wales, Aberystwyth, and in the recently established National Library and National Museum (fig. 10). Founded only in 1907, the state-funded museum and library were victories in a long campaign by Wales's Liberal Nonconformist elite to establish distinctive national institutions.[30] The influence of Ruskin and William Morris had also brought a new aestheticism to progressive politics. Beginning in 1914, David Davies funded *Welsh Outlook*, "A Monthly Journal of National Social Progress" that included generous and international coverage of the arts. This publication expressed no doubt that "the study of painting and sculpture is in a deplorably backward condition in Wales."[31] While an anxiety about a lack of "a national art" and a belief in art's improving qualities were common in late nineteenth-century Wales,[32] this sense of backwardness was new and controversial.[33] The Davies sisters shared the conviction[34] and lent generously to exhibitions between 1912 and 1923, apparently feeling they had a moral and social duty to do so. In 1913, much of what

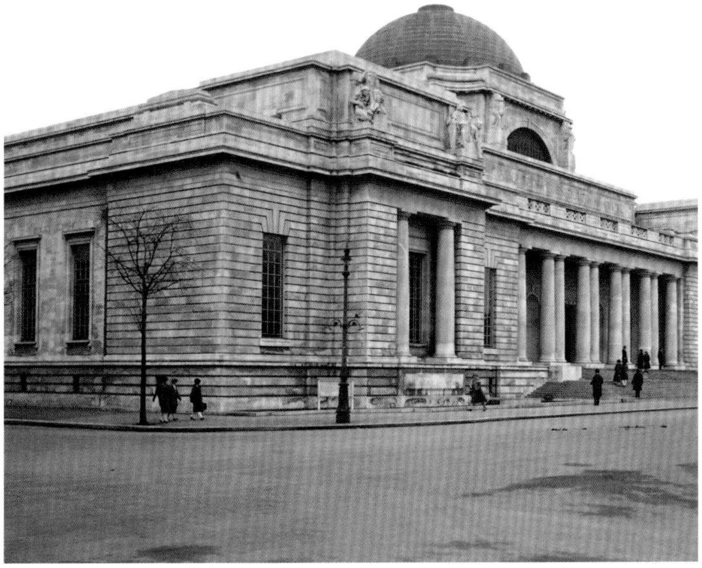

10

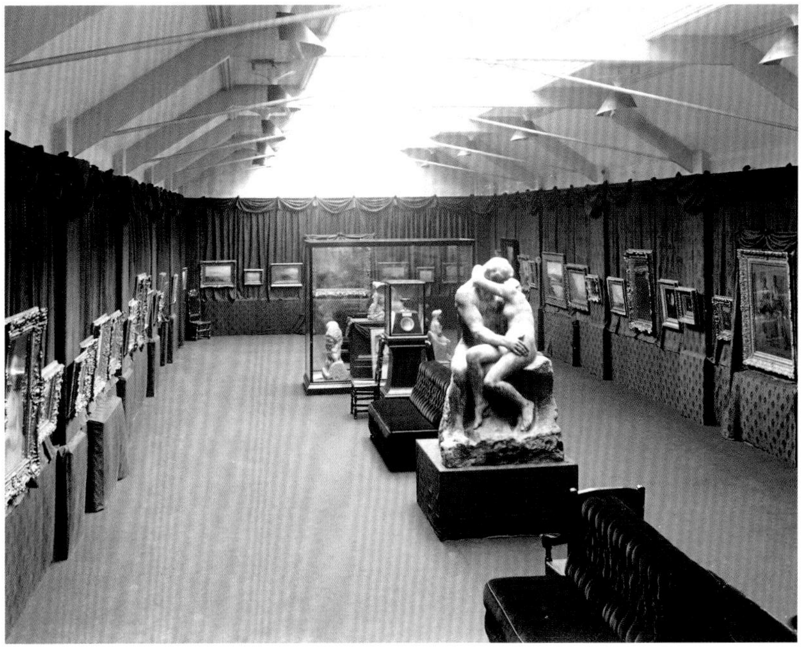

11

they had acquired was shown – anonymously – in *A Loan Exhibition of Paintings* (fig. 11) at the National Museum in February and March 1913.[35] The idea for the exhibition came from Murray Urquhart and Hugh Blaker, and the sisters were persuaded to participate by their friend and confidant Thomas Jones (fig. 12).[36] They met all the costs of the show, which had more than 26,000 visitors in seven and a half weeks. The exhibition included one of the most comprehensive presentations of recent French art yet seen in Britain.[37] Reviews in the British national press were enthusiastic, but a local reviewer could bring himself to approve only of the Meissonier (cat. no. 27).[38]

On 4 August 1914, Germany invaded Belgium, drawing Britain into World War I, which was to destroy the late Victorian world of the sisters' childhood. They promptly ceased collecting, but their ambition to raise the practice and appreciation of the arts in Wales through exposure to European modernism found a new outlet. The plight of Belgian refugees in Britain attracted much sympathy. The Davies family decided that Belgian artists, poets, and musicians should be encouraged to come to Wales. Major Burdon-Evans, their agent, and Thomas Jones were dispatched to Belgium, where they assembled a group of ninety-one refugees, including the sculptor George Minne (1866–1941), and the painters Valerius de Saedeleer (1867–1941) and Gustave van de Woestyne (1881–1947).[39] All three were to spend the rest of the war as refugees, largely dependent on the Davies family for support. Isolated from the Belgian refugee communities in London, and with no contact with other artists, the war years proved to be lonely and difficult ones for them.[40]

Figure 8 Auguste Rodin, *The Kiss*, ca. 1887. Bronze, 72 x 44 in. Amgueddfa Cymru–National Museum Wales (NMWA 2499). Rodin's iconic sculpture of the naked lovers Paolo and Francesca is one of the most significant works in the Davies collection. Gwendoline Davies bought the work from the Georges Petit Gallery in Paris for £3,000 in September 1912. Hugh Blaker urged her to acquire it, declaring, "the bronze is unique," as she hesitated between it and two Venetian Monets. There are two versions of the sculpture in marble. This example was cast in bronze by Alexis Rudier after 1902.

Figure 9 Antonio Mancini, *Portrait of a Girl*, 1898. Oil on canvas, 79 x 35 ⅝ in. Amgueddfa Cymru–National Museum Wales (NMWA 2175). Margaret Davies acquired this painting at the beginning of 1913. It is one of three works by Mancini in the Davies collection. John Singer Sargent described Mancini as the greatest living painter, and he developed an extraordinary technique using wire grilles and thick impasto. The work was lent to Brighton Art Gallery and Museum and Leeds City Art Gallery and may not have been hung at Plas Dinam or Gregynog.

Figure 10 The National Museum of Wales, Cardiff, designed by Arnold Dunbar Smith (1866–1933) and Cecil Claude Brewer (1871–1918) and begun in 1912. Together with their brother, David, the Davies sisters gave £5,000 to the museum's building fund in 1914 and a further £5,000 in 1916. Amgueddfa Cymru–National Museum Wales

Figure 11 *A Loan Exhibition of Paintings* held in the temporary museum in Cardiff City Hall, 4 February to 28 March 1913, the first exhibition organized under the auspices of the National Museum of Wales. Gwendoline and Margaret Davies covered its costs and lent (anonymously) much of their newly formed collection. Amgueddfa Cymru–National Museum Wales

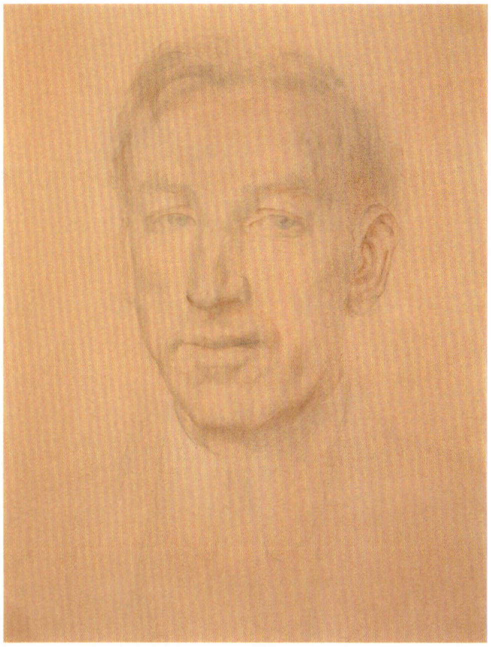

12

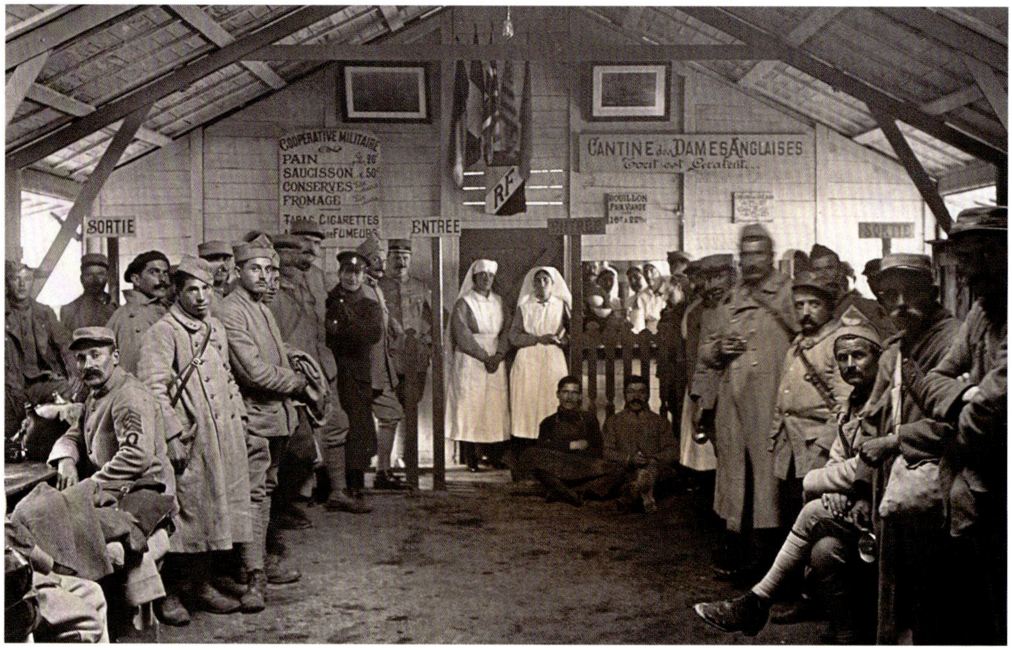

13

During 1915, the sisters became increasingly involved in other charitable war work. Having bought nothing for nearly two years, Gwendoline Davies visited an exhibition of pictures by Augustus John in February 1916. Here was an artist from Wales, admired also by Blaker, whose personal and romanticized version of Primitivism aligned him with elements of progressive art in both France and Britain. She spent £2,350 on ten oils (cat. nos. 22 and 23) and a drawing – almost half the paintings in the show.[41] By now the sisters were "very keen ... to do something in the way of helping" the war effort. Their brother, David, was in France, and they had been greatly distressed by the death of their cousin Edward Lloyd Jones the previous year. Gwendoline Davies volunteered for service with the London Committee of the French Red Cross,[42] and in July 1916, she was sent to Troyes, France, to run a canteen (fig. 13).[43] Margaret joined her in June 1917, and her journals provide a record of their lives at this period. Although travel was difficult, Gwendoline sometimes visited Paris on Red Cross business, which provided an opportunity to visit the Bernheim-Jeune gallery in the Boulevard de la Madeleine. There, over the course of several months, she was to spend over £11,000 on seven pictures. She bought a Daumier and a Carrière in April 1917, as well as paintings by Renoir (cat. no. 40), Manet, Monet (fig. 14), and Puvis de Chavannes.[44] In February 1918, she made the most important purchases of her life – two landscapes by Cézanne, *The François Zola Dam* and *Provençal Landscape* (cat. nos. 7 and 8).[45] Works by Cézanne had been included in a London selling exhibition of Impressionist paintings organized by Durand-Ruel back in 1905, but he had been virtually ignored by British collectors.[46] Even

Figure 12 Paul Artôt, *Thomas Jones (1870–1955)*, ca. 1914. Pastel on paper, 18 ⅛ x 12 ⅜ in. Amgueddfa Cymru–National Museum Wales (NMWA 1792). Thomas Jones was appointed secretary of David Davies's Welsh National Memorial Association to combat tuberculosis in 1910. He was also the editor of the political and cultural journal *Welsh Outlook*. A friend of Gwendoline Davies, Jones traveled to Belgium in September 1914 at the request of the sisters and their stepmother and brought to Wales a group of war refugees, including several artists. He was Deputy Secretary to the Cabinet from 1916 until 1930. Like the Davies sisters, he immersed himself in many charitable and philanthropic projects.

Figure 13 The entrance to the canteen at the railway station in Troyes where Gwendoline and Margaret Davies worked for extended periods beginning in August 1917. Margaret is probably the canteen worker in the Red Cross uniform on the right. Next to the canteen (where everything was free) was the cooperative shop Co-Operative Militaire. Soon after their arrival, to their horror, the cooperative started to sell wine, but Gwendoline persuaded the colonel in command to put a halt to this. Private collection

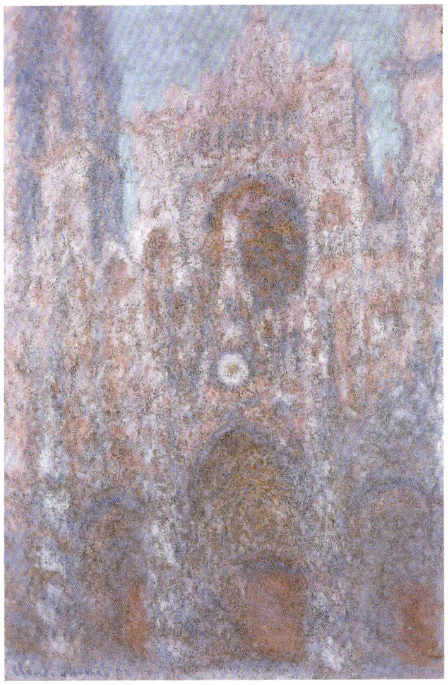

14

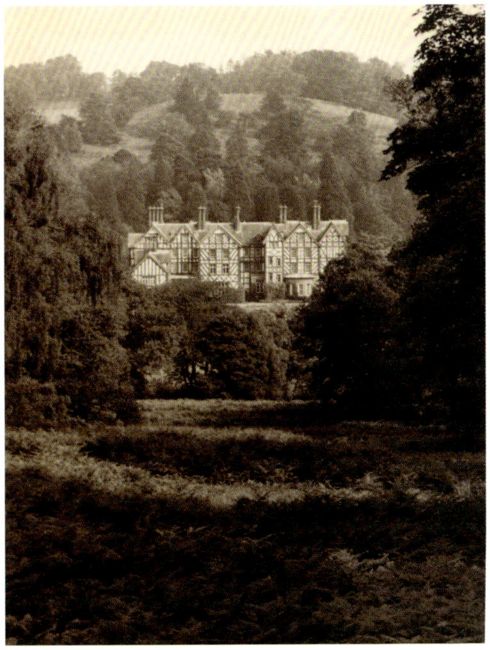

15

in a depressed wartime market, the two landscapes cost £2,500 and £1,250, respectively. A few weeks later came the greatest crisis of the war, as the German spring offensive made alarming progress. Blaker, worried about the safety of Gwendoline's purchases, persuaded her to lend them to an exhibition in Bath.[47] In May 1918, the canteen in Troyes had to care for hundreds of civilian refugees from the German advance, and the sisters were deeply moved by the suffering of sick and hungry women and children. Troyes was full of French and American troops traveling toward the fighting, and when hospital trains evacuating the wounded stopped at the station, the canteen workers boarded them to distribute cigarettes and comforts.

For many British women, World War I brought loss, suffering, and hunger rather than danger and physical hardship, but Gwendoline and Margaret Davies saw its destruction and dislocation firsthand. They had been bombed and shelled, and they had comforted wounded and dying soldiers. They were appalled by the horrors experienced by both British and French troops and shocked at the suffering of civilian refugees. As early as December 1917, Thomas Jones noted in his diary: "I found Miss Davies deeply affected by her life in France and determined to do all she could for the soldiers at home after the war."[48] The stress and long hours of work also affected them physically. Gwendoline later wrote that the war had "knocked my life and health to pieces." In 1919, she decided to establish a place where ex-soldiers and others could learn craft skills in peaceful surroundings. One of the Davies family companies owned a large Victorian country house called Gregynog Hall (fig. 15) only a few miles from their home at Plas Dinam, which the sis-

Figure 14 Claude Monet, *Rouen Cathedral: Setting Sun*, 1892–94. Oil on canvas, 39 ⅜ x 25 ⅝ in. Amgueddfa Cymru–National Museum Wales (NMWA 2482). Gwendoline Davies bought this painting from Bernheim-Jeune in December 1917 for the relatively modest sum of £1,350. Monet's paintings of the great Gothic cathedral were seen as a patriotic statement when first exhibited. The sisters sometimes attended Catholic services when they were in France, and Margaret drew Troyes Cathedral. Gwendoline may therefore have seen this work as a symbol of France.

Figure 15 Gregynog Hall, the Montgomeryshire country house bought by the Davies sisters in July 1920 and intended to be used as a center for arts and crafts and for conferences. It became their home in 1924. Rebuilt in the 1830s, it was later clad in concrete and painted in black and white to resemble a timber-frame house typical of the area. Private collection

ters purchased in 1920. Their plans for Gregynog grew to include music and literature, as well as the visual arts and the promotion of international peace and social harmony. They had not originally intended to make it their home but decided to do so in 1924. During the 1920s and '30s, Gregynog was the venue for many national and international conferences attended by educators, politicians, and welfare campaigners, as well as for an annual festival of music and literature. The sisters entertained a constant stream of visitors. Even Prime Minister Stanley Baldwin stayed at Gregynog in 1936 to recover from the stresses of the Abdication Crisis.[49] Gwendoline and Margaret also founded the Gregynog Press, one of the finest private presses of the day and the only element of their "craft colony" to be realized, which published a run of fine books between 1923 and 1940.[50]

The sisters continued to collect after the war, adding more favorites, such as works by Daumier, Turner, and Augustus John. Margaret extended their holdings of Impressionism by buying two oils (cat. no. 42) and a group of drawings by Pissarro. Gwendoline already owned a painting then ascribed to Gauguin (cat. no. 41), and she acquired two more outstanding Post-Impressionist works from Bernheim-Jeune in 1920, Cézanne's *Still Life with Teapot* (fig. 16) and van Gogh's *Rain–Auvers* (cat. no. 55), again one of the first to enter a British collection.[51] Their appreciation of Cézanne led them to Derain and to Vlaminck but no further, and between 1919 and 1923 they bought a number of old master paintings.[52] Collecting increasingly seemed an indulgence. Gwendoline wrote to Thomas Jones in November 1921: "Thank you for telling us about the John pictures – I have not bought any for 18 months, we simply cannot, in the face of the appalling need everywhere, Russian children, Earl Haig's ex-soldiers, all so terribly human."[53] Her last known purchase is an eighteenth-century landscape by Richard Wilson (1714–1782).[54] Margaret, in contrast, continued to spend modest sums on British followers of Impressionism such as Walter Richard Sickert (cat. no. 42) and Harold Gilman. Some of the sisters' French pictures were lent to exhibitions and to public galleries,[55] and others were kept in their London apartment. Most, however, were brought to Gregynog (fig. 17), where they were seen by visitors, conference delegates, and student groups, contributing to the house's unique atmosphere[56] until their eventual transfer to the National Museum.[57] Perhaps to fill the gaps left by the departure of Gwendoline's paintings in 1952, Margaret bought more frequently in the 1950s. Again, most of her purchases were the work of living British artists, but after selling some of her pictures in 1960, she returned to the French art of her youth, buying two late Impressionist paintings by Sisley (cat. no. 44) and Henry Moret (cat. no. 36), as well as works by Bonnard (cat. no. 3) and Utrillo.[58]

This late group aside, the Davies sisters' collection of modern French art was complete by 1924, when it was the largest of its kind in Britain. Others, notably Samuel Courtauld, were to follow where the sisters had led over the next thirty years. Theirs was not a comprehensive collection of progressive French painting from the 1840s to the early 1900s. Many artists are completely absent (and Degas is represented only by sculpture), and there is no attempt at career coverage (all but one of the Monets are after 1900). It is largely a collection of landscapes, interspersed with sympathetic representations of women and children

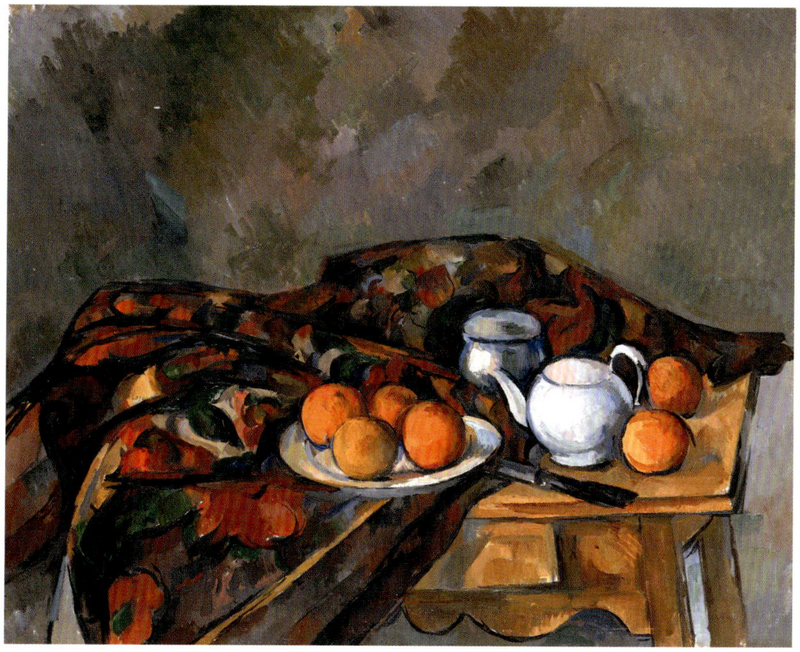

16

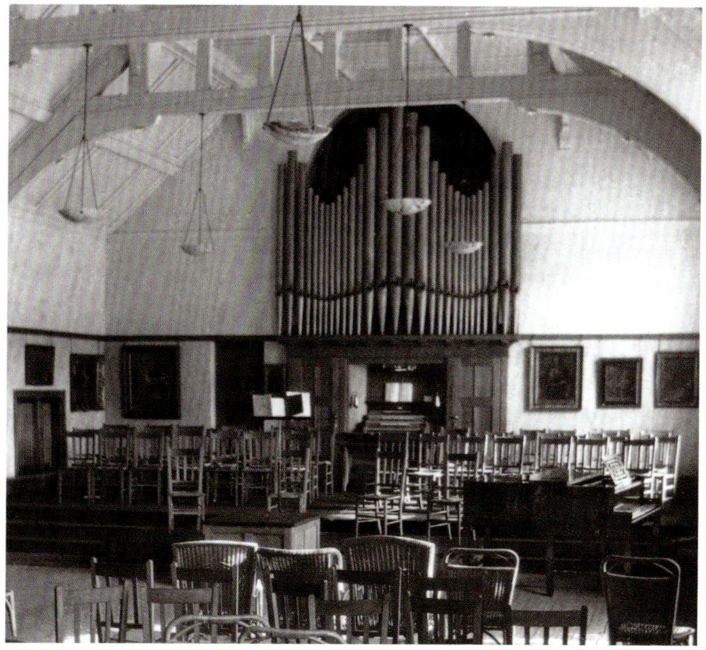

17

and of people at work. There are no images of contemporary Paris life; no bars, theaters, or picnic parties; no nudes; and only one street scene (cat. no. 38). It can be assumed that the collection represents the sisters' personal taste. Gwendoline wrote in 1925: "The great joy of collecting anything is to do it yourself, with expert opinion granted, but one does like to choose for oneself. All the time we have been collecting our pictures we have never bought one without having seen it or at least a photograph before purchase."[59] Murray Urquhart later described Hugh Blaker as "the architect and inspirer" of the Davies collection, but the relationship was a professional rather than a personal one, and the sisters did not always follow his advice.[60] There is no doubt that both Gwendoline and Margaret loved what they felt to be beautiful and believed strongly in the spiritual and moral value of art. Did they fully understand just how remarkable some of their paintings were? Possibly not – they never mixed with artists and only rarely with other collectors. For all their travels and their visiting of exhibitions and dealers, they could be scornful of academic art criticism,[61] and their occasional comments on individual works are pedestrian.[62] All told, however, they had the wealth,[63] determination, and idealism to pursue "things of beauty" with the wider aim of enriching the cultural life of their homeland.

Postscript: The Davies sisters converted a number of loans to the National Museum into a gift in 1940. Gwendoline's collection came to Cardiff after her death in 1951. Margaret's followed in 1963. She also gave Gregynog to the University of Wales.

Figure 16 Paul Cézanne, *Still Life with Teapot*, 1902–06. Oil on canvas, 24 ¼ x 29 ¼ in. Amgueddfa Cymru–National Museum Wales (NMWA 2440). This picture, bought by Gwendoline Davies in Paris for £2,000 in 1920, is one of Cézanne's greatest still lifes, painted not long before his death in 1906. The crockery, cutlery, and fruit relate to the folds of the carpet on the table like motifs in a landscape. Cézanne manipulated perspective, and details, such as the knob on the teapot lid, have been suppressed to emphasize the importance of form over subject matter.

Figure 17 The Music Room at Gregynog. This photograph illustrates the room as it was used for the summer festivals in the 1930s. Manet's *The Rabbit* (1881) is on the left-hand wall, and visitors also remember seeing Monet's water lily paintings and Pissarro's *Pont Neuf, Snow Effect* (cat. no. 38). Amgueddfa Cymru–National Museum Wales

Paul Greenhalgh Recognizing the Modern World: Art, Patronage, Optimism

We often forget what it *is* to be modern, and when we look to the past, we correspondingly forget what it *was* to be modern. The very word conjures up such huge forces and dramatic transformations in the substance and appearance of things: shifts in science, technology, communications, politics, economy, and other material abstractions of existence. We tend, by imagining the world through science fictions – both prophetic and spurious – and by remembering it through the medium of wars and political intrigue, to forget that to be modern is (and was) also a far humbler struggle, a more prosaic attempt to give one's life a shape on a day-to-day basis, by pushing one's way through a quagmire of thousands of endless developments and changes in the condition of things. Art can help us to remember that day-to-day struggle and render it profound.

La Parisienne (cat. no. 39) – the Lady in Blue – looks out at us through 130 years of history; and her gaze says more about the times she lived in than does a library full of books. She is a creature of the burgeoning modern urban environment, a city girl. Even though the artist, Pierre-Auguste Renoir (1841–1919), chose to place her on a blank ground, isolated from her natural environment like a specimen on a glass slide, we can see that she was a creature who embraced the full flow of her times, her whole demeanor showing us her ambition and desires. Her beautiful blue dress and carefully angled bonnet say much. The result of new dye technology that had only recently placed such fabric within her means, the loud, assertive blue is in some ways the real subject of the painting. The style of the dress, in its combination of an older, aristocratic – Rococo – ambience, and the coquettish boldness of the café concert and dance hall, reveals the duplicitous complexity of the social environment. She wants what the privileged few of old had had, but she wants it on her terms.

We know that the model was Henriette Henriot, a young, unknown actress when Renoir painted her but destined to rise to celebrity in the coming years (see fig. 13, p. 37). At this moment in 1874 when Renoir made her *La Parisienne*, the mythic symbol of the world's most modern city, she was a sixteen-year-old feigning rather than embodying confidence. This feigned confidence, fired by the desire to move beyond her initial station in life, is touchingly revealed by her gaze. Undoubtedly, some of the confidence is real, but her physiognomy is wracked by a childlike fear of the unknown, a tentativeness that suggests she is unsure of herself and nervous under the scrutiny of her public. She appears like a creature standing her ground, intimidated but determined to mark her territory.

La Parisienne is one of the great masterpieces of Impressionism collected by two Welsh women in the early part of the twentieth century. The sisters Gwendoline and Margaret Davies – unlikely names for collectors during the golden age of the French avant-garde – amassed an extraordinary collection. After collecting in a fairly wide way across the range of the Western tradition, they focused more directly on the most important names in the Realist, Naturalist, Impressionist, Aestheticist, Symbolist, Post-Impressionist, and Fauvist movements and thus rank among the most important patrons in Europe at a key moment in the history of painting. Having found their feet by around 1910 and having surrounded themselves with shrewd advisers, they amassed the bulk of their collection by the early 1920s.[1] With notable exceptions, they concentrated on the period circa 1850–1914, and principally on French art, with a small number of extraordinary English works.[2]

The central questions raised by this situation, of these extraordinary works and the extraordinary sisters who collected them, have to do with context and motivation. Why did these artists respond to their context, their environment, in this way, and why did the sisters gather paintings by them at that time? In short, what was the relationship between practice, patronage, and the period? As my somewhat generalized list of movements suggests, it was the first great age of "isms," when artists increasingly formed into self-conscious groups and attempted to define their practice in essays, treatises, and manifestos. The span of their collection represents the great – and arguably first – age of professional art criticism, specialized magazines, and public and private galleries. It was also the key age for artistic exploration of modernity. As such, the Davies sisters opted to collect the work of successive generations of artists who – consciously and unconsciously – challenged, modified, and even defied accepted canons of artistic practice, in a quest to create an art that reflected and reported modern life.

And indeed, modern life was something to reflect on and report in the second half of the nineteenth and beginning of the twentieth centuries. As Henriette Henriot sported her new blue dress in front of Renoir, the very conditions of existence seemed to be in flux, in the material and psychological senses of that phrase. The preceding hundred years had set the stage. During the eighteenth and early nineteenth centuries, there had been two traumatic revolutions, an industrial one in Britain and a political one in France. These opened the way for the voracious and ongoing transformation of the fabric of life in Europe and America. In the second half of the nineteenth century, as historian Eric Hobsbawm has noted, the word *capitalism* came into popular use for the first time, to describe the integrated system of economics and politics that was to facilitate the process of transformation.[3] Hobsbawm characterized the "vast and apparently boundless expansion of the world" as "the age of capital" and noted interestingly that "the [British] industrial revolution had swallowed the [French] political revolution." By this, he implied that it was an age obsessed with the economic and social progress of industrialism, to the point at which many at the time and later came to see the obsession as quasi-religious.[4]

Perhaps more than any other genre, landscape art was affected by this world of change. The most obvious visual feature of this age of capital, of which the Davies sisters were so very much a product, was the spectacular growth of cities. Industry and politics had apparently fused to give rise to an urban revolution. London and Paris had essentially become the largest and most sophisticated cities in the world by the turn of the nineteenth century. By the turn of the twentieth, they were far larger still, but by then, they resided in the context of a general urbanization of the Western world. And throughout the entire period, they stood for modernity. When Claude Monet (1840–1926) made his regular sojourns to London to depict the fog and bustle of life on the river Thames (see cat. no. 33) or Camille Pissarro (1830–1903) sat on the left bank of the river Seine to capture the energy of traffic

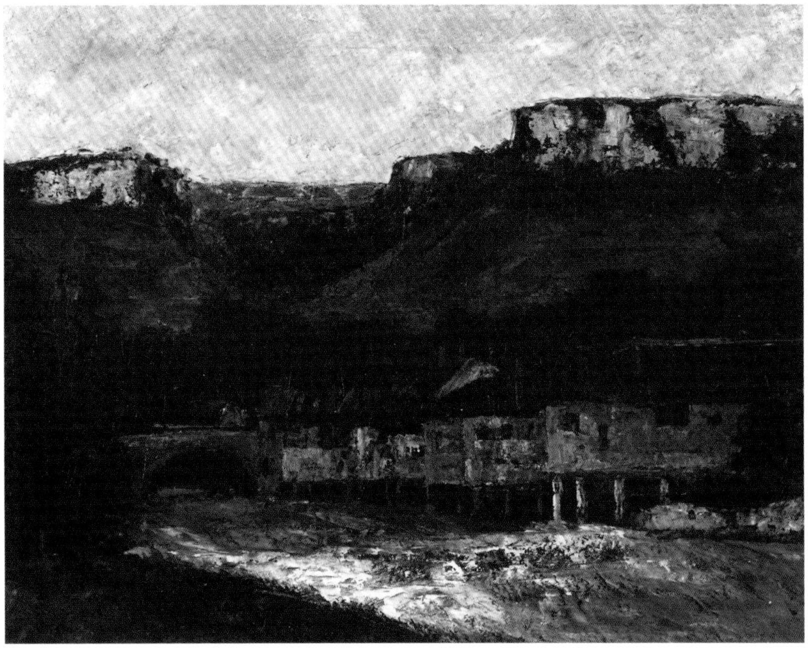

1

and the grand stately facades of Paris – which he seemed to consciously subordinate to the passing hubbub (see cat. no. 38) – they were engaging with life at the heart of the city, and both were celebrating it as the ubiquitous presence of modernity.

As a consequence of this ongoing urban revolution, the social, economic, and cultural space between the countryside and the city became a distinct feature of the age. Indeed, while the contrast between the country and city has been around as a cultural determinant certainly since antiquity,[5] and continues to be one, the second half of the nineteenth century was the period in which the forces of modernization meant that the space between the country and city was not only bound up with social perception, tradition, and lifestyle but also more than ever with the undermining and destruction of the rural economy. Notably, in parts of the French countryside, from the mid-century onward, an already difficult existence became close to intolerable for the peasantry, as the city became increasingly the magnet for a population attracted by the new economic activity. Both landscapes and cityscapes in art reflected the various attitudes that these demographic shifts brought about.

The countryside was depicted as representing many, often contradictory, things. For instance, some artists used it to avoid the modern world; others used it as a vehicle for the exploration of the moral and political implications of modernization; still others reported it in a direct but often celebratory manner. The Davies sisters collected examples of all of these. Among the first group, it was common to negate the reality of the nineteenth century and opt, in the face of the drastic transformation of rural life, to use the land as a vehicle for timeless contemplation. The past and mythic worlds could be used to create scenes that could exist only in art. Perhaps this approach was exemplified by Camille Corot (1796–1875), whose naturalistic vision might combine scenes inspired by, and even directly taken from, sites in the Forest of Fontainebleau, with eclectic hints of various phases of classicism. *The Pond* (cat. no. 10) effortlessly pulls together the worlds of nature and myth.

But those with a moral commitment did not believe the modern world was to be avoided. Gustave Courbet (1819–1877), leader of the Realist movement, was at the forefront of a broad artistic commitment to depict the reality of the land, the plight of the French rural population, and the decay of abandoned buildings (see fig. 1). In a more focused way than Courbet, Jean-François Millet (1814–1875) spent much of his career as a painter showing us that the modern countryside was not Arcadia but could be a place of toil, hunger, misery, and hopelessness. His depictions of rural life usually emphasize the quiet dignity of rural people in the face of backbreaking toil and poverty, and his vision of the landscape is neither epic, welcoming, nor idyllic; his land is a stubborn natural resource that positions man not as fellow traveler but as parasite, an irritant to be resisted and denied. Occasionally, he went way beyond even this, pushing the land and its inhabitants into an extreme condition. In *The Gust of Wind* (cat. no. 32), a terrifying squall rips across the landscape, uprooting a tree and turning its branches and roots into gothic, skeletal claws, bringing a violence to a scene already crippled with a dark melancholy. The

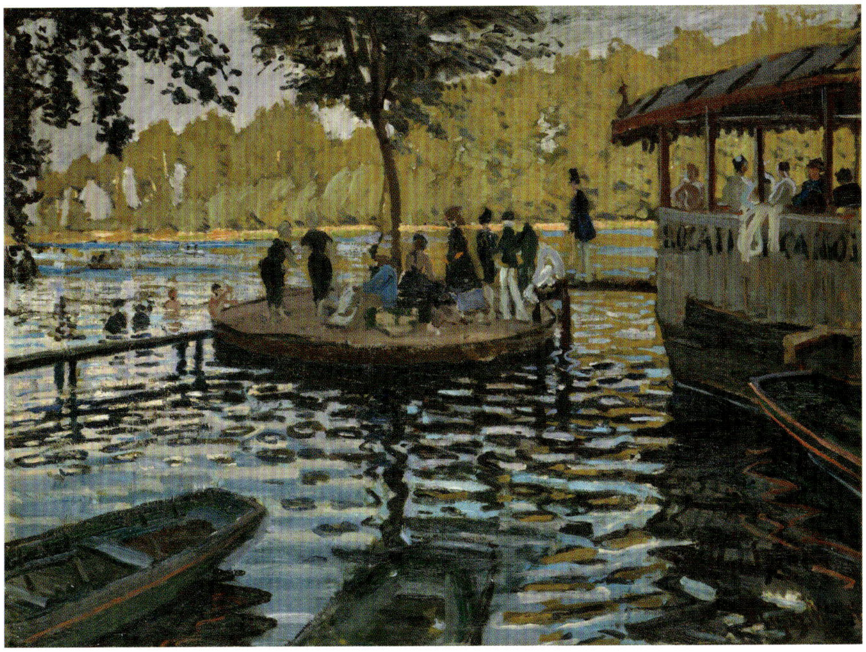

2

Figure 1 Gustave Courbet, *Ornans*, n.d. Oil on canvas, 16 ½ x 19 ⅜ in. Corcoran Gallery of Art, Washington, D.C.; Bequest of George Lothrop Bradley and Helen McHenry Bradley (19.6)

Figure 2 Claude Monet, *La Grenouillère*, 1869. Oil on canvas, 29 ⅜ x 39 ¼ in. The Metropolitan Museum of Art; H. O. Havemeyer Collection, Bequest of Mrs. H. O. Havemeyer, 1929 (29.100.112). Image © The Metropolitan Museum of Art

British painter Walter Richard Sickert referred to this painting as "an astonishing artifice of mystery and terror."[6] This was not a modern Arcadia; it was not designed by Corot; and it is not a place to live in with any comfort.

Impressionist art sits interestingly in these visions of the land. Naturalism and Realism undoubtedly created the environment that allowed Impressionism to blossom and as such affected the idea of the country and the city. Without doubt, Impressionism is in many respects a furthering of the Realist idea but with inflections unique to itself. Drifting into existence at the end of the 1860s, it was initially the product of a small number of young painters, led by Claude Monet, Pierre-August Renoir, Camille Pissarro, and Alfred Sisley (1839–1899). Perhaps a seminal moment for the production of work was Monet's and Renoir's time together in 1869, at the resort of La Grenouillère (see fig. 2), when both their oeuvres achieved a sense of mature resolution. A key moment for the presentation of Impressionism to the world was the first Impressionist exhibition in 1874. Certainly by then, a circle far wider than the artists themselves had a sense of what the new art looked like and what it was about.

Crucially, though outside the scope of this essay, Impressionist art radicalized approaches to color, brushwork, form, and space. Much of its modernity can be found in these breakthroughs, and there were clearly points in time when most of the artists considered Impressionists, especially Monet, completely subordinated subject matter to the exploration of raw natural form through color. During its years of formation, however, Impressionism had a distinct approach to subject matter. Art historian John House has noted of Monet that "in his early maturity he deliberately sought out man-made landscapes, focusing on the contemporaneity of the scenes around him."[7] More deliberately than their immediate forebears, the Impressionists used the landscape neither to escape modernity nor to aggressively address the morality of its effects – in this sense they were not followers of Corot or Millet, respectively – but to show us what they could see in the prosaic yet vibrant scenes in front of them. To a considerable extent, they were interested in the interface of rural and city life, in what House calls "man-made landscapes": scrubland and allotments behind houses and buildings; small fields with barns and outhouses; canals, railways, and industrial riverbanks; domestic gardens; open-air promenades; parks; and town squares. These attempts by urban populations to take possession of plein-air spaces inside or close to urban developments were the very stuff of the new mode of living, and they were what Impressionists like the young Monet and Sisley lived to depict (see cat. no. 44). Similarly, Berthe Morisot's (1841–1895) depiction of a woman and child in a meadow in *At Bougival* (cat. no. 37) shows us the countryside not as heaven or hell, or even rural life per se, but as a green site being visited by urban dwellers for pleasure. Interestingly, even in his later years, when Monet famously retired back into himself, he chose his very man-made garden as his muse, to focus his eye on the poetic potential of water lilies (see cat. no. 34).

Impressionism was an idiom formed around the idea of making the banal special, of taking the small, incremental aspects of the modern world and placing them in front of us. It also depended on the achieve-

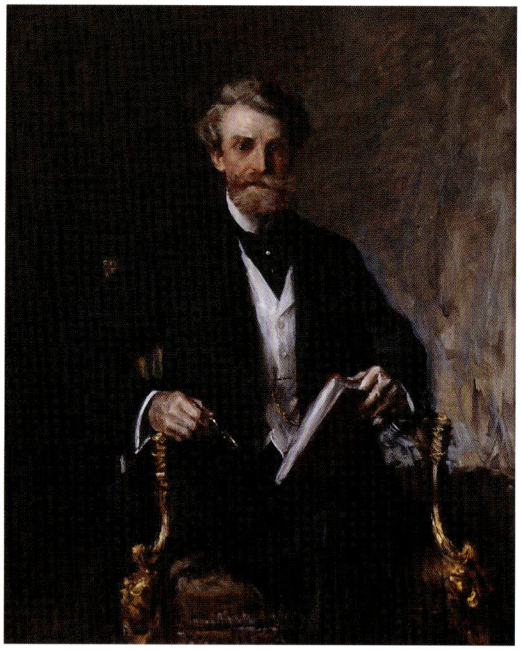

3

ment of instantaneity, the fleeting glance, of capturing the instant without any inertia. In this sense, it was not simply about rendering insignificant things eternal but also about the passing of insignificant time. In its shimmering mobility, it perfectly represented the frenetic time in which it was made.

But this determination to celebrate prosaic modern life lasted only a brief art historical moment: other approaches to modernity came steadily to the fore beginning in the 1880s. After the first blossoming of the style, most of the Impressionists themselves moved on to wrestle with other issues. Monet used an extreme approach to nature to push beyond Impressionism; Renoir combined his Impressionism with Mannerist and Neoclassical impulses to develop a unique style; Pissarro became a Pointillist. The next generation of progressive painters followed their forebears and moved on; among these, however, were artists who did not so much adjust their styles and attitudes as fundamentally challenge the premises of Impressionism. The most important among these were Paul Cézanne (1839–1906), Vincent van Gogh (1853–1890), Georges Seurat (1859–1891), Paul Signac (1863–1935), and Paul Gauguin (1848–1903). They were responsible for movements and individual departures that became collectively named Post-Impressionism. Among other modernist movements, Post-Impressionism set the stage for Fauvism, one of the first avant-garde styles of the twentieth century. Remarkably, the Davies sisters moved along with all these developments and acquired not only later works by the first Impressionists but also key works by the Post-Impressionists, including Cézanne's spectacular *François Zola Dam* (cat. no. 7); one of van Gogh's very last works, the technically extraordinary *Rain–Auvers* (cat. no. 55); Paul Signac's view of St. Tropez of 1918 (cat. no. 43); and Fauvist works by André Derain (1880–1954), Albert Marquet (1875–1947), and Maurice de Vlaminck (1876–1958).

Returning to my earlier questions about the Davies sisters: Why did they collect most of these paintings, a good proportion of them new or almost new when they bought them, and more generally, what was the relationship between patronage and artistic practice in the period? How did they sit as patrons, and therefore as an important part of the infrastructure of the art world, with these numerous disparate ideas about the modern world? Perhaps there are two ways of looking at these questions: first, in terms of the sisters' own lives, and second, in terms of the visible art scene that surrounded them during their own times.

Not atypically, the money that allowed the Davies sisters to buy art came from a powerful business empire. Their grandfather, David Davies, was the quintessential industrialist, a self-made man who acquired his fortune in mines and docks. As a leader in the aforementioned age of capital, Davies's career, and the careers of industrialists like him, had a powerful impact on the lives of millions of people; men like him physically changed the landscape of the regions they lived in. A bronze statue of Davies still stands proudly in Barry, South Wales, a town that could not have existed without him. Their voracious industrialism was at the core of modernity, and therefore it was their activities to which many artists of the period were responding.

Such careers were not necessarily lauded in the arts. For two of the great novelists of the period, the main product of industrial manu-

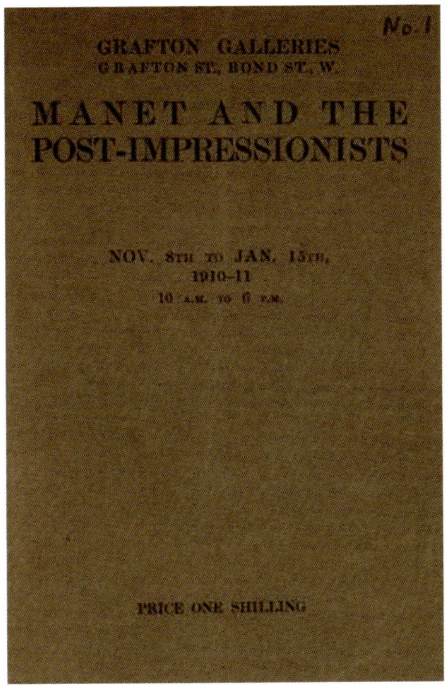

4

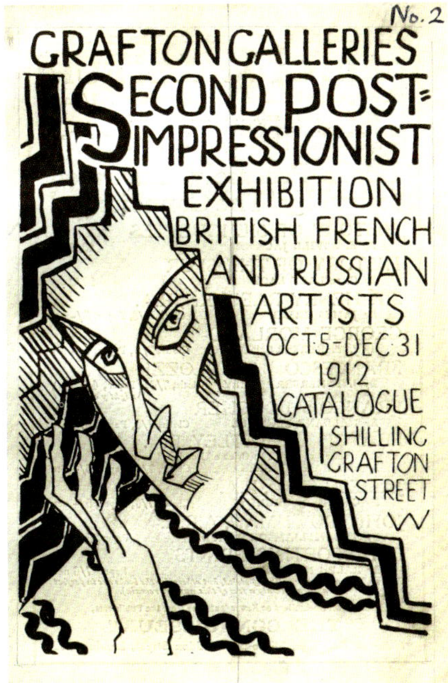

5

Figure 3 William Merritt Chase, *William Andrews Clark*, ca. 1915. Oil on canvas, 50 ½ x 40 ¼ in. Corcoran Gallery of Art, Washington, D.C.; Gift of William A. Clark (17.3)

Figure 4 Catalogue published to accompany the exhibition *Manet and the Post-Impressionsists* held at Grafton Galleries, London, 1910. © Tate Collection, London, 2008

Figure 5 Catalogue published to accompany the *Second Post-Impressionist Exhibition* held at Grafton Galleries, London, 1912. © Tate Collection, London, 2008

facture was a modern form of brutalizing savagery. Charles Dickens was not describing Barry in *Hard Times*, but he could have been: "It was a town of unusual red and black like the painted face of a savage … interminable serpents of smoke trailed themselves for ever and ever, and never got uncoiled."[8] And Emile Zola, even more pertinently in his novel *Germinal*, given his subject, and his personal association with some of the artists whose work Davies's granddaughters collected, described the desperate reality of coal mining and the social destruction it wrought:

> The wicks of their lamps displayed only glowing red tips through their metal screens. You couldn't make out anything clearly. The work space opened out into a large chimney, flat and sloping, on which the soot of ten winters had created a profound night. Ghostly forms moved about, random light beams allowing a glimpse of the curve of a thigh, a brawny arm, a savage face, blackened as if in preparation for a crime …[9]

David Davies, a baron of industrial modernization, begat Gwendoline and Margaret, committed to cultural modernity. In the bigger scheme of things, this was not an unusual scenario in Europe or America. Children and grandchildren of industrial potentates often – usually – gentrified into the cultural sphere, creating a distance between their lives and origins of the fortune that made their lives possible.[10] Nor was it unusual for industrial fortunes to be invested in contemporary art. The great museums of northern England, the heartland of Victorian British industry, including Manchester, Liverpool, and Birmingham, boast fabulous collections of advanced British contemporary art from the mid-nineteenth century, donated to them by wealthy industrialists who collected it when it was new. Interestingly, however, such collectors seemed to tend temperamentally toward one of two approaches to patronage. Some bought art that was wholly different from their own lives and the means through which they acquired their wealth. The Gothic Revivalists, Pre-Raphaelites, and the circle around the artist-designer William Morris, for example, were essentially stylistic escapees from, and haters of, the modern world. Indeed, Manchester, the city literally at the heart of the industrial world in the Victorian age, has an art gallery rich in Pre-Raphaelite art donated by such patrons; and the city fathers chose to build a city hall in high Gothic style, an idiom that flatly negated the century and the ethos that had made Manchester possible. More pertinent still, the Marquis of Bute, one of the great industrial magnates of the nineteenth century, hired William Burges, a Gothic Revivalist and sometime mystic opium addict, to fashion Cardiff Castle in Wales as a medieval fantasy.[11] Some of the British, it seems, wanted to live in Camelot, not Lancashire or the Rhondda Valley.[12]

Other collectors made wealthy by industrialism were far more comfortable embracing art that implied the modern world. The Davies sisters numbered among these, their tastes decisively placing them among those who wished to avoid historicism, escapism, and mysticism. Unashamed of where they came from, they, understandably, do not appear to have dwelled too heavily on Dickens or Zola, but they determined that they wanted to celebrate the world into which they

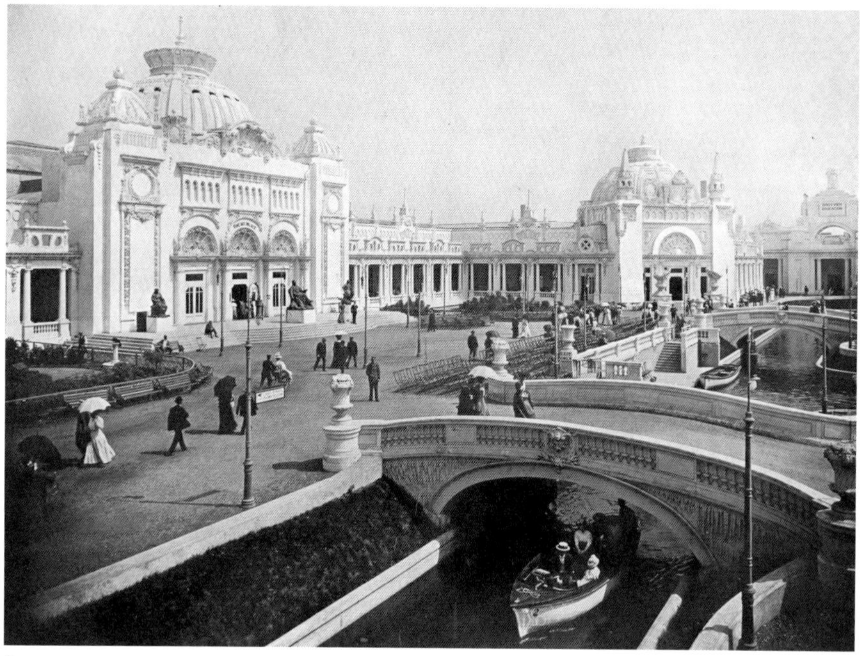

6

were born. And as with many British and American patrons, they were deeply committed to the French idea of culture. In this, they were far from unique. Indeed, and interestingly in the current context, a hauntingly similar story to theirs can be found in the life and career of the American senator William A. Clark. Clark made a fortune in mining (in Montana), entered national politics (like David Davies), fell passionately in love with French culture, and assembled a superb art collection, including a magnificent body of French Realist, Naturalist, and Impressionist work, which he donated at his death to a major public institution, the Corcoran Gallery of Art (see fig. 3).[13]

When the Davies sisters began to collect, it was an interesting moment in the artistic milieu in terms of what could be seen and bought. The major British private galleries, most notably the Sackville and Grafton Galleries, were successfully making the British aware of the avant-garde. With relatively little effort, Gwendoline and Margaret Davies could have seen the most aggressively advanced artists in Europe. For example, perhaps the most seminal exhibition of the period, held at the Grafton Galleries and organized by the critic Roger Fry, gave Post-Impressionism its name and made modernism acceptable, at least to the braver patrons of art. *Manet and the Post-Impressionists* essentially described the move from Impressionism to the next generation and explained the prefix "post" as being a signifier for those artists interested in moving away from direct representation of a thing, toward a more fundamentally abstract mode of expression (see fig. 4). The catalogue essay by Fry explains: "Impressionism encouraged an artist to paint a tree as it appeared … his work often failed to express a tree at all … The 'treeness' of the tree was not rendered at all … ."[14] The exhibition contained quite a few examples of how to achieve "treeness." It presented a liberally inclusive selection, but overall, the exhibition was dominated by Cézanne, Gauguin, and their followers. Among the younger artists, Matisse and his Fauvist colleagues were heavily represented.[15] At the end of 1912, a second Post-Impressionist exhibition, again at the Grafton Galleries, included French, Russian, and British artists and more powerfully carried the story beyond Fauvism into Cubism and Vorticism (see fig. 5). Also in 1912, the Sackville Gallery staged a large exhibition on the Italian Futurists.[16]

These latter two were more aggressively eclectic shows, and part of a wider international "coming-out" of modern art. Such works could be seen in a dozen places in Paris and at a few venues in New York, Berlin, Cologne, and Prague. In 1913, the New York Armory Show splashed modernism across the palettes of American art lovers.

In the mainstream, the single largest exhibition of French art and culture ever staged in Britain opened in London in 1908, in the form of a two-nation World's Fair. The Franco-British Exhibition covered 140 acres in Shepherds Bush (in an area still known as the White City, after the nickname of the exhibition) and had eight and a half million visitors over a six-month period (see fig. 6).[17] Massively reported on, the exhibition presented a very large survey of contemporary French fine and decorative art (see fig. 7). It was a giant, confusing mélange with many agendas, but one of these was to introduce a mass audience to trends in current art. The more advanced art critics rightly realized

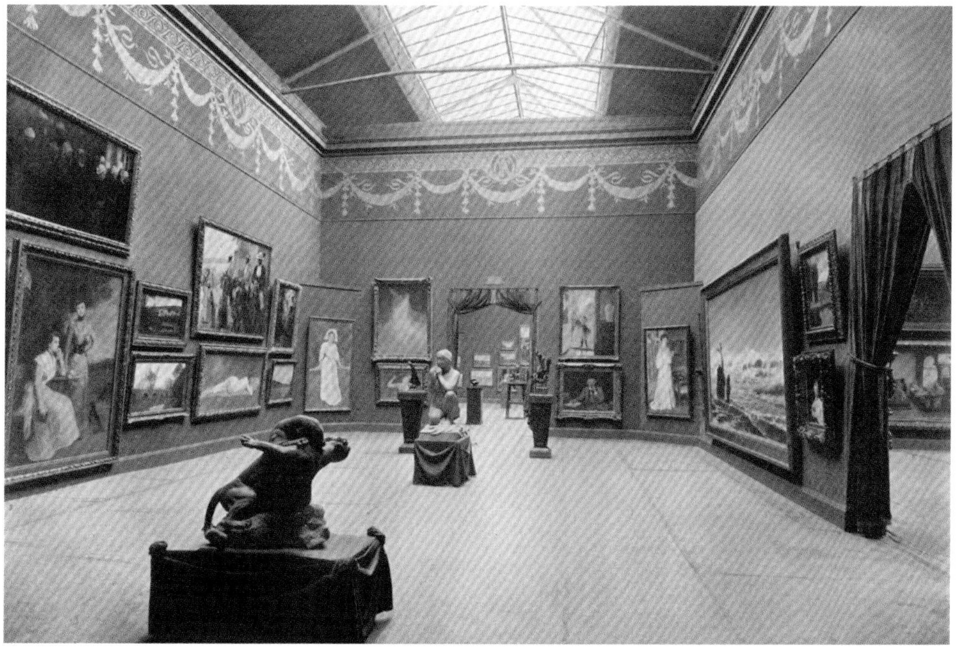

7

Figure 6 The Fine Arts Palace, London, one of the exhibition halls for the Franco-British Exhibition. Reprinted from *The Franco-British Exhibition: Official Souvenir* (London: Hudson & Kearns, 1908).

Figure 7 The exhibition *French Art Selections – Oil Paintings*, part of the Franco-British Exhibition. Reprinted from *Souvenir of the Fine Art Section Franco-British Exhibition 1908*, compiled by Sir Isidore Spielmann (London: Bemrose & Sons, 1908).

that it largely failed to do so. Sir Walter Armstrong, an astute observer of art, wrote in *The Guardian*:

> The freest and most modern spirits are represented but poorly… impressionism is represented of course, but only by comparatively unimportant things – three or four bad Renoirs, one Manet, one good Monet and several poor ones, a Sisley or two – while nothing further down the slope of revolution has been admitted at all, not even a Cézanne.[18]

What is interesting here is the fact that Armstrong, a conservative, perceived Cézanne, who had died only two years before, not as a radical but as relatively mainstream. While it would be a mistake to assume Impressionism and Post-Impressionism had become widely acceptable, they were undoubtedly moving slowly toward this condition. However, mainstream reportage and popular taste in the decorative and fine arts, in the specific period of 1908 to 1914, began a steady slide into a conservatism that was ultimately to wallow in bigotry. As European nationalism heated up in the years before 1914, all the major European nations embraced traditionalism and became increasingly suspicious of all that might be perceived as "foreign." While these were undoubtedly the years of the avant-garde in the most rarefied artistic circles, this was not the case in the larger world.[19]

The Davies sisters, who were already highly unusual, as serious supporters of modern art living outside of the major centers, sat interestingly in this environment.[20] Their taste was brave: admirably and positively modern. They did not live in La Ruche or La Bateau Lavoir, among the Parisian avant-garde; they lived in Plas Dinam. Their daily milieu was one in which their choice of art stood out dramatically; it would have raised eyebrows and demanded justification and defense. Understandably therefore, their taste was not aggressively modernist but was poised between the radical and the conservative. The sisters would not have been alienated by the first Post-Impressionism exhibition but would have been by the second. They never ventured into the aggressive end of Fauvism or the worlds of Cubism, Futurism, or Vorticism, despite the fact that these things were loudly unfolding around them. Such brutally modernist and utopian visions were not for them. On the other hand, they were ultimately far more adventurous than the organizers of the Franco-British Exhibition. In short, they recognized that they lived in the modern world, grasping and enjoying the way some artists reported its effects on normative life; but they refused to pursue modernity to ideological extremes and were not interested in critique, deconstruction, or transformation. With notable exceptions, they did not venture too far beyond the parameters of Impressionism; they clearly enjoyed its prosaic, domestic urban modernity and its optimism.

Gwendoline and Margaret Davies had fundamentally different lives from Henriette Henriot – *La Parisienne* – but they came from the same modern world as she did, and they understood her value system. More than anything, therefore, they were the patrons of modern, optimistic reportage.

Colin B. Bailey Looking Closely at Renoir's *La Parisienne*

How simple it is, how beautiful, and how fresh. Paul Signac, 1898[1]

Renoir's ambitions as a figure painter during the 1860s and 1870s were driven by the challenge to construct a new language of modern painting while respecting the traditional hierarchies of the artistic establishment. Hence his determination to participate in the official Salon, to which he submitted work every year but three between 1864 and 1880.[2] Hence also his preference for large canvases – the stock-in-trade of the history painter, calculated to make an impact in the crowded rooms of the Palais de l'Industrie – to whose formats he returned for the far more intimate installations of the Impressionists. Renoir's *La Parisienne* (fig. 1 and cat. no. 39) exemplifies this paradox: a work scaled for the official Salon and painted with an intransigent's color and audaciousness.[3]

La Parisienne was the largest of the six works that Renoir showed at the inaugural Impressionist exhibition held at Nadar's former studio on the Boulevard des Capucines between 15 April and 15 May 1874.[4] It was the painting that he valued most highly, priced for sale at 3,500 francs – quite unrealistically, as it turned out.[5] With *The Dancer* (fig. 2) and *La Loge* (fig. 3), *La Parisienne* represented Renoir's aspirations to follow in Manet's footsteps as a painter of modern life; his other submissions were calculated to show his abilities in the lesser genres of landscape and still life.[6] Pecuniary value mirrored aesthetic priorities. *The Dancer* was offered for sale at 3,000 francs, *La Loge* at 2,500 francs, and the landscape *Harvesters* (private collection, Zurich) at 1,000 francs. Only the last-mentioned canvas would sell during the run of the exhibition; the others were returned to Renoir, who found buyers for them at much reduced prices in the years to come.[7]

Initially, Renoir had been reluctant to secede from the official arena. His name is not mentioned in Pissarro and Monet's earliest discussions about organizing a group exhibition in defiance of the Salon, nor was he listed as a potential participant in Paul Alexis's article in *L'Avenir National* of May 1873.[8] Indeed, that very month he was experiencing the indignities of the Salon des Refusés, where his megalomaniacal *Riding in the Bois de Boulogne* (fig. 4) was on view in a makeshift pavilion opposite the Palais de l'Industrie.[9] Renoir's change of heart seems to have taken place during the summer of 1873, when he drew closer to Monet and his family and began to paint at Argenteuil. By the winter of that year, he was thoroughly committed to an artists' cooperative that would boycott the Salon and show in an alternative space with neither jury nor prizes.[10] In the earliest drafts of the organization, Renoir is named as one of two *commissaires* responsible with the *gérant* (or manager) for planning and running the exhibition; in the published bylaws, he is listed as a member of the *Conseil provisoire de surveillance*. It was in his apartment on the rue Saint-Georges that these bylaws were drawn up at the end of December 1873, and it was there that the ailing cooperative would be dissolved a year later.[11]

It is not clear exactly when Nadar's former studio – which the photographer had given up in 1871—was chosen as the venue for the Société Anonyme's inaugural exhibition (fig. 5).[12] The earliest press announcements did not list this well-known address, and although Monet, in

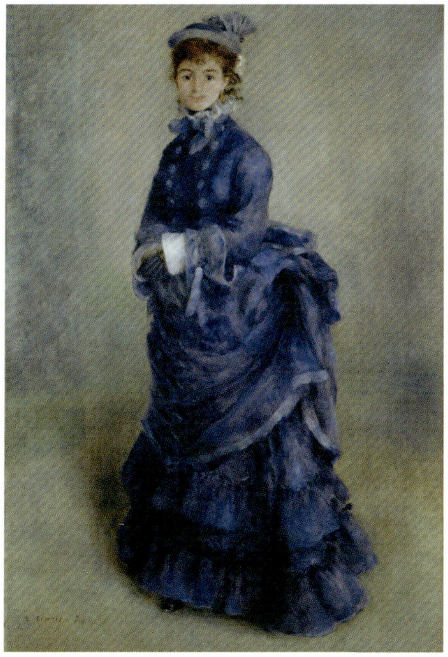

1

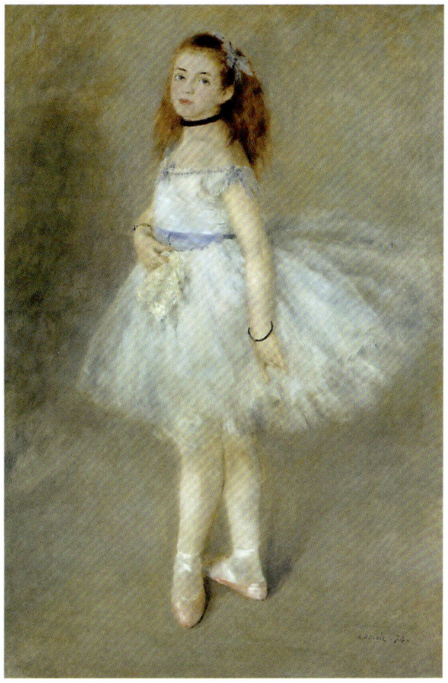

2

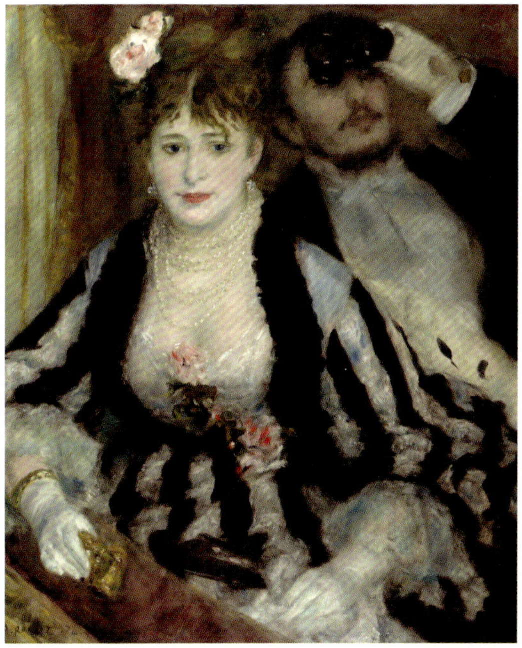

3

old age, recalled that the photographer had offered his premises at no charge, the accounts show that the group paid 2,020 francs in rent and 983 francs for gas lighting (the exhibition was open between ten and six o'clock, and between eight and ten o'clock at night).[13] The advantages of Nadar's establishment lay chiefly in the layout – between six and eight rooms (estimates differ) on two floors linked by a "Chinese staircase" – and the generous natural lighting afforded by the floor-to-ceiling windows that faced the street.[14] The critic Philippe Burty spoke admiringly of the opportunity for the group "to present their paintings almost under the same conditions as in a studio, that is, in good light, isolated from one another, in smaller numbers than in official exhibitions."[15] In his review for *La République française*, he noted that the lighting was similar to that found in a "moderately spacious apartment" *(un appartement moyen)*.[16]

The choice of venue and the relatively brief interval leading up to the exhibition – the bylaws were drawn up on 27 December 1873, but it is unlikely that Nadar's studio was "booked" until February of the following year – played a part in determining the subjects that Renoir chose and the manner in which he painted them. His three principal submissions must have been executed in less than four months, and thus he was prepared to paint in a more abbreviated and higher-keyed manner than in his rejected submissions to the official Salon the year before. While *La Loge* has a relatively elaborate paint surface, both *The Dancer* and *La Parisienne* are quickly executed, on light grounds, with brushwork visible and traces of impasto alternating with the most summary laying in of color.[17]

Figure 1 Pierre-Auguste Renoir, *La Parisienne*, 1874 (cat. no. 39)

Figure 2 Pierre-Auguste Renoir, *The Dancer*, 1874. Oil on canvas, 56 ⅛ x 37 ⅛ in. National Gallery of Art, Washington; Widener Collection (1942.9.72). Courtesy Board of Trustees, National Gallery of Art, Washington

Figure 3 Pierre-Auguste Renoir, *La Loge*, 1874. Oil on canvas, 31 ½ x 25 in. The Samuel Courtauld Trust, Courtauld Gallery, London

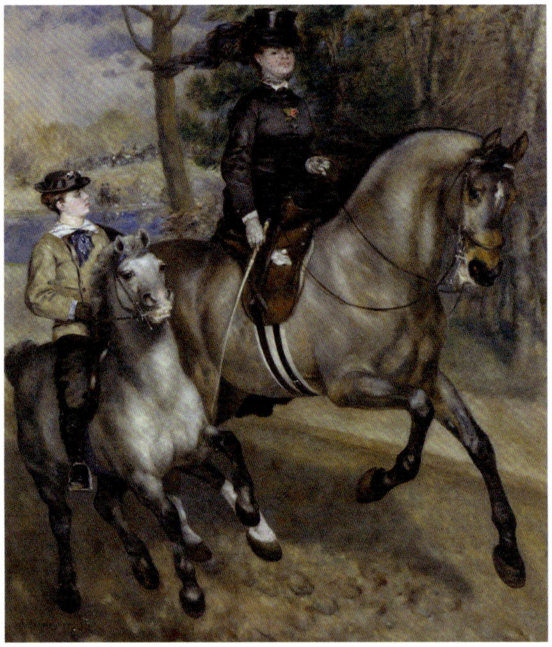

4

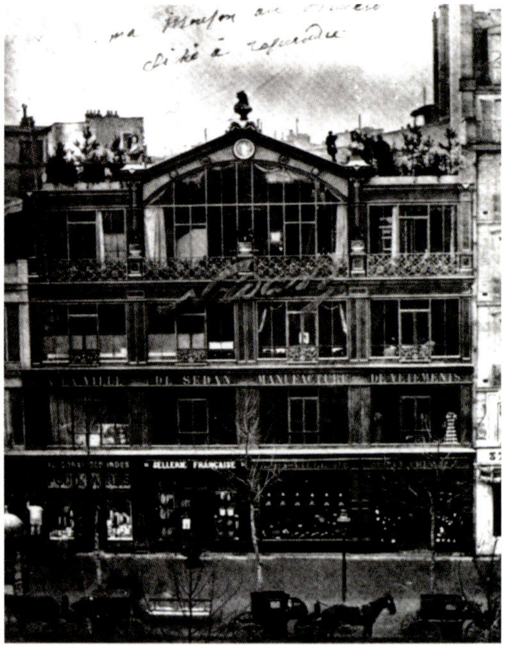

5

Renoir could be assured that his pictures would be well presented, since the Société's bylaws specified that works would not be "skied" as in the official Salon. Hanging was to be on two levels at most, with the privilege of having a work "on the line" *(à la cimaise)* determined in each room by drawing lots.[18] Once decided, the arrangement within the room was alphabetical, as in the Salon. Critics seem to have appreciated the less crowded hang: "At every corner, well lit and without having to crick one's neck *(sans torsion de cou)*, one finds a striking work that is never banal."[19] Both Degas and Pissarro had very strong opinions about how the works should be displayed,[20] yet it was Renoir who was left to hang the exhibition on his own; he complained to Philippe Burty that he was "up to his eyes in this complicated installation."[21] Although no floor plan of the Société Anonyme's inaugural exhibition has survived – and the catalogue is ordered alphabetically rather than by room – it is possible to gain a sense of how Renoir's works were shown from the rich journalistic record. The artist's pictures appear to have been displayed in the first room of the ground floor of the exhibition, with *La Parisienne* hanging on the same wall as *The Dancer*, which was placed opposite the doorway and thus enjoyed the sight line from the adjoining rooms.[22] The hang encouraged one reviewer to treat Renoir's three principal canvases as part of a series: "Now turn your head, and you will see the two of them, the little girl and the young lady, grown up, blossoming and potent, in the canvas that M. Renoir entitles *L'Avant-scène*" (the alternative title for *La Loge*).[23]

La Parisienne shows a young model dressed from head to toe in an outdoor morning toilette of striking blue silk, with matching toque and choker. She wears gloves of the same color, trimmed with fur (possibly squirrel), the edge of which peeks out from beneath the bright starched cuff on her left hand (fig. 6). Her fashionable day ensemble consists of a jacket worn over a double-layer skirt, with the overskirt pulled back into the bustle in the back and the underskirt trimmed with two pleated flounces at the front. The double row of buttons that continues from her collar to the end of the overskirt is almost military in style; despite the banded edges of the overskirt and the ribbons hanging off the cuffs, the design of the dress is relatively simple. The absence of accessories and of figured patterns on the material confirms that this outfit, while stylish, is not couture.[24]

Although Renoir does not seem to have slavishly copied his prototype from the pages of a fashion magazine, the dress worn by his *Parisienne* was not simply of his own invention. In 1873, bright blues and mauves seem to have been in high fashion, as were the shaped bodice, bustle skirt, and pleated hem.[25] In Emile Zola's *Ventre de Paris*, published that year, Cadine, a flower seller of Les Halles, gazes covetously at the fabrics in a department store, "the pieces draped and set off to advantage by the window dressers, some *soft blue* or apple-green silk," from which she dreams of making a Sunday dress, trimmed with pink ribbons.[26] Certain elements of the dress worn by Renoir's model – and materials strikingly similar in color – appear in the plates of *Journal des Demoiselles*, although these ensembles are more elaborate and feature more luxurious fabrics and accessories than in the painting (figs. 7 and 8). The Kyoto Costume Institute owns a faille day dress with silk taffeta ribbons and black braid on the hem

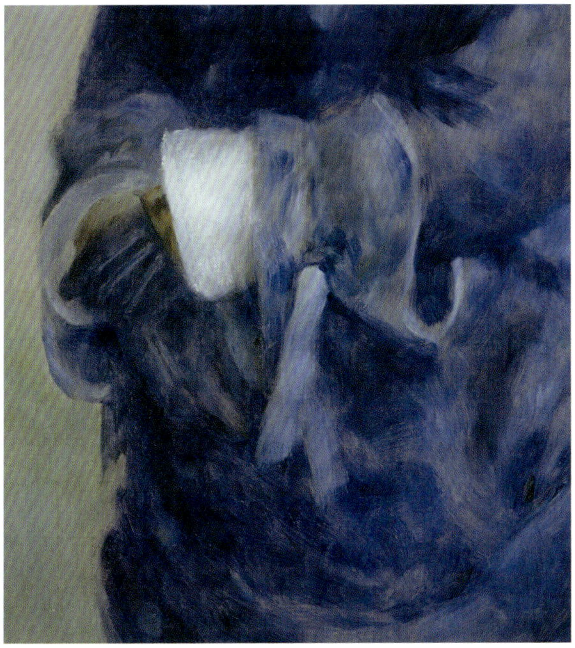

6

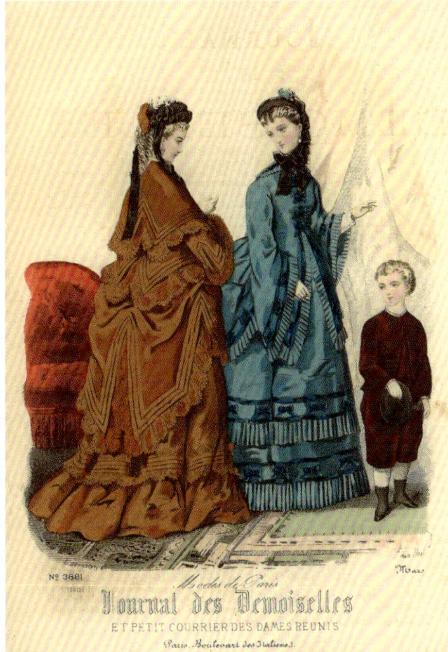

7

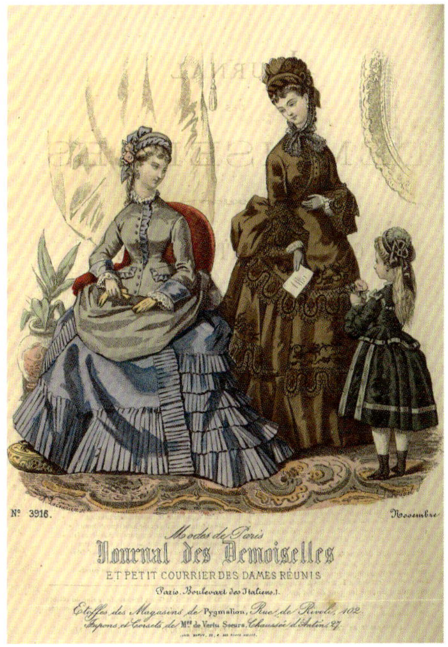

8

dated to about 1874, which, while not of precisely the same design, is very close in overall shape and construction (figs. 9 and 10).[27] The Kyoto model differs from that worn by Renoir's Parisienne in its bodice with a single row of buttons, its tight sleeves with no cuffs, and an overskirt less flamboyantly draped in the bustle. Strikingly similar, however, is the color of the fabric, a coal-tar hue known as *bleu de Lyon*, "which dyes silk readily and retains its blue color by artificial light."[28] Such high-keyed fabrics were possible because of the synthetic, aniline dyes pioneered in England in the late 1850s by William Henry Perkins and used in dress design throughout Europe during the following decades.[29]

In recognition of this, perhaps, several critics referred to Renoir's striking figure as "la Dame en bleu"; cobalt was certainly among the artist's favorite pigments in the 1870s and is here mixed liberally with white.[30] Renoir was working on a commercially primed canvas, of a width slightly greater than the standard format, whose white ground he toned with the application of a thin red glaze.[31] Initially, he situated his model in a more defined setting – a curtain at left, a column at right (?) – also laid in in blue wash but subsequently painted out. If Renoir had intended to evoke an urban promenade, or the interior of a fashionable department store, he suppressed such anecdotal details, thereby distancing his subject from the minutiae of conspicuous consumption. As Arsène Alexandre noted in May 1892, "She is shown without any indication of setting or milieu, against one of those changeable backgrounds that blends into a complex shade of grey beloved by the artist."[32]

As with *The Dancer*, Renoir's handling is a bravura (and assured) performance in which conventional details are handled in an

Figure 4 Pierre-Auguste Renoir, *Riding in the Bois de Boulogne*, 1873. Oil on canvas, 103 x 89 ⅛ in. Hamburger Kunsthalle, Hamburg, Germany. Photo Bildarchiv Preussischer Kulturbesitz / Art Resource, NY

Figure 5 Nadar's studio, ca. 1870. Albuman print. Bibliothèque nationale de France

Figure 6 Detail of *La Parisienne* (cat. no. 39)

Figure 7 *Journal des Demoiselles*, March 1873. © The Kyoto Costume Institute

Figure 8 *Journal des Demoiselles*, November 1873. © The Kyoto Costume Institute

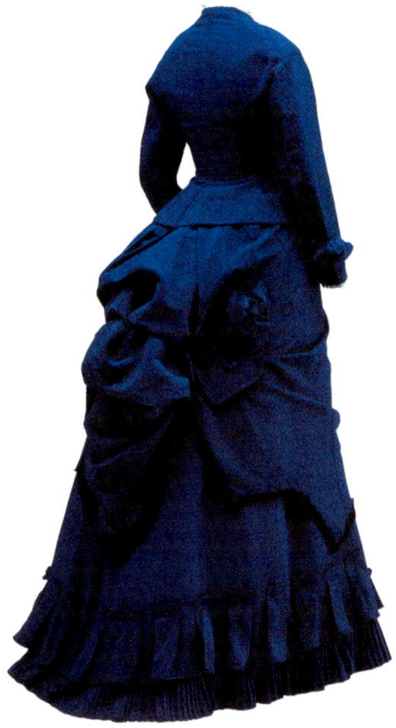

9

extremely sketchy way. In keeping with the tenets of the New Painting, his modeling of the figure is coloristic, with details of *La Parisienne's* face outlined in blue-green, her hair in green-yellow, and the shadows in the folds of her costume inflected in green (fig. 11). Renoir's treatment of the complicated engineering of the silk ensemble is a tour de force – his father had been a tailor, his mother a dressmaker – and despite the lack of a setting, the figure is fully anchored in the indeterminate space. If the subject of the chic *parisienne* was already something of a visual cliché, with mainstream genre painters happy to exploit the frisson of the unaccompanied woman on display for unseen male admirers (see fig. 12), Renoir's treatment of it was notably restrained and demure. The transgressive qualities of the figure in *La Parisienne* are primarily painterly; there is propriety in her appearance, her gaze is unthreatening, and it is hard to see her as a blatant example of "commodified femininity."[33] Indeed, for the reviewer of the first Impressionist exhibition writing under the pseudonym of Jean Prouvaire (Victor Hugo's insurgent), Renoir's standing figure was not coquettish enough. With the exception of her hat, "daringly" tilted over one ear, he complained: "We hardly even see the tip of her ankle boot, which peeps out like a little black mouse. Her dress does not reveal enough of her body. There is nothing more annoying than locked doors."[34]

Criticism of *La Parisienne* in the other reviews of the first Impressionist exhibition was laconic but generally favorable. While scathing about the exhibition overall, de Gantès praised *La Parisienne* as "well composed and forthrightly painted"; and de Lora admired Renoir's "pretty standing figure, an effect of blue upon blue that is astonishing."[35] Certainly, Renoir's abbreviated manner drew attention, and Armand Silvestre was troubled by the sketchy quality of both *The Dancer* and *La Parisienne*: "The figure should not be systematically treated in such a summary fashion."[36] Ernest Chesnau was the only writer to consider the painting a "failure."[37]

Renoir's title of *Parisienne* placed the work securely within the orbit of a literary and cultural type. His female *flâneur* descended from the flirtatious, elegant urban consumer variously popularized in Théodore de Banville's verse and prose poems, Zola's novels, journalistic illustration, and the fashion press.[38] Yet Prouvaire cautioned that Renoir's picture might also be read as a portrait: "The face, strangely old-looking and childish at the same time, meets us with a false smile, yet the figure has an innocence about her. One could say that this little person is doing her best to be kittenish."[39] While Renoir chose not to present himself as a portraitist at the first Impressionist exhibition, "the little person" who modeled for his *Parisienne* can be identified as Marie-Henriette-Alphonsine Grossin (1857–1944), an aspiring actress, not yet seventeen years of age, recently back in Paris after a tour in the provinces. Grossin began appearing in minor roles at the Théâtre de l'Ambigue-Comique in 1875 – at which point she adopted the stage name of Henriot – and she was the model for no fewer than eleven of Renoir's paintings in the mid-1870s. Her career as a successful vaudeville comedienne took off only in the late 1880s, when she was "discovered" by the actor-director André Antoine, the creator of the avant-garde Théâtre-Libre in the rue Blanche, who cast her in the most coquettish roles.[40]

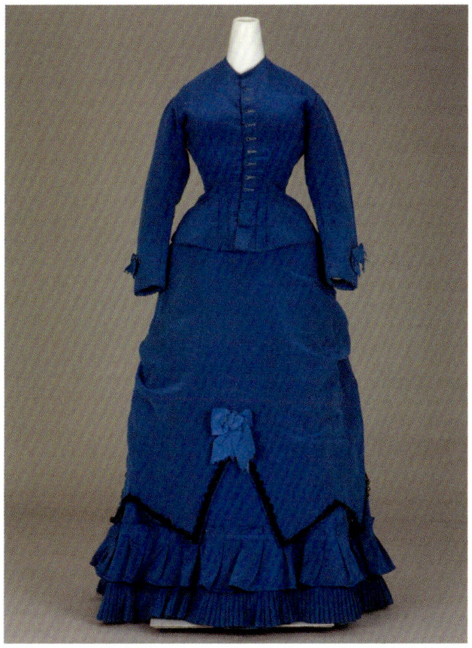

10

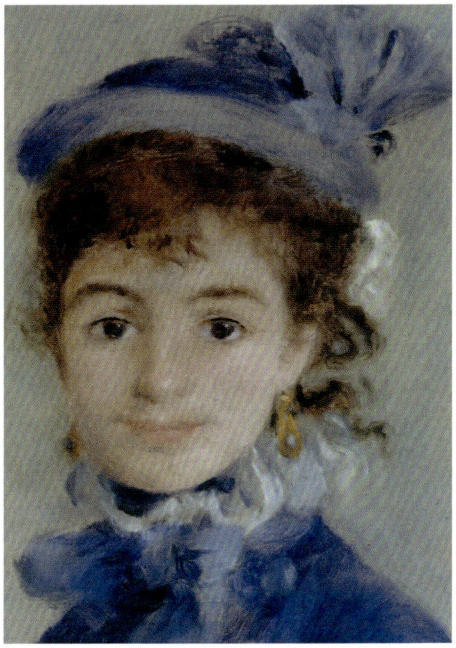

11

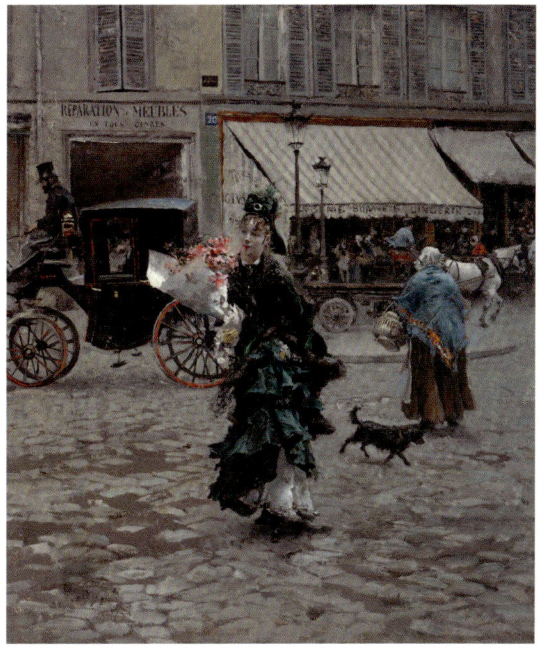

12

A dark-eyed and not particularly beautiful actress with a full jaw (fig. 13), born out of wedlock to a milliner, in 1874 Marie-Henriette had the physical characteristics Renoir most admired and was of an age to appeal to him (Renoir had recently broken with the Le Coeur family after making advances to their fifteen-year-old daughter).[41] His most romantic portrayal of her, the delicate and vaporous *Portrait of Madame Henriot* (fig. 14), most likely painted in 1875, was also the only portrait of her by Renoir that the model owned.[42] Appropriately, in this work, far more attention is focused on Henriot's face than it is in *La Parisienne*, but the voluptuousness of Renoir's portrayal may also have been inspired by criticism of the earlier painting. In his depiction of Henriot's bare arms and ravishing décolletage, might Renoir not have been responding at some level to Prouvaire's complaint that his *Parisienne* had been too resolutely clothed?

Although Degas considered the first Impressionist exhibition a commercial and critical success, few of the works sold during the run of the exhibition at the (inflated) prices assigned to them by the participants.[43] Renoir's *Parisienne* was a case in point. It was acquired in October 1874 for the sum of 1,200 francs – a third of the initial asking price – by the industrialist and collector Stanislas-Henri Rouart (1833–1912).[44] Two weeks before the first Impressionist exhibition opened, Rouart had agreed to purchase Renoir's *Riding in the Bois de Boulogne*, which had failed to find a buyer since its appearance at the Salon des Refusés of the previous year, for the sum of 2,000 francs (to be paid in three installments).[45] The slightly lower price for *La Parisienne* was in keeping with the market for Renoir's ambitious single-figure paintings; in May

Figure 9 *Day Dress* (back view), ca. 1874. Faille, silk taffeta. Kyoto Costume Institute (AC2196 1979-09-1AC). © The Kyoto Costume Institute. Photo Takashi Hatakeyama

Figure 10 *Day Dress* (front view), ca. 1874. © The Kyoto Costume Institute

Figure 11 Detail of *La Parisienne* (cat. no. 39)

Figure 12 Giovanni Boldini, *Crossing the Street*, 1875. Oil on canvas, 18 1/16 x 14 3/4 in. The Sterling and Francine Clark Art Institute, Williamstown, Massachusetts

1873, Duret had paid the same amount (1,200 francs) for *Lise with an Umbrella* (Museum Folkwang, Essen), unsold since its appearance at the Salon of 1868.[46] In the early 1870s, Manet's canvases were for the first time able to command the sums that Renoir had assigned to his three principal submissions to the first Impressionist exhibition. As Duret would remind the painter Camille Pissarro in June 1874, the discerning art lovers who had collected their work were of a different breed from the rich amateurs able to pay large prices: "It will be many years, I think, before you can expect to sell your paintings regularly for between 1,500 and 2,000 francs."[47]

A school friend of Degas, and an engineer who pioneered the introduction of metal tubing and refrigeration into France – the Paris Morgue was a major client – Rouart was an amateur landscape painter of some distinction, who had sent work to each Salon between 1868 and 1872.[48] He also exhibited alongside the Impressionists in the spring of 1874, where – because of the alphabetical hanging arrangement – his landscapes were displayed next to Renoir's figure paintings (just as his two landscapes had hung with Renoir's *Riding in the Bois de Boulogne* at the Salon des Refusés in 1873).[49] Rouart's familiarity with both of Renoir's monumental modern-life paintings – and his decision to purchase them – may in part be associated with the quiddities of installation that had made temporary neighbors of Renoir and himself for the run of the respective exhibitions. While Rouart would go on to assemble an impressive collection of nineteenth-century painting – which included masterpieces by Millet, Degas, and Corot – he cannot be said to have had a particular affinity for Renoir since *La Parisienne* was the last work by the artist that he would acquire.[50]

After its appearance in the first Impressionist exhibition, *La Parisienne* went on public display in Paris on only one more occasion, in Renoir's mid-career retrospective of 110 works organized by Durand-Ruel in May 1892.[51] Rouart's collection was certainly accessible to those with an interest in Barbizon and Impressionist paintings, and at least two visits by artists are documented. In January 1898, Renoir accompanied his students Jeanne Baudot and Julie Manet to Rouart's *hôtel particulier* at 34 rue de Lisbonne, near the Parc Monceau. Julie Manet was struck above all by the many figure paintings by Corot, greatly admired by Renoir and for which Rouart's collection was renowned. "Now I understand M. Renoir's enthusiasm; the greatness of Corot's genius was apparent to me for the first time; until now I thought I loved his work but I did not appreciate him in the way he should be appreciated."[52] She was most taken by Renoir's *Riding in the Bois de Boulogne* but also noted "a woman in blue and another thing" by the artist.[53]

The following month (February 1898), Edouard Vuillard introduced Paul Signac to Rouart's collection, which he pronounced "une profusion de merveilles." Unlike Julie Manet, Signac was most impressed by Renoir's *Parisienne*, commenting: "A large portrait of a woman in blue by Renoir painted in 1874. The dress is blue and of a purity and intensity that makes the flesh tones appear almost yellow by contrast, and somewhat green from the reflections. The play of colors is admirable. How simple it is, how beautiful, and how fresh. It is as if this painting, done twenty years ago, had just emerged from the artist's studio."[54]

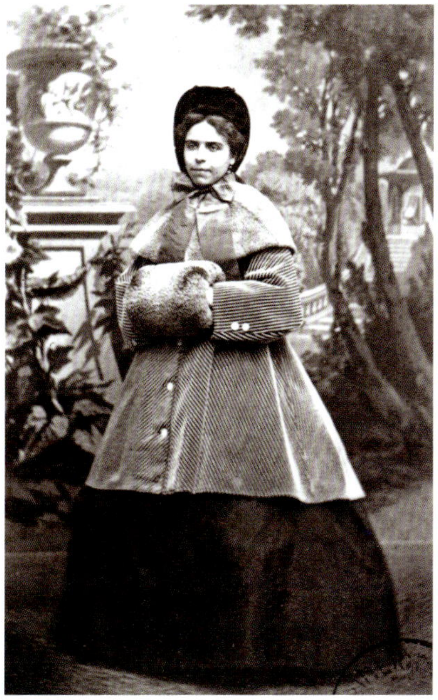

13

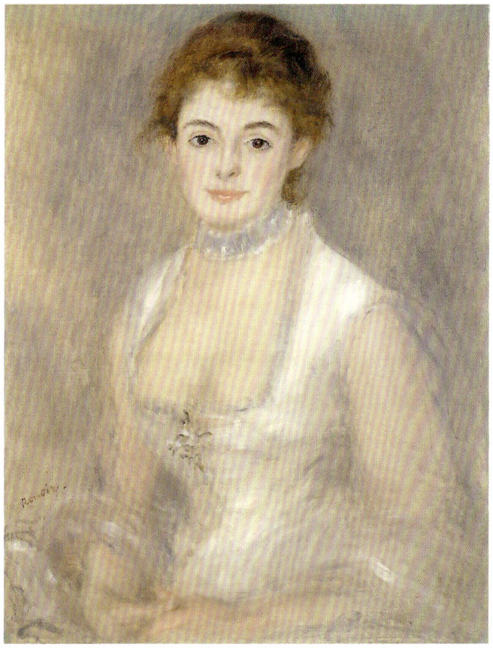

14

At the sale of Rouart's collection between 9 and 11 December 1912, *La Parisienne* was acquired by Knoedler and Durand-Ruel jointly for 56,000 francs (plus commission).[55] This sale was noteworthy for the high prices fetched by Rouart's Impressionist pictures, above all Degas's *Dancers Practicing at the Bar* of 1876–77 (Metropolitan Museum of Art, New York), for which the Havemeyers paid the astonishing sum of 478,500 francs (Mary Cassatt had advised them to bid up to 200,000 francs).[56] Renoir, wintering in Cagnes at Les Collettes, was kept apprised of the details of "papa Rouart's auction, this sensational sale that has amazed everyone."[57] On 17 December 1912, Georges Durand-Ruel informed him that the gallery had acquired *La Parisienne* in concert with the London branch of Knoedler & Co., which it had finally convinced to enter the market for the New Painting. "We also pushed your other painting, *Riding in the Bois de Boulogne*, as high as we could go and then we let [the Berlin art dealer] Cassirer buy it for 95,000 francs."[58] Gwendoline Davies would pay the equivalent of 125,000 francs for the picture in June 1913, when she acquired it for £5,000 from the Grosvenor Gallery on 51A New Bond Street. She may have considered the price a bargain. The previous August, her adviser, Hugh Blaker, had encouraged this burgeoning interest in "the Impressionists of 1870": "Very few English collectors, except Hugh Lane, have bought them at all, although much of their best work is in America already. I expect you also know the work of Sisley, Pissarro and Renoir. These can still be got quite cheaply."[59]

Figure 13 Photograph of Henriette Henriot by Georges Numa, 1874. Courtesy Bibliothèque de l'Arsenal, Paris

Figure 14 Pierre-Auguste Renoir, *Portrait of Madame Henriot*, ca. 1875. Oil on canvas, 26 x 19 ⅛ in. National Gallery of Art, Washington; Gift of the Adele R. Levy Fund, Inc. Courtesy Board of Trustees, National Gallery of Art, Washington

Catalogue

Bargue Bevan Bon
Corot Daumier Derain John M
Monet Moret Morisot Pissarr
Sisley Smith Stevens Turner

rd Boudin Carrière Cézanne
net Mauve Meissonier Millet
Renoir Seguin Sickert Signac
n Gogh Vlaminck Whistler

Bargue With a historic veneer designed to elevate the work's status in the traditional hierarchy of painting, the action takes place at a non-specific point in the eighteenth century.

1 Charles Bargue (1826–1883)
The Artist's Model, 1874
Oil on board, 9 ¼ x 6 ½ in. (23.8 x 16.5 cm)
Miss Margaret S. Davies Bequest, 1963 (NMWA 2425)

Charles Bargue began his career as a popular lithographer. He studied under Jean-Léon Gérôme, with whom he wrote *Drawing Course (Cours de Dessin)* (published between 1866 and 1871),[1] a didactic publication upholding the principles of formal training for artists and guiding students through the rigors of working from plaster casts, master drawings, and from life. Bargue's output in oils was small, comprising single-figure Orientalist scenes and historic genre paintings such as this, most of which now reside in private collections.

Notable for its freedom of brush and invention of color, *The Artist's Model* is an oil sketch for *The Opinion of the Model*, a work of the same year that is now lost.[2] The sketch is typical in style, size, and subject of popular painting in France in the mid- to late nineteenth century, and the domestic scale of both this sketch and the finished piece is indicative of the purchasing power of the bourgeoisie, who formed an eager market for this type of painting. With a historic veneer designed to elevate the work's status in the traditional hierarchy of painting, the action takes place at a non-specific point in the eighteenth century. As is clear from the finished version (though not in the present sketch), the artist sits in a Rococo interior, painting a scene that recalls Boucher, Fragonard, and the art of the ancien régime. The historic setting is supported by the artist's costume and coiffeur. The model, however, appears to be something of an anachronism, not least because she holds a Japanese fan, which places the work firmly within a nineteenth-century frame of visual reference. As it was the relocation of flesh to a historical context (however vague) that enabled artists to bridge the conceptual gap between titillation and artistic merit, this may explain why the oil sketch's risqué depiction of swathes of back and ankle was not followed through to the finished work in which the model is rather more substantially covered.

With much the same appeal as Meissonier, Bargue was still in vogue at the beginning of the twentieth century, and Margaret Davies may have seen his work in Paris. She acquired *The Artist's Model*, which was formerly in the collection of Alexander Young, in 1910, securing Meissonier's *Innocents and Card Sharpers* (cat. no. 27) in the same year. These two stylistically similar purchases are indicative of the conservatism in the early years of the sisters' collecting.

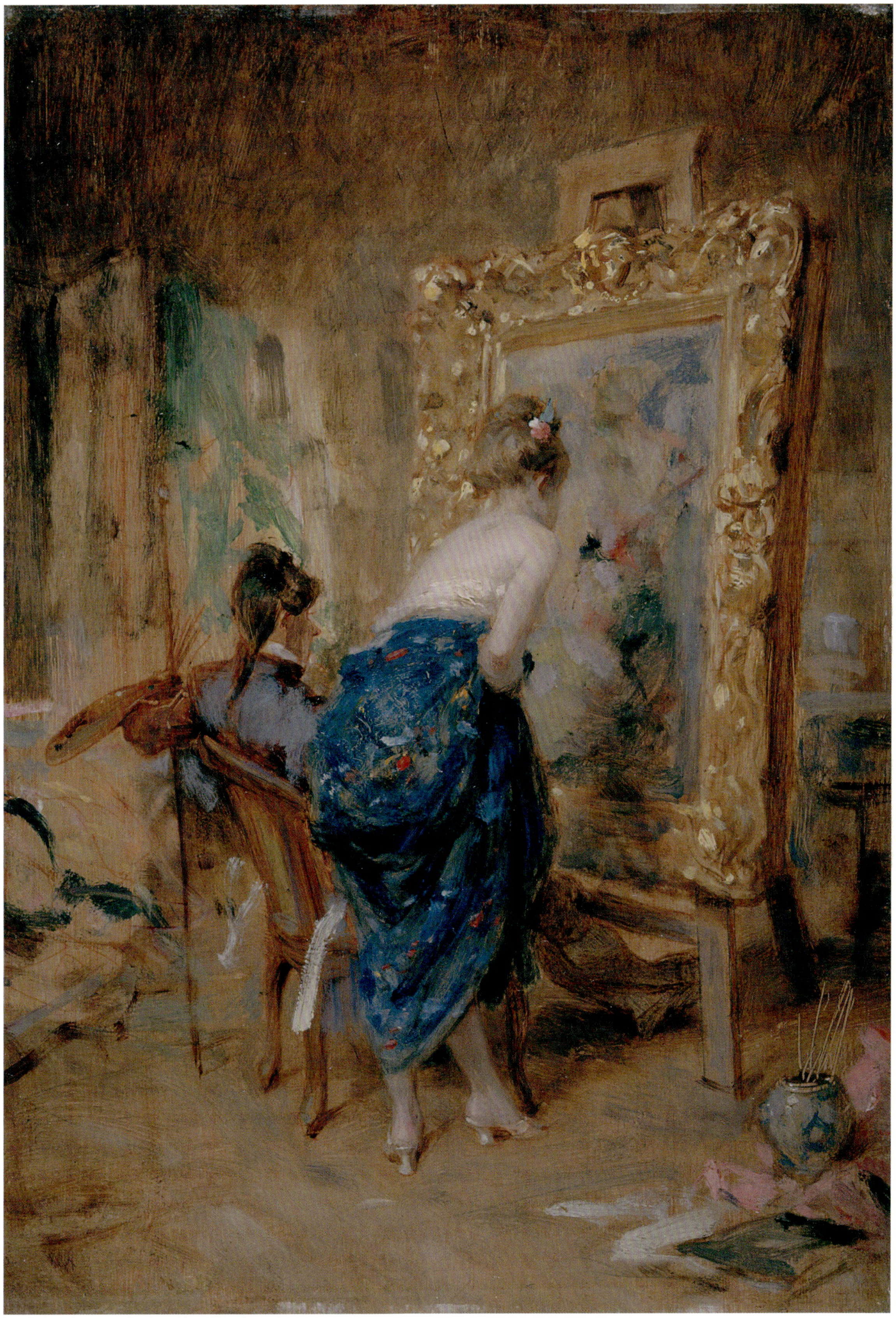

Bevan The painting's flat, hard-edged shapes and chalky palette are most suggestive of the work of the Nabis, who were followers of Gauguin.

2 Robert Polhill Bevan (1865–1925)
Maples at Cuckfield, Sussex, 1914
Oil on canvas, 20 ¼ x 24 ⅛ in. (51.4 x 61.2 cm)
Miss Margaret S. Davies Bequest, 1963 (NMWA 2085)

Robert Bevan was a founding member of the Camden Town Group, which included Walter Richard Sickert and Harold Gilman. The group sought to depict the urban quotidian with a Post-Impressionist verve and was one of a number of early twentieth-century British artist groups bound together by stylistic or ideological concerns. Such artistic alliances were vital to the development of modernism in Britain, functioning as both a forum for peer review and an opportunity for independent exhibition. In 1914, Bevan, along with Gilman and Charles Ginner, formed the breakaway Cumberland Market Group, which reflected Bevan's propensity for painting horses and horse sales. This painting dates from that time, a period during which Bevan's distinctive style reached its maturity.

Maples at Cuckfield, Sussex was painted at the artist's family home in Cuckfield, Sussex, where Bevan stayed with his wife, the Polish artist Stanislava Karlowska, in the summer of 1914. It is one of three canvases dating from this stay, which depict the same view. The two others are both titled *The Town Field, Horsgate:* one is now owned by the Reading Museum in Reading, England, and the other is in a private collection. The similarity among these three works is marked, with their jagged pools of shadow and angular cattle, though *Maples* is marginally more limited in palette, being composed almost entirely of mint green, pink, and purple to conjure the sensation of rural hush on a hot, still day.

Maples at Cuckfield, Sussex and its related canvases occupy something of a midpoint for Bevan between his early softer Fauve style and a later, semi-abstract, almost Vorticist approach to the landscape. The painting's flat, hard-edged shapes and chalky palette are most suggestive of the work of the Nabis, who were followers of Gauguin. In the early 1890s, Bevan had spent time at Pont-Aven, where he met Gauguin, and his stylistic development does to an extent follow that of the older artist. Gauguin's aim for the reduction of art to the essentials of color, surface, and form can clearly be seen in *Maples at Cuckfield, Sussex*, as can the Nabis' interest in pattern and design. Earlier oils by Bevan of this scene have a more fluid naturalism and painterly interest. The 1914 canvases see Bevan heavily refining both color and shape, reflecting Roger Fry's aesthetic ideals of formalism, which were key to modernism in Britain in the early 1910s. *Maples at Cuckfield, Sussex* was purchased by Margaret Davies in 1954, the year after Gwendoline's bequest entered the National Museum of Wales. With the knowledge that her collection was also destined for the same location, Margaret began acquiring British work of the early twentieth century with a view to enhancing the fledgling collection at the museum.

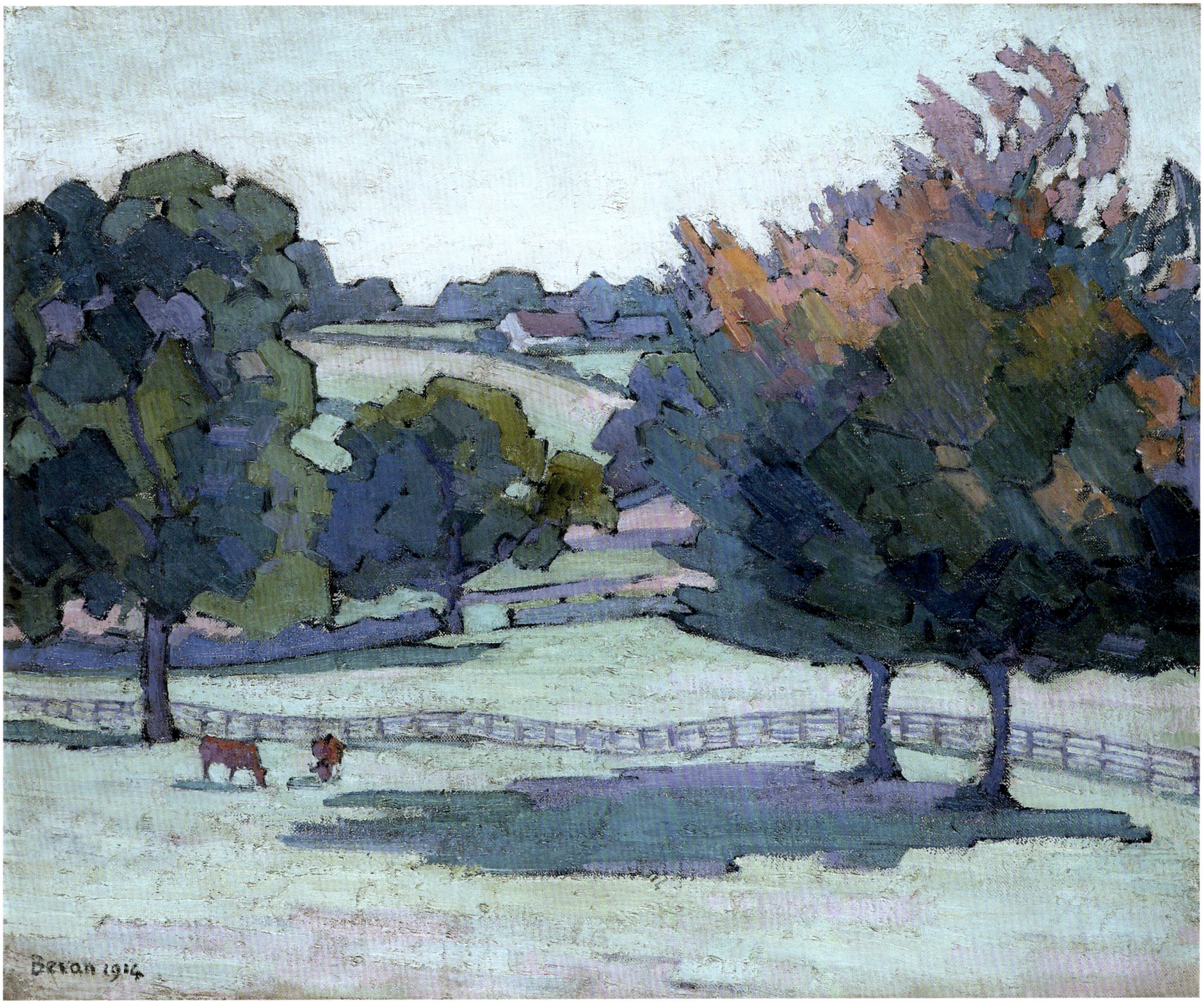
Bevan 1914

Bonnard The timbered terrace in these Vernonnet views becomes, in Bonnard's oeuvre, almost as familiar as the figure that inhabits them – the painter's future wife, Marthe.

3 Pierre Bonnard (1867–1947)
Sunlight at Vernon, 1920
Oil on canvas, 18 ½ x 24 ½ in. (47 x 54.5 cm)
Miss Margaret S. Davies Bequest, 1963 (NMWA 2164)

Sunlight at Vernon depicts the house that Bonnard had been renting at Vernonnet, near Vernon, since 1910, and which he purchased in 1912. The small, half-timbered structure, which he called Ma Roulotte (My Trailer), was close to Monet's home at Giverny (the two men became close friends) and was a recurring motif in Bonnard's work between 1910 and 1928. Inspired by Monet's repetitive approach to subject matter, Bonnard attempted to interpret Ma Roulotte under differing atmospheric conditions. He painted both the interior and exterior, sometimes together, as cool rooms lead through to bright gardens and vice versa. This relationship became a main preoccupation in his work; yet unlike Monet, Bonnard did not paint en plein-air, preferring instead to work from memory. He described his process thus: "I have all my subjects to hand. I go and look at them. I take notes. Then I go home. And before I start painting I reflect, I dream."[3] The expressive, psychological dimension of this working practice could not differ more from the immediacy of his Impressionist predecessors, placing Bonnard, a leading Nabi in the 1890s, firmly within the broader environs of Symbolism. Also, as Bonnard moved around France fairly regularly after 1911, these works were not often painted in situ.

This painting shows the artist's garden in a wild state, which was how he preferred it to be. The pink-tinged sky suggests the early evening light as it bounces off the timber, heightening the surrounding greenery. The timbered terrace in these Vernonnet views becomes, in Bonnard's oeuvre, almost as familiar as the figure that inhabits them – the painter's future wife, Marthe, whom he had met in 1893 but did not marry until 1925. It is most likely that she is the small figure visible at the bottom right of the canvas, disappearing, as in other versions at Vernonnet, into the wild garden.

Sunlight at Vernon was previously owned by the writer J. B. Priestley, whose artistic tastes were similar to those of the Davies sisters. The painting was purchased by Margaret in 1960, under the title *Le Potager* (The Kitchen Garden), with funds raised through the sale of other artworks, including Monet's view of the Grand Canal (now in the collection of the Fine Arts Museum, San Francisco). This late, relatively expensive purchase suggests an attempt by Margaret to fill a gap in her collection, which was by this point destined inevitably for the National Museum of Wales, the intimate subject matter seamlessly fitting in with the Impressionist and Post-Impressionist collecting of the sisters' early years.

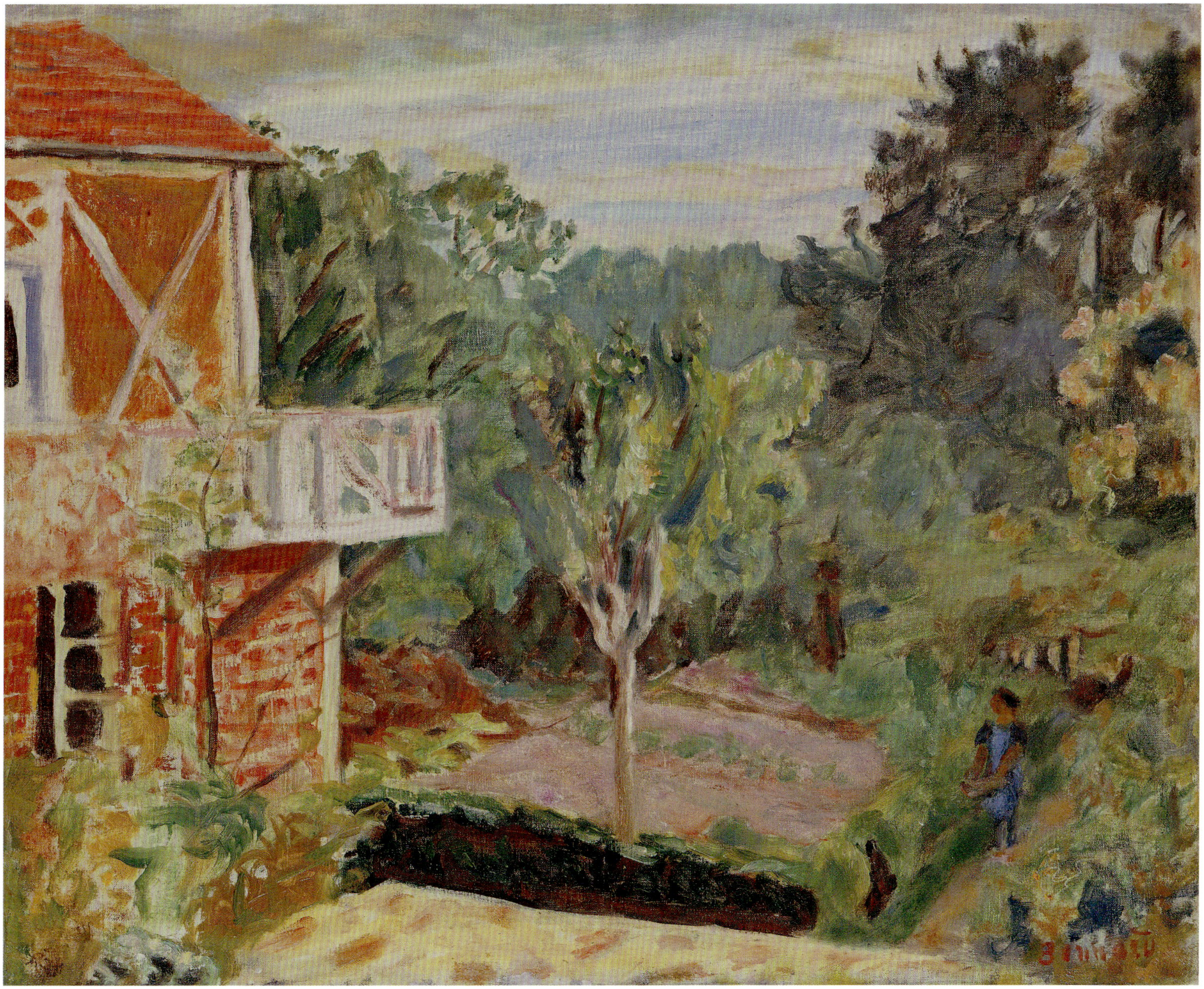

Boudin Described as a "pre-Impressionist," Boudin had been painting en plein-air since 1853, so it is likely this work was painted in situ.

4 Eugène Boudin (1824–1898)
Venice, the Molo, 1895
Oil on canvas, 14 ⅛ x 22 ¾ in. (36 x 58.1 cm)
Miss Gwendoline E. Davies Bequest, 1951 (NMWA 2432)

Like many artists associated with Impressionism, Boudin came to Venice late. He was well into his sixties at the time of his first visit in 1892. Described as a "pre-Impressionist," Boudin had been painting en plein-air since 1853, so it is likely this work was painted in situ. It shows the mouth of the Grand Canal and the Molo, the large stone quay at the entrance to Saint Mark's Square. To the right is the Zecca (the mint), built by Jacopo Sansovino in 1536, and the Giardini Reali; and at the center left are the Dogana and the church of Santa Maria della Salute. At the left of the picture can be seen shipping on the Giudecca Canal, which in the 1880s was starting to become the hub of industrial Venice.

Boudin's feelings for the city, as articulated in a letter of June 1895 to his friend Bonjean, describe a dual sensation of disappointment and discovery:

> Today a storm wraps everything in a grey and dull mist … but sometimes the sun shines and gives us some warmth. But the waters, which don't resemble those of the Mediterranean, are mostly green and do not differ from the waters of the Channel. Aside from that, what a magnificent country – with its splendid palaces, this city is a real museum – the only things that strike a false note in this setting are our great modern steamers. They come too often, to our sensitive eye and place themselves in front of this beautiful line of silver-toned palaces … like the Doges Palace, so delicate in the lace-like tracery of their sculptural decoration … [4]

This letter, which was given to Margaret Davies on her purchase of two other works by Boudin in 1924, describes perfectly Venice as seen in this picture, with its muted palette and extensive use of grays and greens. Boudin's comment regarding the "false note" of the modern steamers suggests that while he painted with an Impressionistic technique, he did not embrace modern subjects with quite the same vigor. Boudin was lodging on the Calle San Zaccaria,[5] very near the spot where this was painted, and as a result, numerous versions exist, each depicting different atmospheric conditions. Larger canvases are in the Phillips Collection, Washington, D.C., and the Musée du Québec.

Gwendoline purchased *Venice, the Molo* from the dealer Durand-Ruel in November 1912. Venice was clearly a special place for the Davies sisters. They visited numerous times, and Margaret's existing diary from 1909 is full of incident, including gondola rides and the rebuilding of the *campanile* in Saint Mark's Square, which had collapsed in 1902. This love is reflected in their purchasing, and between 1912 and 1913 they bought six oils depicting the city, including four Monets (cat. no. 35), a Whistler (cat. no. 58), and this Boudin. Gwendoline paid 7,000 francs (about £280) for this work.

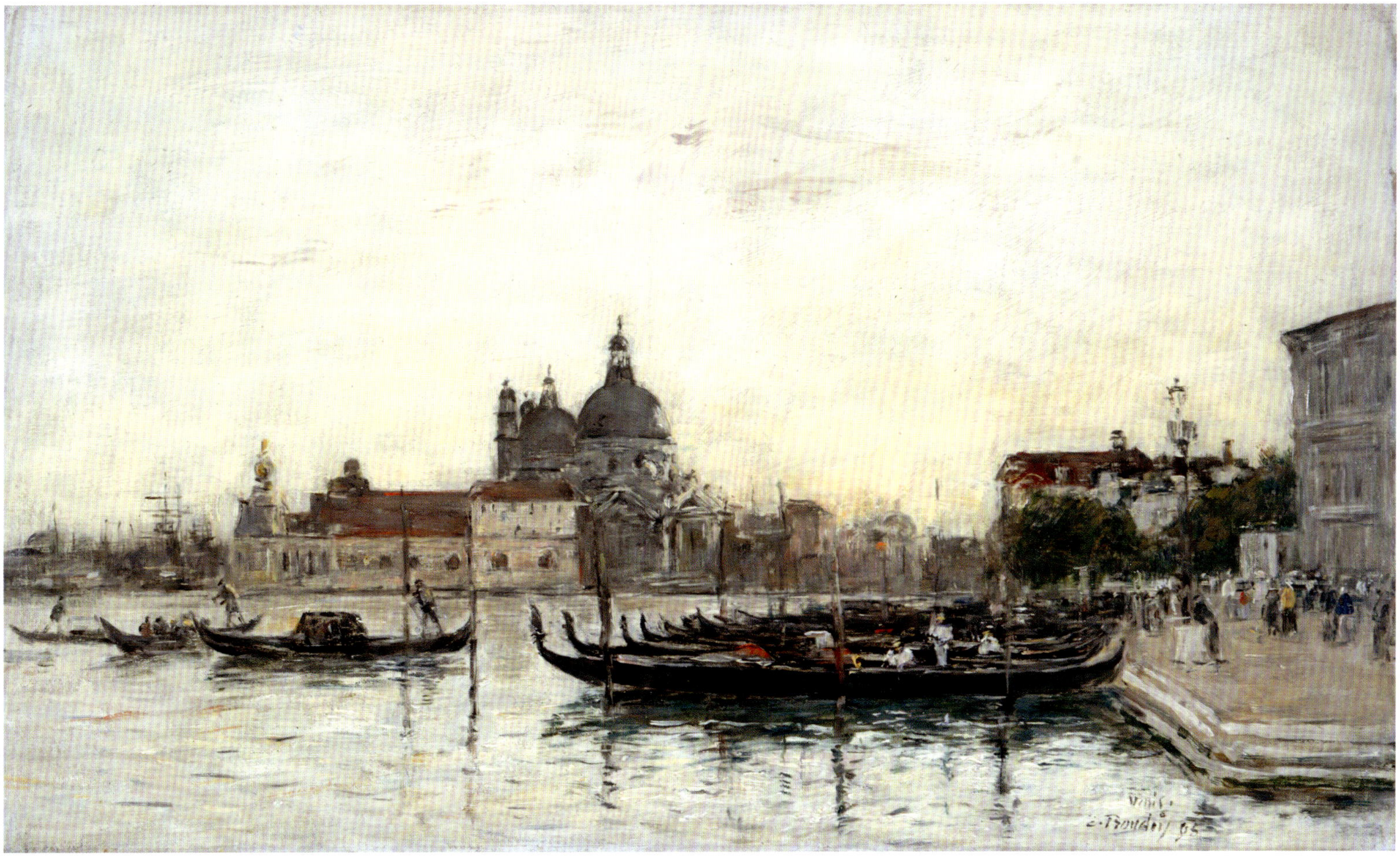

Carrière Neither a portrait nor an attempt to directly illustrate a subject, *Maternity* is an evocation of a broader concept of motherhood, an emotional state.

5 Eugène Carrière (1849–1906)
Maternity, early 1890s
Oil on canvas, 21 ⅝ x 29 ¾ inches (54.8 x 75.5 cm)
Miss Gwendoline E. Davies Bequest, 1952 (NMWA 2174)

Born in Alsace, Carrière originally studied under Alexandre Cabanel at the Ecole des Beaux-Arts and in the late 1870s spent time in London, where he was impressed by the work of Turner. In the 1880s, he began to refine his palette dramatically, which resulted in effects such as the brown and gray mist of *Maternity*, which gives the impression that the viewer is observing the painting's subject through smoke or in a dream. *Maternity* is thought to date from the early 1890s and is based on an earlier work by Carrière of the same subject titled *Le Sommeil* (location unknown) and an etching given the explicitly Symbolist title *Réalités ayant la magie du rêve* (Realities with the Magic of a Dream; location unknown). The title of this etching is crucial as a means of understanding Carrière's intention for *Maternity*, showing as it does the artist grappling with a key aspect of fin-de-siècle thought – despite depicting the artist's wife and child, *Maternity* is neither a portrait nor an attempt to directly illustrate a subject but rather an evocation of a broader concept of motherhood, an emotional state. *Maternity* can be viewed therefore in relation to Bergsonian theories of consciousness and reality,[6] as the artist makes an (ultimately paradoxical) attempt to articulate inner experience.

Carrière cut an individual but commercially successful figure in the Symbolist milieu. His choice of subject was limited, if not repetitive – mostly small-scale variations on the theme of his family, which would have had a sentimental domestic genre appeal to the purchasing public. Yet by fusing the naturalistic and the dreamlike, he was working firmly within the late nineteenth-century aesthetic, winning respect from other artists. He exchanged paintings with Gauguin, for example,[7] and was friends with the sculptor Rodin. The hazy chiaroscuro of Carrière's painting can be likened to the effect of Rodin's marbles, both giving the sense of objects appearing organically from the background – in Carrière's case from dark to light; in Rodin, from formless to formed. Although stylistically dissimilar and certainly with differing ideas about the role of color, Carrière's work also bears comparison with that of Bonnard, whose intimate domestic scenes were approached from a like-minded concept. Carrière achieved considerable commercial success in his lifetime and was at the height of his fame when he died in 1906. He was still a sufficiently popular contemporary figure for Gwendoline Davies to buy six of his works between 1913 and 1920 though his reputation declined later in the twentieth century.

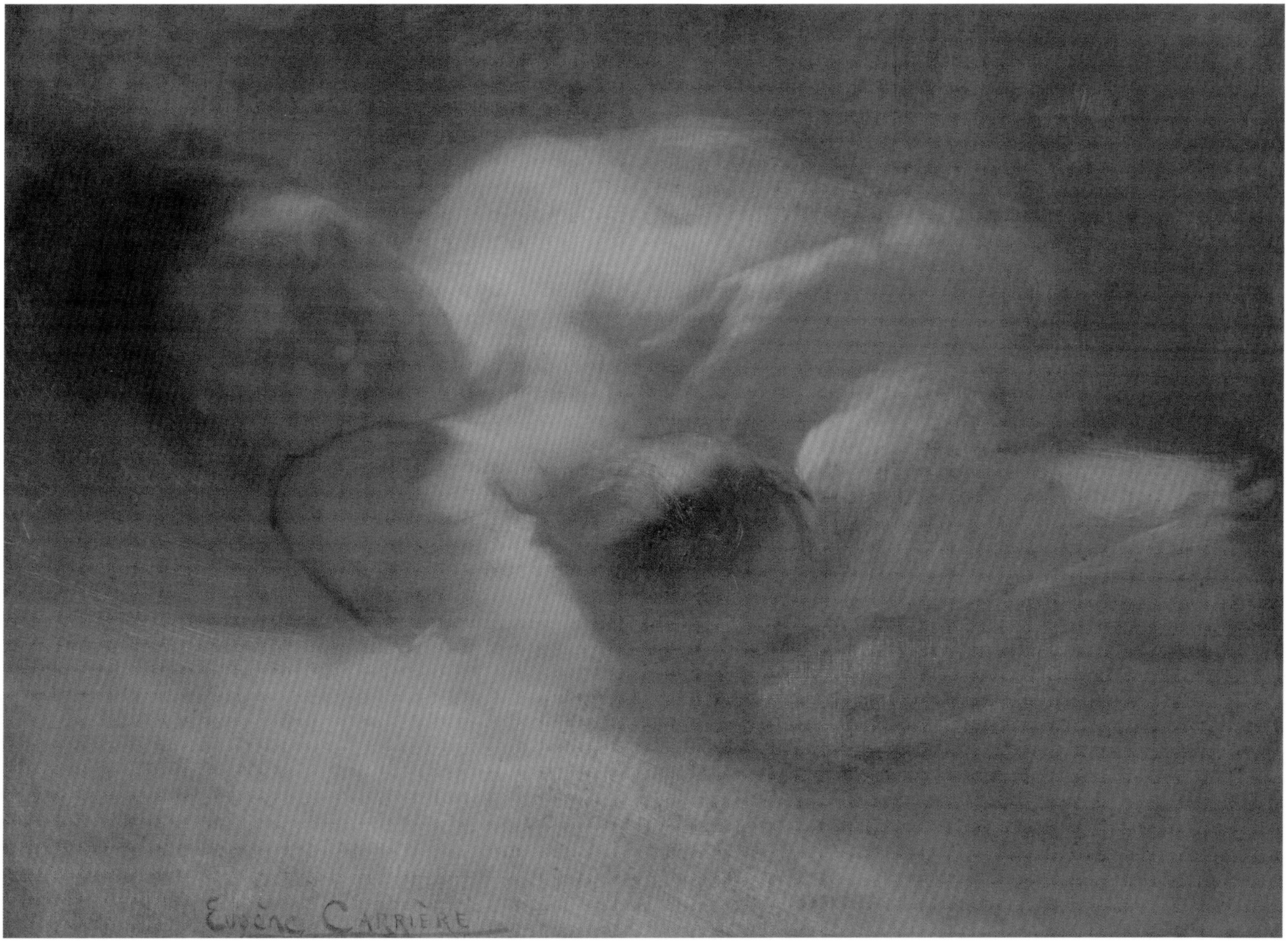
Eugène CARRIÈRE

Carrière Carrière removed extraneous detail from his paintings in order to express emotion over narrative; here the rendering of the two figures is reduced to the essentials of heads and hands.

6 Eugène Carrière (1849–1906)
Maternity (Suffering), ca. 1891–92
Oil on canvas, 32 ⅛ x 25 ¾ in. (81.6 x 65.4 cm)
Miss Gwendoline E. Davies Bequest, 1951 (NMWA 2434)

Popular in the nineteenth century, the image of the sick child frequented genre scenes to elicit pathos amid the picture-buying public, or, for example, in the case of Edvard Munch as an expression of fin-de-siècle existential anxiety. In 1886, Carrière had submitted a different, more naturalistic version of this subject to the Paris Salon, where it had been widely praised and was bought by the state.[8] This later version dates from the 1890s, when the artist had refined his palette and removed extraneous detail from his paintings in order to emphasize emotion rather than narrative; here the rendering of the two figures is reduced to the essentials of heads and hands.

Maternity (Suffering), like *Maternity* (cat. no. 5), was painted using as models the artist's wife, Sophie, and one of his children. Unusually for the "Maternity" series, however, here the artist depicts an older child rather than a baby. Carrière is often likened to Odilon Redon, but Redon himself somewhat pejoratively likened Carrière to Jean-Baptiste Greuze,[9] referring to Carrière's rather maudlin depictions of children. Carrière's later style, however, ensures that his pictures never quite lapse into gross sentimentality. Although Carrière was distinctly anti-clerical, he made numerous depictions of Christian iconography, and there is certainly something of the Madonna and child in this work. Both in style and symbolism, there are visual links between the present work and the oil sketch of the *Pietà* from 1895 (particularly in respect to the current title and its emphasis on suffering), now in a private collection, while the circular composition that encloses the figures was also used by Carrière in his 1896 image of a young girl on the occasion of her first communion (*La Première Communiante*; Metropolitan Museum of Art).

Carrière's reputation was such that on his death in 1906 the Paris Salon dedicated a whole room to him, though the repetitive nature of his subject matter could lead to confusion. This work was exhibited under the title *Amour maternel* and was illustrated in the *Gazette des Beaux-Arts* although their rapturous description of it seems to refer to a different painting, *Le Baiser*, which was at the time in the collection of Madame Jeanne Chausson, the wife of the composer Ernest Chausson. The Chaussons were friends of Carrière, and he painted their portrait as a family (Musée de Lyon). Although markedly different in many respects, *Le Baiser* is comparable to *Maternity (Suffering)* in that it depicts a similar child of the same age, unusual depictions in Carrière's oeuvre. Alongside *The Footbath*, *Maternity (Suffering)* was the first picture by Carrière bought by Gwendoline. She went on to procure an additional five, the gentle subject matter clearly of great appeal to her.

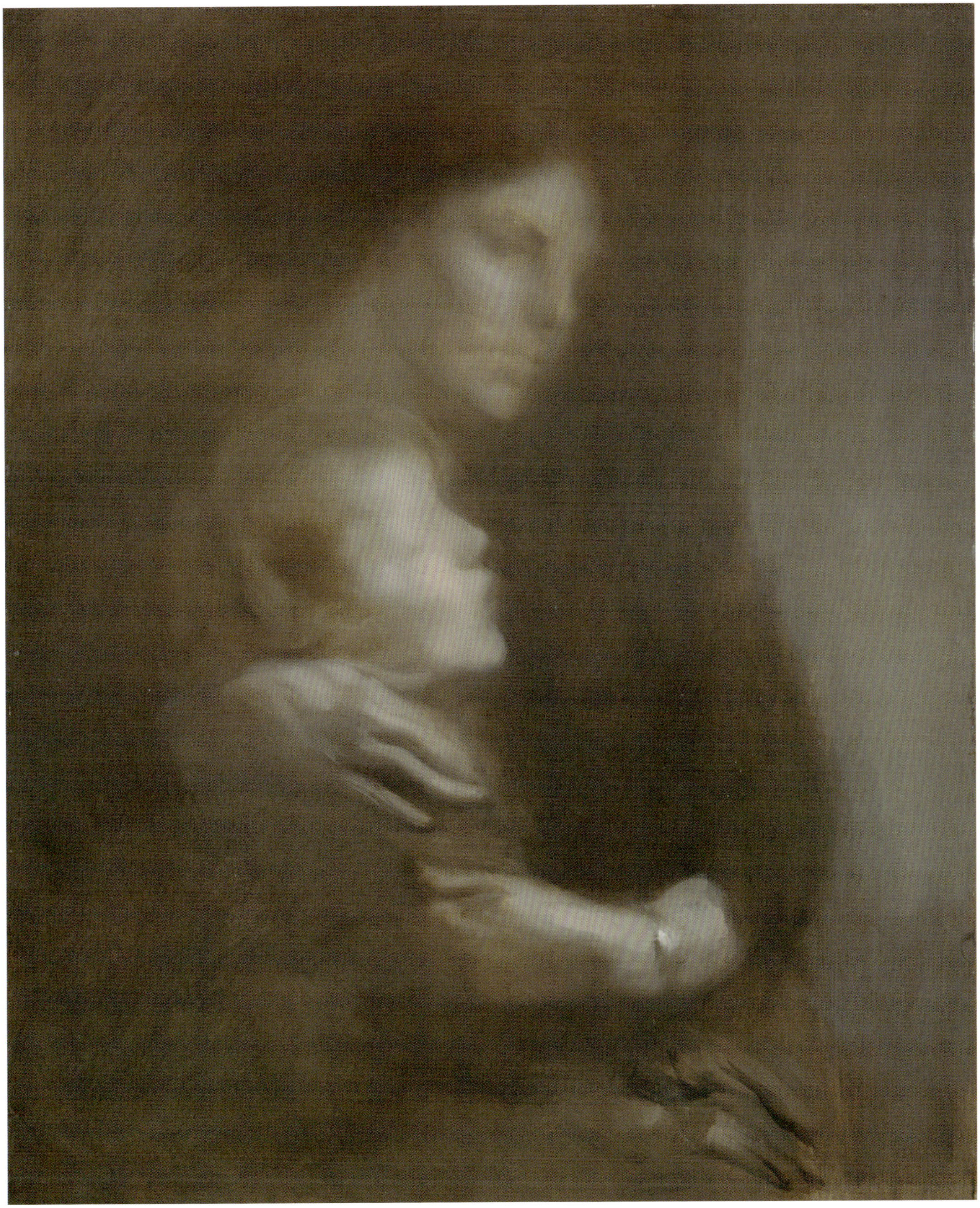

Cézanne The landscape has been manipulated for formal ends – the central *S* arrangement, instigated by the row of cypresses in the foreground, tapers to the mountain beyond.

7 Paul Cézanne (1839–1906)
The François Zola Dam, ca. 1877–78
Oil on canvas, 21 ⅜ x 29 ¼ in. (54.2 x 74.2 cm)
Miss Gwendoline E. Davies Bequest, 1951 (NMWA 2439)

The precise location of this view has been the subject of considerable debate, and the title has been altered on numerous occasions. Although it has long been known as *Midday, L'Estaque*, current scholarship suggests that the painting's original purchase title, *Le Barrage François Zola* (The François Zola Dam), is indeed correct.[10] If so, this is Cézanne's only known view of the dam, which lies about five kilometers outside Aix-en-Provence. Although uncertainty has arisen from discrepancy regarding exact location, a precise match was never likely to be found – it is one of Cézanne's compositions that, in the words of Roger Fry, conciliates "the opposing claims of design and the total vision of nature."[11] In *The François Zola Dam*, the landscape has been manipulated for formal ends – the central *S* arrangement, instigated by the row of cypresses in the foreground, tapers to the mountain beyond, while a vertical anchor is provided to the left by the tree, the boxlike form, and the geometric gray area (the dam itself) directly above it. The red-roofed house is probably an invention, designed to provide "rhyming" contours with the blue mountain behind.

Despite previous suggestions, the support is not paper but a fine linen canvas and is covered by the artist with a smooth cream ground that gives the surface its uniform appearance. The paint is relatively thickly applied, and the technique is a mixture of Cézanne's characteristic striated brushwork and thicker strokes of saturated color. The painting was first owned by Gauguin, who acquired it in 1883 and described it as "quite simply a marvel."[12] He used the composition in a design for a fan, now in the Ny Carlsberg Glyptotek, Copenhagen, and the more general influence of Cézanne's work can be seen in Gauguin's work from this period.

Gwendoline Davies purchased *The François Zola Dam* from Bernheim-Jeune in Paris, in February 1918.[13] The painting was the subject of some controversy in the early 1920s, a controversy that demonstrates how progressive the sisters' collecting had become by that time. With Cézanne's reputation as a modern master established, Gwendoline offered the work for loan in 1921 to the National Gallery, London, which, unwilling to accept it, passed it to the Tate Gallery, which also rejected the proposal.[14] This prompted something of an outcry, leading the *Burlington Magazine* to assert that "a gallery of modern foreign art without a Cézanne is like a gallery of Florentine art without Giotto."[15] Roger Fry, the likely author of these words, championed both Cézanne and this work, saying, "It seems to me one of the greatest of all Cézanne's landscapes, and I dare hardly say how high a place that gives it for me in all known examples of landscape art."[16] Pressure forced the Tate to capitulate, and the painting duly went on display in 1922, for sixteen years. It has been suggested that this inspired Samuel Courtauld, who a year later began to amass his outstanding collection of Cézanne's works.[17]

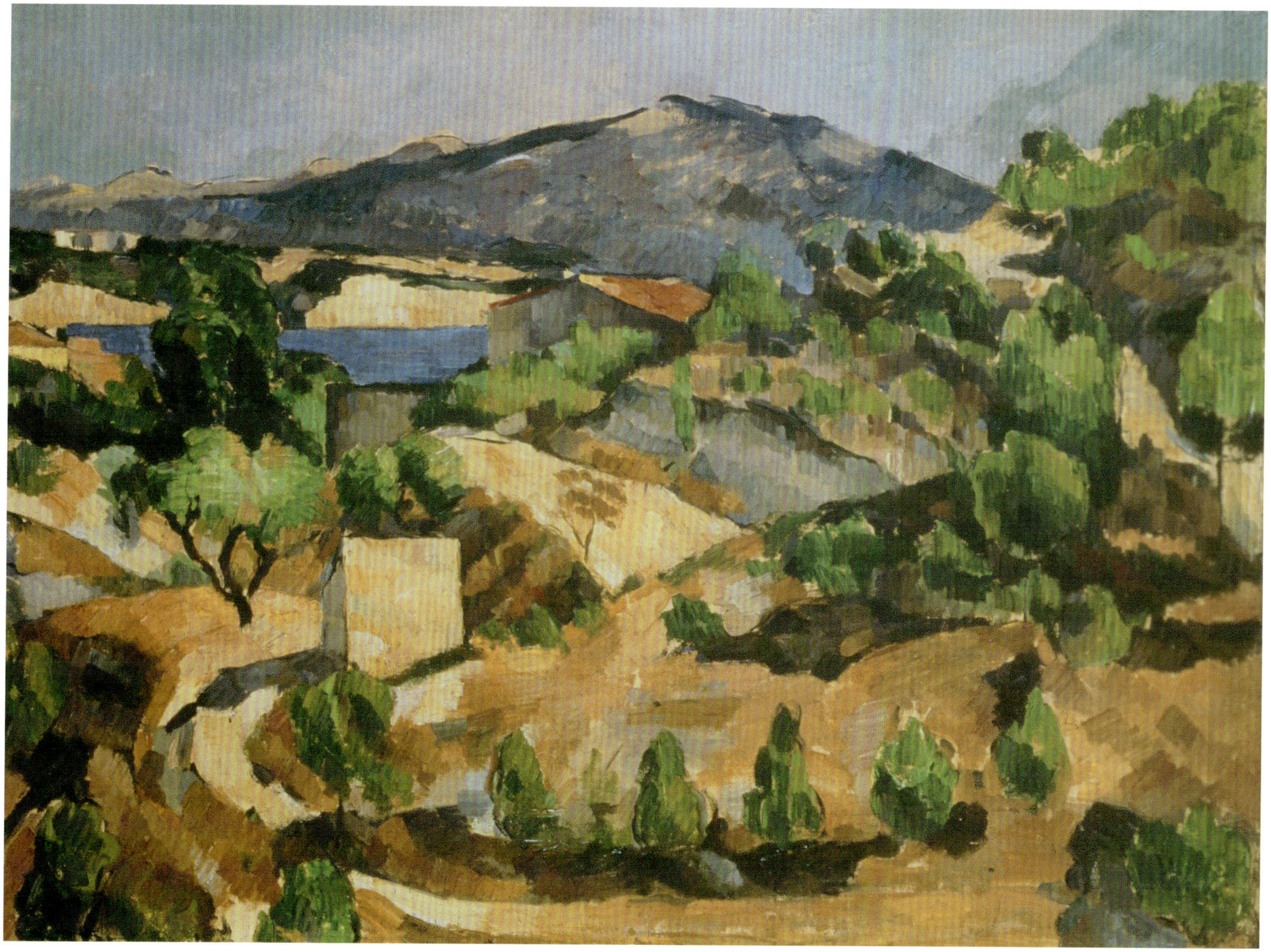

Cézanne The spatial effects disrupt every conventional expectation of the viewer, as the lighter areas of sky and foliage within the center band appear to float while the darker areas recede.

8 Paul Cézanne (1839–1906)
Provençal Landscape, ca. 1887
Oil on canvas, 31 ⅞ x 25 ⅝ in. (81 x 65.2 cm)
Miss Gwendoline E. Davies Bequest, 1951 (NMWA 2438)

In 1886, upon the death of his father, Cézanne's inherited wealth enabled him to settle in his native Provence and fully devote his energies to painting. Although the location of this scene is unknown, the brushwork and color make it datable to the late 1880s, and it was therefore probably painted in the grounds of the Jas de Bouffan, an estate of approximately thirty-seven acres, outside of Aix-en-Provence, which Cézanne's father had purchased in 1859 and where the artist spent much of his time.

Provençal Landscape is a deceptively simple work depicting a copse on a hot day, yet, as with *The François Zola Dam*, every aspect of the canvas has been carefully worked through, and every brushstroke has its place. While the striated and multi-directional brushwork gives the painting a bright dynamism, it also emphasizes the flatness of the canvas to the extent that the foreground takes on the quality of textile. Perspectively, Cézanne disrupts every conventional expectation of the viewer through spatial effects that make the lighter areas of sky and foliage within the center band of the canvas appear to float while the darker areas recede. The foreground is irregular in itself, with a lone tree coming from the broad expanse of scorched earth, breaking the horizontal line that demarcates the main body of the copse, while the taller trees to the right of the picture destabilize the unnatural sense of balance that would otherwise overwhelm the scene. The lines of the trees in the central panel are both mirrored and subverted – the two central curving trees reflect each other, but their "rhyming" is staggered to evoke in the viewer a sense of visual balance rather than an absolute knowledge. The slanting, almost triangular composition of the trees can be compared with the various landscapes in Cézanne's late *Bathers* series.

The terracotta-green-blue triumvirate is typical of Cézanne's work from this period; while the immediate appearance is one of distinct bands representing earth, trees, and sky, the repetition of blue, from the top down through the trees, provides visual coherence of design throughout. Although the canvas is quite densely covered, Cézanne has left small areas of the cream ground uncovered, which provides highlights.

There are no other works in Cézanne's oeuvre that seem to relate particularly to this landscape although various groups of trees exist. Like *The François Zola Dam* (cat. no. 7), *Provençal Landscape* was purchased in 1918 from Bernheim-Jeune. In 1920, Gwendoline added to the group by purchasing a still life and three watercolors, including two views of bathers that are still in the collection of the National Museum of Wales.

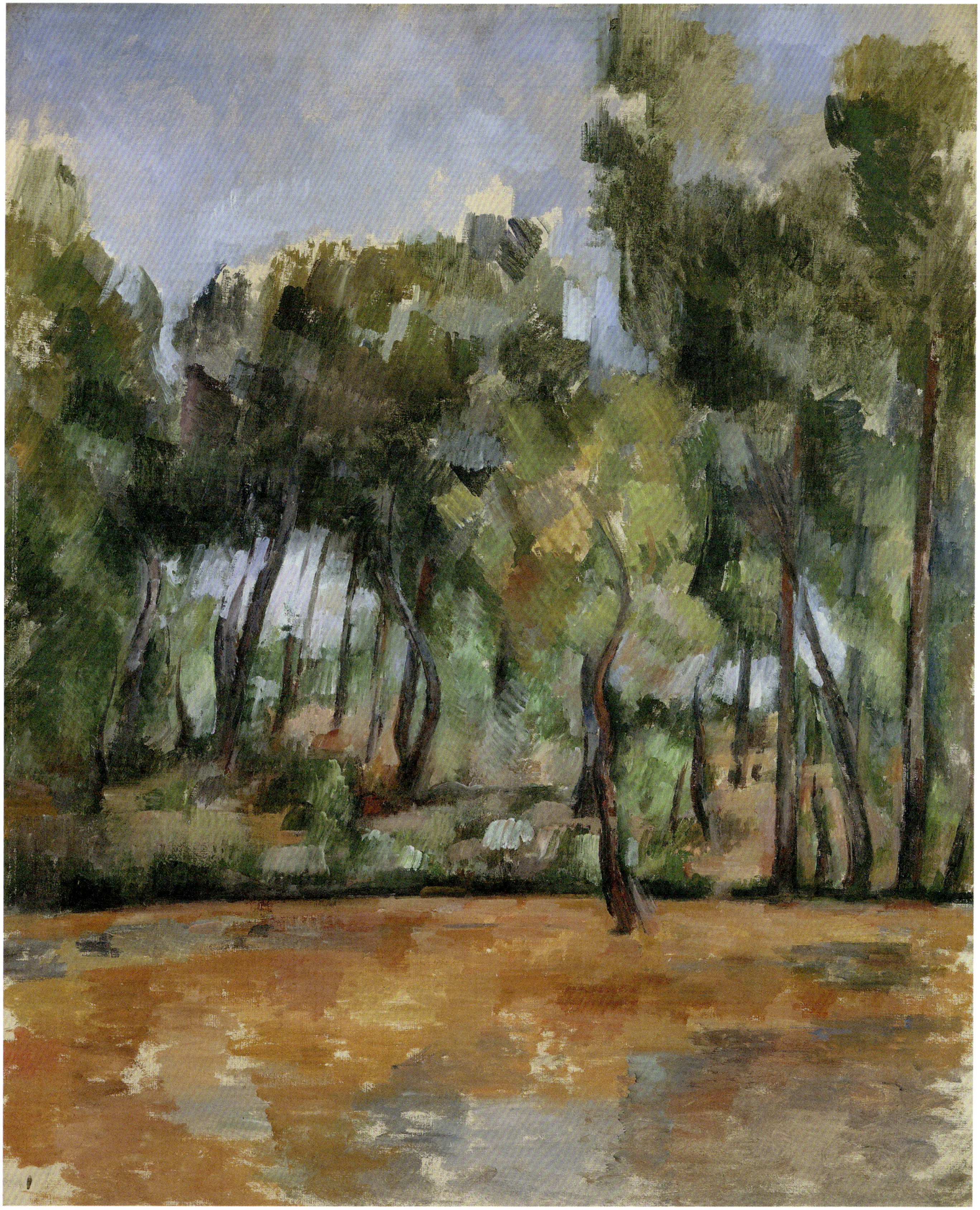

Corot By the time this work was painted, Corot had developed his later style of translucent, almost shimmering landscape effects.

9 Camille Corot (1796–1875)
Castel Gandolfo, Dancing Tyrolean Shepherds by Lake Albano, 1855–60
Oil on canvas, 19 ⅜ x 25 ¾ in. (49.2 x 65.5 cm)
Miss Gwendoline E. Davies Bequest, 1951 (NMWA 2443)

In this scene, Corot's ability to fuse naturalism with the forms of classical landscape can be clearly seen. Born in Paris, Corot studied first at the Académie Suisse and then with Achille Michallon and Jean-Victor Bertin. From 1825, he traveled three times to Italy, where he made studies of the landscape and people. Lake Albano and Castel Gandolfo resided well within the canon of classical landscape painting subject matter, having been depicted by Poussin among others. Because Corot made his final visit to northern Italy in 1843, the present work, which dates from more than ten years later, was certainly painted from memory. From the early 1850s, Corot's work could be divided into three categories – studies from nature, historic works for the Salon, and the more commercial picturesque landscape scenes.[18] This work, which was commissioned by a M. de Chastellux in 1855, falls into this last category.

Corot's first attempt to depict Castel Gandolfo in oil is probably a small study, without any pastoral figure accompaniment (Metropolitan Museum of Art), that dates from between 1826 and 1828. Although painted almost thirty years later, the present work is much more in the vein of Claude Lorrain, Poussin, and classical landscape style. It does, however, demonstrate that Corot had by this time developed his later style of translucent, almost shimmering landscape effects. The all-pervading gray/green/silver tones in this work are pricked by the bright red and yellow of the dancer's headscarves. A very similar scene of dancers by Lake Albano, painted around the same time though slightly smaller, is *Les Danseurs de Castel Gandolfo* (private collection). The principal differences are the costume and instruments – the figures wear Neoclassical garments and play historic instruments, whereas the present work is more contemporary in its presentation.

Gwendoline Davies bought the painting in London in October 1909, as *Castel Gandolfo, with Tyrolean Shepherds Dancing by Lake Albano*. Because of the incongruity of Corot depicting shepherds from the Tyrol in a Roman landscape, it has been suggested that the title has been subject to a misreading and that the painting in fact shows Tivolean shepherds.[19] At £6,350, *Castel Gandolfo* was one of the most expensive works Gwendoline purchased. On seeing works by Corot in the Louvre, Margaret admired "the beautiful light in them all, and the softness, and the touch of colour which the figures give."[20]

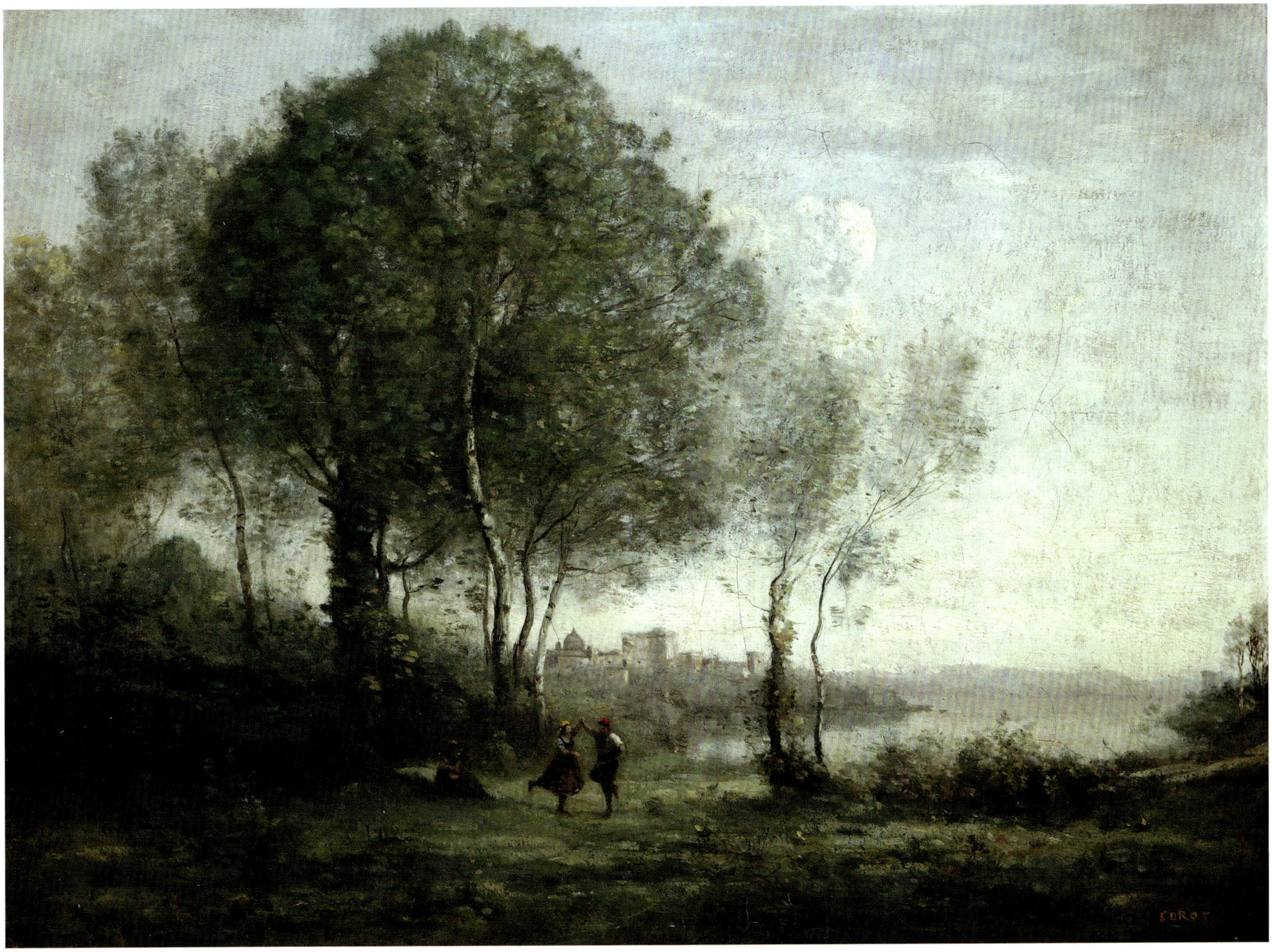
COROT

Corot The artist's ability to give the impression of having painted directly from nature is undoubtedly one of the strengths of Corot's later technique.

10 Camille Corot (1796–1875)
The Pond, 1860s
Oil on canvas, 15 ½ x 26 ½ in. (39.4 x 67.3 cm)
Miss Gwendoline E. Davies Bequest, 1951 (NMWA 2442)

The Pond dates from the 1860s, by which time Corot had settled into the most commercially successful phase of his career, producing lyrical landscapes that fused classical compositional technique with the contemporary naturalism of Barbizon – a combination of idealization and observation. Although like *Castel Gandolfo* (cat no. 9), this work is a landscape with figures, it does not present a recognizable view or have a narrative thread, and the figures are purely incidental.

The Pond exemplifies Corot's highly sought-after mature technique. In contrast to the solid, more defined forms of his earlier landscapes, the brushwork here is feathery, the impression hazy, and the tonal range limited to browns, greens, and grays. The diaphanous mist of the foliage on the extremities of the tree branches has the delicate appearance of watercolor or even of having been painted onto glass. (In order to achieve this effect, Corot would mix his colors through with white.) In *The Pond*, as in *Castel Gandolfo*, Corot has cut through the tonal uniformity by picking out tiny flashes of color, almost indiscernible in the headgear of the foreground figure and in the yellow of the head covering of the tiny figure to the right who moves away from the viewer. Corot's approach to landscape was thus:

> When faced with nature, begin by looking for form, then values and tonal relations, colour and execution; and subordinate the whole to your original feelings ... Faced with any particular landscape or object we are moved by a certain elegance or grace. We should never let go of that emotion, and even when seeking truth and precision, we should never forget to reclothe it in the form in which it struck us.[21]

The Pond is indeed an example of Corot submitting to the "first impression." Because he was so closely connected with Barbizon and an early exponent of plein-air painting, it is tempting to think that this work was painted outdoors. However, much of his commercial later work, such as this, was composed in the studio from memory, using what he had learned from his early close observation. The artist's ability to give the impression of having painted directly from nature is undoubtedly one of the strengths of Corot's later technique. This is particularly marked in the artist's conveyance of atmospheric suggestion, in the white wintry light that pervades his canvases but never appears bleak.

This painting was Gwendoline's first purchase. It was acquired for her by Hugh Blaker from a sale at Christie's, and she paid the not inconsiderable sum of £2,730. Corot's ongoing popularity coupled with Hugh Blaker's expert eye ensured that this was a good starting point for amassing a collection, and although an undoubtedly safe bet, *The Pond* marked the beginning of what would be a crucial interest in modern French landscape painting.

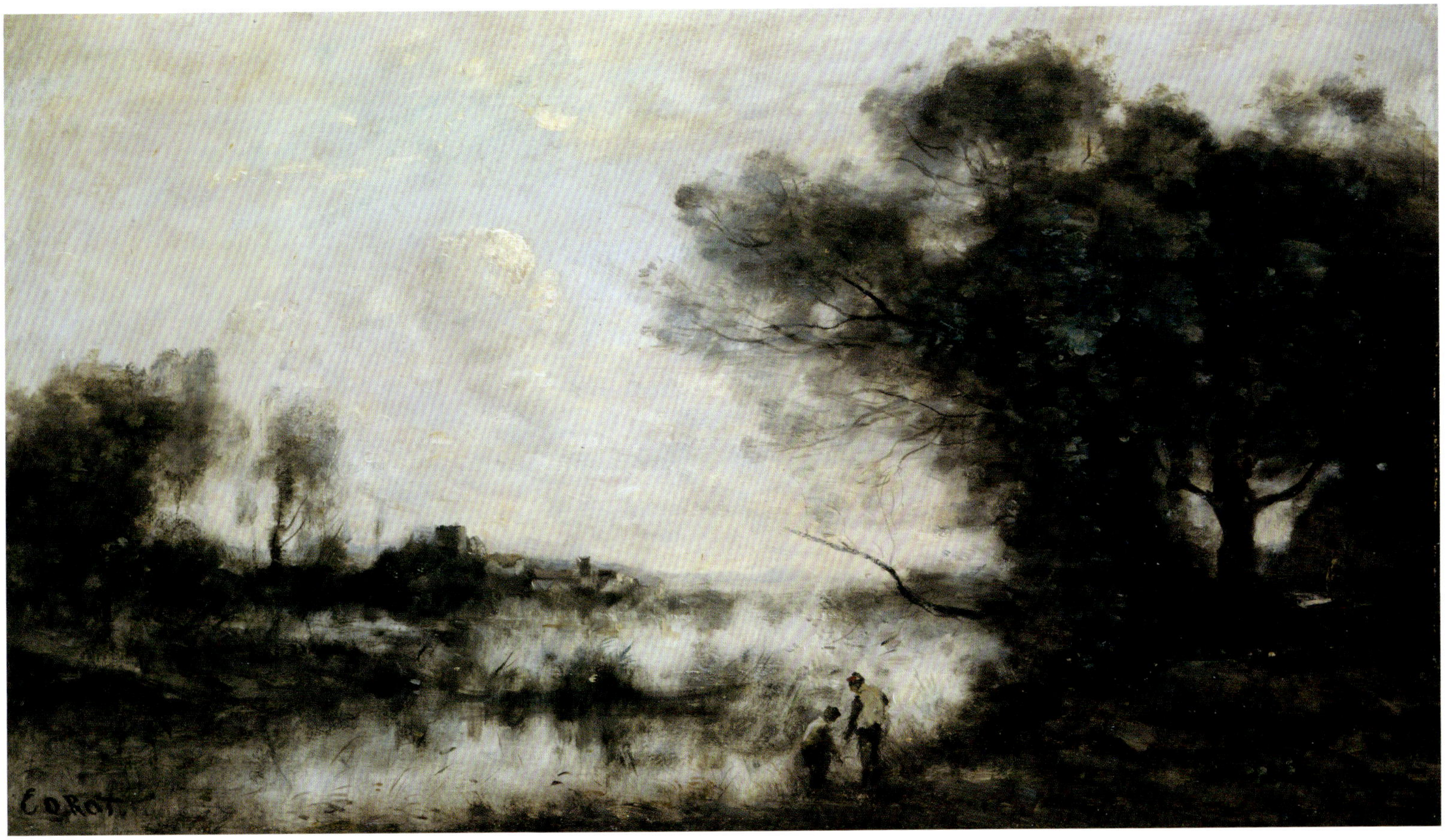
COROT

Corot With no figures to provide narrative or coloristic interest, Corot adds both variety and vigor by use of a vibrant pink blossom across the foreground right of the picture.

11 Camille Corot (1796–1875)
Distant View of Corbeil, ca. 1870
Oil on canvas, 9 ⅞ x 13 ⅜ in. (25.1 x 33.8 cm)
Miss Margaret S. Davies Bequest, 1963 (NMWA 2441)

Although *Distant View of Corbeil* represents a named place, the dating of this work suggests it was not painted en plein air but was more likely completed from a combination of studies and memory. During the late 1860s, Corot's ill health meant that the artist was largely restricted to studio painting, a confinement that was exacerbated by the Franco-Prussian War and the siege of Paris from 1870 to 1871.[22]

Corbeil, which lies on the Seine, midway between Paris and Barbizon, was, when Corot depicted it, well known as a manufacturing town with extensive flourmills and a corn warehouse. There is a similar view, *Corbeil vu de loin: Derrière les arbres, le matin* (Hunterian Museum & Art Gallery, Glasgow), which is given the same date of about 1870. If indeed both works represent the same location, it becomes more likely that they were not painted entirely en plein air. Although the overall suggestion is very similar, there are significant perspectival differences, and the inclusion of a large tower to the left of the Glasgow scene (identified as a flourmill) is absent in the Cardiff work.

Although Corot's subject matter and basic style remained constant, it is interesting to compare the technique of this late scene to both *The Pond* (cat. no. 10) and *Castel Gandolfo* (cat. no. 9). Structurally, the classical landscape model is far less pronounced than in either of the earlier works. If it has a historical model, it is better likened to the greater naturalism of earlier Dutch landscapists. While the Seine still curves through the center of the work, leading the eye through the middle and background, the formal structure and placement of the trees are not nearly so rigid, and gone also are the figures, leaving an empty and Impressionistic foreground section. With no figures in the composition to provide either narrative or coloristic interest as in the previous works, Corot adds both variety and vigor by use of a vibrant pink blossom across the foreground right of the picture. Overall, the handling is softer and less glassy and demonstrates Corot's extraordinary painterly skill.

Distant View of Corbeil was purchased by Hugh Blaker on behalf of Margaret Davies in June 1910. At the time of acquisition, it was identified as *Joinville sur Marne*. At the same time, she augmented this landscape purchase with works by Millet, Jozef Israels, and Narcisse-Virgile Díaz de la Peña – an indication that the sisters were now actively forming a collection.

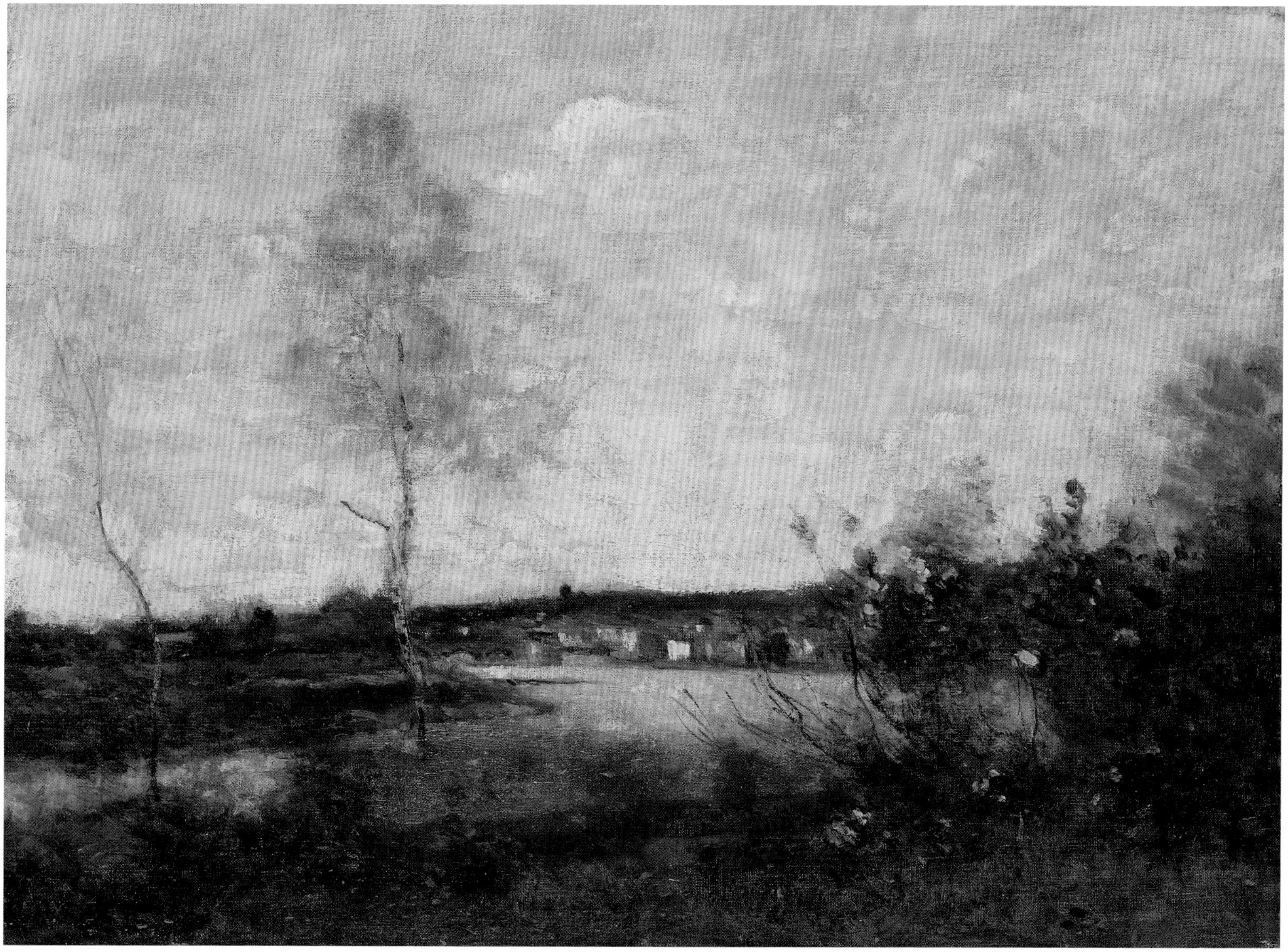

Daumier An interest in moonlit scenes pervaded European Romanticism at the time and is a theme Daumier had explored in earlier lithographs.

12 Honoré Daumier (1808–1879)
The Night Walkers, 1842–47
Oil on board, 11 ⅜ x 7 ⅜ inches (29.1 x 18.9 cm)
Miss Gwendoline E. Davies Bequest, 1951 (NMWA 2452)

While his fame rested primarily on his work as a caricaturist, in the mid-1840s Daumier began to work in oil. *The Night Walkers* is regarded as one of the earliest examples of this technique in his oeuvre. Something of an enigma, this nocturnal scene shows a top-hatted gentleman and companion regarding the moon by the side of the Seine. The difference in the attire of the two figures suggests differing social strata; it has also been suggested that there is something of Don Quixote and Sancho Panza about the figures,[23] a reference to Daumier's later artistic preoccupation with Cervantes's novel. An interest in moonlit scenes pervaded European Romanticism at the time[24] and is a theme Daumier had explored in earlier lithographs.

While much of Daumier's graphic work is datable through publications, his oils have historically been far more difficult to locate chronologically. *The Night Walkers* is no exception but is now accepted by most scholars as dating from the mid-1840s,[25] when Daumier first began to execute works in oil – the definition of detail through line rather than tone and color hinting at his unfamiliarity with the medium. It has been stylistically linked to another Daumier in the Davies sisters' collection, *Workmen on the Street*, which exhibits the same strong graphic element described as "drawings made with the point of the brush and then toned."[26] *The Night Walkers* was painted on thin oak panel with a white ground, while the figures are outlined in black crayon and paint. Infrared photography has shown that this work originally featured a single figure in the center of the canvas. The head was placed next to the head of the left-hand walker, and the form is still just visible. The reason for the change of composition is not known, but the existing contrast between the dark figures in the lower right of the image and the bright moon in the upper left creates a pleasing balance that demonstrates Daumier's compositional skill.

The Night Walkers was formerly owned by the industrialist, painter, and collector Henri Rouart, whose collection went up for sale at the Galerie Manzi-Joyant in December 1912. This was Gwendoline Davies's first purchase of work by Daumier – between them, the sisters purchased eighteen works in a variety of media by him, though only twelve came into the collection of the National Museum of Wales.

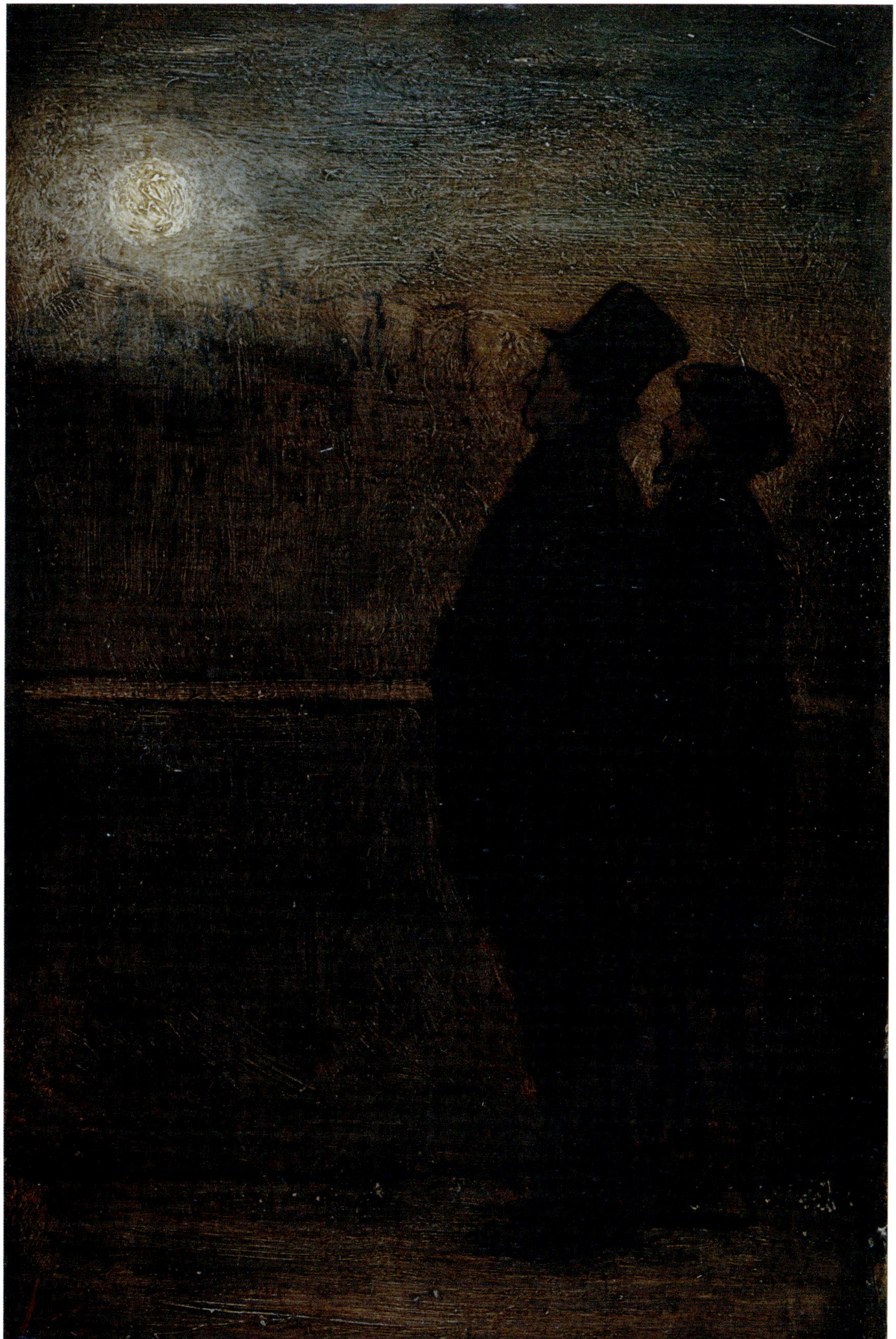

Daumier Although the work predates Cubism, the economic use of lines and volumetric form give it a very modern feel.

13 Honoré Daumier (1808–1879)
Head of a Man, ca. 1850
Black chalk on laid paper spotted with iron gall ink,
7 ¼ x 5 ⅞ in. (18.5 x 15 cm)
Miss Gwendoline E. Davies Bequest, 1951 (NMWA 1680)

Through his work as a caricaturist, Daumier published nearly four thousand lithographs that commented on French politics and bourgeois life. His work was highly admired and appreciated for the insight it offered into the follies of both public and everyday life. Daumier was first critically recognized as an artist and exceptional draftsman when an exhibition of his work was organized by friends a few months before he died. Since then, his reputation has grown, and his work has influenced numerous artists.

K. E. Maison identified this work as a study for the head of the central figure in the painting *La famille sur la barricade* (Národní Galerie, Prague). It is also related to the oil painting *Head of a Man* (cat. no. 15), purchased by Gwendoline Davies in 1914. In addition, there is a highly finished drawing of the same figure in a private collection in Paris. If this is the first drawing for this figure, it is interesting to see how Daumier is working out the main lines, alignment, and features of the face before adding in the detail. However, it is also possible that this drawing was done after the painting and that here Daumier is simplifying the composition. Although the work predates Cubism, the economic use of lines and volumetric form give it a very modern feel. The figure in the painting retains the same sense of angularity and solidity.

Gwendoline Davies purchased this drawing in December 1922 from an exhibition at the Lefevre Gallery, London, along with *Two Studies for the Return of the Prodigal Son* (cat. no. 18) and *A Lawyer, Walking* (cat. no. 20). There is no correspondence to confirm that she was aware that the work was related to one of her oil paintings; however, the likeness of the general composition no doubt drew her to it.

Both Gwendoline and Margaret Davies collected works on paper, and together they bequeathed seventy-four watercolors and drawings to the National Museum of Wales.[27] Since Daumier was renowned for his draftsmanship, it made sense for the sisters to purchase his drawings as well as his paintings. The sisters were not specialist collectors of watercolors and drawings but tended to buy works by artists they were interested in, many of whom were also represented in their paintings collection.[28]

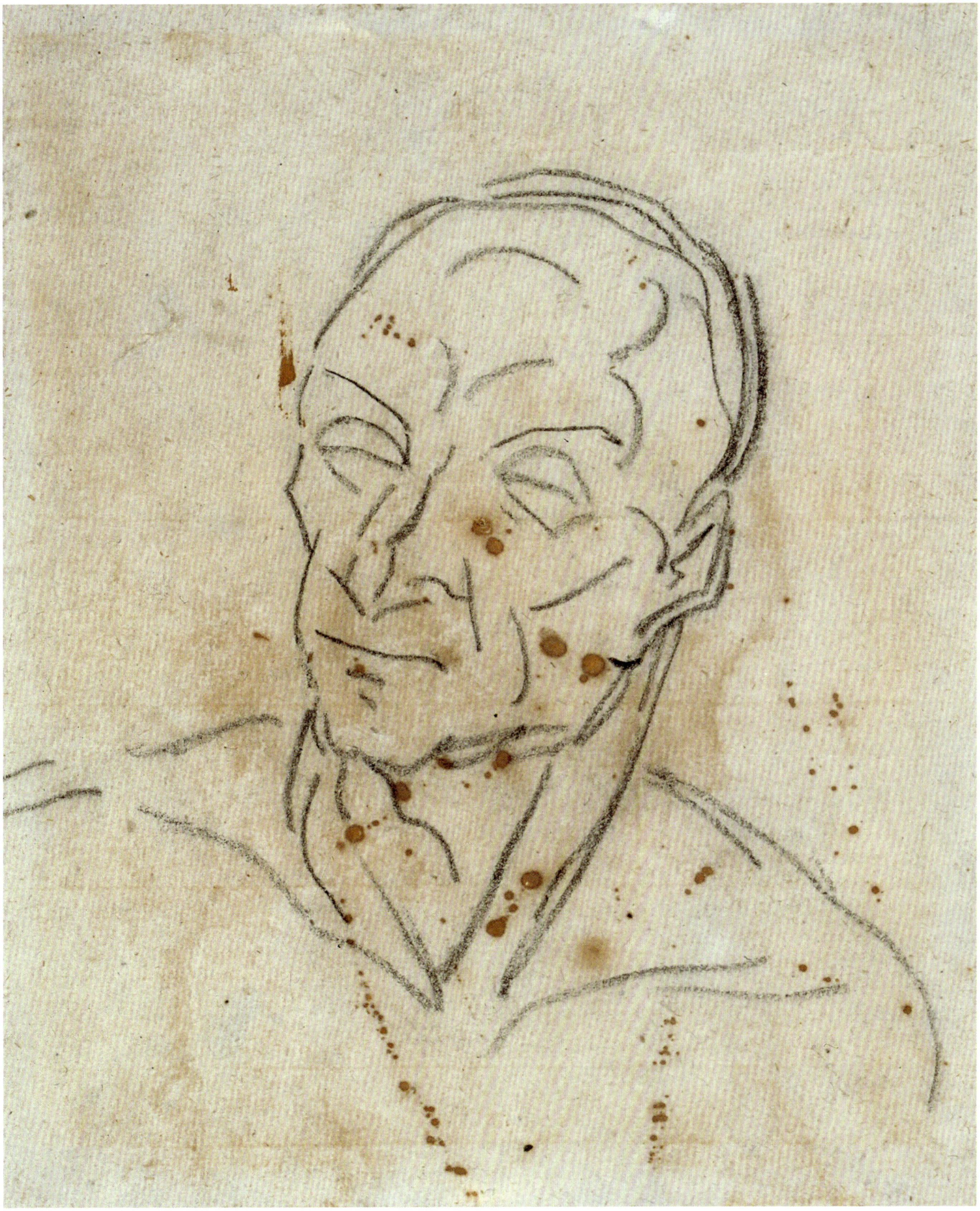

Daumier Historically, the attribution to Daumier was doubted, but recent research reveals the work to be typical of the artist in both technique and material.

14 Honoré Daumier (1808–1879)
The Heavy Burden, 1850–60
Oil on panel, 15 ⅝ x 12 ⅝ in. (39.7 x 32.2 cm)
Miss Gwendoline E. Davies Bequest, 1951 (NMWA 3891)

Like *The Night Walkers* (cat. no. 12), *The Heavy Burden* shows two figures by a wall at the side of the Seine, only in this image it is a woman struggling against the elements with a bundle of laundry, accompanied by a child. There are numerous versions of this composition;[29] the present version is probably most closely related to a monochrome oil on panel in the Burrell Collection in Glasgow, Scotland, titled *Le fardeau*. The Cardiff version is the only one of this particular group in which the woman wears a headscarf, although a different arrangement, in which the figures climb a set of steps up from the river, also shows this sartorial feature.[30] The difficulty of dating Daumier's oil paintings has been mentioned elsewhere, but a contemporary account from a visitor to Daumier's studio in 1852 describes "a washerwoman dragging a little girl along the quayside, blown by a great wind – an *ébauche* so sad in feeling that one might say the bundle of linen stuck under her arm was en route for the pawn shop,"[31] which provides an approximate date for the series as a whole. The light area that spreads from the upper right of the picture is occupied in other versions with tall buildings.

Historically, the attribution to Daumier was doubted,[32] but recent research[33] reveals the work to be typical of the artist in both technique and material. It was begun as a watercolor on paper, and x-ray photography has revealed that the original composition depicted the woman and child viewed from behind, walking to the left, an arrangement that Daumier had used previously in a charcoal drawing, now in a private collection. The original position of the child's head is still partially visible, and the head scarf, which K. E. Maison had described as possibly the action of a weak painter attempting to "unsuccessfully soften the grim look of the broad and heavy working class woman," is shown to be covering an area of damage that would have occurred during the mounting of the paper on to the panel. The case is further strengthened in that this technique, that of mounting paper onto a surface and reworking in oil, can be observed in another version of the scene at the Musée des Beaux-Arts in Dijon.

Like *A Third Class Carriage* (cat. no. 19), the present work is a sketchy version of a scene that was worked up more fully by Daumier in other versions. Gwendoline Davies bought *The Heavy Burden* from the Grosvenor Gallery, London, in March 1914. It is notable that while images of peasant life and labor are a clear feature of the Davies sisters' collection (see, for example, cat. nos. 26 and 28), they are almost exclusively rural scenes. This is the only one that takes place in an urban setting.

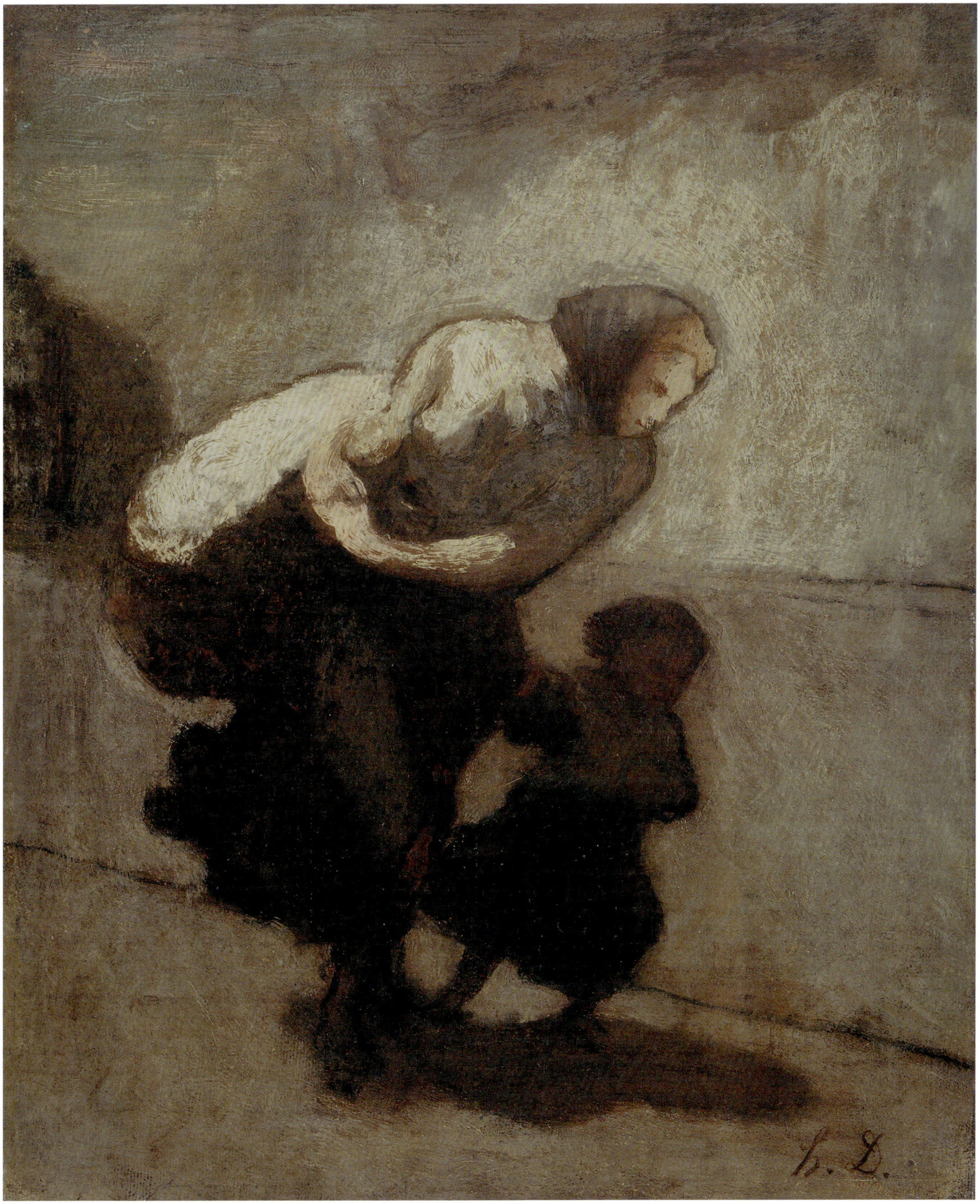
h. D.

Daumier *Head of a Man* is painted on to a red ground that is left exposed in certain areas, providing an overall feeling of warmth in the work.

15 Honoré Daumier (1808–1879)
Head of a Man, ca. 1852–56
Oil on canvas, 10 ⅞ x 13 ⅞ in. (27.5 x 35.5 cm)
Miss Gwendoline E. Davies Bequest, 1951 (NMWA 2456)

Daumier was a committed republican and no stranger to political subjects through his work as a caricaturist for *Le Charivari*. In the 1830s, he spent a short period in prison for producing a satirical lithograph of the king. The present image, which depicts the loosely painted head of a man in a waistcoat and shirtsleeves, looking down to the right, is directly related to the central figure in *La famille sur la barricade* (oil on panel; Národní Galerie, Prague) and *Le lutteur de barricades* (oil on canvas; private collection). The former shows a half-length image of a figure similar to the present work with two young boys, in the midst of a bustling crowd. Both these paintings were inspired by the 1848 revolution that led to the Second Republic, although Daumier did not create them until the Second Empire, when the promise of the republic must have seemed like a distant memory.

The difficulty of dating Daumier's work has raised questions as to whether this work predates *La famille sur la barricade* or not. Despite its sketchlike attributes, mainstream scholarship does not believe the present work to be a study for the Prague work, as its quality and vigor suggest it was taken up as a subject at a later date (ca. 1855–56). It is notably more sophisticated in execution than the same head in the "barricades" painting, although this has since been disputed by Michael Pantazzi, who posits the earlier date as the more likely.[34]

Head of a Man is painted onto a red ground left exposed in certain areas, which provides a warmth to the work as a whole. Within the Davies collection, *Head of a Man* is connected to the drawing of the same name (cat. no. 13). It is most likely that the drawing predates the oil, but the most directly related work to the present painting is a different chalk drawing, almost identical in its rendering, which is now in a private collection. Gwendoline purchased *Head of a Man* from Wallis & Son, London, in 1914.

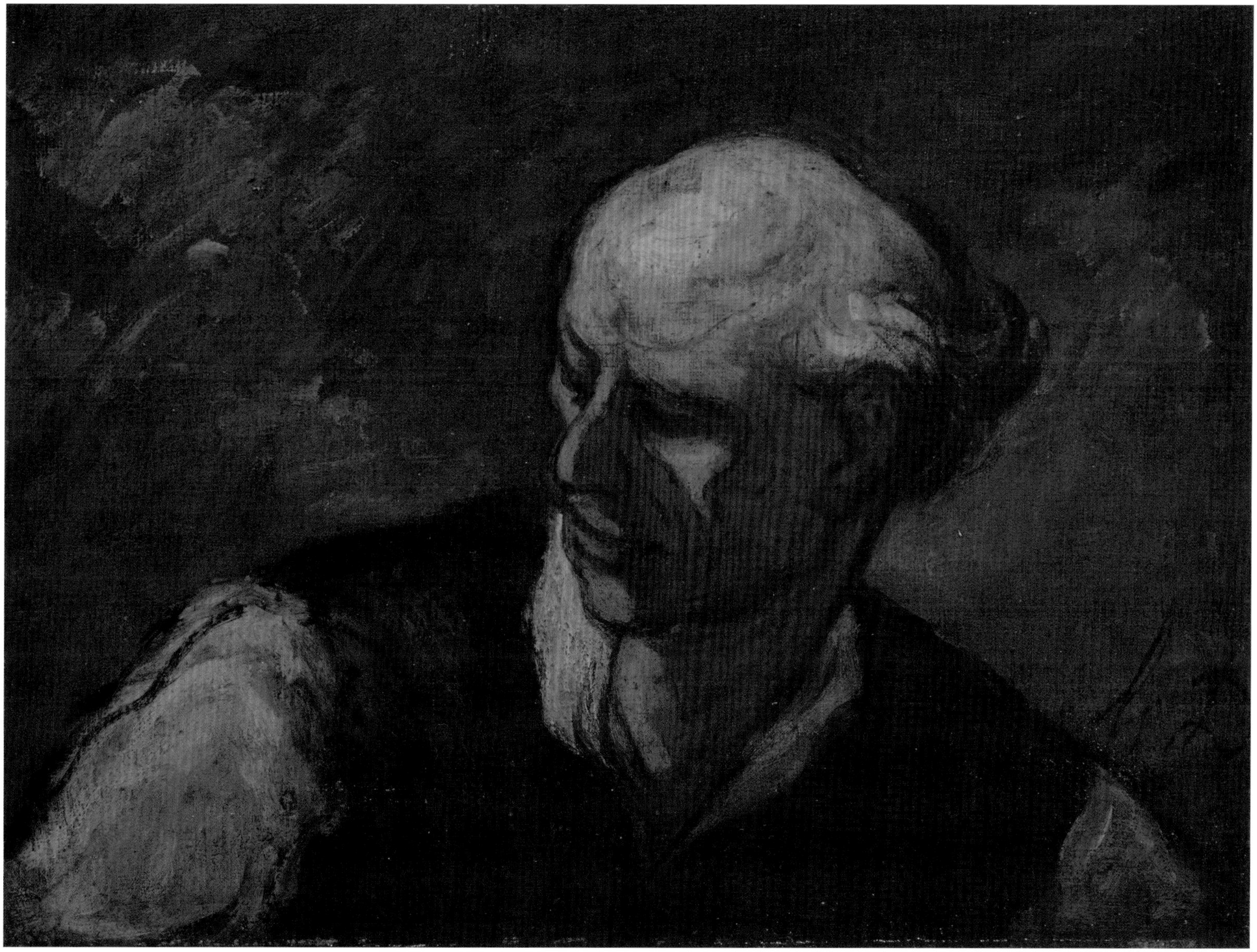

Daumier Far from being purely observational, *The Watering Place* has a distinctly narrative aspect to it, coupled with a romanticism that recalls the work of Géricault.

16 Honoré Daumier (1808–1879)
The Watering Place, ca. 1855–60
Oil on board, 17 ⅝ x 21 ⅞ in. (44.9 x 55.8 cm)
Miss Margaret S. Davies Bequest, 1963 (NMWA 2451)

Like *The Night Walkers* (cat. no. 12) and *The Heavy Burden* (cat. no. 14), this Daumier oil painting shows the banks of the Seine. From about 1846 to 1863, Daumier kept a studio on the Quai d'Anjou and from his window would have observed many riders watering their horses. This is one of numerous works depicting the scene, though none are particularly similar. Despite its title and inspiration, *The Watering Place* has a distinctly narrative aspect to it, coupled with a romanticism that recalls the work of Géricault. The focus of the work is the figure of a man on a white horse, startled by a dog that barks in the shadows at the lower left while his companions water their horses uninterrupted, partially hidden from view. Daumier's use of atmospheric contrast in this work produces a dramatic effect; the central horse and rider are bathed in bright light while the others remain in shadow. *The Watering Place* was described in *The Connoisseur* as a work in which "the drama of the commonplace … produces a minor epic."[35]

It has been noted that equestrian subjects feature rarely in Daumier's work,[36] though there is a small group of works that could be described as related to the present one, for example, the single figure *Un Homme sur un Cheval Blanc* (now in a private collection). It has also been observed that Daumier's depictions of horses from this period are all of stocky and robust work horses – the effect described by Laughton as being that of a realist subject invested with romantic overtones,[37] which is in many ways the perfect description of much of Daumier's work in oil. There is also the large body of work based on Cervantes's *Don Quixote* in which the wiry, almost alien equine form could not differ more from those in the present work, whose central white horse can be compared to works by Géricault and classical sculpture in its form and energy.[38] X-ray photography shows that the main horse's leg position was changed several times during painting.

A comparison of the oil technique of *The Watering Place* with that of an earlier oil, such as *The Night Walkers*, demonstrates how Daumier's technique as an oil painter had developed during the 1850s – the tonal variation and areas of light and shade, seen particularly in the horse and the muscularity of the central rider, are much more skillfully handled. Margaret bought *The Watering Place* from Colnaghi in July 1914, under the title *By the Seine*.

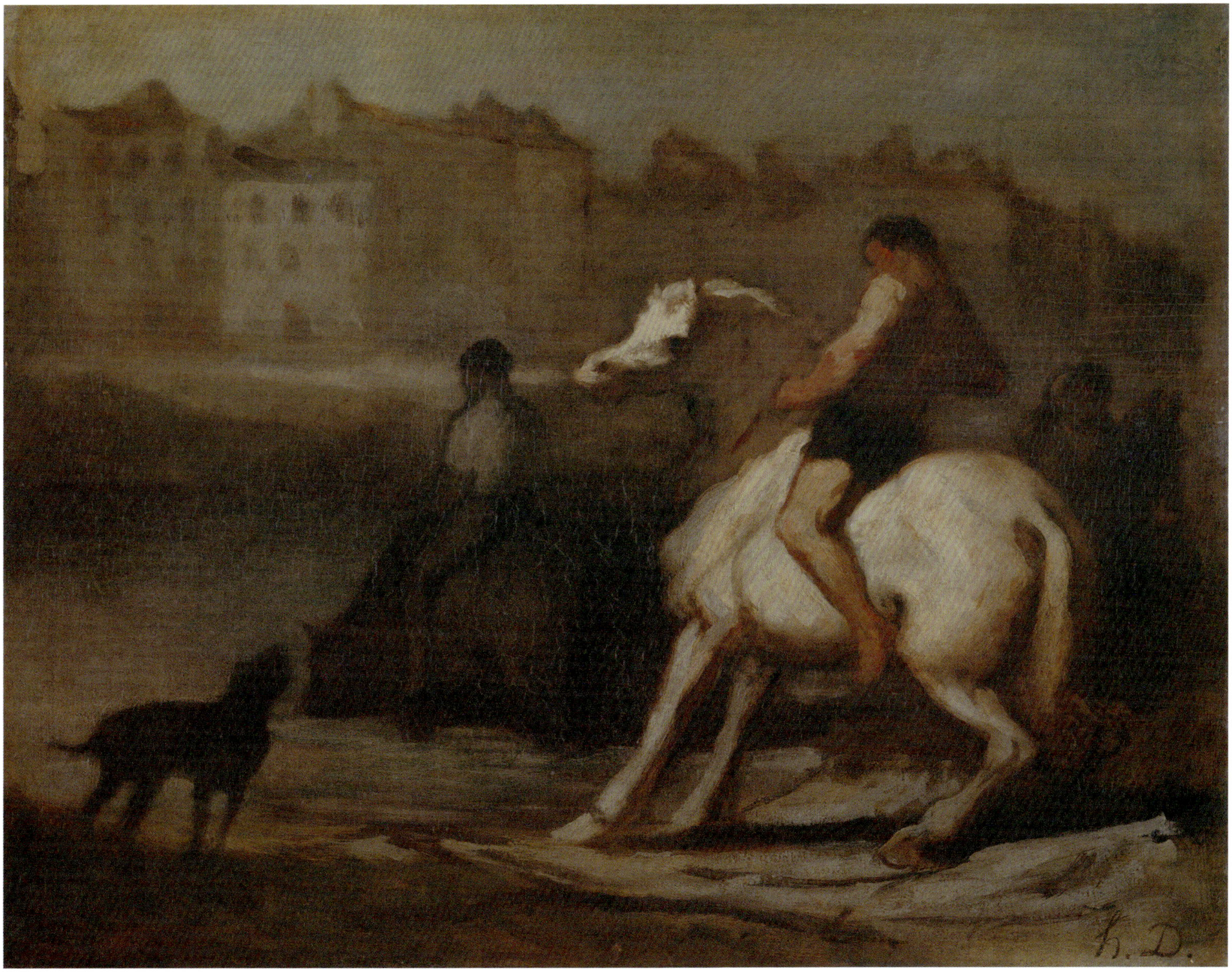
h. D.

Daumier Daumier's skill as a caricaturist is best seen in the second figure from the left, where with only a few lines he captures an expression of self-importance and satisfaction.

17 Honoré Daumier (1808–1879)
The Lawyer and His Client, ca. 1862–64
Watercolor, ink and wash and crayon on two sheets of laid paper joined together, 9 ½ x 9 ⅜ in. (24.1 x 23.8 cm)
Miss Gwendoline E. Davies Bequest, 1951 (NMWA 1679)

Daumier addressed many subjects of everyday life in his drawings: ordinary people at work, in railway carriages, singing, drinking, eating, playing games, dancing, talking, bathing, and playing. However, he is perhaps best known for his portrayals of lawyers and law courts.

In 1831, at only twenty-three, Daumier was himself in court for contemptuously caricaturing the French king, Louis-Philippe. He was sentenced to six months in prison. This firsthand experience obviously fueled an interest in the judicial system, and he became a frequent visitor to the courts, particularly the Palais de Justice de Paris. In 1845–48, Daumier published the series of lithographs titled "Les Gens de Justice" (Men of Justice), which examines the legal "type." He explored gestures and expressions of lawyers and their interactions with the clients. The success of the series led him to readdress the subject many times, particularly in the 1860s.

Daumier made a number of works of lawyers talking with their clients. Here the client is a humble woman who worriedly rubs her hands together as she addresses her lawyer, who looks over his shoulder, paying little attention, as if rushing off to something else. Daumier's skill as a caricaturist is best seen in the second figure from the left, where with only a few lines he has captured an expression of self-importance and satisfaction.

This composition began with two figures, the female client and the lawyer she is addressing. Daumier later extended the composition by adding paper to the left side and drawing the two additional lawyer figures in the background.

Although works by Daumier are very difficult to date, this watercolor was probably produced in the period after he was fired from the journal *Le Charivari* in 1860 and when he produced a number of more worked-up watercolor images to sell. He would have been able to better exploit his skill as a draftsman in these works than in his oil paintings and sell them at an affordable rate. A contemporary account of a visit to Adolphe-Victor Geoffroy-Dechaume's studio records, "Daumier is presently in terrible straits. At Geoffroy's there were about a dozen of his drawings, which he is selling for 50 francs each and which he does in pen, slightly embellished with muted colours."[39]

Gwendoline and Margaret Davies were arguably the principal British collectors of Daumier's artist's work at the time. As early as 1909, their adviser, Hugh Blaker, was drawing their attention to his work when he came back from Paris "obsessed with Carrière [and] Daumier."[40]

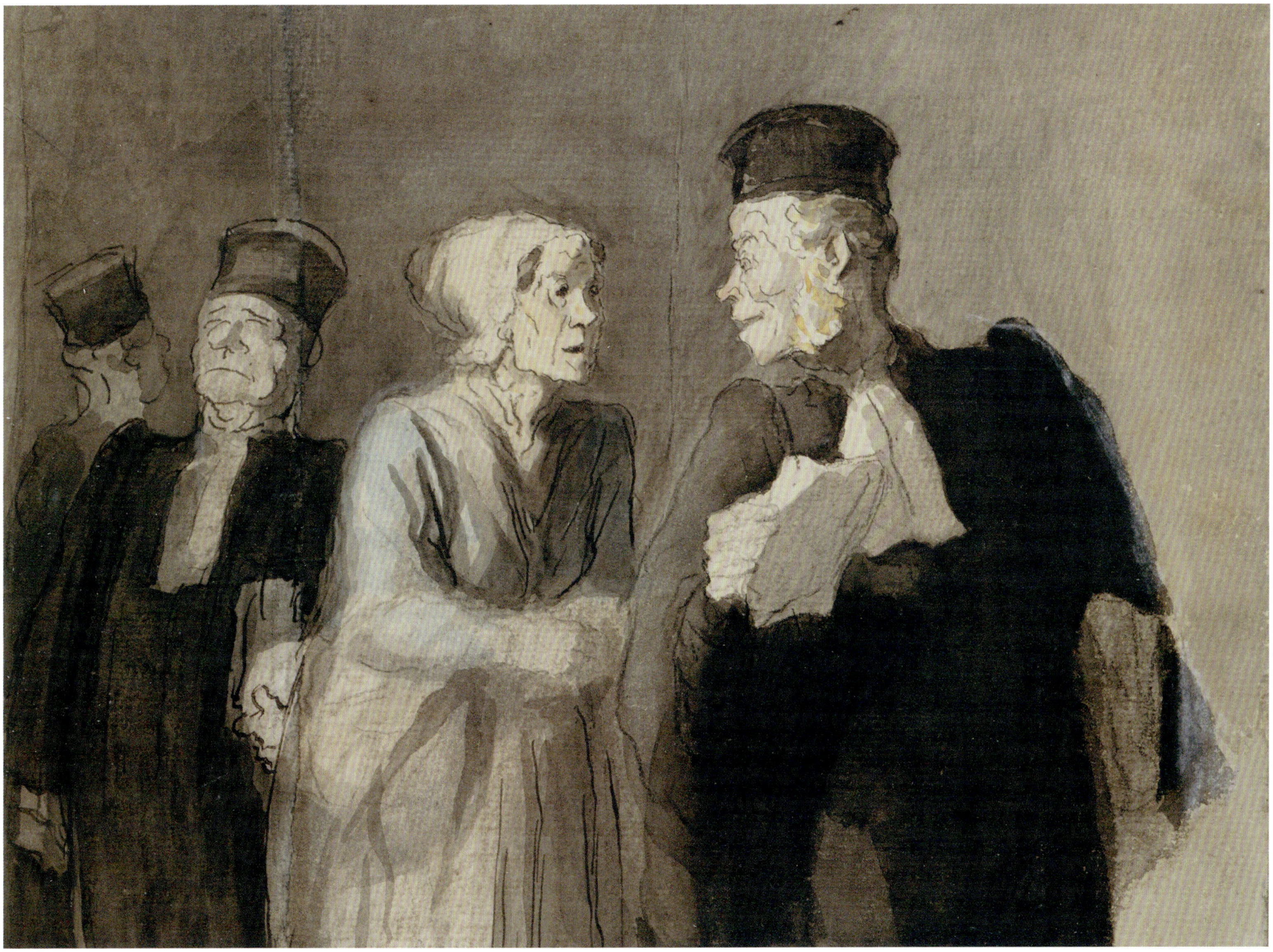

Daumier As a caricaturist, Daumier was accustomed to reducing a story to a single image and to capturing the main focus in an arrested moment.

18 Honoré Daumier (1808–1879)
Two Studies for the Return of the Prodigal Son
(verso: *Three Sketches of Heads in Chalk*), 1863
Ink and wash on laid paper, 8 ¼ x 5 ¼ in. (21.1 x 13.2 cm)
Miss Gwendoline E. Davies Bequest, 1951 (NMWA 1678)

This sheet shows two small-format studies from the famous parable of the Return of the Prodigal Son at the exact moment that the Prodigal Son returns and is embraced by his father. Daumier explored the composition of the two figures in several sheets, many of which are in the National Gallery of Art, Washington, D.C. In each of them, Daumier tries out positions and poses for the two figures and explores the physical representation of repentance and perhaps of submission. Most of Daumier's drawings of the subject show the son facing the father, who places his hands on his son's back and shoulders. Here, it is unclear whether the father's support is exaggerated, as he almost literally holds his son up, or whether this, in fact, represents the son carrying his father back in to the family home following their reunion.[41] It is a very emotive pose. The wash framing device is used to suggest a doorway. Daumier was probably working toward a painting of the subject, but no such picture is known. Before its current identification, the subject of this work was previously thought to be *The Good Samaritan* or *The Blind Man and the Cripple*. The work had the latter title when Gwendoline Davies purchased it.

The choice of a biblical subject is unusual for Daumier and marks a departure from his observations of everyday life. It is perhaps the humanistic nature of the story and the expression of emotion and character that drew Daumier to it. He was perpetually fascinated by the interaction of individuals. As a caricaturist, Daumier was accustomed to reducing a story to a single image and capturing the main focus in an arrested moment.

On the verso of this sheet are three head sketches or caricatures – experiments that are typical of Daumier's graphic work. The artist seems to have drawn heads almost continuously, exploring physical features and expressions.

Gwendoline Davies purchased this work in 1922 from the Lefevre Gallery, London, along with *Head of a Man* (cat. no. 13) and *A Lawyer, Walking* (cat. no. 20).

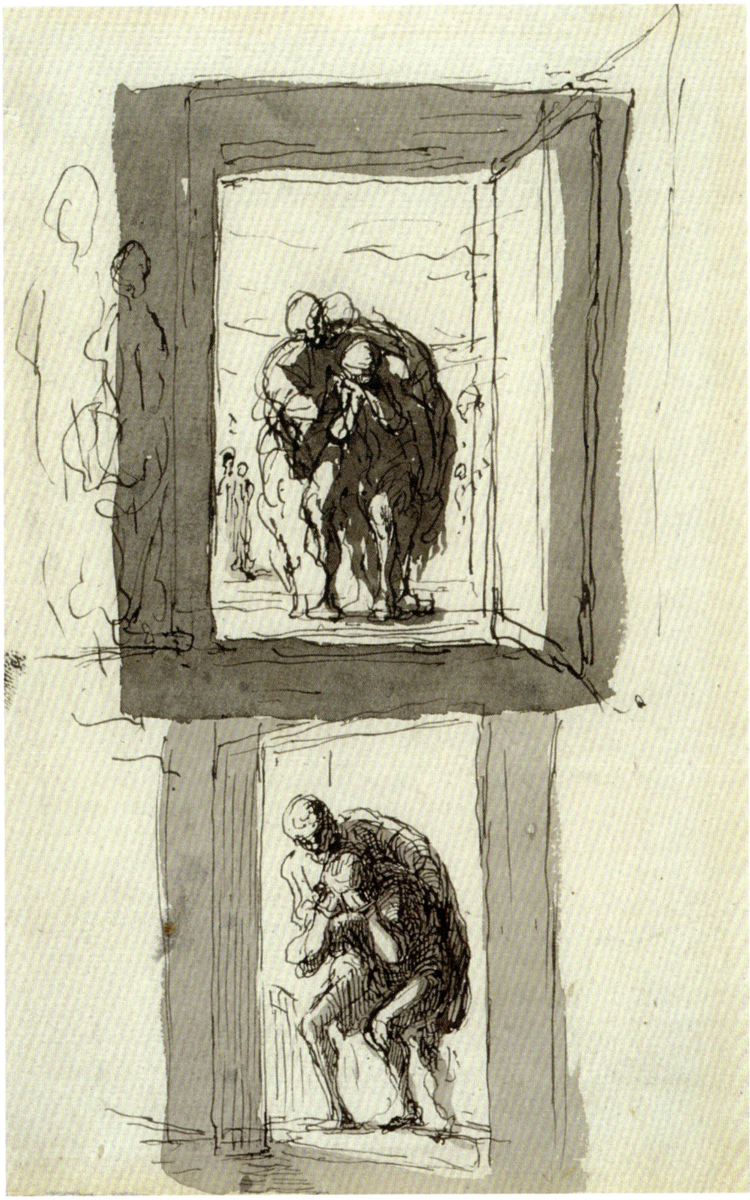

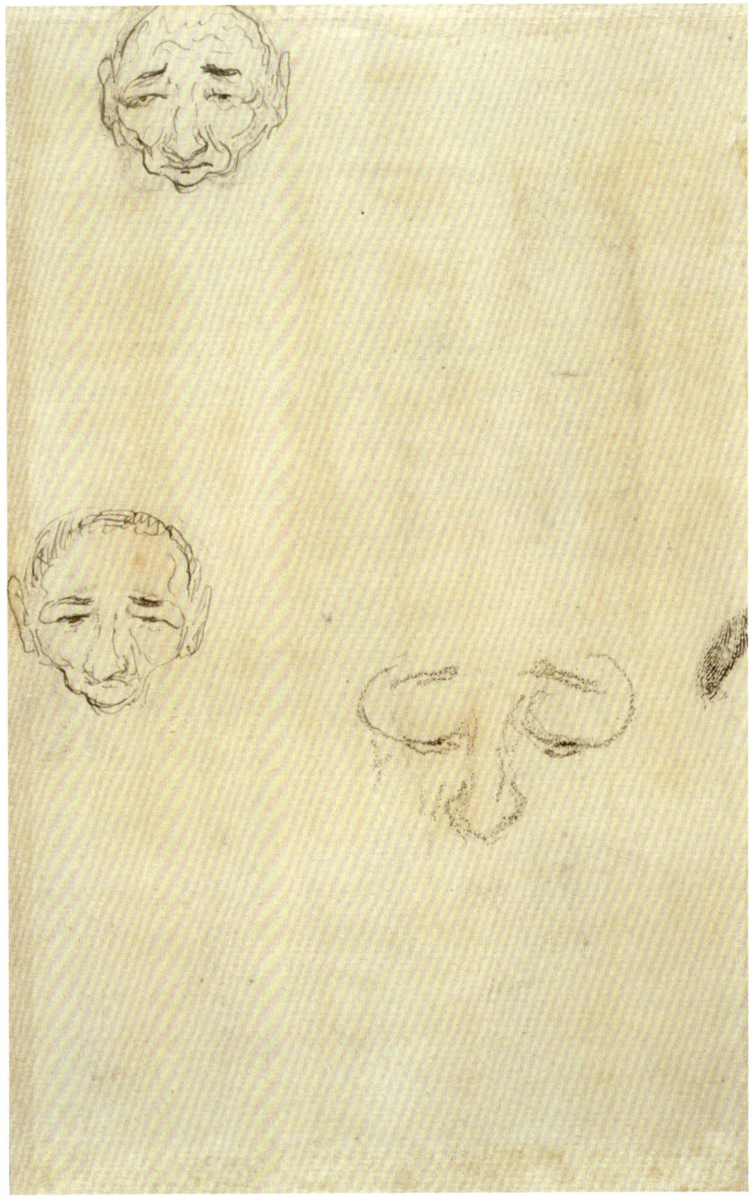

Daumier In contrast to other versions of this subject, the work is very much a study, composed of discrete depictions of individuals rather than a homogenous group.

19 Honoré Daumier (1808–1879)
A Third Class Carriage, ca. 1865
Oil on board, 10 ⅜ x 13 ¼ in. (26.4 x 33.6 cm)
Miss Gwendoline E. Davies Bequest, 1951 (NMWA 2455)

Public transport was, in many ways, the ideal subject for Daumier, allowing as it did for the illustration of a broad range of types. He had been working on the theme of railway carriages during the 1860s, and the present work dates from about 1865. In 1864, he was commissioned to produce three drawings, representing first-, second-, and third-class carriages.[42] The Cardiff version of this last theme, *A Third Class Carriage*, is painted on oak panel, and the dense white lead ground is typical of Daumier's working methods in oil. With pervading red tones, the scene shows five figures, the most prominent being a red-haired female in a striking blue dress. Daumier has also used black bitumen, creating patches of inky density, most notable in the figure on the left of the canvas who has been blacked out entirely. While other versions of this subject have a graphic, almost caricature-like quality to them, the present work is very much a study in oils and seems to be composed of discrete depictions of individuals rather than a homogenous group.

Although this version does not relate to any other versions of the scene, Maison confirms the Daumier attributions,[43] which are further supported by recent research on a group of three Daumiers in the collection of the National Museum of Wales.[44] An underdrawing can be identified in the upper right-hand section, beneath the reddish-brown wash, and Michael Pantazzi has subsequently identified this as a version of a series of compositions based on Don Quixote and Sancho Panza made between 1864 and 1866 (ink and wash, Staatliche Kunsthalle Karlsruhe; crayon, Zdenko Bruck Collection, Buenos Aires; oil and crayon on panel, private collection). The visible lines form part of a tree, and traces run through into the right-hand figure. The central figure with the dense black hat relates to the figure of Sancho Panza in other versions of the underdrawing. While many copies of the third-class carriage subject exist, the identification of the underdrawing seems to confirm a positive attribution to Daumier.

This was the last work by Daumier acquired by either Davies sister. Hugh Blaker purchased it in November 1919 from a sale at Christie's on Gwendoline's behalf. A few months earlier, in July, Margaret had also bought a more finished version of this scene, which she sold in 1960 and which now resides in the Fine Arts Museum of San Francisco and is generally regarded as one of Daumier's finest examples of the subject.

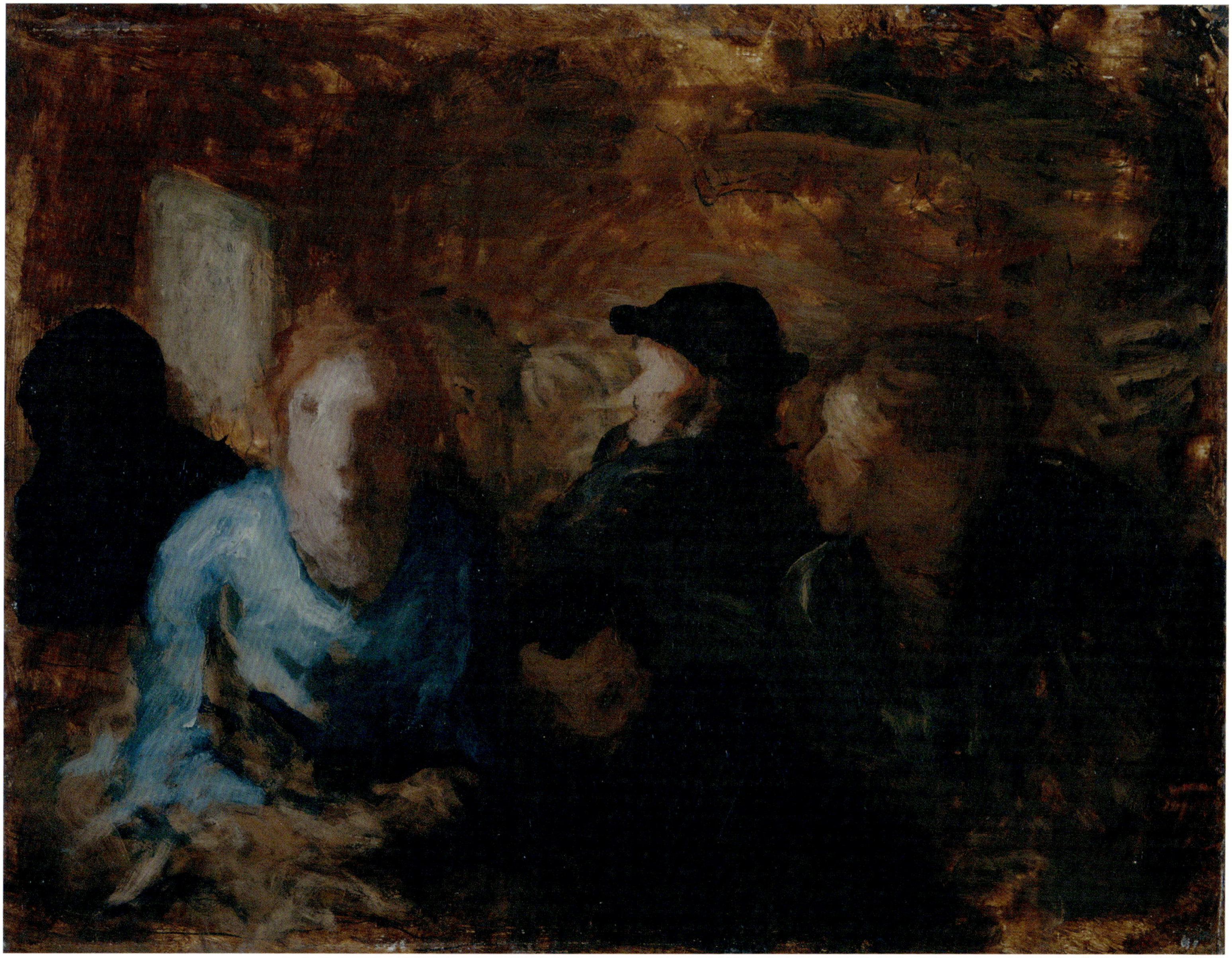

Daumier Daumier has used ink for the precise rendering of the head, which is contrasted with chalk used to suggest the lawyer's gown.

20 Honoré Daumier (1808–1879)
A Lawyer, Walking, ca. 1865
Ink and chalk on laid paper, 15 ¾ x 10 ⅜ in. (40 x 26.3 cm)
Miss Gwendoline E. Davies Bequest, 1951 (NMWA 1681)

In the course of his career, Daumier returned repeatedly to his favorite subjects, images of lawyers being one of these. He drew and caricatured both known people within the judicial system, and "types," exploring generalized postures and expressions. In much of his work, such as this example, he gives prominence to flamboyant poses. The figure's pompous stance and haughty expression give the lawyer an overall look of self-importance, superiority, and power.

Daumier has used ink for the precise rendering of the head, which is contrasted with chalk used to suggest the lawyer's gown. He frequently employed this technique of using both chalk for general areas and ink for detailed work. The arched stance of this lawyer also appears in other works, including drawings of actors and musicians. His face is in profile, adding to the sense of detachment. As always, Daumier focuses not on the details of the figure's clothes but concentrates on the essentials of character, suggesting a "type."

Like most of Daumier's graphic output, this work is probably a drawing in its own right and not a study for an oil painting or a more finished watercolor. Similarities in stance and expression can be seen with other figures of lawyers by the artist.

This drawing, which has also been known as *The Public Prosecutor*, is one of three purchased by Gwendoline Davies in December 1922 from an exhibition of works by Daumier held at the Lefevre Gallery, London.

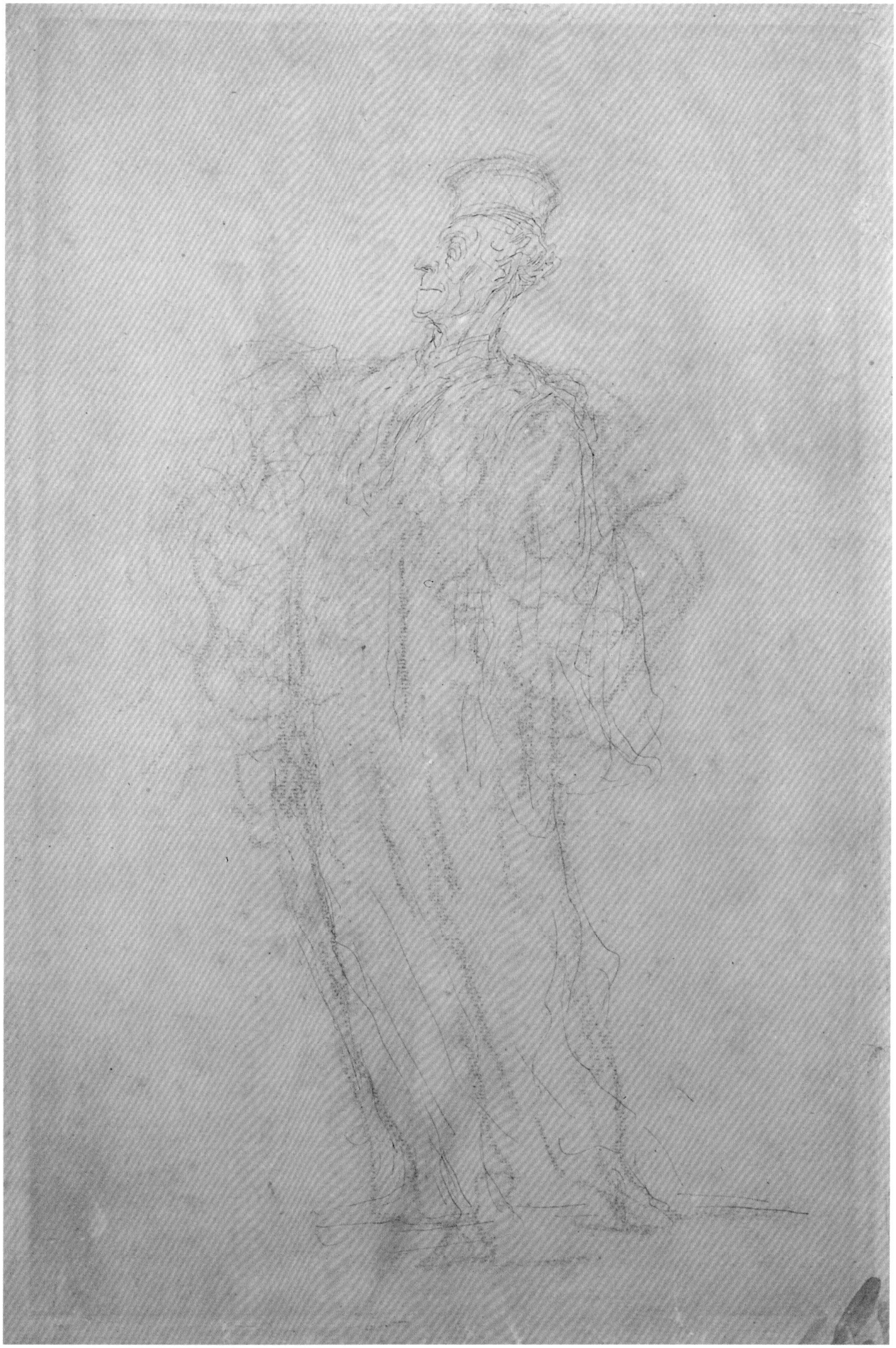

Derain After 1907, when Derain abandoned his Fauvist palette, he turned first to African art and later to old master paintings, which both influence the style of this portrait.

21 André Derain (1880–1954)
Madame Zborowska, 1919
Oil on canvas, 29 ⅞ x 21 ⅛ in. (76 x 53.8 cm)
Miss Margaret S. Davies Bequest, 1963 (NMWA 2163)

Hanka (Anna) Zborowska (dates unknown) came from a wealthy Polish aristocratic family. After moving to Paris to become a teacher, she married the poet and art dealer Léopold Zborowski.[45] Painted regularly in the late 1910s and early 1920s, Madame Zborowska was on numerous occasions a model for Modigliani (Zborowski was his dealer) and was also painted by Henri Hayden. She sat for Derain on this occasion in 1919, and he also painted her husband in 1922. After 1907, when Derain abandoned his Fauvist palette, he turned first to African art and later to old master paintings, which both influence the style of this portrait.

Madame Zborowska is typical of the classicism favored by European artists in the aftermath of World War I and seems to correspond most closely to Italian painting of the period. Madame Zborowska has the same elongated body parts as figures by Modigliani (the exaggerated, sloping shoulders also being characteristic of early Italian art); the pale, contemplative air of Morandi; and the dry, fresco-like quality of Mario Sironi. Derain worked in thin tempera using a sponge to soften contours, and the simplicity of the muted color scheme is maintained by the limitation of background tones to reflections of those in the foreground. The sitter's dark hair sits on washed-out black, and her terracotta-colored dress is placed against a paler ground, creating an atmosphere of calm serenity. There is another Derain canvas that is almost certainly Madame Zborowska but is more sharply defined and includes greater background detail.

This is one of two paintings by Derain owned by the Davies sisters, the other being a landscape, *The Church at Vers* (1920). It is unusual amid their purchases of twentieth-century European art in that it was bought very shortly after it was painted, an example of the sisters buying truly "contemporary" work. It is not known why this particular image appealed to Margaret, but shortly before, in 1919, Gwendoline had procured two paintings by Vlaminck (see cat. nos. 56 and 57) from an exhibition organized by Léopold Zborowski; it is possible Margaret was making the connection when she bought this portrait. Observing the collection as a whole, it is notable that while the sisters owned more than ten paintings by leading Fauves Derain, Vlaminck, and Albert Marquet, the only actual Fauve painting in the collection, *La ciotat* (1907) by Othon Friesz, was not purchased until 1948, suggesting that the vibrancy of pure Fauvism was perhaps too avant garde for their early taste.

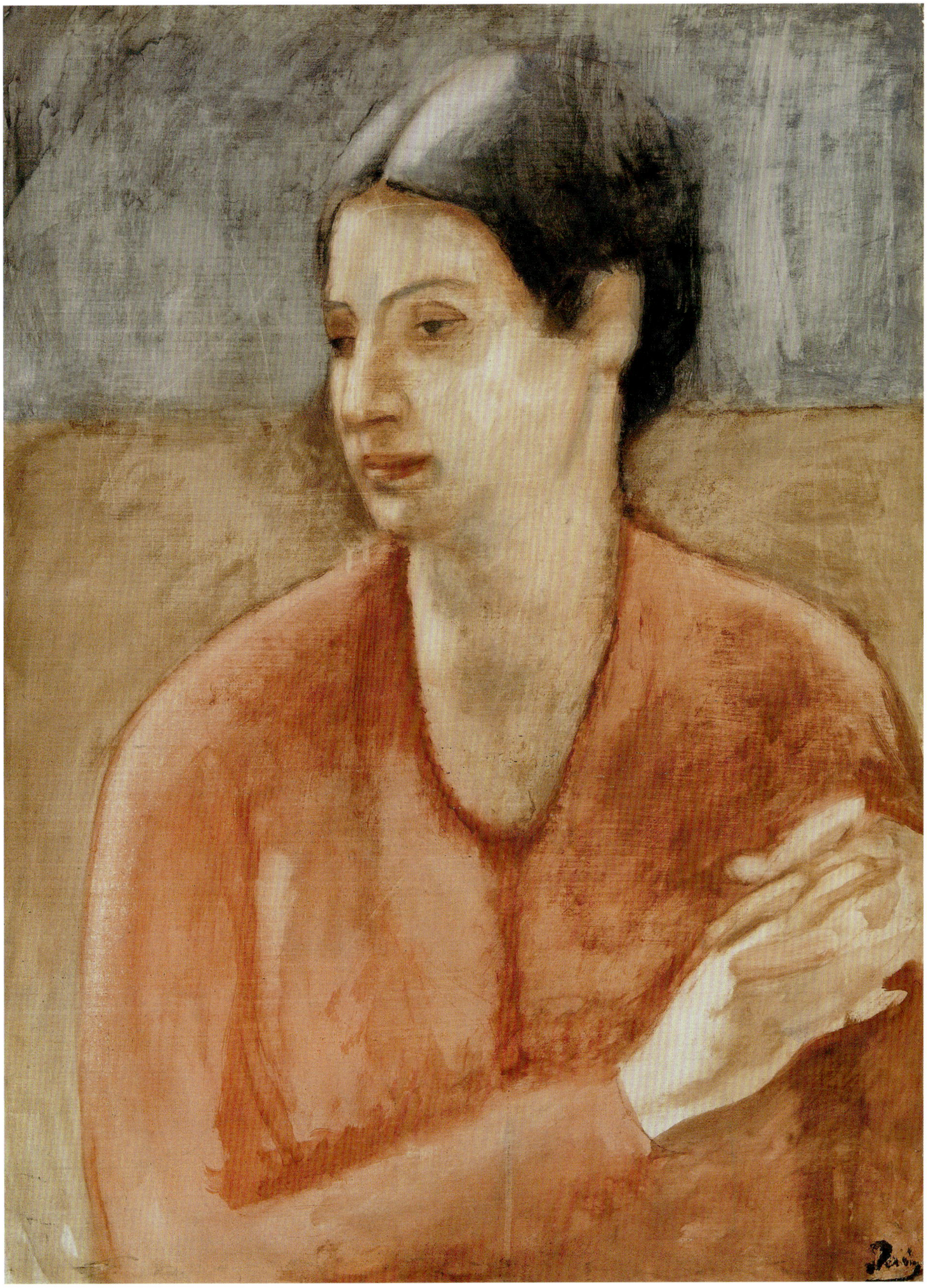

John The chalky nature of the paint gives this image a fresco-like quality, while the composition imbues Dorelia with the air of a *cinquecento* Madonna.

22 Augustus John (1878–1961)
Head of Dorelia, ca. 1911
Oil on plywood, 16 x 13 ⅛ in. (40.7 x 33.3 cm)
Miss Gwendoline E. Davies Bequest, 1951 (NMWA 162)

Born in Tenby, a small seaside town in southwest Wales, Augustus John attended the Slade School of Fine Art in London with his sister, the artist Gwen John (1876–1939). He exhibited at the New English Art Club from its inception in 1899 and was a founding member of the Allied Artists Association, which was at this time progressive but became increasingly conservative. *Head of Dorelia* is an excellent example of the artist's early intimate and characterful portraits of his family and friends, though later in the decade, he trod a strange path between the über-bohemian and new establishment, working as a portraitist while exercising his penchant for painting "outsiders" and large-scale fantasy works. Dorelia McNeill (1881–1969), whom he met in 1903, was a friend of John's sister, Gwen. At the time, John was married to a Slade contemporary, Ida Nettleship, and with Dorelia they lived as a painful ménage-à-trois until Ida's early death in 1907.[46] Dorelia became John's common-law wife and muse until his death more than fifty years later.

Contemporary labeling suggests the work was painted in 1911. Dorelia's hairstyle certainly suggests a date no later than this,[47] and it could even be earlier. In terms of technique, composition, and material, it is very similar to a portrait of John's son Caspar at the Fitzwilliam Museum, Cambridge, England, which dates from about 1909. To make this study, John would have drawn directly onto unprimed plywood, the grain of which is still fully visible, blocking in with unmodulated areas of color that highlight the picture surface. The pencil underdrawing is still discernible. The chalky nature of the paint gives this image a fresco-like quality, while the composition imbues Dorelia with the air of a *cinquecento* Madonna. An excellent draftsman, John was also a bold and increasingly lurid colorist. This early work shows an acute sensitivity in this area and is quite different stylistically from many of his other paintings. Between 1910 and 1912, John became close to the artist J. D. Innes (1887–1914), and while there was certainly some mutual influence in the landscape images of the two artists, it appears to reveal itself in this portrait also. John's use of color and almost naïf style here are highly reminiscent of the younger artist's work.

John produced many images of Dorelia. *Head of Dorelia* is related to a smaller oil, *Dorelia by the Caravan* (1911), which is now in the collection of the Fitzwilliam Museum. The National Museum of Wales has an extensive collection of works by John, a small part of which was purchased and bequeathed by the Davies sisters. Gwendoline Davies bought *Head of Dorelia* in 1916, at the same time purchasing nine other oils, including *Self-Portrait* (cat. no. 23), and one drawing. This was the largest body of a single artist's work that Gwendoline bought and demonstrates the high regard in which she held John and her interest in promoting contemporary Welsh art. Interestingly, neither sister purchased any work by his sister, Gwen, whom recent history has shown to be the more highly regarded and who remains, arguably, one of the most important women artists of the twentieth century.

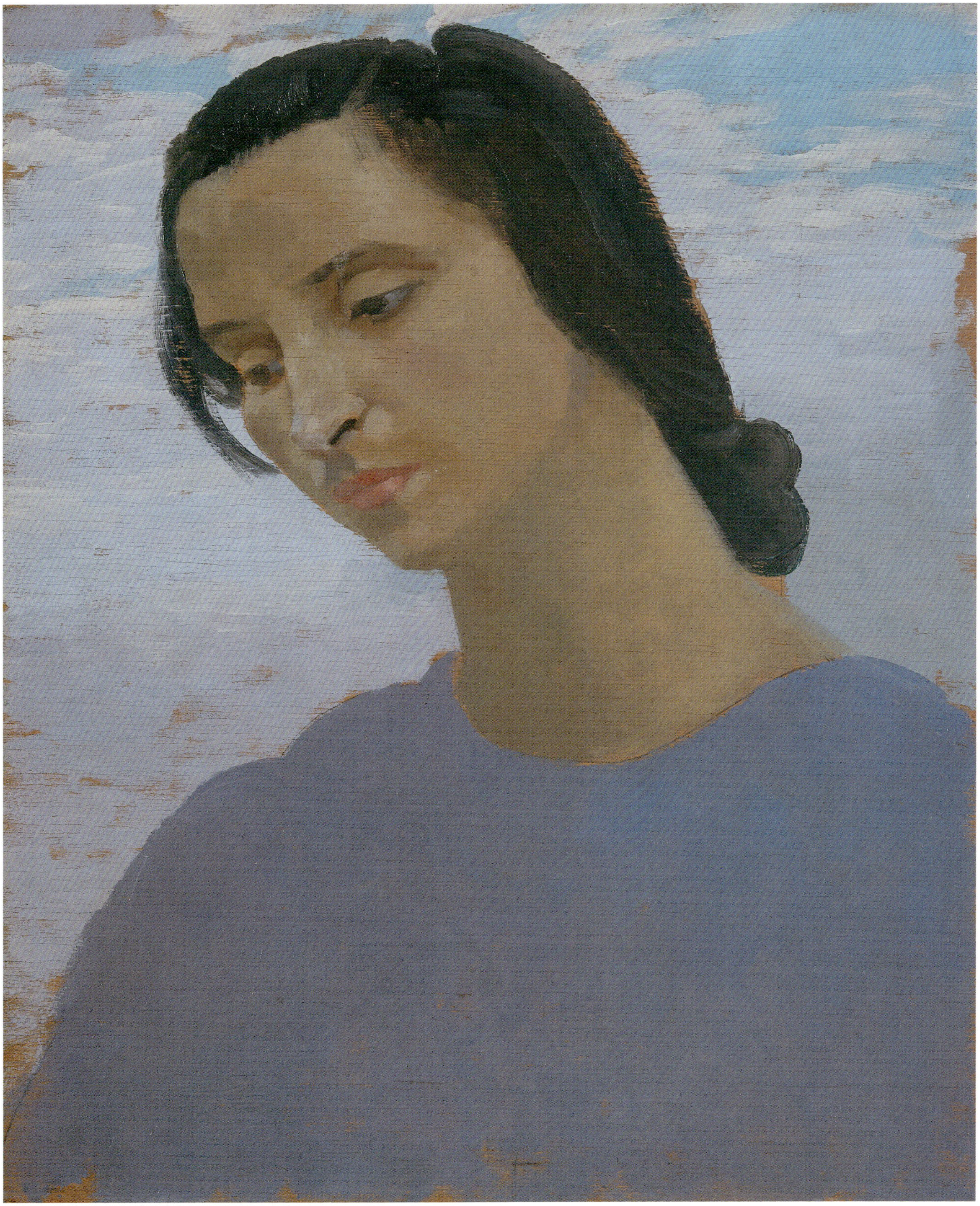

John The brushwork shows John's skill as a colorist, the unblended strokes forming a multi-tonal patchwork across the surface of the canvas.

23 Augustus John (1878–1961)
Self-Portrait, 1913
Oil on canvas, 24 x 20 ⅛ in. (61.1 x 51.1 cm)
Miss Gwendoline E. Davies Bequest, 1951 (NMWA 158)

John painted this self-portrait in 1913, when he was in his mid-thirties. The date has been ascertained from contemporary labels on the reverse, and this was also the year he exhibited in the Armory Show in New York. John both had his portrait painted and painted his own on many occasions, though they become less frequent later in his oeuvre. With the subject depicted bust-length, confident, and dressed in the uniform of the trade, the present picture is, in many respects, a classic artist's self-portrait. The artist's right arm is raised in the act of painting; his brow appears furrowed in concentration. Although this work demonstrates John's technical skill, it is notable that his earlier self-portrait drawings and etchings, which show the artist in a variety of different poses and costumes, are perhaps the more interesting. Much in the way that Courbet and Rembrandt made repeated variations on their self-imaging, so did John in these earlier works, as if either searching for an artistic identity or reveling in his ability to change it at will.

As can be seen from the present work, John's appearance was striking. On his return to the Slade School of Fine Art in 1899, following a period of convalescence after a diving accident, his contemporary, the artist William Rothenstein, described him thus:

> He looked like a young faun; he had beautiful eyes, almond-shaped and with lids defined like those Leonardo drew, a short nose, broad cheek bones, while over a fine forehead fell thick brown hair, parted in the middle. He wore a light curling beard and his figure was lithe and elegant … A dangerous breaker of hearts he would be.[48]

In this self-portrait, the paint is applied freely onto the coarse weave canvas, with some areas remaining exposed. The brushwork shows John's skill as a colorist, the unblended strokes forming a multi-tonal patchwork across the surface. Stylistically, this self-portrait is completely different from the portrait of Dorelia (cat. no. 22) and does not quite have its charm. When this work was exhibited at the Chenil Gallery, London, from where Gwendoline purchased it in 1916, a review in the *Times* newspaper, under the heading "Empty Accomplishment," noted how "Mr. Augustus John continues to mark time with great professional skill."[49] It is worth observing the fundamental difference between this portrait and that of Dorelia. While the image of Dorelia relates far more closely to the gypsy and fantasy works that show John as a purveyor of the avant-garde, this safe self-portrait bears far more resemblance to the glossy, technical excellence of his more commercial portraiture.

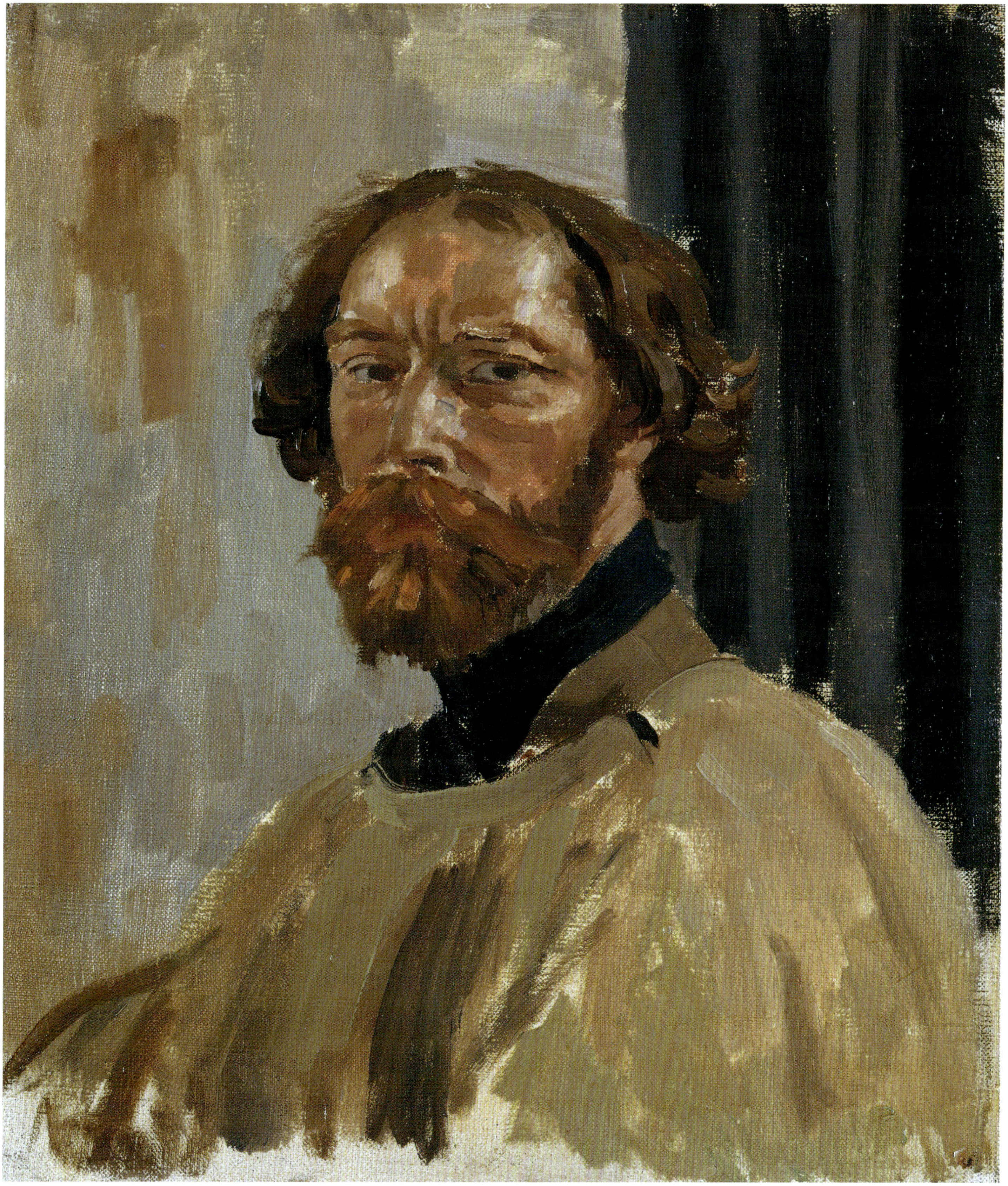

Manet It has been suggested that this was Manet's first "Impressionist" scene – there is no underdrawing, and the hastily applied brushstrokes suggest form rather than describe it.

24 Edouard Manet (1832–1883)
Effect of Snow at Petit-Montrouge, 1870
Oil on canvas, 24 ¼ x 19 ⅞ in. (61.5 x 50.5 cm)
Miss Gwendoline E. Davies Bequest, 1951 (NMWA 2468)

In September 1870, the Prussian Army laid siege to Paris in a move that would end the Franco-Prussian War. Manet volunteered for the National Guard at the outbreak, sending his family to the Pyrenees for the duration. The siege lasted for four months, ending in victory for Prussia. This work shows the church of Saint Pierre de Montrouge at Petit-Montrouge in the fourteenth *arrondissement*, where Manet visited his brother Eugène, also a guardsman, in late December. The church was built in the 1860s and so was relatively new – and serving as a field hospital – when this work was painted during the siege, only to be damaged in heavy fighting during the Commune six months later, in May 1871.[50]

Manet wrote not only of the bitter cold and hunger but also of the boredom. A comparison of this deserted, frozen image with the violence of his depictions of the events of the Commune six months later demonstrates two entirely different facets of conflict.[51] At least half of this canvas shows a sprawling, snow-covered waste ground, the monochrome sepia tones of the sketch emphasizing the bleakness, but with typical Manet-like juxtapositions of black and white. It has been suggested that this was Manet's first "Impressionist" scene – there is no underdrawing on the fine-woven linen canvas, and the hastily applied brushstrokes suggest form rather than describe it. He inscribed the painting *A mon ami H. Charlet* while the paint was still wet, most likely a dedication to an as-yet unidentified fellow guardsman.

Manet had written during the siege how he planned to "start some sketches from life. They will be souvenirs that one day will have value."[52] It is not clear if he meant because of the artist or the context, but either way, *Effect of Snow at Petit-Montrouge* is the only known surviving work from this period. There is another painting, now lost, called *La gare du chemin de fer à Sceaux*, which was last seen around 1944.[53] It bears the same date, is the same size, and is stylistically identical to the present canvas but is in landscape rather than portrait format. Despite its title, it is unlikely that it depicts the railway station at Sceaux, being much more likely to show a view closer to the present one.[54]

Originally called simply *Eglise de Petit-Montrouge*, this work was purchased by Gwendoline Davies in 1912, the year in which the sisters began to acquire Impressionist art. At a time when their only Impressionist purchases were the Venetian Monets, this work was a bold and unusual choice but, as it transpired, an extremely farsighted one.

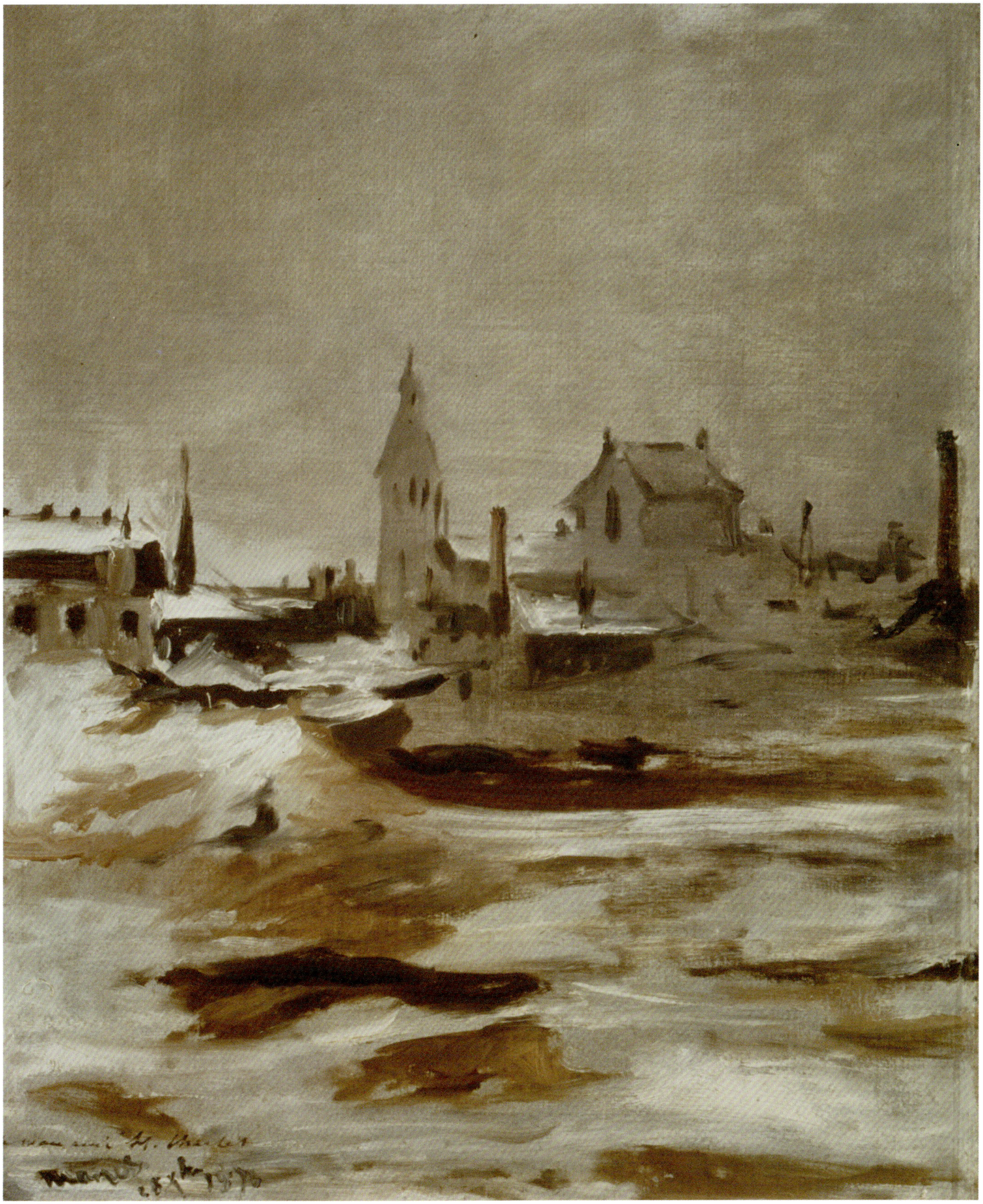

Manet While Argenteuil was seen as a place of "modern" pleasures, Manet's work hints at the flip side of this social shift and pursuit of leisure.

25 Edouard Manet (1832–1883)
Argenteuil–Boats, 1874
Oil on canvas, 23 x 31 ½ in. (58.5 x 80 cm)
Miss Margaret S. Davies Bequest, 1963 (NMWA 2467)

During the summer of 1874, Manet stayed at the family home in Gennevilliers, two miles away from the town of Argenteuil. Famed for its boating and regattas, Argenteuil was popular with well-heeled Parisians wishing to escape the city and was a rapidly expanding location for weekend tourism. As a painter of modern life and pursuits, Manet duly followed. He had assisted Monet in finding a house in Argenteuil, and that summer, Manet, Monet, and sometimes Renoir, who was also visiting, would paint together on the banks of the Seine, producing superficially similar yet utterly different representations of the location.

Argenteuil–Boats is related to *The Seine at Argenteuil* of 1874 (private collection, on extended loan to the Courtauld Gallery, London), which shows a wider view, with a woman and child on the bank at the lower left-hand side of the picture watching the boats. In the Courtauld view, Manet's brushwork and palette can be compared to that of Monet, but the present work is far closer stylistically to Manet's work of the previous decade, with its opaque blocks of color, eschewal of transitional tones, and emphasis on creams and brown-blacks. It is assumed (though it has been noted circumstantially[55]) that Manet painted this en plein-air; yet structurally, although it has the looseness of Impressionism and plein-air painting, Manet's tightly knit compositional touches from the 1860s are firmly in evidence, for example, in the way in which the boats recede with complete uniformity, the masts lined up in perfect parallel, creating a visually arresting (but very unlikely) set of reflections in the water.

Manet painted some of his most famous images during his summer sojourn, including the intriguing *Argenteuil* (Musée des Beaux-Arts, Tournai, Belgium), whose simple title belies the enigma of its subject matter. Similarly, *Argenteuil–Boats* cannot be read simply as an oil sketch or a straightforward landscape. While much of Monet's work at Argenteuil shows its recreational aspect as a place of "modern" pleasures, Manet's work hints at the flip side of this social shift and pursuit of leisure. The vessels on the far bank are laundry houses, catering to the influx of visitors, which, as Paul Hayes Tucker has observed, jar with the natural forms surrounding them.[56] Thick smoke billows from almost invisible chimneys in the distance (which, in *The Seine at Argenteuil*, are visible but dormant), echoed in the swathes of brown shadow and reflection that dominate the middle ground, acting not only as a visual metaphor for industrial pollution but dividing the canvas into foreground and background, a subtle juxtaposition of leisure and labor.

Margaret Davies purchased *Argenteuil–Boats* from Bernheim-Jeune, Paris, in 1920, at the same time acquiring van Gogh's *Rain–Auvers* (cat. no. 55). This was the final purchase of work by Manet of either sister, adding to their earlier landscape of Petit-Montrouge (cat. no. 24) and a late still life, *The Rabbit* (1881), purchased in Paris in 1917.

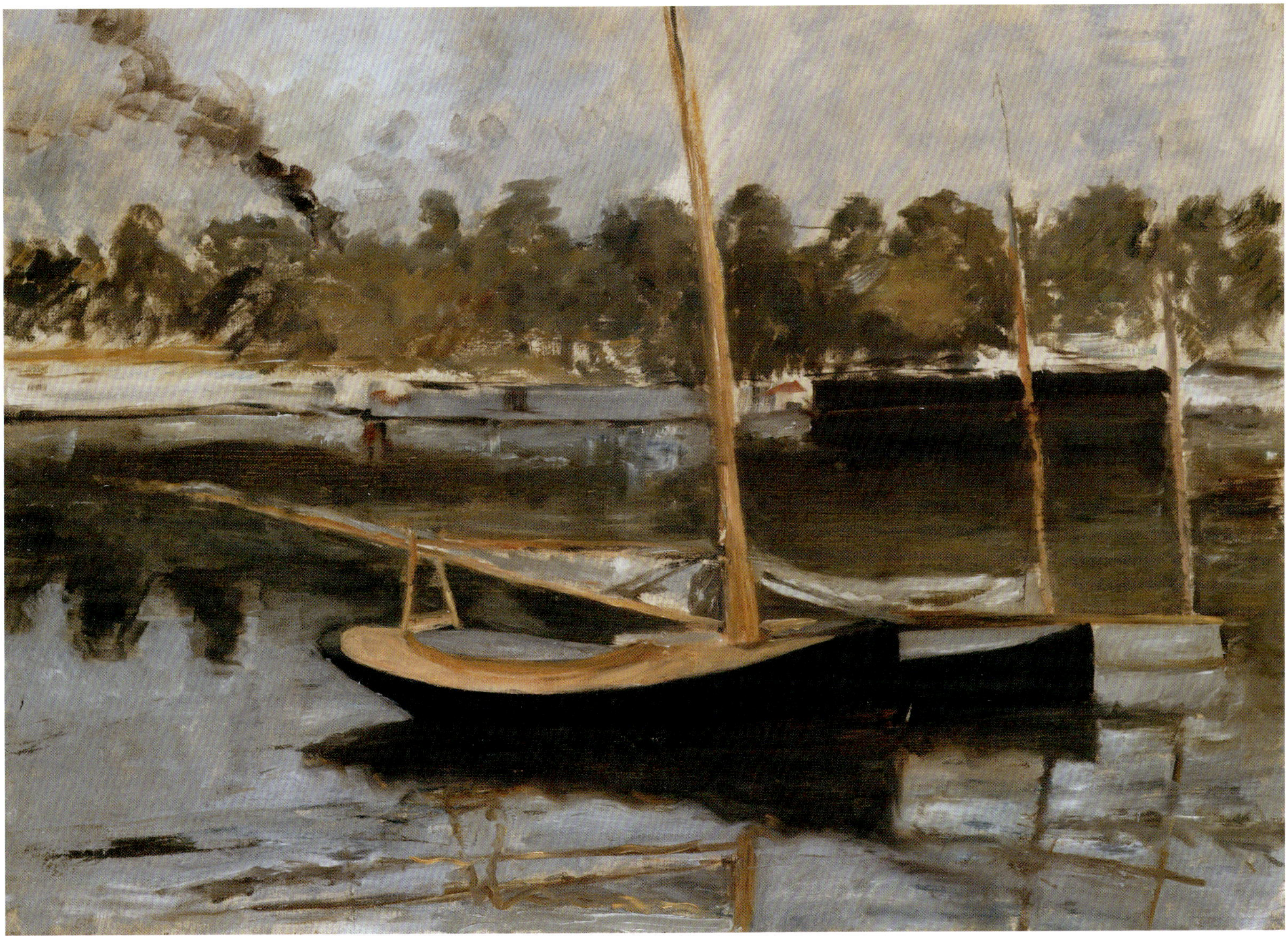

Mauve It is most likely that this work dates from the period after 1882 when Mauve first began visiting the town of Laren, where sheep grazed on the vast heathland.

26 Anton Mauve (1838–1888)
The Shepherdess, 1880s
Oil on canvas, 12 ¼ x 19 ¾ in. (30.2 x 50.2 cm)
Miss Gwendoline E. Davies Bequest, 1951 (NMWA 2225)

Born in Zaandam, Holland, Anton Mauve was a member of the Hague school that flourished between 1860 and 1890 and which included Jozef Israels and Jacob Maris. Mauve's work influenced the early realism of van Gogh, who was his cousin by marriage, and although he was extremely popular in his day, Mauve's reputation has suffered through comparisons with the work of his more famous relative. Although he spent his entire life in the Netherlands, Mauve would have had contact with the work of the Barbizon school through paintings and prints at the Hague branch of Goupil & Sons, where van Gogh had worked and where Mauve's own work was sold.[57] Mauve was very much influenced by Millet, and the Barbizon style can be clearly seen in this painting, though the October 1907 issue of *The Studio* noted that while Mauve was "not a pioneer, he was no imitator, not even the disciple of another painter. His art was distinctly national, its development logical and personal."[58]

Mauve, who traveled the Netherlands painting rural and animal scenes, first began to paint en plein-air in the early 1860s in the village of Oosterbeek, where a community of artists would gather each summer. He did not date any of his paintings, so it is difficult to assess them in any kind of chronological order, but it is most likely that this work dates from the period after 1882 when Mauve first began visiting the town of Laren, in the Gooi area, where sheep grazed on the vast heathland. Mauve settled there in 1885, and his paintings of sheep after this time were so popular with the buying public that he became almost unable to cope with the demands, being required to produce on one occasion twelve sheep canvases in three weeks for an English dealer.[59] It is very possible that this small canvas is one such work.

This early purchase by Margaret Davies, in May 1909, was acquired on her behalf by Hugh Blaker. As Mauve was then a leading modern Dutch painter, the acquisition demonstrates the sisters' preference for small but fashionable works at this time. *The Shepherdess* represents the type of work the sisters acquired in the first few years of their collecting and is just one of a number of sheep and shepherding scenes. In addition to a portrait by George Romney, the same year the sisters' collecting comprised works by Constable, David Cox, and Millet, all very similar in subject matter.

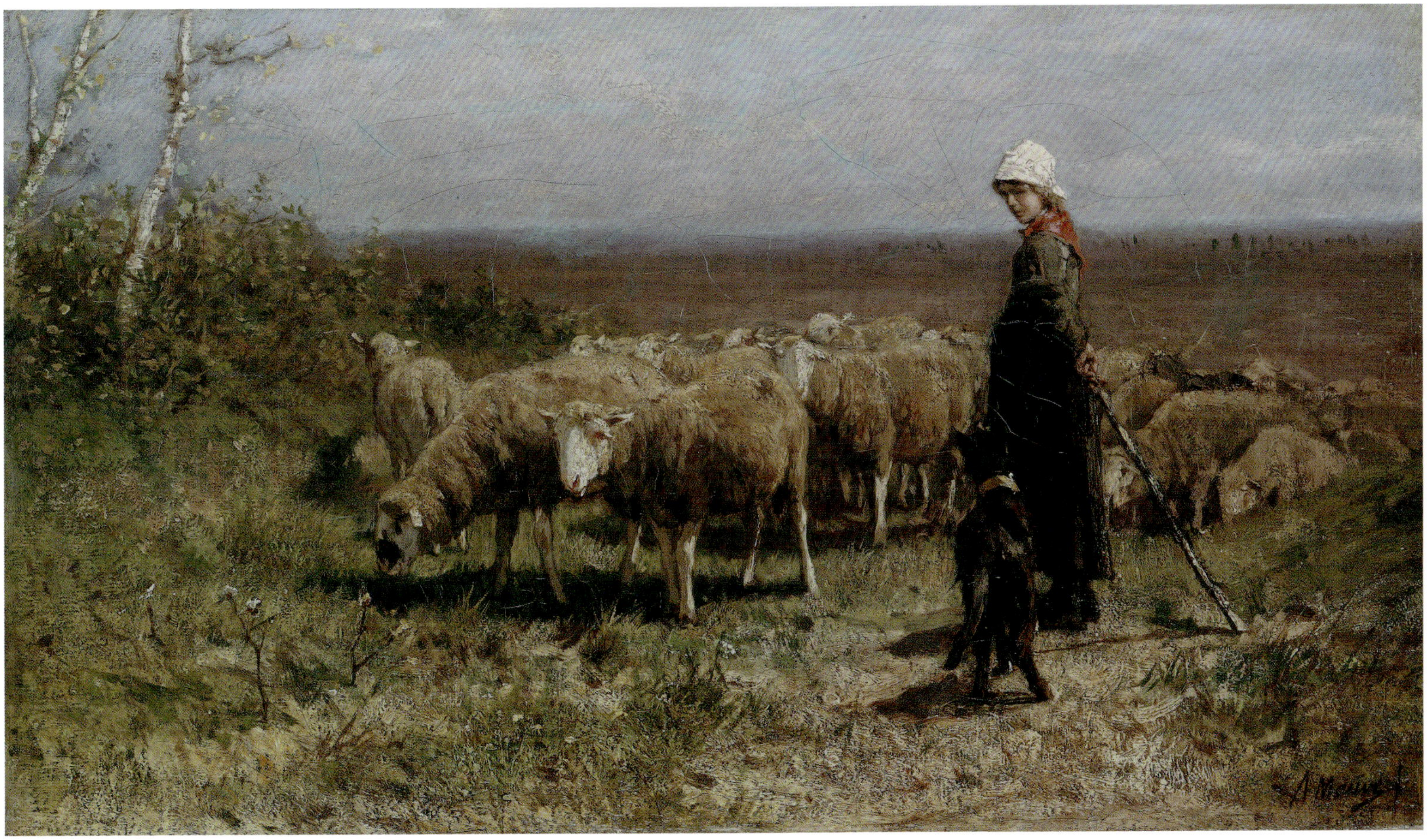

Meissonier Meissonier evokes a considerable tension – there is even perhaps the threat of violence, as the figure to the right places a hand on his sword, as if anticipating a scuffle.

27 Jean-Louis-Ernest Meissonier (1815–1891)
Innocents and Card Sharpers, 1861
Oil on board, 9 ½ x 12 ⅝ in. (24.2 x 32.2 cm)
Miss Margaret S. Davies Bequest, 1963 (NMWA 2471)

The work of Meissonier was popular during the Second Empire of Napoleon III. Through his small, historic genre scenes evoking the worlds of Chardin and Vermeer, he gained public and state acclaim and was the first artist to receive the Grand Cross of the Legion of Honor in 1889.[60] Meissonier worked in microscopic detail, depicting either eighteenth-century bourgeois or, as in the present work, cavalrymen of the Louis XIII period. Meissonier was ultra-conservative, and his particular brand of photographic realism was in many ways the antithesis of progressive forms of art in France at the time, such as the work of his contemporaries Gustave Courbet and Edouard Manet.

Historically, card playing has been a popular subject in western art, providing as it does a context for drama, emotion, and narrative. In this image, also known as *Innocents and Sly Ones*,[61] the fresh faced "innocents" to the right come up against the more experienced, bearded cardsharpers to the left in a game of Piquet. Meissonier evokes a considerable tension as the two young men choose their next move – there is even perhaps the threat of violence, as the figure to the right places a hand on his sword, as if anticipating a scuffle. The compositional device of a central table balanced on either side by figures was a favorite of Meissonier's (as in, for example, *A Game of Chess*; Hamburger Kunsthalle), though he usually involved just two figures rather than a more complex group such as this.

Margaret Davies had admired the work of Meissonier in the Louvre during the sisters' European trip of 1909. She had commented on "the fineness in his painting to every detail, whatever it may be"[62] and asked their adviser, Hugh Blaker, to find her an example. The price of *Innocents and Card Sharpers*, at £5,250, reflects how highly desirable Meissonier still was twenty years after his death. This purchase also demonstrates how in the first few years of collecting the sisters were making safe, fashionable purchases. This is one of three small historic genre scenes of a similar type bought by the sisters in the early years of their collecting, the other two being *The Artist's Model* by Charles Bargue (cat. no. 1) and *The Engraver* by Carl Seiler (National Museum Wales).

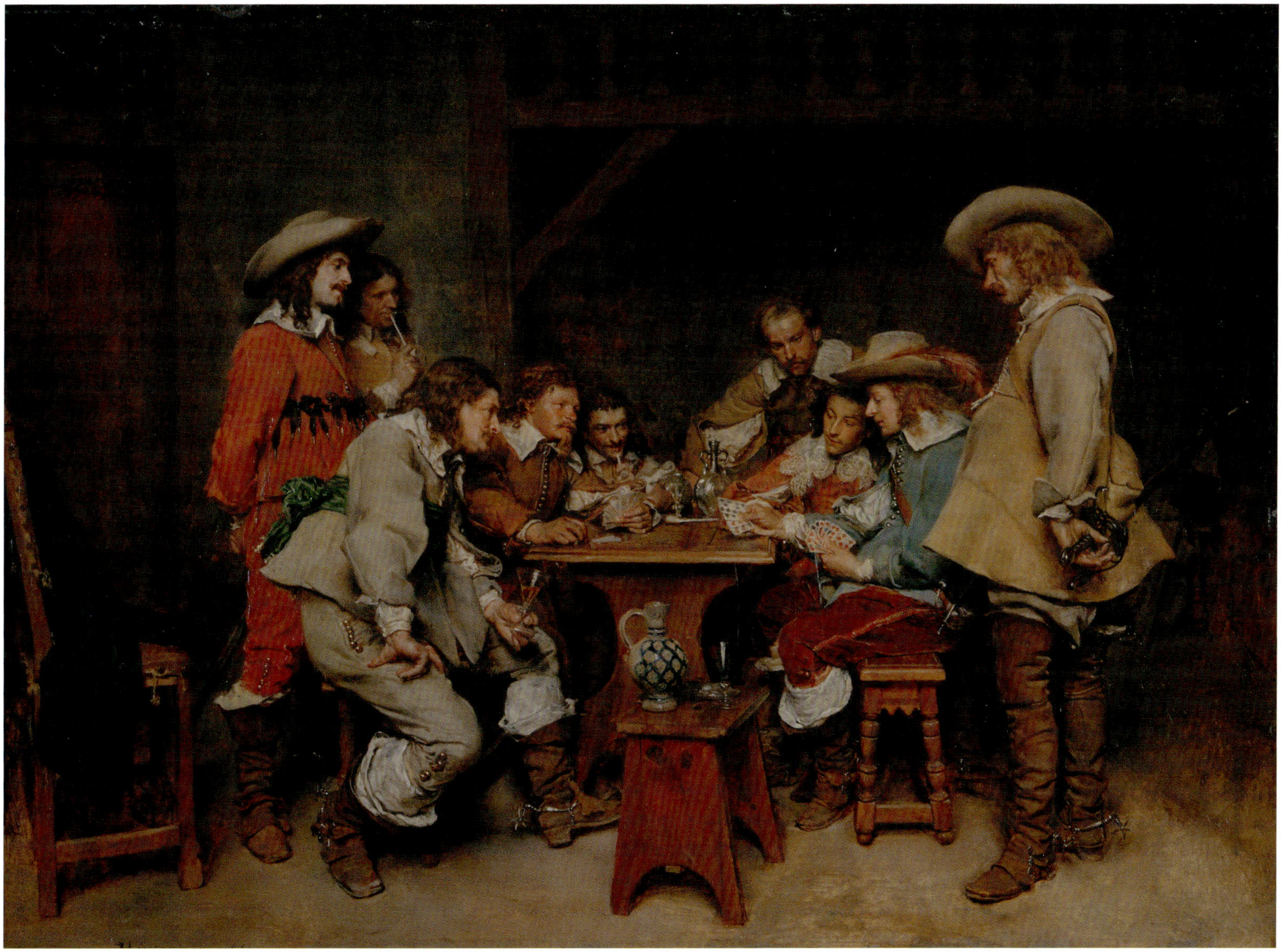

Millet Although picturesque, *The Seated Shepherdess* also hints at the grind of rural life, which would become more pronounced in Millet's later work.

28 Jean-François Millet (1814–1875)
The Seated Shepherdess, 1840–50
Oil on board, 7 ⅜ x 9 ⅝ in. (18.7 x 24.4 cm)
Purchased by National Museum Wales, 1991 (NMWA 585)

Millet grew up in a farming community in Normandy and would have worked on his family's farm as a youth. He moved to Paris in the 1830s to study art, but beginning in the late 1840s, he became progressively more disenchanted with urban life and industrialization; and in 1849 he moved to the village of Barbizon about thirty miles outside of Paris on the edge of the Forest of Fontainebleau. Here, Millet and artists such as Corot, Daubigny, and Rousseau painted directly from nature. The depiction of peasant life in nineteenth-century France underwent a paradigm shift in the 1840s – the idealized countryside was gradually replaced by images that showed not only the true rigors of rural life but also its inhabitants as a tangible, solid force – which in the wake of the 1848 revolution caused not a little conservative disquiet.

It has often been observed that despite the fact that Millet's work followed this shift – particularly in his later pieces (see cat. no. 31) – he was no social reformer. Stylistically, this work can be seen to occupy a sort of middle ground in Millet's rural output. While the small scale, attractive color, and relaxed allure of *The Seated Shepherdess* would have appealed to the picture-buying public, Millet also hints at the grind of rural life, which would become more pronounced in his later work – the figure's skin is sunburned and her hands are large and prominent, a sign of one inured to manual labor. There are certain similarities between this work and *The Goose Girl at Gruchy* (cat. no. 30), both of which show central figures in a state of almost classical repose, while their animals remain untended behind.

The attribution to Millet is strengthened by recent x-ray photography, which has revealed the presence of a previous composition below the present image, that of a man digging (a subject Millet would return to on many occasions). The vertical brushstrokes at the center of the work show where the figure was overpainted. Formerly in the collection of Henri Rouart, *The Seated Shepherdess* was exhibited at the major Millet retrospective at the Ecole des Beaux-Arts in 1887. At the Rouart sale of 1912, it was recognized as one of the most important works by Millet in his collection.[63] The painting was bought for Margaret Davies from the sale by Wallis & Son, though it never formed part of her 1963 bequest. It was purchased by the National Museum of Wales in 1991 to join the existing group of Millets from the sisters' collection.

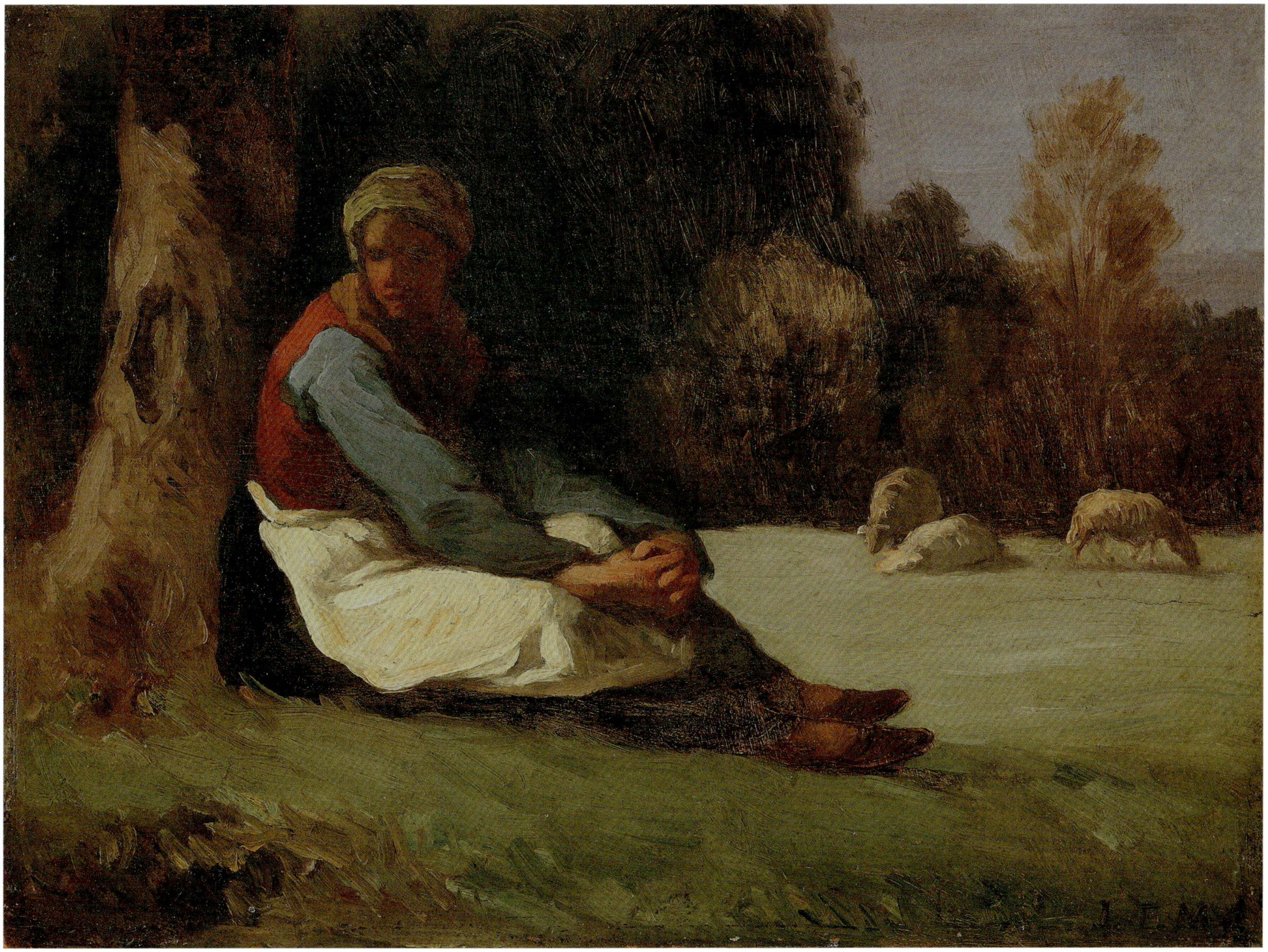

Millet *The Good Samaritan* is notable for its economy of detail, which was to become a feature of Millet's work.

29 Jean-François Millet (1814–1875)
The Good Samaritan, 1846
Oil on canvas, 16 x 12 ¾ in. (40.6 x 32.4 cm)
Miss Gwendoline E. Davies Bequest, 1951 (NMWA 2477)

Millet was originally from Cherbourg. Though he spent most of his life in Barbizon, between 1837 and 1849 he lived in Paris, where he studied under the artist Paul Delaroche (1797–1856). *The Good Samaritan* dates from the latter part of this period. Although best known for his works depicting peasant life, during his time in Paris, in addition to portraiture, Millet focused on biblical and literary scenes – subjects more suited to Salon tastes. The Davies collection also includes *The Shooting Stars*, an illustration of the fifth canto of Dante's *Inferno*, from the same period.

Despite its narrative subject, *The Good Samaritan* is notable for its economy of detail, which was to become a feature of Millet's work. Painted on a small canvas, the image shows two men, one struggling to carry the other, who hangs limply in his arms like a rag doll. There is no physical context to speak of other than a wall, behind which the moon rises, appearing to illuminate the two figures whose shadows suggest an additional light source to the left. The picture is rendered more enigmatic by Millet's decision to depict the men from the back, their faces remaining unseen.

This work came from the celebrated collection of Alexander Young, which was sold at Christie's, London, in June and July 1910. While the biblical subject of the Good Samaritan would seem an obvious choice for the devout Davies sisters, their purchase of this particular work is peculiar given the 1910 sale catalogue's description of it thus: "A sturdy peasant dressed in a blue blouse and buff breeches, carrying a bundle slung over his back, is supporting an inebriated comrade." This challenges the view that it is a representation of the biblical story of the same name, suggesting a more general depiction of the phrase that has come into general usage, that of performing a good deed for someone in trouble. With knowledge of the teetotal sisters' ideals and religious belief, it is unlikely they would have purchased a work depicting drunkenness, suggesting that when Gwendoline acquired this work from Wallis & Son, London, shortly afterward, she had not seen the initial description and only the work itself. It is notable that subsequent descriptions of the painting make no reference to inebriation.

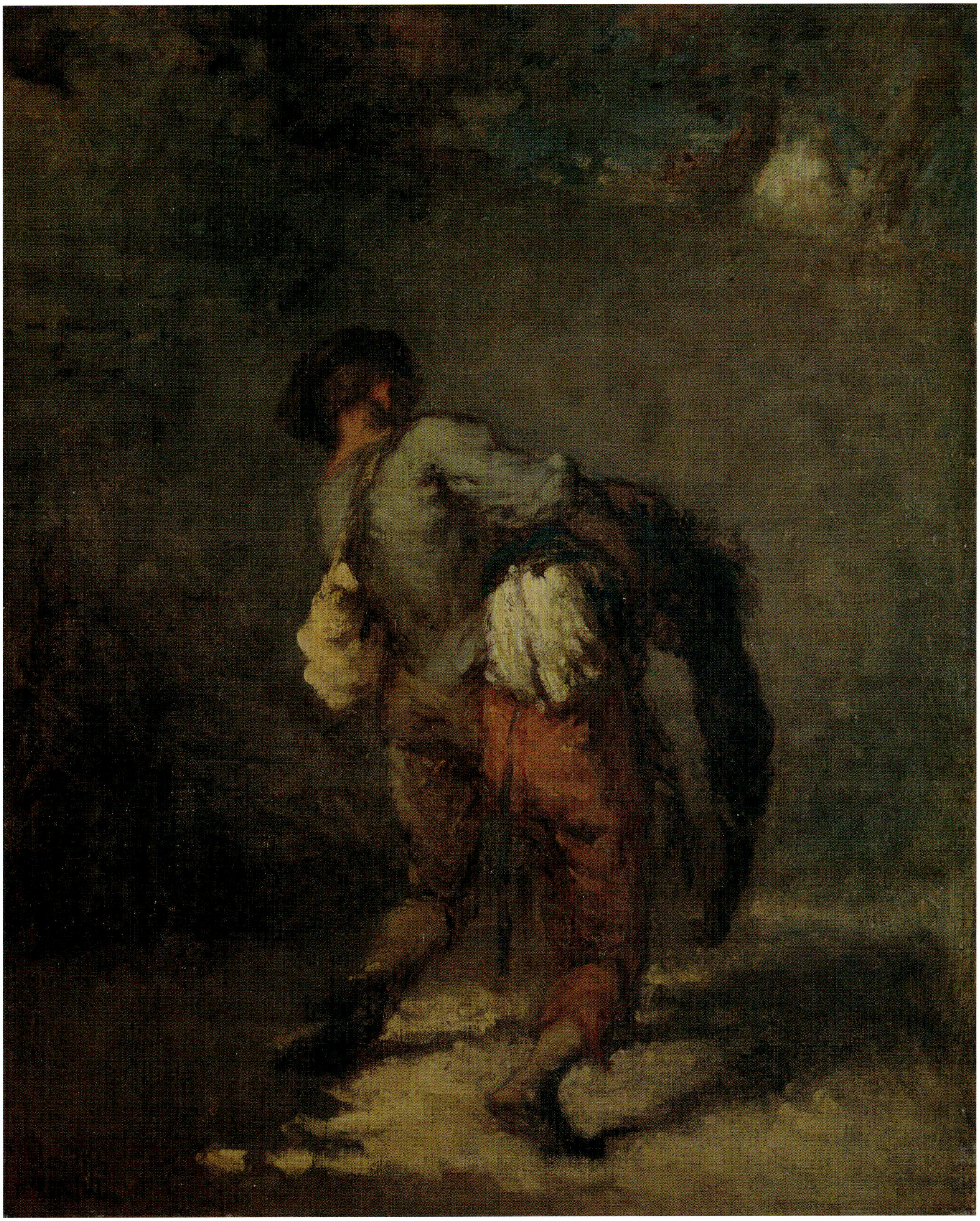

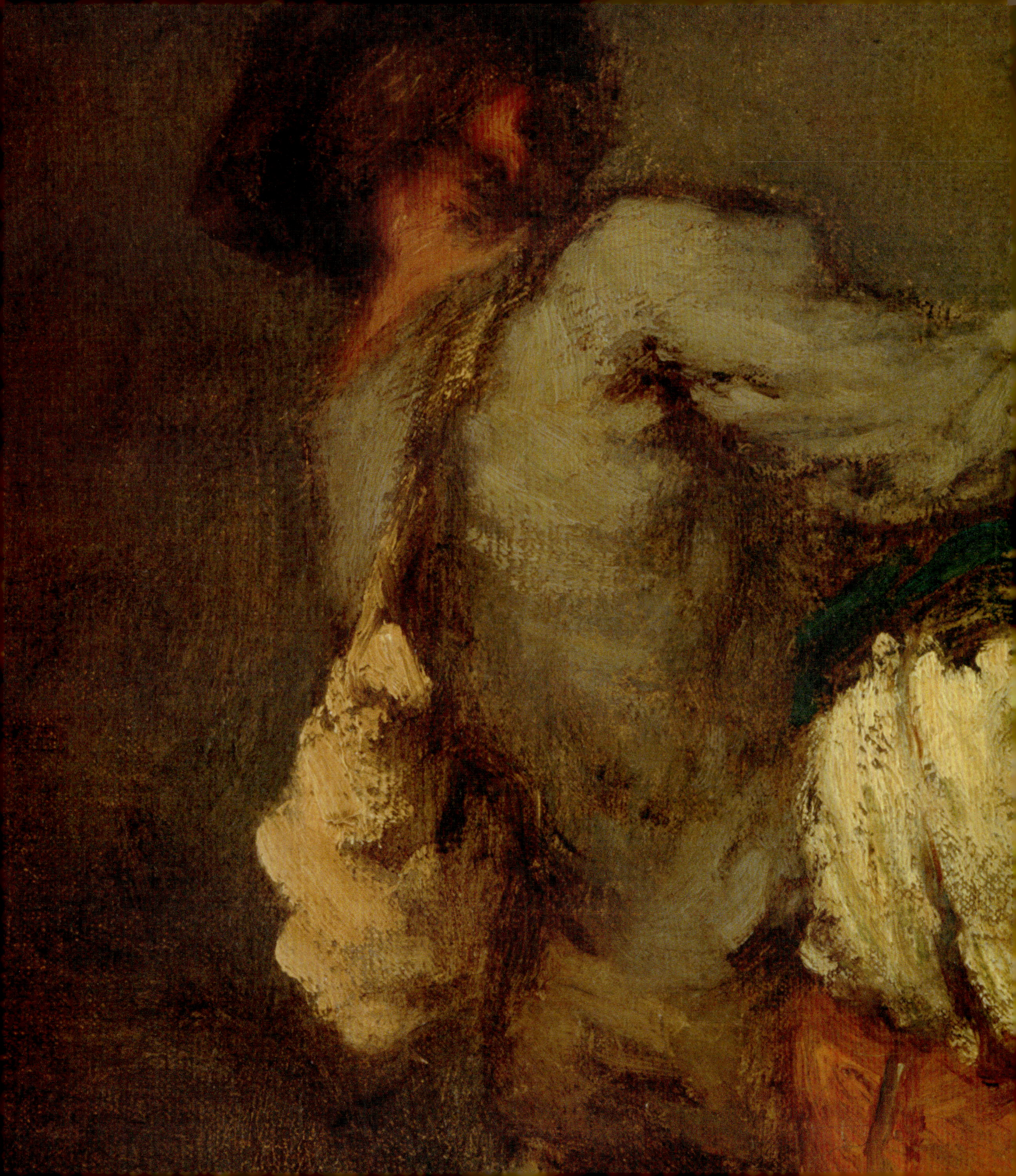

Millet The work is suffused with a sense of rural hush – the screaming geese form a direct contrast with the contemplative pose of the goose girl herself.

30 Jean-François Millet (1814–1875)
The Goose Girl at Gruchy, 1854–56
Oil on canvas, 12 ⅞ x 9 ¾ in. (32.8 x 24.6 cm)
Miss Gwendoline E. Davies Bequest, 1951 (NMWA 2479)

This small painting shows the hamlet of Gruchy near Cherbourg, where Millet was born. During the summer of 1854, he returned to the family home for the first time in almost ten years,[64] and it is most likely that this work was begun there, though it was probably finished back at Barbizon. It is often noted that while Millet frequently recorded the hardship of peasant life, his works are more nostalgic than polemical, often recalling events witnessed in his youth. *The Goose Girl at Gruchy* is explicitly such a scene.

The image shows a girl minding geese, pensively leaning on her shepherding crook, while her charges play in the stream. Behind, Gruchy sits on top of a sharply rising hill. Millet frequently depicted goose girls and wrote of a later version of the subject, "I am at work on my Geese ... I want to make the screams of my Geese ring through the air. Ah! Life, life! The life of the whole!"[65] The present image shows a wholly different focus for the artist, as the work is suffused with a sense of rural hush. The screaming geese to the right of the picture form a direct contrast with the contemplative pose of the goose girl herself, who leans on a stick and appears oblivious to the chattering and splashing. Beginning in the 1840s, Millet often depicted peasants leaning on garden implements, and while in later works this was an illustration of exhaustion and backbreaking labor, in earlier depictions such as this one, the action demonstrates more of a bucolic reverie.

Millet painted the work on a light ocher ground. Although the colors are in fact more saturated than in many of his previous works, there is a curious soft-focus edge to *The Goose Girl at Gruchy* that is absent from other works and which evokes an odd sense of nostalgia and idealization, though this has also been described as a damp mistiness.[66] A related drawing is in the collection of the Musée Bonnat, Bayonne, on the reverse of which is a chalk drawing depicting a peasant resting on a shovel – itself bearing some relation to the present image of the goose girl.

Formerly in the collection of Scottish collector Sir John Charles Day, *The Goose Girl at Gruchy* was the first work by Millet in the Davies sisters' collection, purchased by Gwendoline in 1909. Aside from the two works by Turner acquired the previous year, at more than £5,250, it was the most expensive painting that either had hitherto purchased.

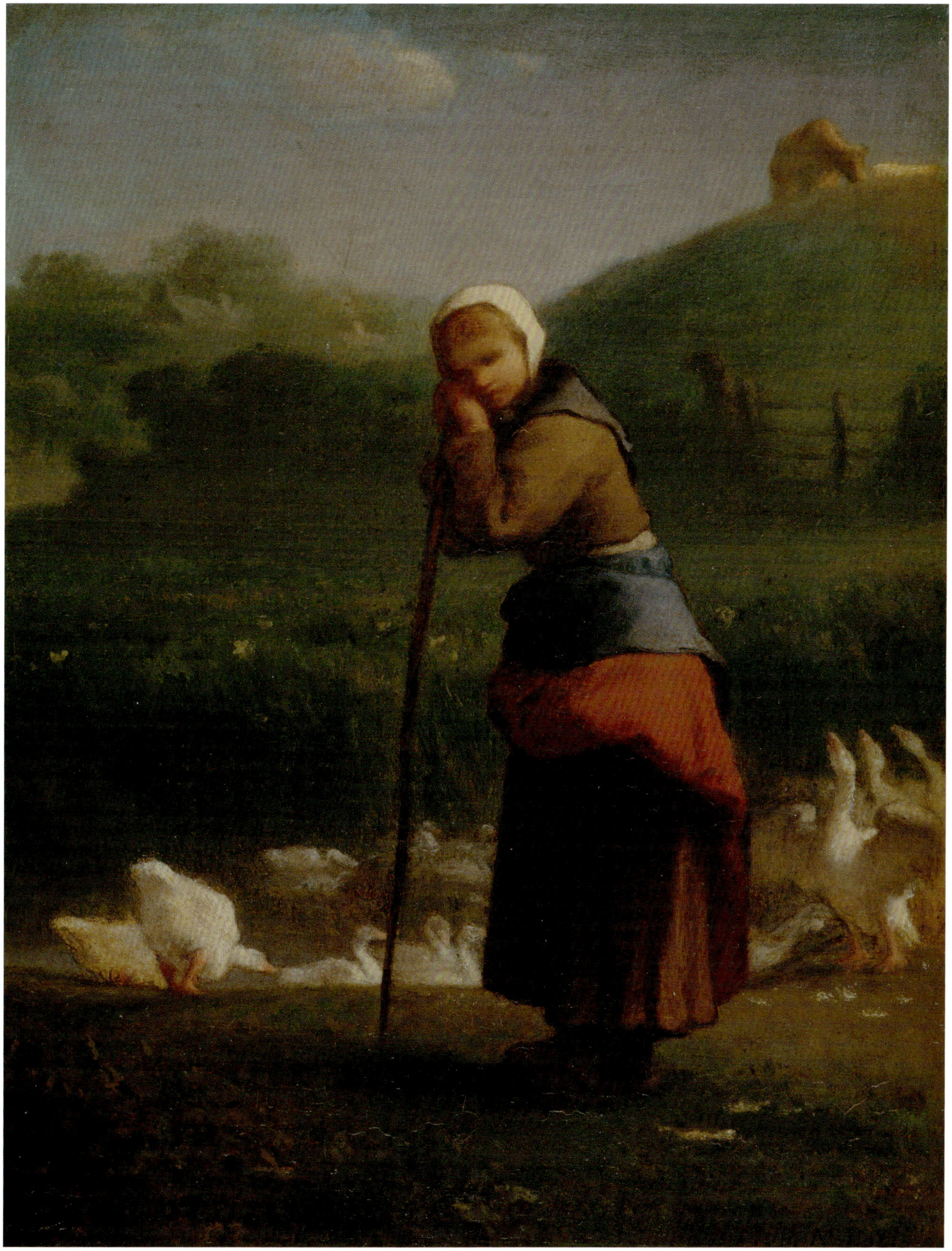

Millet The faceless figures trudge across the canvas in an act of backbreaking labor, the economy of detail contributing to the starkness of the image.

31 Jean-François Millet (1814–1875)
Winter: The Faggot Gatherers, 1868–75
Oil on canvas, 32 ¼ x 39 ⅜ in. (81.8 x 100 cm)
Miss Gwendoline E. Davies Bequest, 1951 (NMWA 2478)

Winter: The Faggot Gatherers is believed to have been painted between 1868 and 1875, remaining unfinished on Millet's death in 1875. While many artists, including Millet himself during his early career, presented peasant life and labor in more idyllic, nostalgic terms, here we see the lengths to which he had moved beyond this. As early as 1851, Millet had written in a letter about "a poor, heavily laden creature with a bundle of faggots advancing from a narrow path in the fields. The manner in which this figure suddenly comes before one is a momentary reminder of the sad condition of human life, toil."[67] In this work, the faceless figures trudge across the canvas in an act of backbreaking labor, the economy of detail and unfinished nature of the work adding to the starkness of the image. *Winter: The Faggot Gatherers* is a large work, measuring a meter wide, but the figures, particularly the principal foreground study, seem hunched into and restrained by the canvas. The heavy black outline of the central peasant recalls the work of Daumier, whom Millet admired.

It has long been suggested that *The Faggot Gatherers* was commissioned by the industrialist Frederic Hartmann in 1868 and intended to represent Winter as part of a set of four seasons.[68] However, recent research has suggested otherwise,[69] offering as a potential alternative *La Porte aux Vaches by the Snow: Solitude* (Philadelphia Museum of Art), which does appear be to an immediately more coherent part of the existing group. The size and formal structure of the present painting have contributed to doubts over whether it does in fact represent the unfinished *Winter*, but no firm attribution either way has been satisfactorily sustained. A black crayon drawing of this scene, dated 1863–64, is in the collection of the Museum of Fine Arts, Boston. The use of infrared photography has also revealed that the canvas was originally intended for the portrait of a woman, whose head can be just ascertained directly above the figure on the far right.[70]

The Davies sisters were fond of images of peasant life and labor, though earlier purchases, such as Anton Mauve's *The Shepherdess* (cat. no. 26) and Millet's *The Goose Girl at Gruchy* (cat. no. 30), show a more idealized, bucolic representation of such scenes. Like other works in their collection, this painting was originally in the collection of Henri Rouart, and Gwendoline acquired it from Wallis & Son in December 1912, along with two other works by Millet, including *The Seated Shepherdess* (cat. no. 28), and a Daumier (cat. no. 12).

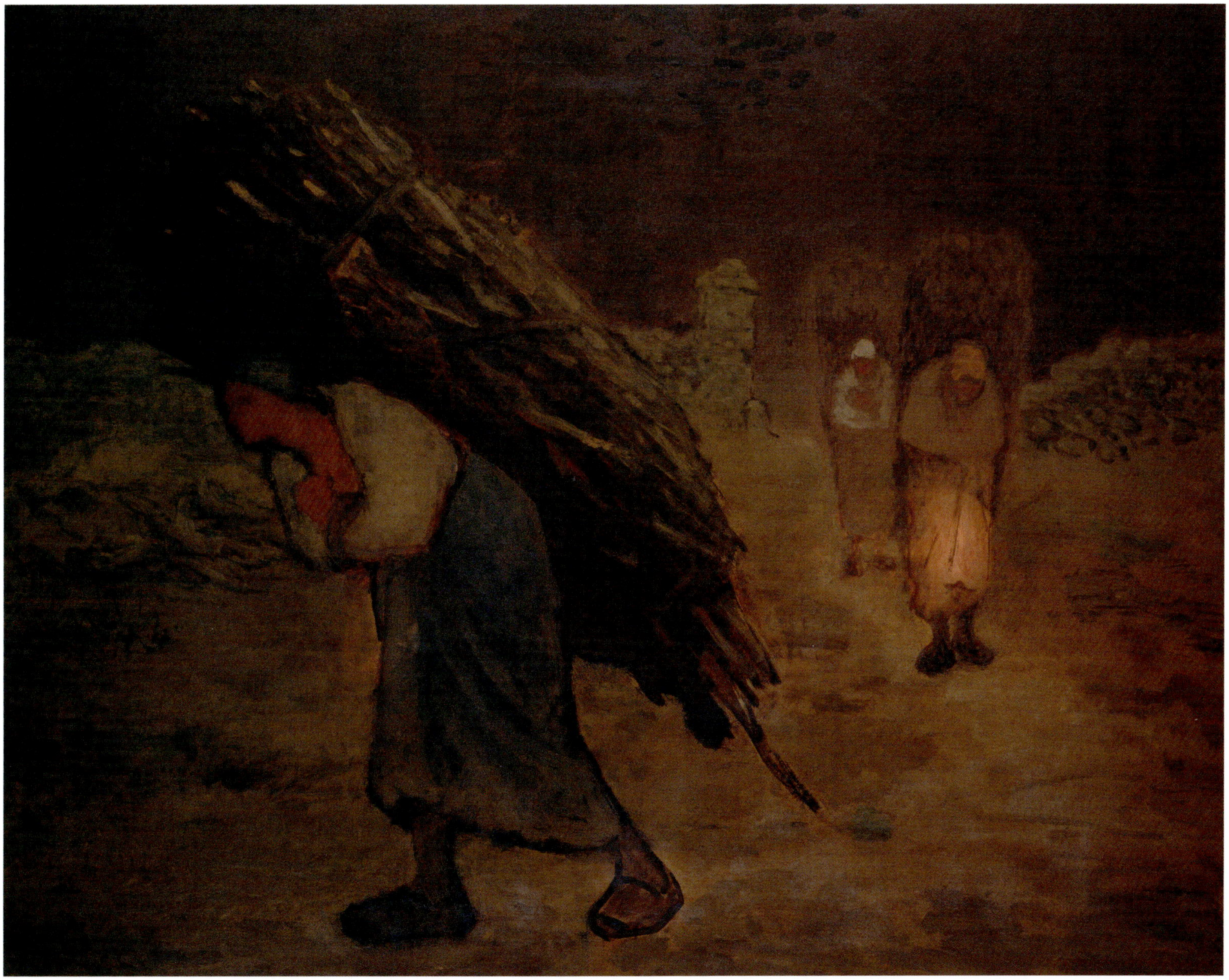

Millet The eye of the drama is in the middle ground, high on the horizon, which emphasizes the classic Romantic struggle of man against the forces of nature.

32 Jean-François Millet (1814–1875)
The Gust of Wind, 1871–73
Oil on canvas, 35 x 46 ⅛ in. (89 x 117 cm)
Miss Margaret S. Davies Bequest, 1963 (NMWA 2475)

Painted toward the end of Millet's life, *The Gust of Wind* can be viewed as a subversion of the painter's early pastoral scenes, such as *The Goose Girl at Gruchy* (cat. no. 30). The painter Walter Richard Sickert viewed the work as a foretelling of Millet's own death,[71] but it can perhaps also be read pessimistically in light of Millet's views of the French peasant, whom he saw as a traditional and moral force in an age of increasing change. Even so, *The Gust of Wind* (Le Coup de Vent) is a curiously gentle title that does not entirely convey the level of destruction being wreaked by the natural phenomena depicted.

For an artist so associated with Realism, this is a highly charged Romanticist work heavy with the sublime, as the tiny figure of a shepherd runs for cover from a falling tree, its roots ripped from the ground. The fate of the shepherd, who seems at any moment about to be struck by a large branch that has come adrift from the main body of the tree, remains unclear. While the foreground brushwork is concentrated on describing the effects of the storm on the rocky ground and the wind-lashed pond, the eye of the drama is in the middle ground, high on the horizon, which emphasizes the classic Romantic struggle of man against the forces of nature. The contrasting light from the horizon gives the painting an apocalyptic feel, but it is also the suggestion of a haven, illuminating as it does a far-off village. *The Gust of Wind* reflects the work of Millet's fellow Barbizon painters Théodore Rousseau and Narcisse-Virgile Díaz de la Peña, whose work Margaret also bought an example of early in 1910.

Sickert wrote of *The Gust of Wind*: "I doubt if any modern but Millet would ever have even thought of selecting the moment when a tree has been torn up by the roots, and is in the act of falling, for pictorial representation … The roots are lifted out of the ground with the bulk of the earth that contained them, and the whole terrifying object is painted at the brief moment, when it is silhouetted, free, against the sky."[72] The location for this painting has been identified as the high plateau running through the center of La Hague,[73] and there are three related drawings for this work, all in crayon – two are in the Louvre, the other in the Royal Museum of Fine Arts, Copenhagen.

The picture was originally in the collection of Henry Rouart. In the account of the Rouart sale in *The Studio* (July 15, 1913), it was noted that *The Gust of Wind* did not reach the estimated sale price, suggesting that the subject might have been "a little too severe … for the taste of some of the purchasers," which indicates an intrinsic conservatism in the general art market at the time. This was a late purchase of work by Millet. Margaret did not acquire it until 1937, by which time Gwendoline had ceased collecting altogether. It was bought from the collection of Hugh Blaker, the sisters' adviser, who had in turn not acquired it until 1924.

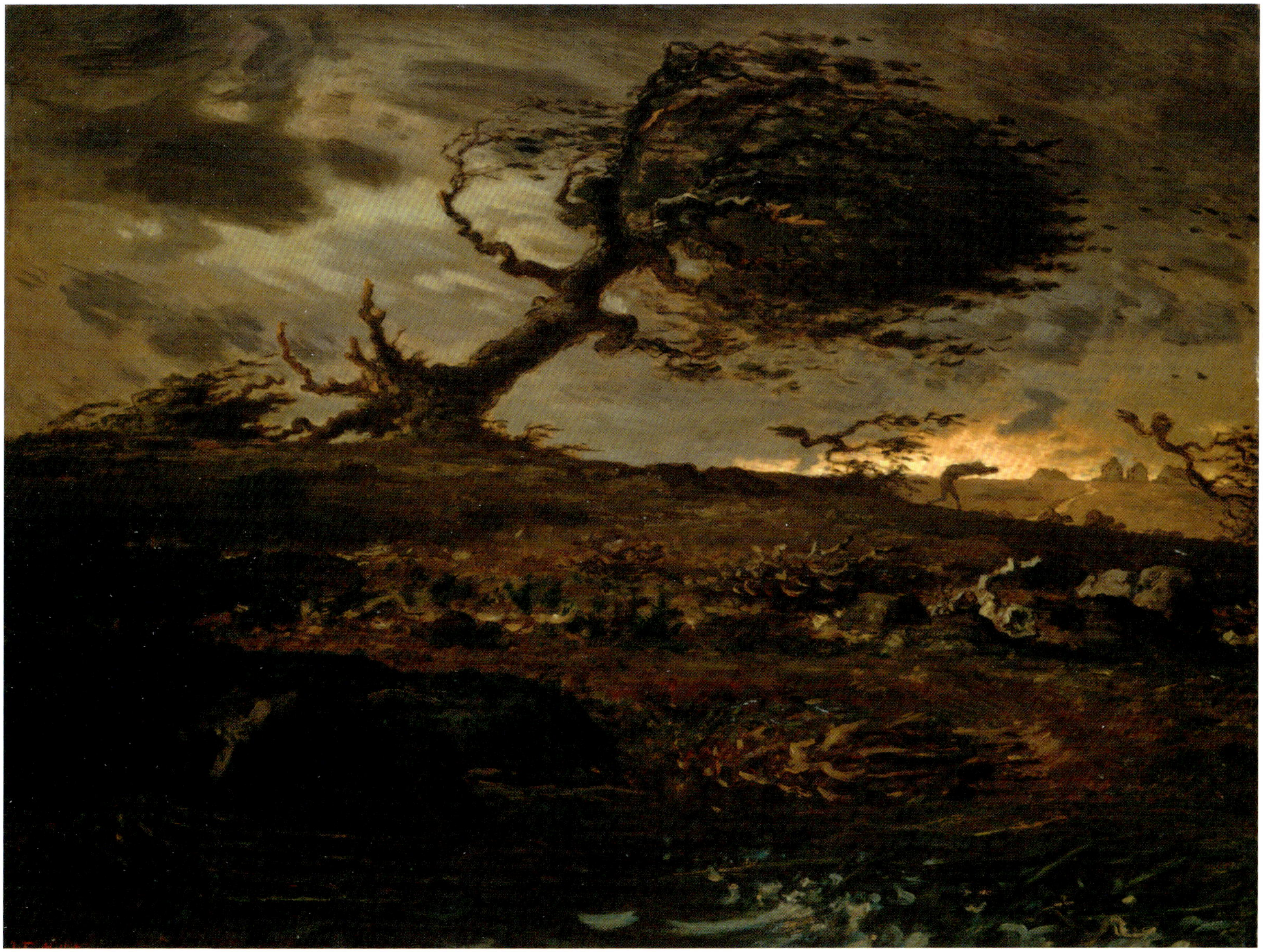

Monet The detail is reduced to the bridge, boats, and distant architecture, all of which act as visual anchors around which the interchangeable haze of sky and water fluctuates.

33 Claude Monet (1840–1926)
Charing Cross Bridge, 1902
Oil on canvas, 25 ¾ x 32 ⅛ in. (65.5 x 81.5 cm)
Miss Margaret S. Davies Bequest, 1963 (NMWA 2483)

Monet first visited and depicted London in the autumn of 1870 during the Franco-Prussian War. Although he returned prior to 1899, it was not until then that he began work on his extensive and important series of London views, of which the present work is an example. Monet's debt to both Turner and Whistler in his London scenes has recently been fully explored,[74] and it has been suggested that this visit might have been inspired by Whistler's set of lithographs of the city from 1896 in which he depicted similar views. Monet arrived in late autumn and stayed at the Savoy Hotel, where his sixth-floor room afforded him a panoramic view of the river; it was from this room that his views of Charing Cross Bridge were executed. Monet painted the Thames in three series: Waterloo Bridge, the Houses of Parliament, and Charing Cross Railway Bridge and the view upstream toward the Houses of Parliament.

Monet's later paintings were primarily concerned with the articulation of atmospheric nuance. The artist was eternally frustrated by the changing London weather and featured Charing Cross Bridge in no fewer than thirty-five canvases. All are morning scenes, demonstrating the infinite variety of his practice. John House has noted how Monet omitted Cleopatra's Needle (an obelisk on the Victoria Embankment) from all but two of his Charing Cross views,[75] as indeed it is absent in this one. The detail is reduced to the compositional devices of the bridge itself, the distant Houses of Parliament, the two boats, and the small section of the Embankment, all of which act as visual anchors around which the interchangeable haze of water and sky fluctuates. In addition to the effects of fog, Monet has depicted, to the left of the canvas, the smoke coming from a train on the railway bridge, which dissipates into the general mist. While some artists might consider the London fog a hindrance, for Monet these "pea-soupers" were an intrinsic part of the landscape, and he said of them "without the fog London wouldn't be a beautiful city. It's the fog that gives it its magnificent breadth."[76]

Charing Cross Bridge was in Monet's possession until 1910, when he offered it as a prize in a charity raffle.[77] By later that year, it was with the dealer Paul Durand-Ruel, from whom it was purchased by the Duke of Marlborough, who sold it to the French Gallery where it was bought by Margaret in May 1913, mistakenly titled *Westminster Bridge*. This was the first non-Venetian subject by Monet that the sisters collected and demonstrates their developing interest in his later work, followed up later that year with another Venetian view – the Palazzo Dario (cat. no. 35) – and three pieces from his "Waterlilies" series (see cat. no. 34).

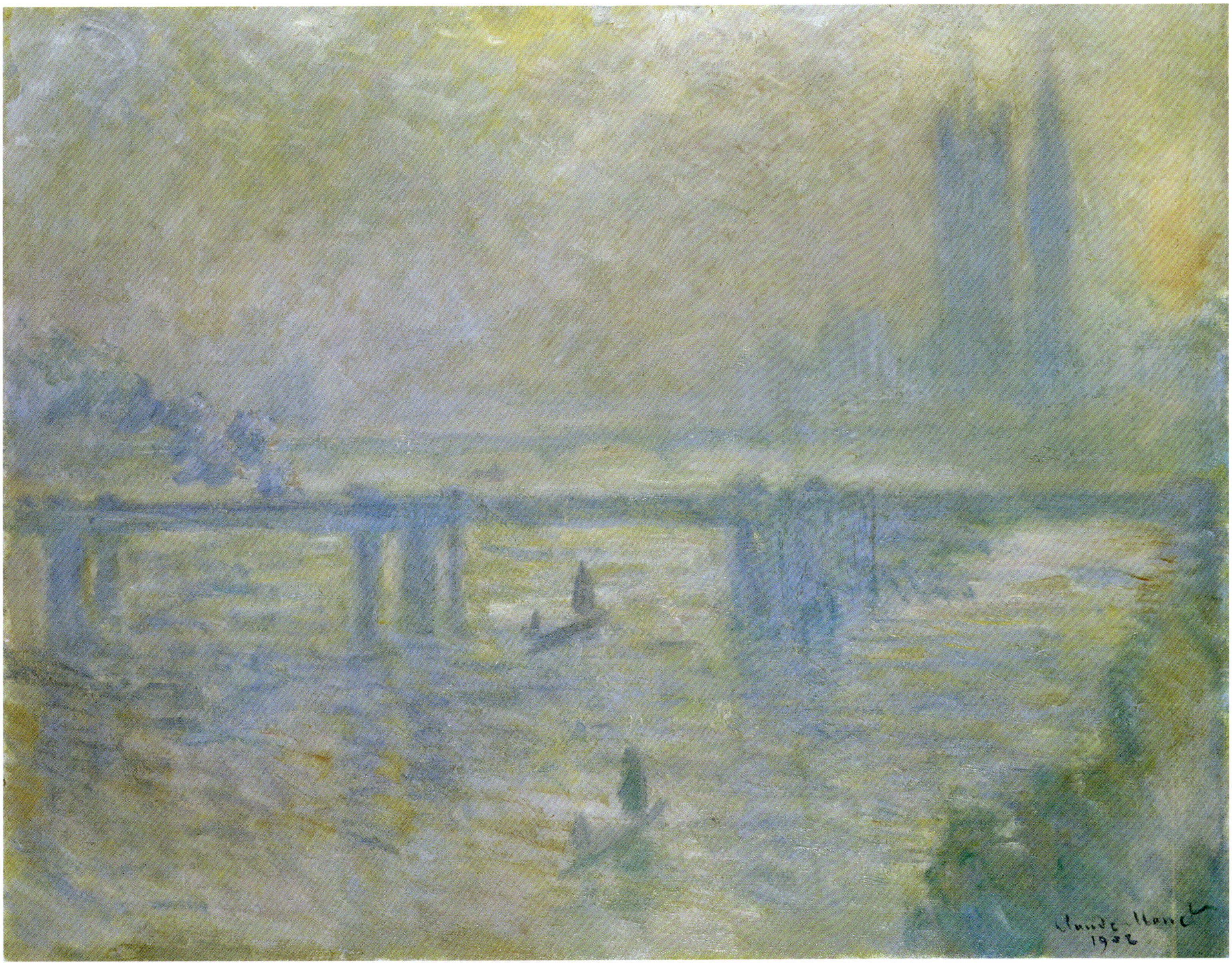
Claude Monet

Monet From his vantage point on the bridge, Monet could view not only the pond's surface with its floral groupings but the reflections above and the depths below.

34 Claude Monet (1840–1926)
Waterlilies, 1906
Oil on canvas, 32 ⅛ x 36 ½ in. (81.5 x 92.7 cm)
Miss Gwendoline E. Davies Bequest, 1951 (NMWA 2487)

It was not until 1888 that Monet began to paint works of art in series – among them, haystacks, Rouen Cathedral, and Venice – but by far the largest and most intense were his studies of light and water on the lily pond at Giverny, where he and his family had moved in 1883. In 1893, after some bureaucratic wrangling, Monet finally gained official permission to construct a pond and Japanese-style bridges in a meadow he had acquired adjoining his property at Giverny. In 1899, he began painting the garden on a regular basis. These earlier images of the pond at Giverny show the bridge and Japonica and constitute comparatively more conventional views of the scene. In 1903, he abandoned the bridge and began to paint canvases showing sections of the pond from an overhead perspective, the lack of tangible reference points and central focus blurring the lines between figurative and abstract works in a way his earlier paintings had not.

The six-year gap between the garden's establishment and Monet's attempts to depict it elapsed because of the length of time it took the garden to mature. A gardener was hired for the sole purpose of maintaining the pond, ensuring the removal of extraneous plant life and algae to keep the surface of the pond clear, and rinsing the lilies to clean the dust from the flowers.[78] He was also instructed to take care that the floating groups of flowers remained circular in shape, with enough space between each grouping that a clear area of water could be viewed. Before dawn, Monet's canvases would be set up so the artist could take advantage of the first light. He would sit on the bridge looking down at the pond, which afforded him a view not only of the surface with its floral groupings but also of the depths below and reflections from above. Although such engineering of nature from an Impressionist seems strange, clearly what Monet sought, particularly in his later years, was form and color, light and water (see cat. nos. 33 and 35) – the exact rendering of natural phenomena now being a concern of the past.

This is one of three of the "Waterlilies" series purchased by Gwendoline – the remaining two date from 1905 and 1908. She bought the set for £3,370 from the Parisian dealer Bernheim-Jeune. The present work, the central canvas of group, with its overall tones of blue, shows the lilies as dark patches on the surface of a light pond, almost like a photographic negative. The earlier 1905 variation owned by Gwendoline offers an inversion of the present work, while the later 1908 canvas depicts a merging of forms that renders the lilies almost indiscernible, picked out by highlights of white. All three canvases hung in the music room at Gregynog Hall, the sisters' home.

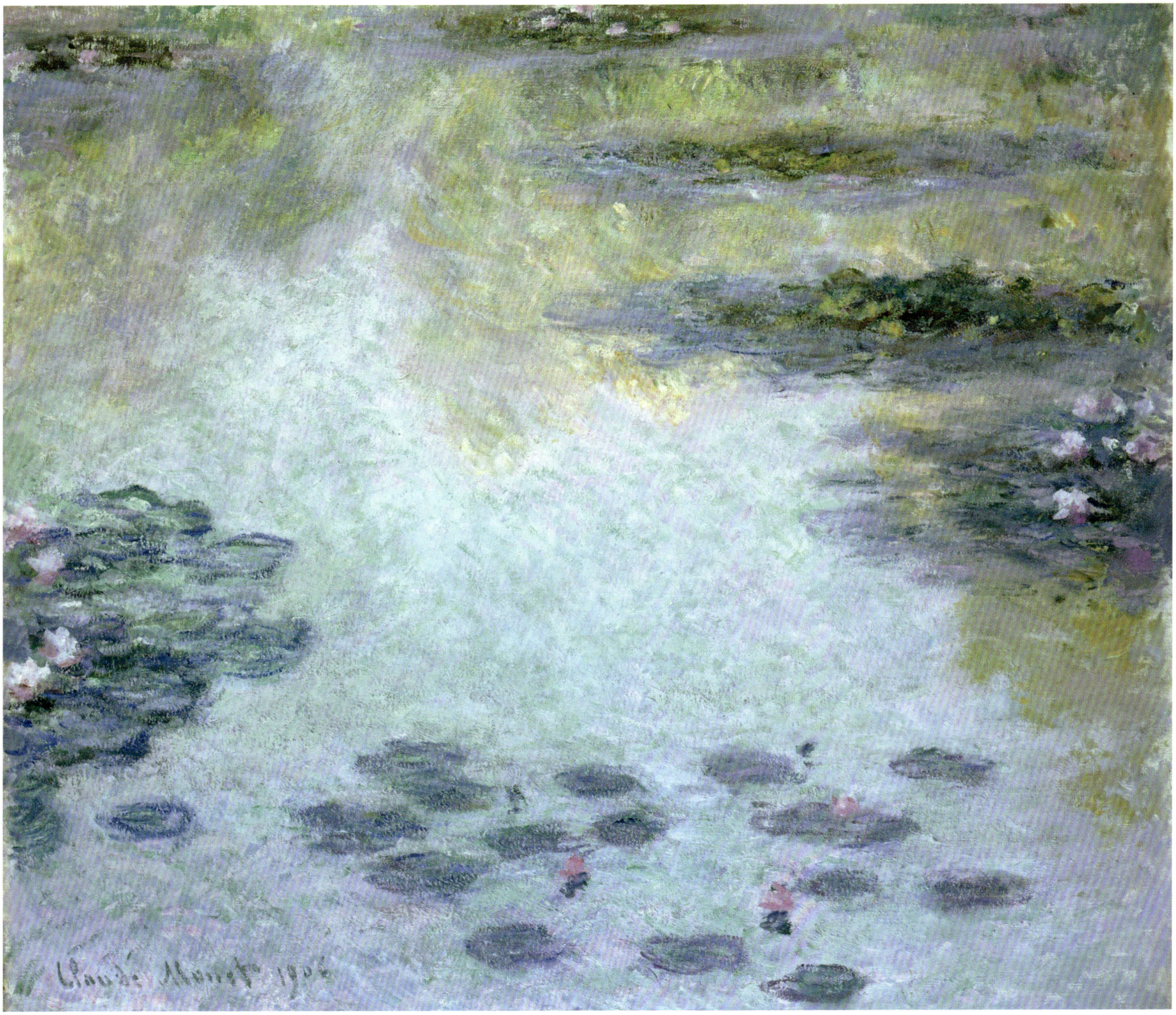

Monet Long periods studying the lily pond at his home at Giverny had enabled Monet to refine his technique for articulating the effects of light and reflection on water.

35 Claude Monet (1840–1926)
The Palazzo Dario, 1908
Oil on canvas, 36 ⅜ x 28 ¾ in. (92.2 x 73 cm)
Miss Margaret S. Davies Bequest, 1963 (NMWA 2481)

For most of his working life, Monet resisted the charms of Venice, but in October 1908 with his second wife, Alice, he traveled there on the invitation of Mr. and Mrs. Charles Hunter.[79] He stayed for more than two months and during his stay began thirty-seven canvases, as if making up for lost time. "What a pity I never came here when I was younger, when I was still full of daring!" he wrote. "But I am having a delicious time and can almost forget that once I was not the old man I am now."[80] The Palazzo Dario, whose facade had undergone renovation between 1905 and 1906, was built in 1497 for Giovanni Dario, Secretary of the Venetian Senate. Its highly decorative marble oculi were much admired by John Ruskin.

By this stage in his career, Monet worked mainly in cycles of repeated motifs, and he made four different versions of the Palazzo Dario: the present work and another in a private collection show a vertical view; the remaining two are landscape format. A pencil sketch relating to this work, now in the Musée Marmottan, Paris, is Monet's only surviving Venetian drawing.[81] In the Cardiff painting, the palace itself is cropped and cut midway by a gondola whose *felze* (the covered central area) mirrors the arches of the windows and connects the upper and lower parts of the canvas. Long periods studying the lily pond at his home at Giverny (see cat. no. 34) and the Thames in London (see cat. no. 33) had enabled Monet to refine his technique for articulating the effects of light and reflection on water, which he further developed in his Venetian scenes.

Although the canvas is dated 1908, it is unlikely that it was completed until 1912. On return from Venice in 1908, Alice's health declined and the Venetian works stayed in storage. Although Monet had hoped to return to Venice, he did not, as sources have suggested, return in 1909. Alice died in 1911, and Monet remembered the period in Venice with great fondness, which probably explains the backdating of the canvases. *The Palazzo Dario* was exhibited in *Claude Monet: Venise* at Bernheim-Jeune in 1912, from where it was bought by Durand-Ruel in 1912 and sold to Margaret Davies in July 1913, for £1310. While in Venice in 1909, just a few months after Monet, Margaret had written in her diary how the "water … seems to be made up of several different colors, here it is blue, then again green, further on it seems a shade of mauve and all around glistens patches of sunlight in silver streaks …,"[82] observations that chime particularly well with Monet's own interpretation.

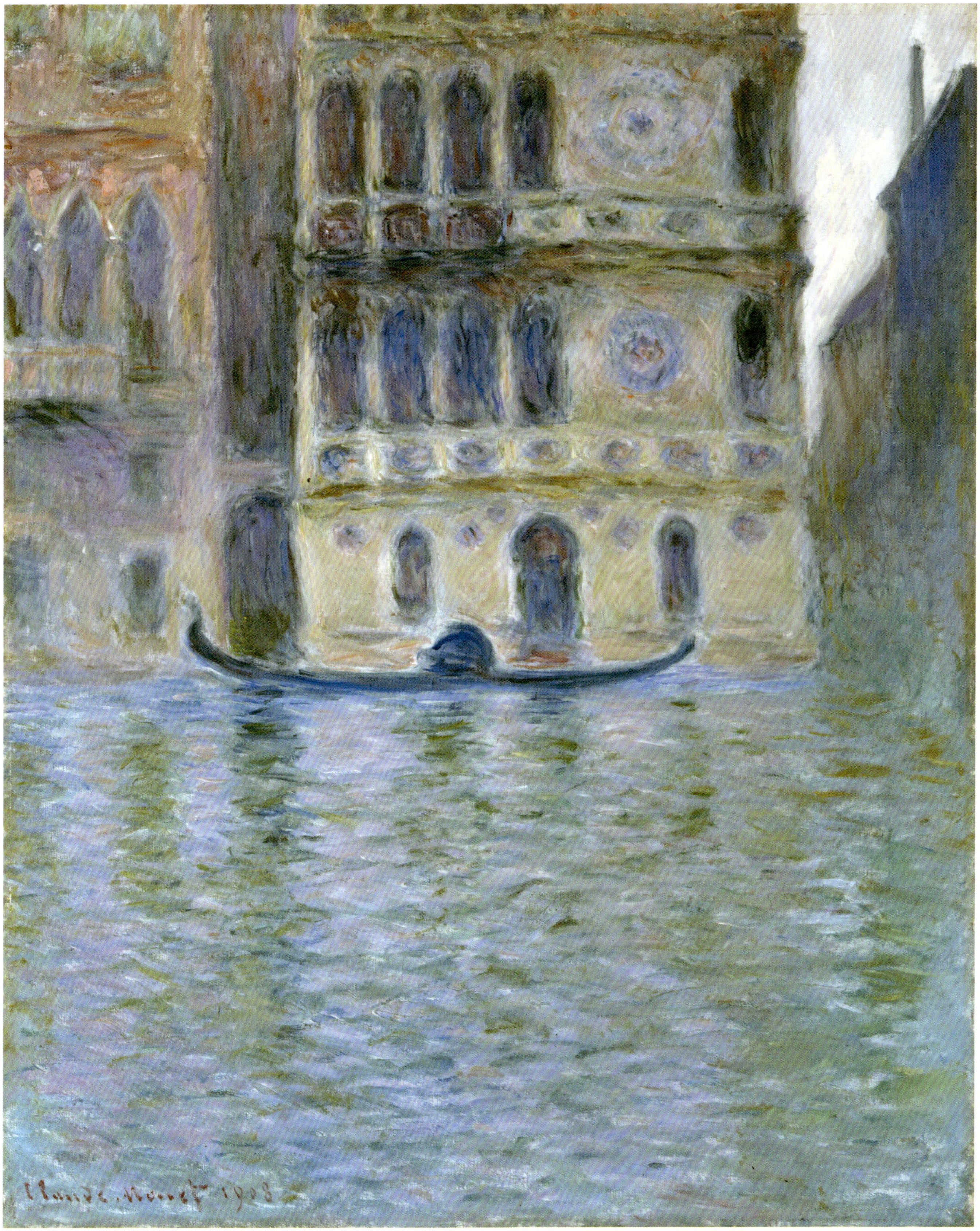

Moret Stylistically, Moret's oil paintings reflect Gauguin's work from the early 1880s, when the older artist was still working in a semi-Impressionist style.

36 Henry Moret (1856–1913)
Village in Clohars, 1898
Oil on canvas, 21 ½ x 25 ⅝ in. (54.6 x 65.1 cm)
Miss Margaret S. Davies Bequest, 1963 (NMWA 2490)

Born in Cherbourg, Henry Moret studied in Paris with Jean-Léon Gérôme, exhibiting at the Salon of 1880. He spent most of his life in Brittany in the area around Pont-Aven. Stylistically, Moret's oil paintings reflect Gauguin's work from the early 1880s, when the older artist was still working in a semi-Impressionist style, particularly in the areas of long, thin brushwork. Monet was also an influence on Moret's style, which is apparent both here and in other oils, and in 1895, he came to the attention of the dealer Durand-Ruel, with whom he found a ready market for his work.[83]

This image shows the village of Clohars, with the thatched cottages and stone walls typical of the local area. Clohars is next to Le Pouldu, one of the principal locations for Gauguin and the Nabis. It is most likely that this oil was begun in 1897 and finished in 1898, the date on the canvas. There is a related watercolor that shows an identical scene, *Route et village de Clohars* (Musée de Pont-Aven), which was painted in the same year, and a comparison of these two works reveals a great deal about Moret's style. The artist's skill and inventiveness as both a draftsman and a colorist are perhaps more evident in his watercolors and graphic work, which show the influence of Cloisonnism and a style not dissimilar to the strong lines of Emile Bernard and Armand Seguin (see cat. no. 41). His oil style was far more akin to Impressionism and works well in his seascapes, but in *Village in Clohars*, it has somewhat mixed results. The varied brushwork is successful in some cases – the sun-baked mud road – but confusing in others. For example, the combination of color and stroke used to create the stone wall running from left to center of the painting makes the subject difficult to identify. The influence of Monet is most evident in the trees, which flutter against the thatched roofs, and in the depiction of light.

Village in Clohars was a late purchase by Margaret Davies, made in 1959, and was one of three final French Impressionist and Post-Impressionist acquisitions, along with Sisley's *Moret-sur-Loing (Rue de Fosses)* (cat. no. 44) and Bonnard's *Sunlight at Vernon* (cat. no. 3).[84] There is no real clue as to why Margaret chose this particular painting. It has been suggested that it may have been chosen to complement the Seguin[85] (cat. no. 41, then believed to be by Gauguin), which is possible, but it seems equally likely that its aesthetic qualities, which are similar to both the Sisley and the Bonnard – and Impressionistic style (coupled with a very reasonable price tag of £750) – made it an attractive purchase.

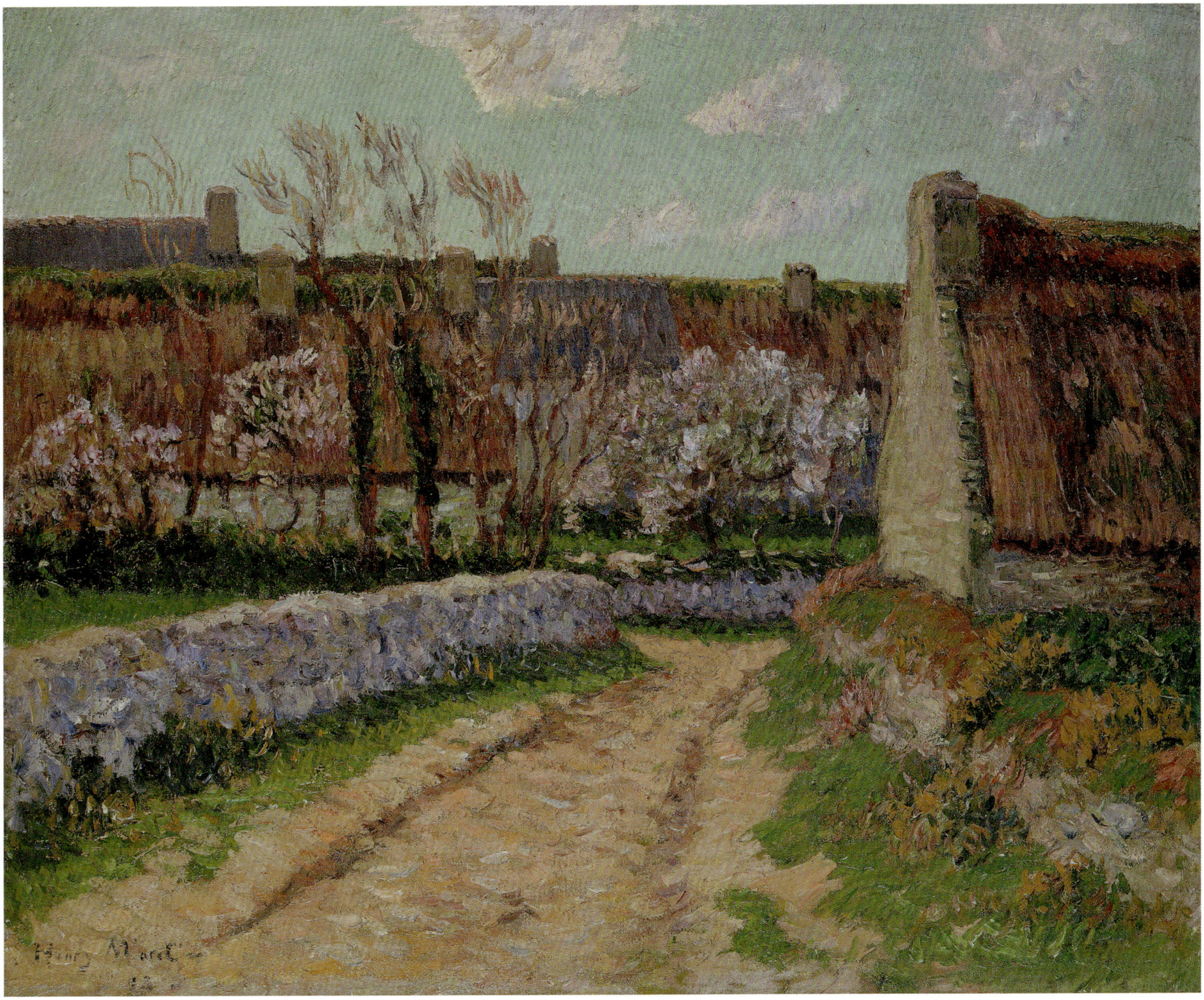

Morisot The brushwork perfectly articulates the sense of a wild garden – the figures are framed and almost consumed by their surroundings.

37 Berthe Morisot (1841–1895)
At Bougival, 1882
Oil on canvas, 23 ⅝ x 28 ¾ in. (60 x 73.1 cm)
Miss Margaret S. Davies Bequest, 1963 (NMWA 2491)

One of the exhibiting artists at the first Impressionist exhibition of 1874, Berthe Morisot was a friend of Edouard Manet, who painted her on numerous occasions (for example, in *Berthe Morisot with a Bouquet of Violets*; Musée d'Orsay, Paris). Although the pressures of bourgeois convention led her to marry – she married Manet's brother, Eugène, in 1874 – this also enabled her to fully pursue her career as an artist. She was both highly skilled and prolific, functioning within one proscribed paradigm – painting explicitly "female" subjects according to the social conventions and restraints to which, as an upper-middle-class woman, she was subject (mother and child depictions feature heavily in her oeuvre) – and adapting it to another through working at the forefront of progressive technique. While it is debatable whether, as a woman, she was ever perceived as an equal by her peers, she showed work in every Impressionist exhibition except one – *At Bougival* appeared in the seventh exhibition, in 1882 – and won considerable acclaim from both the establishment and within Impressionist circles.

In 1881, Morisot and her family rented a house at Bougival, ten miles west of Paris, and the house's gardens are featured frequently in her work. This image of the painter's daughter, Julie, giving a flower to her nanny, Paisie, was painted in the garden of a next-door neighbor, Dr. Robin. The handling is exceptionally free, and the variegated directional brushwork perfectly articulates the sense of a wild garden and long grass – the two figures are framed and almost consumed by their surroundings. The blue, brown, and white tones of the figures are dispersed throughout the canvas (which receives only a scant covering in the outer parts), giving unity to the formal structure. On the reverse of this canvas are the beginnings of a similar, hastily executed Impressionist landscape. A strikingly similar composition from a year later, in 1883, shows what appears to be the same location, only this time showing Julie with Eugène Manet, not Paisie.

Figure-based works are comparatively rare in the Davies sisters' Impressionist collection. Although one could argue the case for Renoir's *La Parisienne* (cat. no. 39), they did not acquire the types of contemporary Parisian figure-based scene that characterized Impressionism. *At Bougival* represents an intimacy and timelessness, representative of the figure-based scenes that they acquired. It is not known from where or for how much Margaret purchased *At Bougival*, but it was certainly before 1927, and its acquisition most likely falls between 1912 and 1923, the years in which the sisters acquired the bulk of their Impressionist painting. It was, until 1936, the only work by a woman artist in the collection.

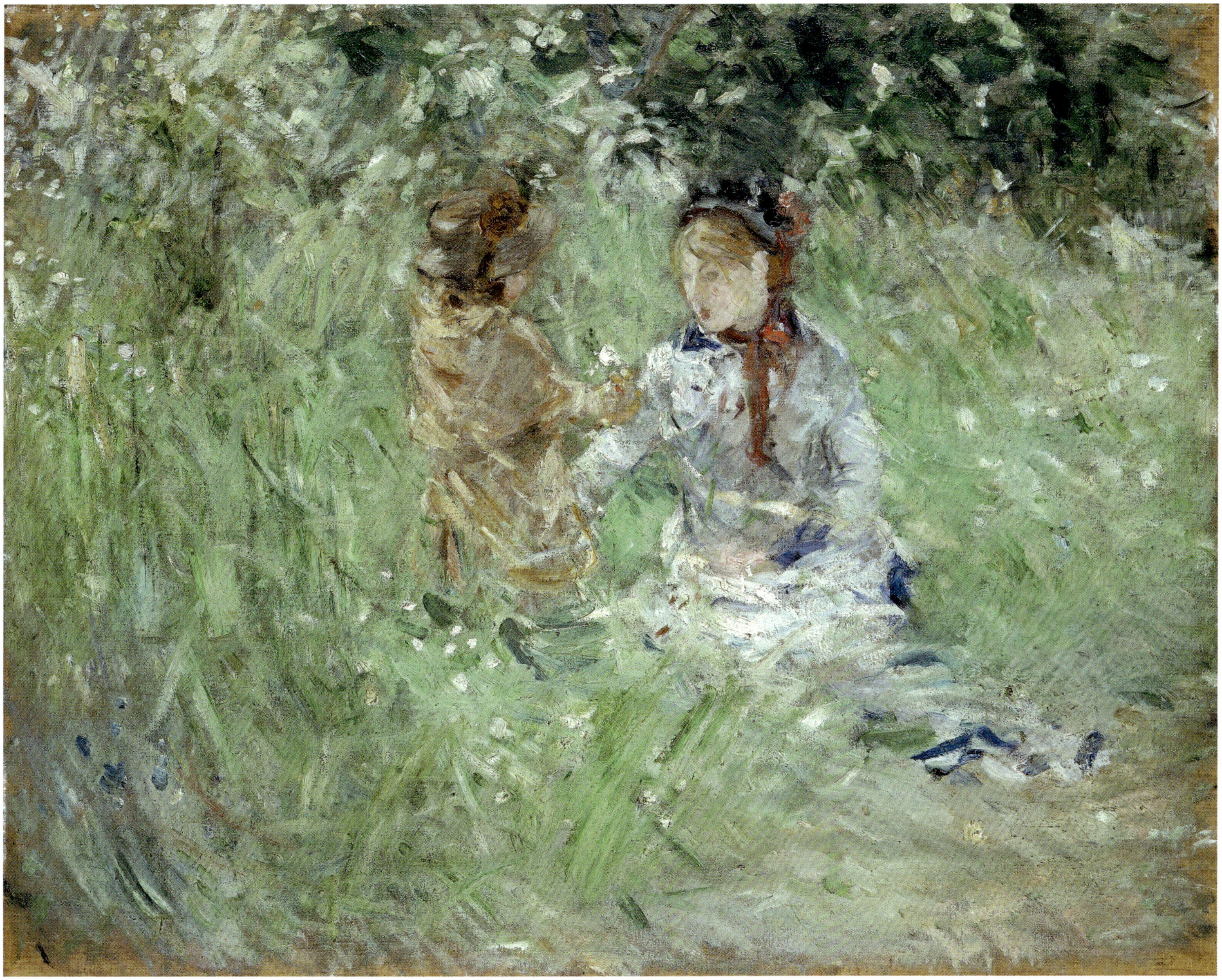

Pissarro While the scene buzzes with the energy of the crowd, it does not show incident and detail – the figures are reduced to anonymous single paint strokes.

38 Camille Pissarro (1831–1903)
Pont Neuf, Snow Effect, 2nd Series, 1902
Oil on canvas, 21 ⅜ x 25 ¾ in. (54.4 x 65.5 cm)
Miss Margaret S. Davies Bequest, 1963 (NMWA 2493)

Pont Neuf, Snow Effect, 2nd Series belongs to a series painted by Pissarro between 1900 and his death in 1903. He had rented a north-facing apartment in the Place Dauphine on the Ile de la Cité and produced in total thirteen canvases[86] showing the north side of the Pont Neuf under differing atmospheric conditions. As a major thoroughfare with high volumes of pedestrians and traffic, the Pont Neuf was an ideal subject for Impressionism. Pissarro's high vantage point enabled him to work with multiple perspectives, showing the iconic architecture of the bridge, the life upon it, and the panorama of the right bank of the river. Pissarro was much taken with his location and, in tandem with the Pont Neuf views, painted a parallel but distinct series of views facing northwest across the Square du Vert-Galant and down toward the Louvre.

The same format and scope are used for each of the Pont Neuf works. Just to the right of the canvas is the Samaritaine department store, whose distinctive red flags can be seen in many other versions from this series. The snow effect is created by the use of a limited palette and tends toward the contrasts of black, white, and cream, while the figures that move about under snow-covered umbrellas are the least distinct renderings of figures in the series. Pissarro painted directly onto canvas to create this scene, and the unprimed support is occasionally visible under the pigment. Intriguingly, the reverse side of the canvas reveals a partially completed still life of flowers on a table, painted onto a primed ground, which was clearly abandoned halfway through.

This painting is unique among the sisters' collection of Impressionist work in that it is a depiction of modern Parisian life. Crucially, however, while the scene buzzes with the energy of the crowd, it does not show incident and detail – the figures are reduced to anonymous single paint strokes, and the bridge itself becomes the focal point. *Pont Neuf, Snow Effect, 2nd Series* was bought by Margaret Davies from the Leicester Galleries, London, in 1920. She purchased an additional oil, from the artist's Rouen series (*Sunset, Port of Rouen*, also in the collection of the National Museum of Wales) and six drawings, of which two entered the national collection.

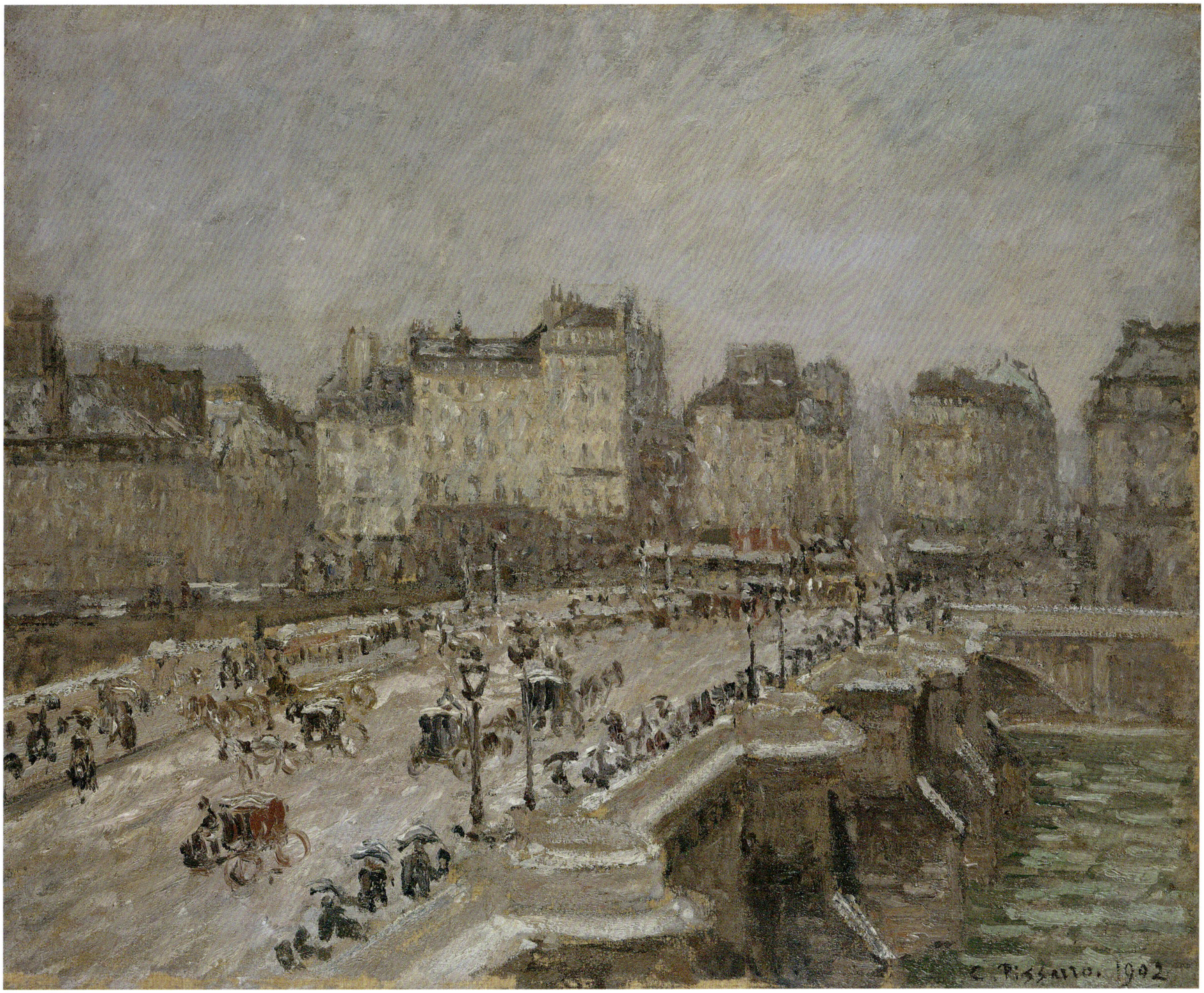
C. Pissarro. 1902

Renoir The painting recalls the portraits and single-figure compositions of Manet and Velázquez and also reflects the influence of Japanese prints.

39 Pierre-Auguste Renoir (1841–1919)
La Parisienne, 1874
Oil on canvas, 64 ⅜ x 42 ⅝ in. (163.5 x 108.5 cm)
Miss Gwendoline E. Davies Bequest, 1951 (NMWA 2495)

Perhaps the best-known Impressionist work in the sisters' collection is Renoir's *La Parisienne*. The painting is a full-length depiction of the actress Henriette Henriot (1857–1944), who posed for Renoir on numerous occasions, notably in *Portrait of Madame Henriot* (fig. 14, p. 37).[87] *La Parisienne* was first shown at the so-called first Impressionist exhibition of 1874 at the photographer Nadar's studio, where it received mixed reviews. With a plain, single-toned background against which the sitter is suspended like a fashion plate, the painting recalls the portraits and single-figure compositions of Manet and Velázquez and also reflects the influence of Japanese prints.

The work was first exhibited under the title *La Parisienne*, though by 1892 it was known as *La Dame en Bleu*[88] (and is still popularly known as *The Blue Lady*). However, the title *La Parisienne* is vital to an understanding of the painting and its milieu. More explicit than even a named portrait could be, the title overtly directs us to a "type" and by association to a visual manifestation of a shift in the social order in the wake of the Second Empire: *La Parisienne* is a fashionable, urban woman – a modern woman – who looks directly at the viewer with confidence, meeting and holding their gaze.

Both under- and overpainting show that Renoir's original concept for the work was somewhat different – the earring and upper eyelashes were added after the painting had been varnished, as were small areas of hair just below the subject's hat. Such details focus attention on the head and face of the model, in addition to making her more immediately glamorous. The rendering of the face is remarkably sharp next to the nebulous gray of the background and the blue costume. Infrared investigation has shown the original presence of a vertical form, possibly a doorway, to the left of the work, and what appears to be drapery, or a curtain, to the right, suggesting that a conventional portrait background was originally intended.

In the context of the Davies collection of Impressionist and Post-Impressionist works as a whole, *La Parisienne* occupies an interesting position for a collection that circumvents any classic scenes of Parisian life. Its subject makes it one of the most "modern" works the sisters collected. The painting was formerly in the collection of Henri Rouart and was purchased by Gwendoline Davies from the National Portrait Society's exhibition at the Grosvenor Gallery in 1913. It was considered to be a Renoir masterpiece at the time, and the price tag of £5,000 reflected this. *La Parisienne* was the most expensive Impressionist purchase made by either sister.

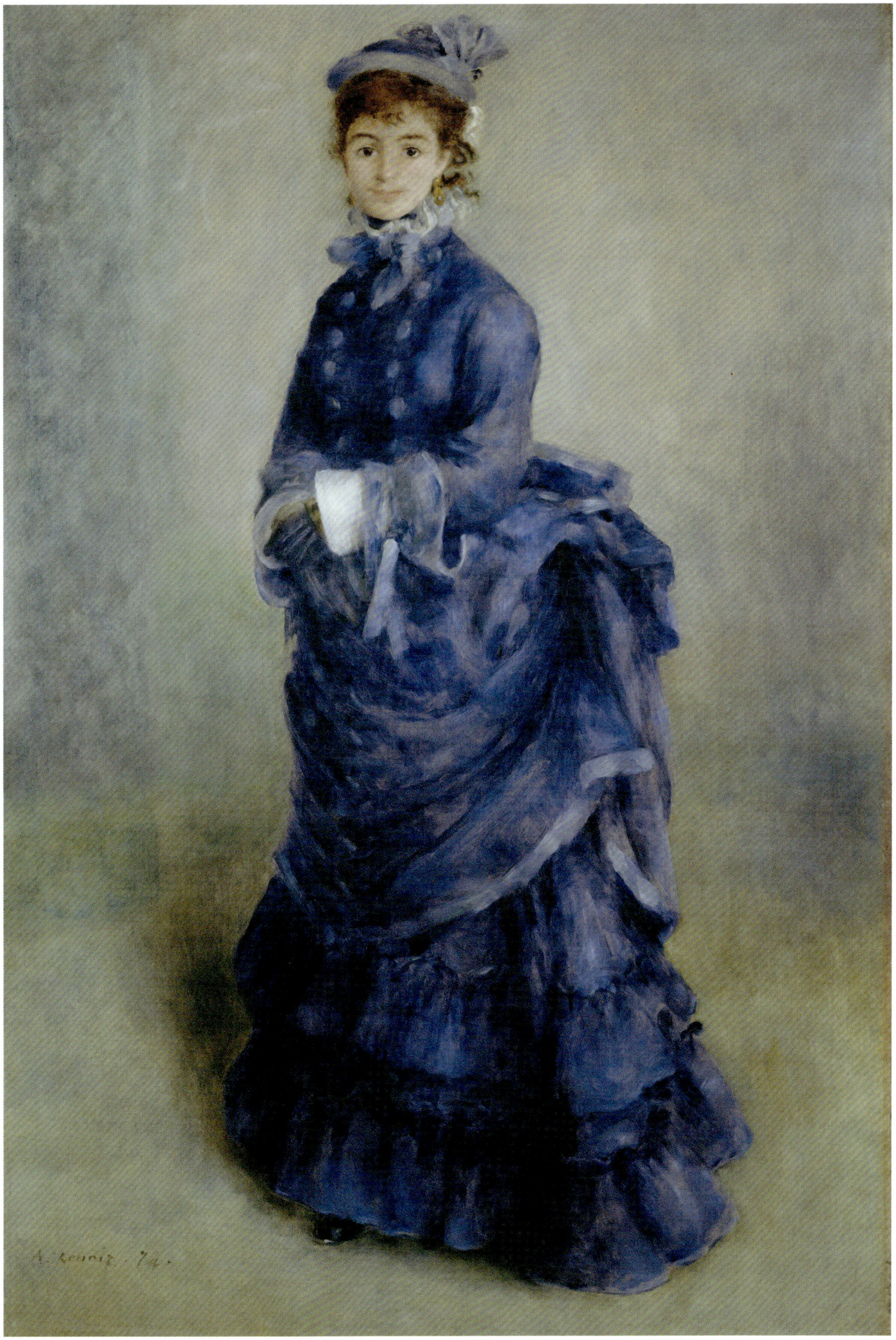
A. Renoir. 74.

Renoir His late works, particularly his nudes, show the clear influence of Titian and Rubens and, in terms of color and looseness, the work of Delacroix.

40 Pierre-Auguste Renoir (1841–1919)
Conversation, 1912
Oil on canvas, 17 ¾ x 25 ⅝ in. (45.1 x 65 cm)
Miss Gwendoline E. Davies Bequest, 1951 (NMWA 2494)

Sometimes assigned to Renoir's "red" period because of the exceptionally warm tonalities employed, *Conversation* dates from 1912, during the last part of the artist's career. It was probably begun in the garden of the house at Essoyes in Burgundy, where Renoir spent his summers.[89] By this time, Renoir had acquired the status of a modern master, but he was also suffering from crippling arthritis, and this forced him to paint more broadly. Beginning in the 1890s, he had relinquished his Impressionist concerns to focus on maintaining the lessons of old master painting. His late works, particularly his nudes, show the clear influence of Titian and Rubens and, in terms of color and looseness, the work of Delacroix. For some time, he had been working to eradicate absolute geometry from his painting, calling for formal irregularity as the only way to achieve a true reflection of nature.[90]

In terms of its title, *Conversation* is puzzling – the picture was bought by Gwendoline Davies as *Jeune Homme et Jeune Femme Assis*, which seems to make better sense as neither figure seems animated by the act of speaking. The contemplative atmosphere contrasts with the ebullience often associated with Renoir's late work. With her dress slipping from her shoulders, the female figure appears somewhat disheveled, although Renoir's penchant for depicting nudes and female flesh during this period might provide more of an explanation than the suggestion of anything else. The formal arrangement highlights the curved line of the woman's shoulders, enclosing softly knotted limbs and folds that contribute to the sensuality of the image as a whole. The subject matter perhaps serves as an updating of the eighteenth-century *fêtes galantes* of Antoine Watteau and Jean-Honoré Fragonard – an idea that has been explored in relation to Renoir's earlier intimate depictions of figures in a landscape.[91] *Conversation*, as an enigmatic pastoral idyll, seems to demonstrate a natural extension of this theme.

Structurally, this painting makes an interesting comparison with Morisot's *At Bougival* (cat. no. 37). Both are unusual within the broader Impressionist and Post-Impressionist Davies collection in that they are specifically rather than incidentally figure-based. It is likely that the air of quiet intimacy that pervades both works appealed to the sisters' sensibilities. This 1917 purchase by Gwendoline was the sisters' third and final purchase of a work by Renoir, joining *La Parisienne* (cat. no. 39; Gwendoline, 1913) and *Young Girl In Blue* from about 1883 (Margaret, 1914) to represent the varying stages of his career.

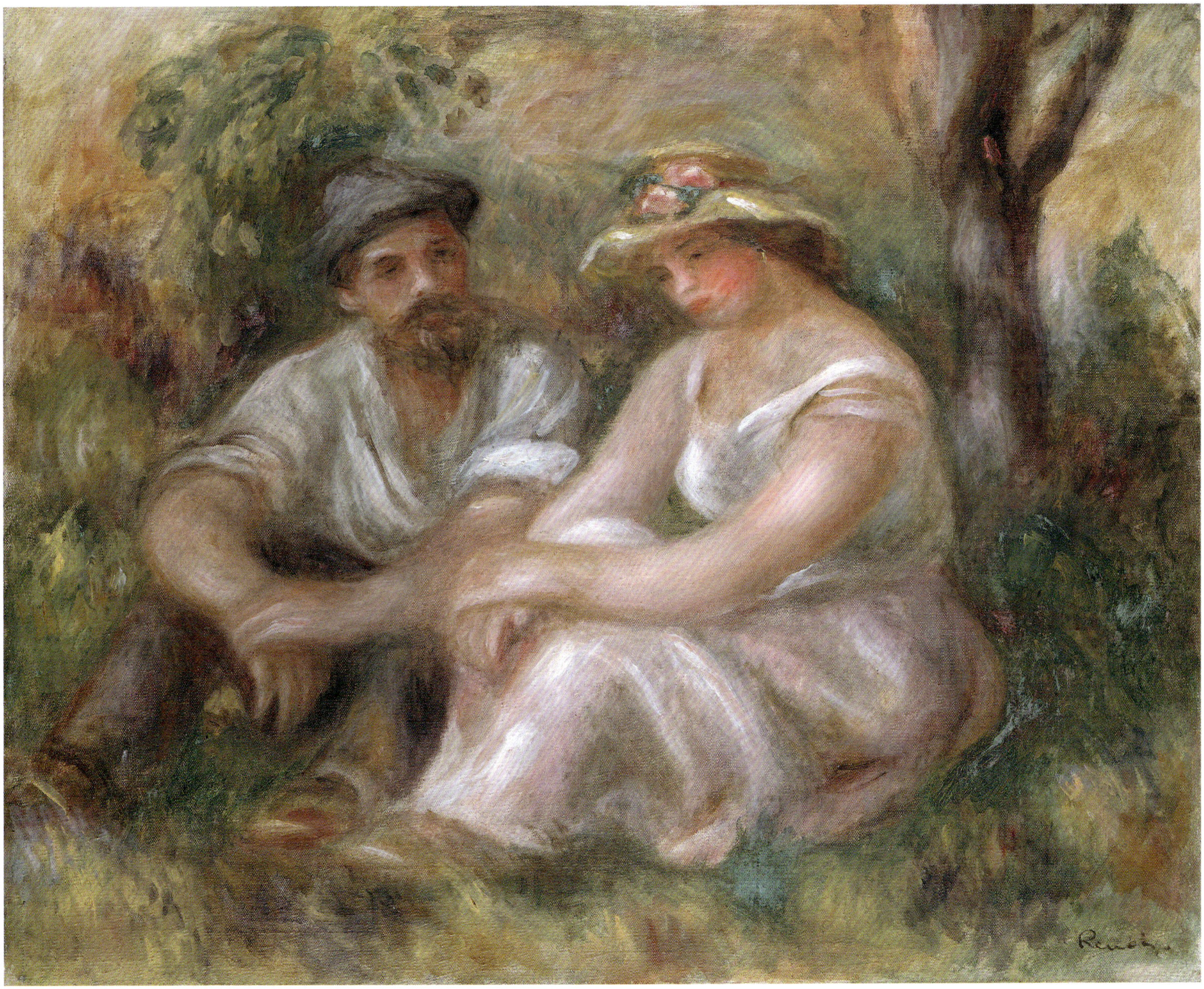

Seguin The stacked, almost jigsaw-like construction of the forms, with an emphasis on surface, reflects the Nabis' interest in the decorative arts and the Cloisonnism of Gauguin.

41 Armand Seguin (1869–1903)
Breton Peasant Women at Mass, ca. 1894
Oil on canvas, 21 ⅞ x 15 ⅛ in. (55.5 x 38.5 cm)
Miss Gwendoline E. Davies Bequest, 1951 (NMWA 2500)

Originally attributed to Gauguin, *Breton Peasant Women at Mass* is now ascribed to Armand Seguin. Seguin was born in Paris and trained at the Ecole des Arts Décoratifs before becoming a successful printmaker. Like many artists of his generation, he was drawn to the community at Pont-Aven in Brittany and visited regularly during the 1890s. Although not himself a member, Seguin worked with the Nabis and described artists such as Bonnard, Denis, and Vuillard as "companions of his youth."[92] Seguin first met Gauguin in 1894, becoming a follower and pupil. Although undated, *Breton Peasant Women at Mass* is thought to originate from this period.

Seguin made numerous images of Bretons in traditional costume, though none quite as intense as this. The stacked, almost jigsaw-like construction of the forms, with blocks of color and an emphasis on surface, reflects the Nabis' interest in the decorative arts and the Cloisonnism of Gauguin, while the composition, that of two faces in profile, is one that Seguin used on numerous occasions, including an etching of two Breton women at prayer, variously titled *Deux Bretonnes, de profil* and *Bretonnes en prière* (Archives Arsène Bonafous-Murat, Paris).

Financial necessity forced Seguin to concentrate on printmaking, and as a result his oil paintings are rare. It has been noted that he never really established his own style, and his oils reflect the work of not only Gauguin but also of contemporaries Paul Sérusier, Emile Bernard, and Maurice Denis. In a letter, he wrote, "Every day, every night I dream of the canvases that I cannot execute, and yearn with all my strength to do so."[93] This image, with its emphasis on drawing and visible pencil line, is clearly the work of someone more at home with graphic art than oil painting.

The picture was purchased by Gwendoline, and it is likely that the human, contemplative nature of the subject appealed to her, particularly at a time of war. It was acquired in 1916, as by Gauguin, from the wife of the artist Alfred Thornton, who had met Gauguin in Brittany in 1890. Although the work is now known as clearly by another hand, the reasons for the original attribution are obvious, particularly with the apparent provenance of the purchase. *Breton Peasant Women at Mass* was exhibited as a Gauguin at the Victoria Art Gallery in Bath from 1918 to 1920, where it drew much admiration and was compared with the work of Filippino Lippi. It was re-attributed to Seguin in 1960.

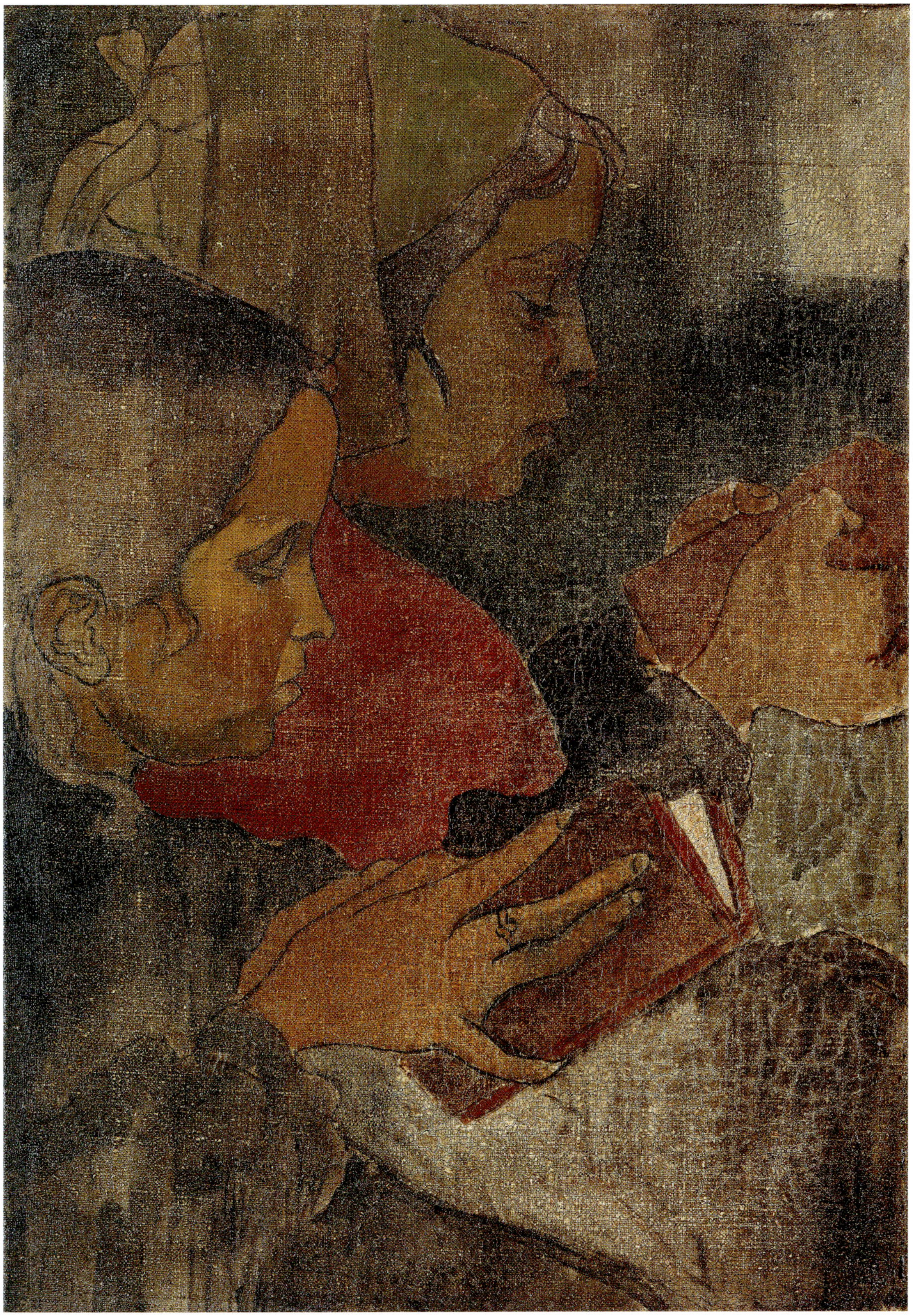

Sickert Although Sickert also painted the grander views of Venice, this image of the Dario has a faintly shabby air, which fits with his interest in the less conventionally picturesque.

42 Walter Richard Sickert (1860–1942)
Palazzo Eleanora Duse, Venice, 1904
Oil on canvas, 21 ¾ x 18 ⅛ in. (55 x 46 cm)
Miss Margaret S. Davies Bequest, 1963 (NMWA 193)

Sickert was for years described as a "British Impressionist," a tag that does no justice to his highly individual approach to painting. As a major figure in modern British art in the early twentieth century, his work can be seen as an attempt to reconcile the articulation of modern life with the seemingly contradictory objectives of formalism. He was friends with Degas, and the composition of many of his pictures, as if seen through a door or from the wings, shows the French artist's influence. Sickert studied with Whistler, and it was while helping to print Whistler's Venetian etchings that he was inspired to travel and tackle the subject himself. Beginning in 1895, Sickert spent numerous periods in Venice. Although called *Palazzo Eleanora Duse*, the image in fact shows the Palazzo Dario to the right, and to the left, the Palazzo Barbaro-Wolkoff, in which the famed actress Eleanora Duse (1858–1924) had an apartment. During his periods in Italy, Sickert painted outdoors; this view was most likely captured from a boat. The scene and viewpoint, from near the Palazzo Corner della Ca' Grande, is the same as that in Monet's *Palazzo Dario* (cat. no. 35),[94] which was painted just a few years later, in 1908.

Although Sickert did paint traditionally grand and popular views such as San Marco and Santa Maria della Salute, this image of the Dario has a faintly shabby air, which fits with his interest in the less conventionally picturesque, accentuated by an absence of architectural detail on either building. Most curious are the areas of brown where the intricate marble roundels that characterize the right-hand side of the facade should be. The roundels underwent renovation in 1905–06, and it is possible therefore that Sickert shows them boarded up and ready for their restoration.[95] However, circular underpainting suggests, equally possibly, that Sickert either painted them in initially or was merely looking to give just an impression of them to maintain the picture's formal integrity.[96] In either case, while most artists before and at this time painted a "fantasy" Venice, Sickert shows a truer picture of faded grandeur, a city effectively in decline. However, his depiction of the Venetian light as it bounces off the sides of the buildings is spectacular, revealing his affection for the place he described as "the loveliest city in the world."[97]

Margaret Davies did not purchase this work until 1935, so it does not fall in with the group of Venetian views acquired between 1912 and 1913 (cat. nos. 4, 35, and 58). It was the only work by Sickert that she purchased. At around the same time, she also acquired works by his contemporaries Vanessa Bell and Harold Gilman. It is notable that, aside from the work of Augustus John, neither sister chose to acquire work by avant-garde British artists during their collecting in the 1910s.

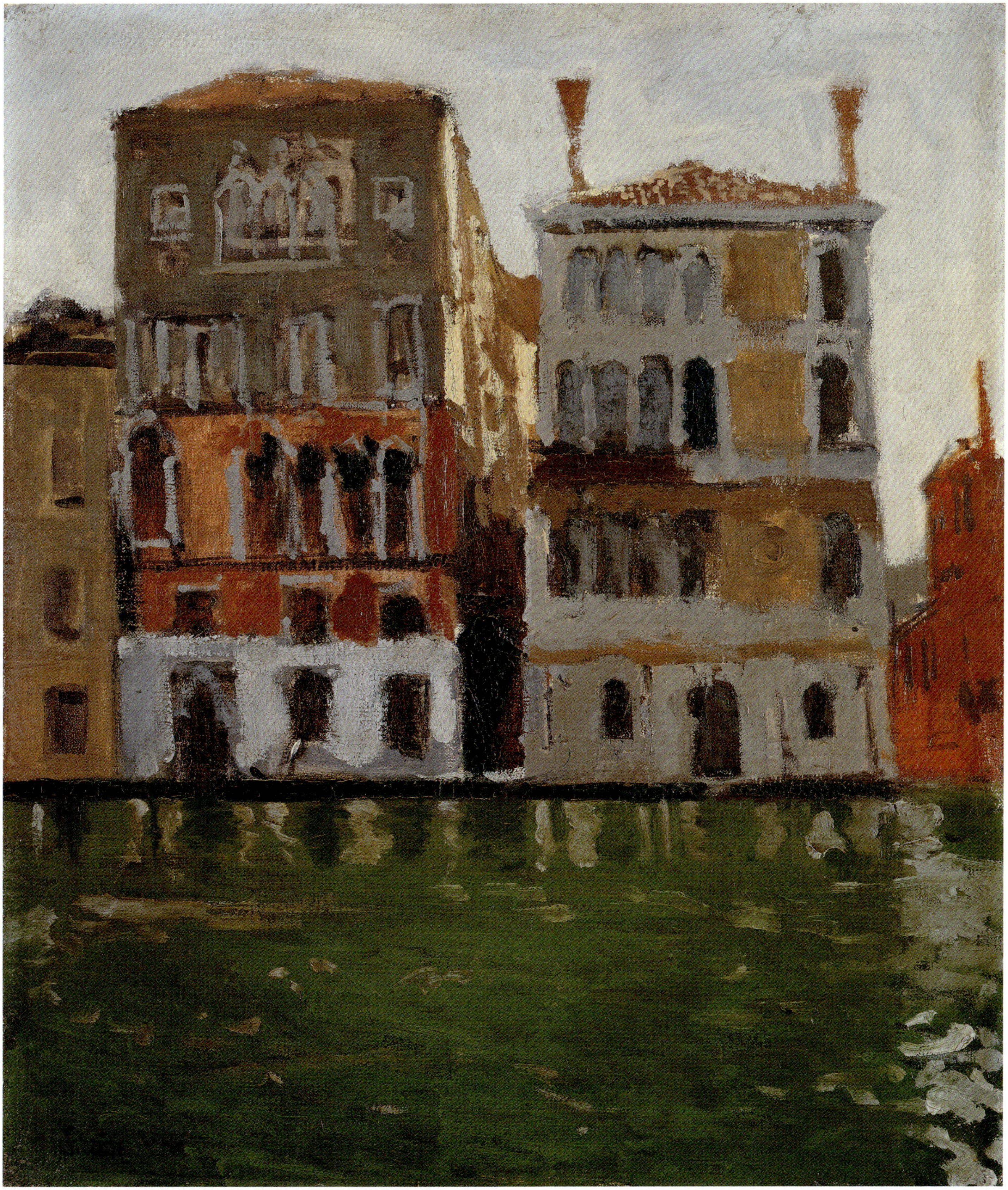

Signac Signac has juxtaposed bright, pure colors in short strokes; the result is a light yet vivid view that is typical of his watercolor style.

43 Paul Signac (1863–1935)
St. Tropez, 1918
Watercolor and crayon on wove paper, 10 ⅝ x 16 in. (27.1 x 40.7 cm)
Signed in pencil, lower left: *P Signac St. Tropez 1918*
Miss Gwendoline E. Davies Bequest, 1951 (NMWA 1710)

Signac was born in Paris. He did not follow his father and grandfather in the family's successful saddlery business and by adolescence had already shown an interest in the paintings of the Impressionists. He visited avant-garde exhibitions and later said that it was the painting of Claude Monet, which he had seen at an exhibition in 1880, that had led him to become an artist.

Signac had no formal training but instead taught himself through the study of other artists. He enjoyed painting en plein air and chose subjects with personal associations, such as Montmartre in Paris, a district famous for its bohemian artists and writers, where he had lived as a child and a young man. He was soon executing and exhibiting paintings in the Impressionist style. In 1884, at the inaugural meeting of the Société des Artistes Indépendants, an exhibiting organization set up to rival the Salon in Paris, he met Georges Seurat; this meeting was to have a profound impact on his work. He was highly impressed with Seurat's theories of color and soon became a dedicated follower. Both Seurat and Signac participated in the eighth and final Impressionist exhibition in 1886; however, the work of both artists moved beyond Impressionism. Signac experimented with developing their shared style of Divisionism, in which small dabs of pure color (they used no earth colors) are placed side by side and as a result combine and blend in the viewer's eye. This became known as Pointillism or Neo-Impressionism.

Signac was influenced by a number of other contemporary artists. In 1885, he met Pissarro, with whom he corresponded about the development of the Neo-Impressionist style and watercolor painting. He also worked with van Gogh in Paris in 1887. He set out his theory of art in his book *D'Eugène Delacroix au Néo-impressionisme*, published in 1899. Its examination of the purity of color, Divisionism, and the theory of color opposites attracted much attention among young artists as an explanation of Neo-Impressionism. Signac was to influence numerous younger artists, including Matisse, who stayed with him in St. Tropez in 1904.

By the 1890s, Signac was making his first serious attempts at watercolor painting, and by 1892 he began to exhibit. His watercolors and drawings were always as important to him as his oil paintings, and his first one-man show in 1894 was composed of watercolors. The critics noticed these works and praised them for their simplicity and vibrancy.

Signac divided his time between Paris and the south of France, where he endlessly painted harbor scenes and seascapes. He was also a keen sailor and would travel the coast, making watercolors along the way.

This watercolor postdates the artist's experiments with Pointillism. He has still juxtaposed bright, pure colors but in short strokes rather than dots; the result is a light yet vivid view that is typical of his watercolor style. It is inscribed *St Tropez*. By 1913, Signac had separated from his wife and had left her their villa in St. Tropez to base himself in Antibes. When purchased by Gwendoline Davies in February 1920 from the Eldar Gallery, in London, the work was titled *Antibes*.

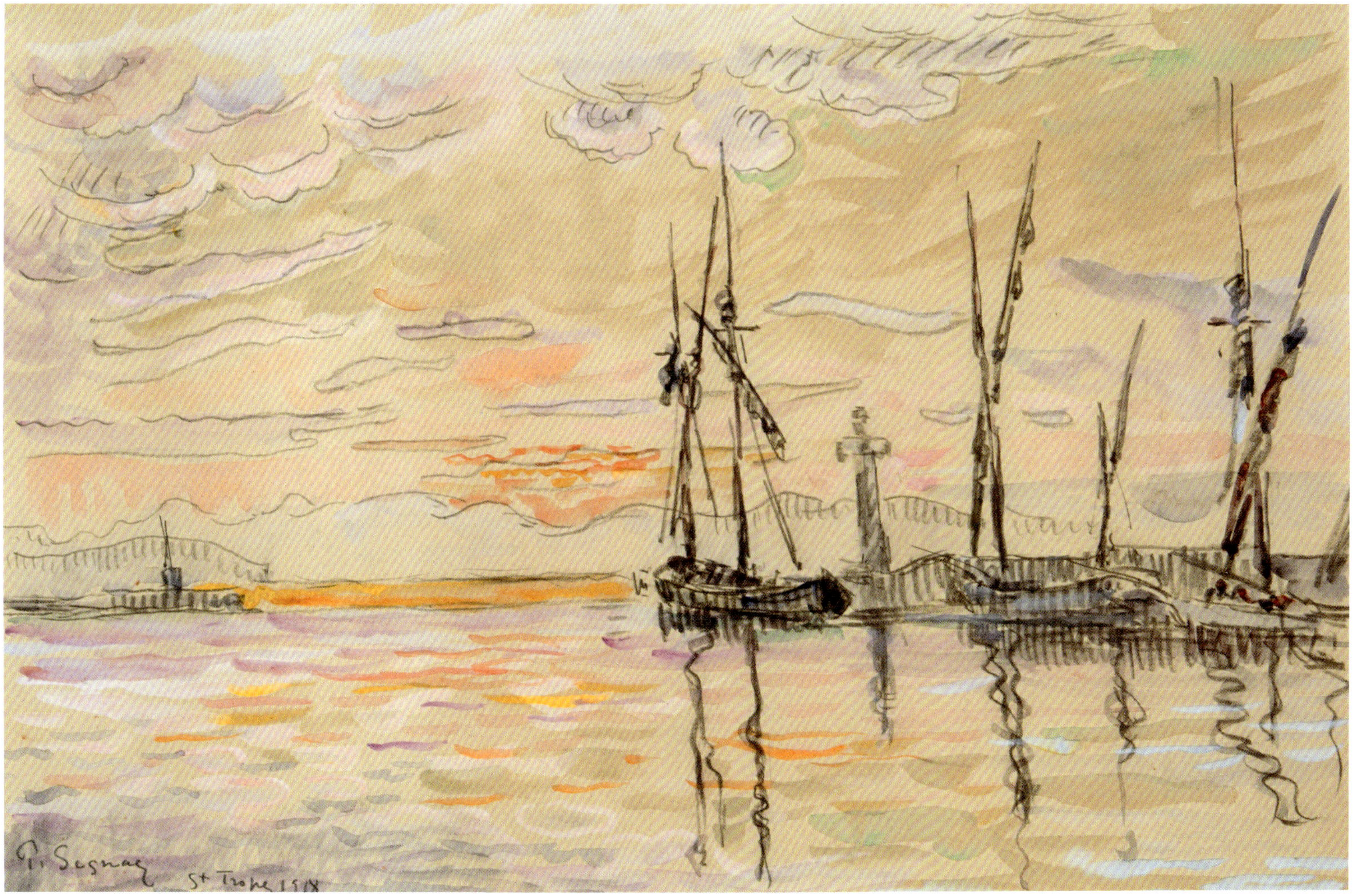
P. Signac
St Tropez 1918

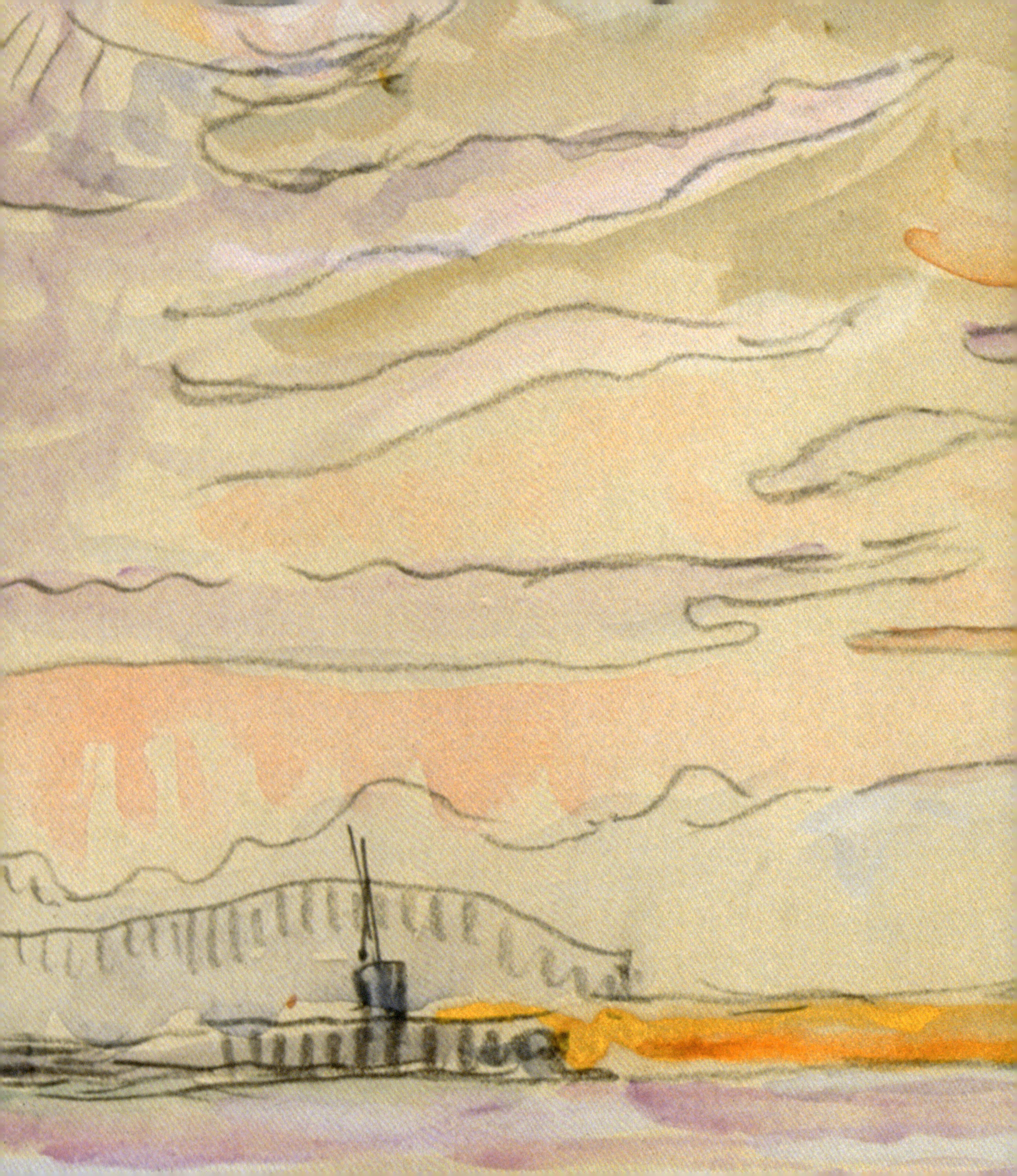

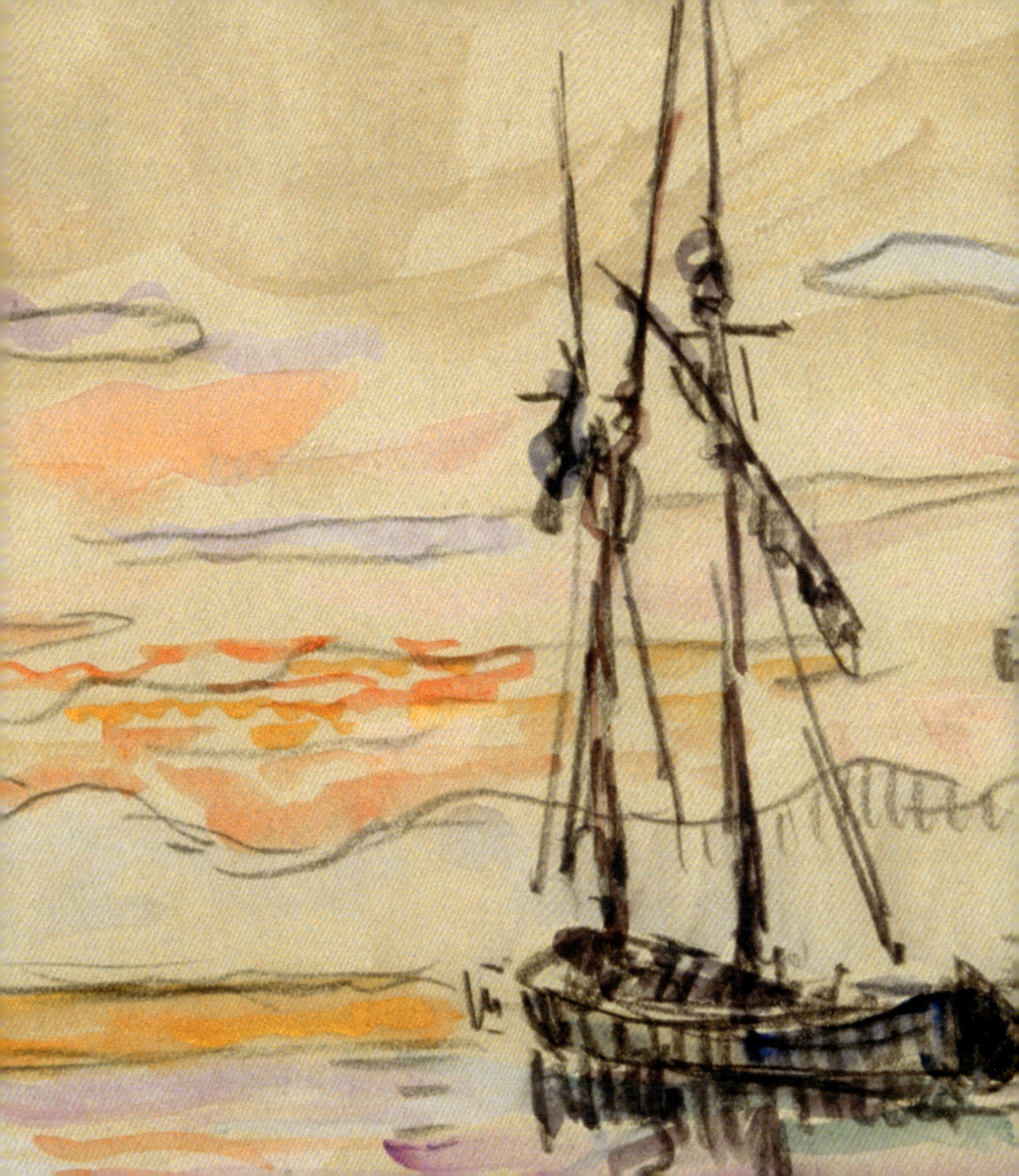

Sisley Monet's early influence can be detected in the depiction of the foliage, but Sisley's rendering of the other aspects of the picture have more in common with Neo-Impressionism.

44 Alfred Sisley (1839–1899)
Moret-sur-Loing (Rue de Fosses), 1892
Oil on canvas, 15 ⅜ x 18 ⅜ in. (39 x 46.7 cm)
Miss Margaret S. Davies Bequest, 1963 (NMWA 2502)

Described by van Gogh as the most "discreet and gentle of the Impressionists,"[98] Alfred Sisley was also one of the most dedicated yet underrated exponents of Impressionist technique. In 1889, he and his family settled permanently in the town of Moret-sur-Loing near the Forest of Fontainebleau. The town is the subject of most of his later works, with the exception of those made during and following his visits to England and Wales in 1897; he wrote that "at Moret my art has undoubtedly developed most."[99] By the time this work was painted, the artist and his family had settled in the rue de Montmartre. Sisley's images of Moret tend to focus on repeated views of local landmarks – the river, the bridge, and the church – but the present work is a much more intimate street scene.

Sisley remained devoted to the techniques of Impressionism, continuing to paint en plein air until his death. The present work was painted outdoors from a position outside the old schoolhouse.[100] The focus here is the rendering of light effects, depicting the street in tones of red and pink, which suggest a bright autumn morning, the season confirmed by the scattered leaves beneath the trees. *Moret-sur-Loing* exhibits the more varied brushstrokes that characterized the last decades of Sisley's life. Monet's early influence on Sisley's technique can be detected in the formation of the trees and the rapidly painted leaves, but his rendering of the other aspects of the picture – the blocks of solid, almost unnatural color – have more in common with Neo-Impressionism. Curiously, the perspective is difficult to reconcile visually. The figures in the center of the canvas appear miniscule in relation to their surroundings.

While Hugh Blaker had recommended Sisley to the Davies sisters when they were beginning to acquire Impressionism, the artist's work clearly did not strike a chord with them. Blaker had written to them, "I … am delighted you are thinking of getting some examples of the Impressionists … I expect you already know the work of Sisley, Pissarro and Renoir. These can still be got quite cheaply."[101] Despite Sisley's interest in Constable and Turner, and the fact that he was the only Impressionist painter to visit Wales (two views of which have since entered the museum's collection), *Moret-sur-Loing (Rue de Fosses)*, their only example by Sisley, was not purchased until 1960 and was the last work by a major Impressionist painter that Margaret collected. She bought it in 1960, the same year as Bonnard's *Sunlight at Vernon* (cat. no. 3), when she was acquiring pieces by artists whose work she and her sister had not purchased in the early years.

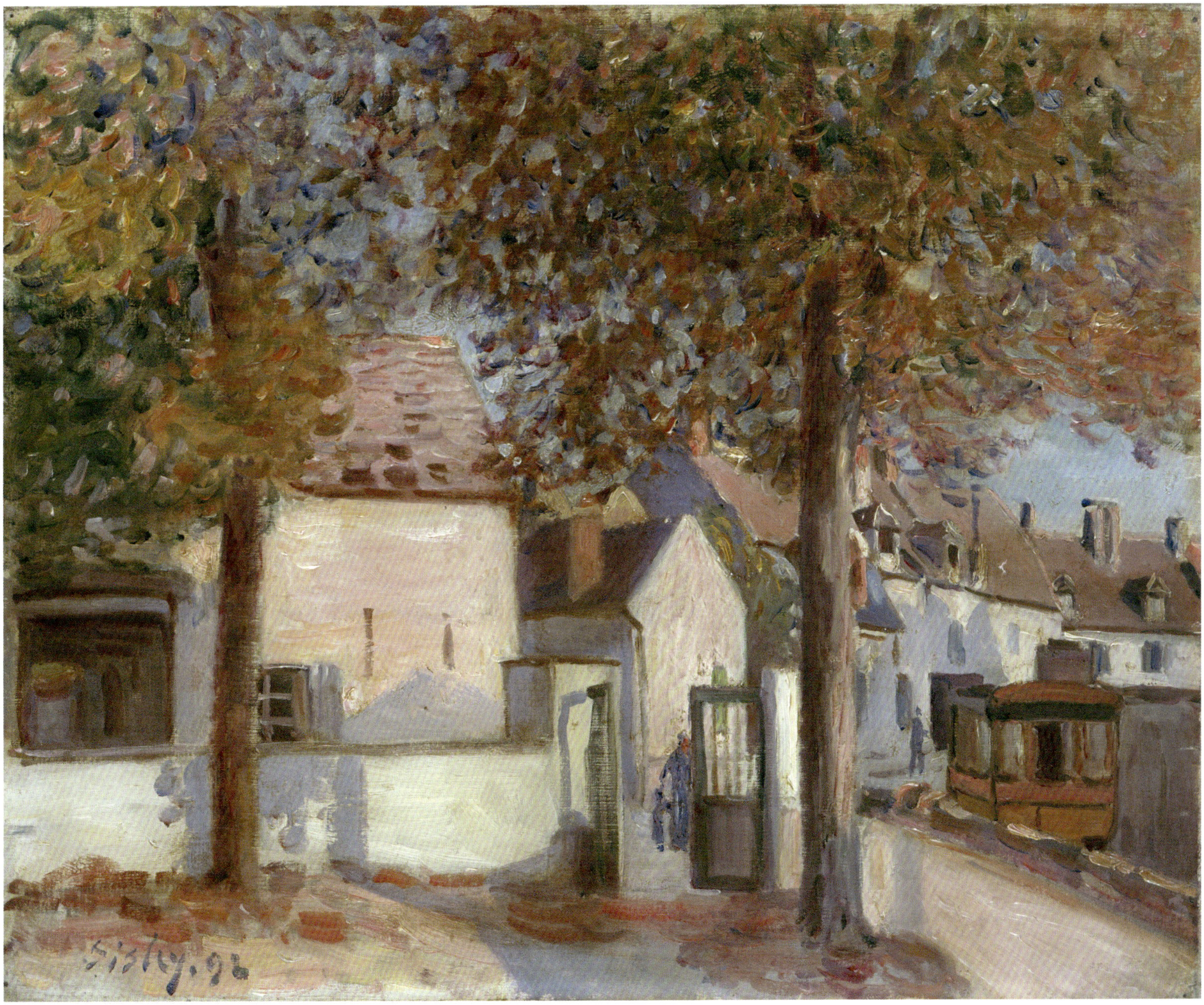
Sisley.92

Smith Reflecting the ideals of modernism, *Apples on a Wicker Chair* is more an exercise in color and form than an attempt at still life.

45 Matthew Smith (1879–1959)
Apples on a Wicker Chair, 1915
Oil on canvas, 16 ½ x 20 in. (41.9 x 50.8 cm)
Miss Margaret S. Davies Bequest, 1963 (NMWA 2049)

Born in 1879 in Halifax, West Yorkshire, Matthew Smith studied at the Slade School of Art before traveling to France, where he lived in Pont-Aven, Paris (enrolling at the Ecole de Matisse) and Grez-sur-Loing. *Apples on a Wicker Chair* was painted in 1915, the year after Smith had returned to Britain and when he was renting a studio at 33a Fitzroy Street, Bloomsbury, then the hub of progressive art in London. Sickert became a good friend, as did the sculptor Jacob Epstein. Smith would also have mixed with his neighboring artists, but while he exhibited with the London Group (which had no overriding ethos but that "all modern methods may find a home"),[102] he cut a singular figure in practice, though his methods certainly chimed with many of the concerns of his peers.

Reflecting the ideals of modernism, *Apples on a Wicker Chair* is more an exercise in color and form than an attempt at still life, and the subject was one that Smith painted numerous times with strikingly different results. He worked from life but with a highly imaginative approach to color that owed much to Fauvism. This can be seen in the proliferation of red coupled with green, violet with orange, and blue with yellow. With the plate of fruit at the top of the canvas, the composition suggests a viewpoint virtually on top of the subject, confusing the sense of perspective and emphasizing the flat of the canvas. The violet shadows are probably equally caused by the proximity of artist to subject as they are from the light source that creeps in above the fruit, while the wicker weave of the chair accentuates the paint strokes, provoking a further awareness of the picture surface. In a more abstracted version of this scene owned by the Tate Gallery, the fruit is surrounded by a flat background design of multi-directional hatching that mirrors the pattern of the wicker in the Cardiff version. Although believed to date from 1915, it could be slightly later – possibly directly postwar when Smith returned to Fitzroy Street and concentrated on still lifes of fruit. A 1919 version (*Apple on a Blue Dish*; private collection) shows the same dish.

This was a late purchase by Margaret Davies, in 1961. Although during the 1910s the sisters acquired the work of contemporary French artists, none of the principal works in their collection from this iconic period in British art were purchased contemporaneously. Perhaps they were not thought to be a good investment, an oversight Margaret sought to rectify after Gwendoline's death. Her late acquisition policy favored twentieth-century British artists, including pieces by Spencer Gore, Paul Nash, Stanley Spencer, and a further two (late) still lifes by Smith. The National Museum of Wales was at this time making its first purchases of modern British art, and this later focus by Margaret suggests she was concentrating on work that would reflect and augment this area of their collection.

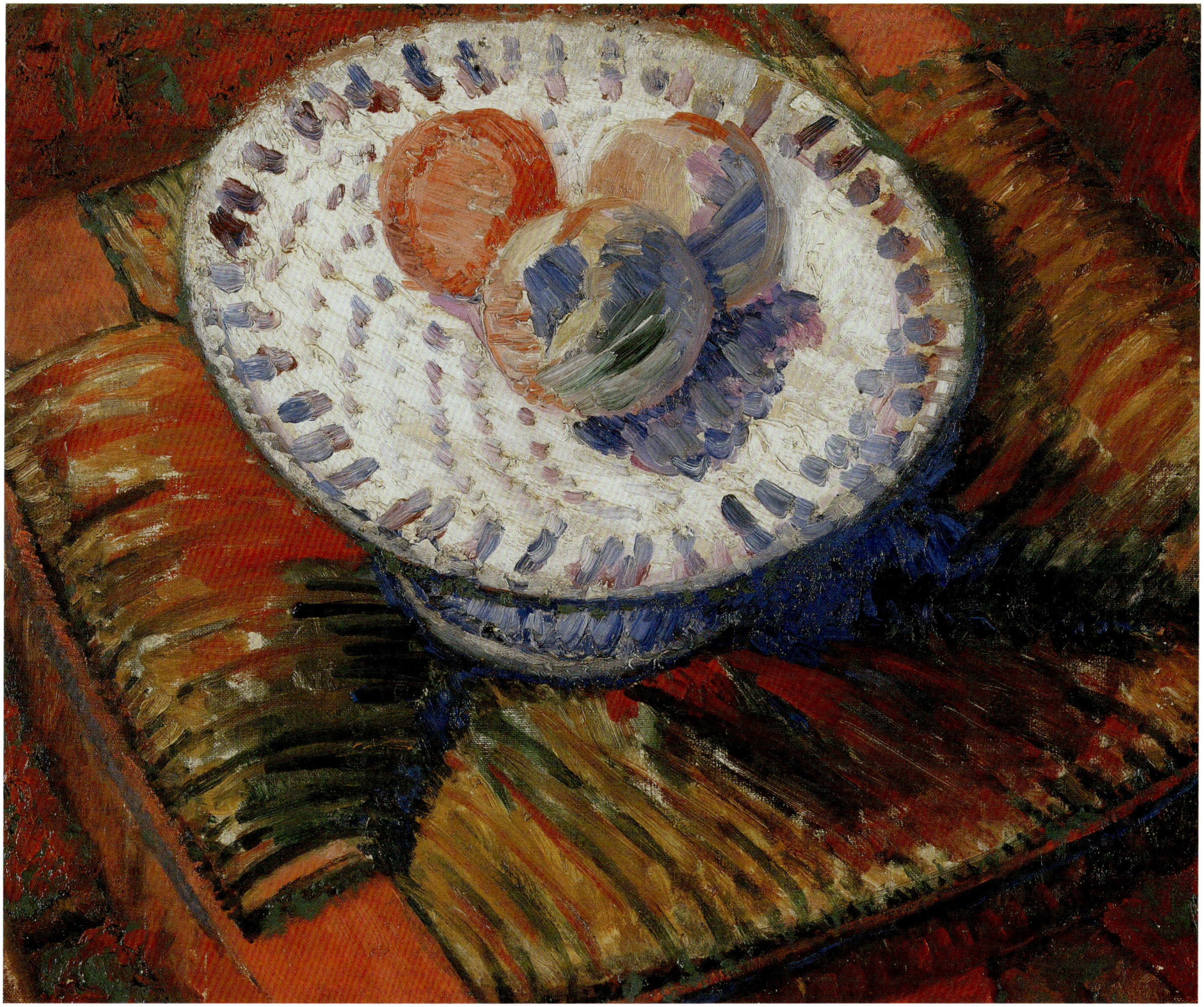

Stevens Stevens was an early enthusiast of Japonaiserie, which can be seen here in the flatness of the rendering and the lack of background detail.

46 Alfred Stevens (1823–1906)
Seated Girl, undated
Oil on canvas, 8 ½ x 6 ⅜ in. (21.6 x 16.2 cm)
Miss Margaret S. Davies Bequest, 1963 (NMWA 2503)

Alfred (Emile Léopold) Stevens – not to be confused with the English sculptor of the same name and period – was a student in Brussels with the Neoclassical painter François-Joseph Navez before moving to Paris in 1844. He found success during the Second Empire with his bourgeois depictions of fashionable women lounging in interiors. A typically fin-de-siècle description of Stevens's narrow depiction of "womanhood" is given by Camille Lemonnier as the type that "breathes an atmosphere of poison, stifles in mystery, pain, and perfumes …"[103] *Seated Girl*, however, is a comparatively straightforward image. Like *The Artist's Model* by Charles Bargue (cat. no. 1), it is a much looser oil sketch than is generally associated with the artist, which in the present work shows the influence of Manet, with its absence of transitional tones and contrasts. This is clearly a finished work as it is signed with the artist's characteristic monogram, but its simplicity, freshness, and lack of incidental detail are rare in the artist's oeuvre.

Like Manet and Whistler, Stevens was an early enthusiast of Japonaiserie, which can be seen here in the flatness of the rendering and the lack of background detail. In *Seated Girl*, the figure's coiffure is somewhat at odds with the voluminous white smock she is dressed in – a hint at the style for which Stevens made his name. She is quite sharply lit, accentuating the contrast of the white material with the background gloom. While the visible light source comes from the upper right corner of the canvas, there are also strong highlights on the front of her face, hand, and knee.

Margaret purchased *Seated Girl* from Wallis & Son in 1918, a joint purchase with a work by the fashionable Dutch artist Matthijs Maris (1839–1917), painter of the very popular (but now unheard of) *He Is Coming* (1874), which the sisters acquired a few years earlier in 1913. In 1958, Margaret purchased an oil sketch titled *Mother and Child* by the French artist Paul Delance, which, in addition to being almost identical in terms of size, also has strong compositional and stylistic similarities with the Stevens sketch.

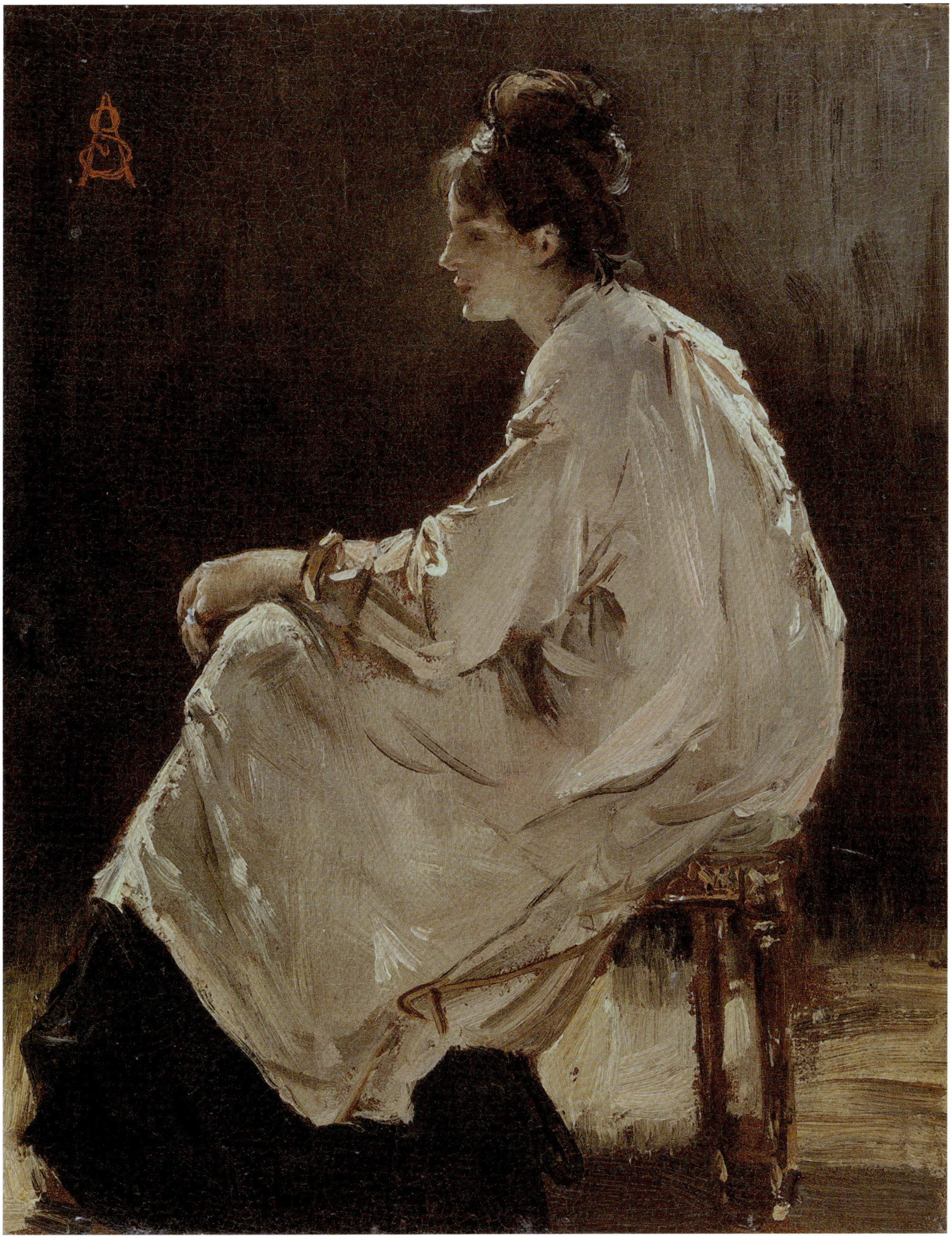

Turner He transformed the use of watercolor, developing new techniques to create luminous and vibrant works.

47 Joseph Mallord William Turner (1775–1851)
Rye, Sussex, 1824
Watercolor with scraping out on wove paper,
5 7/8 x 9 1/8 in. (14.8 x 23.1 cm)
Miss Gwendoline E. Davies Bequest, 1951 (NMWA 1742)

One of Britain's greatest artists, Turner was as renowned for his mastery of the medium of watercolor as for his paintings in oils. He transformed the use of the medium, developing new techniques to create luminous and vibrant works.

This view of Rye on the southern coast of England exemplifies Turner's dramatic treatment of light and form. The town to the left is still in sunlight while a storm coming in from the right has overshadowed the foreground and led people to hurry off the causeway to escape the waves. As well as making skilled use of watercolor, particularly in depicting the sky, Turner has also employed scraping out, literally scratching the surface pigment to reveal the light color of the paper below as a highlight (rather than using a white pigment).

The scene shows the point where the Royal Military Canal meets the River Brede at a junction between the road from Winchelsea to Rye and the road to Winchelsea Beach. Men in the foreground scramble to safety; one has fallen in the sea. This image probably depicts an incident when a temporary dam to protect the construction of the junction was swept away by the spring tide. The canal was begun in 1804 as a defensive barrier in response to the increasing threat of invasion by Napoleon Bonaparte's French armies, although the threat had passed before the dam was finished.

Early in his career, Turner recognized that reproduction prints would bring his art to a much wider audience. This image was engraved by Edward Goodall for the series "Picturesque Views of the Southern Coast of England" in 1824. This was Turner's first major topographical series, and he submitted thirty-nine watercolors for it. The project was commissioned by the brothers George and William Bernard Cooke and was published in parts between 1814 and 1826.

Rye, Sussex was the first watercolor Gwendoline Davies acquired and also the first work by Turner to enter the Davies sisters' collection. It was purchased by their adviser, Hugh Blaker, on Gwendoline's behalf from Christie's for £220 in June 1908.

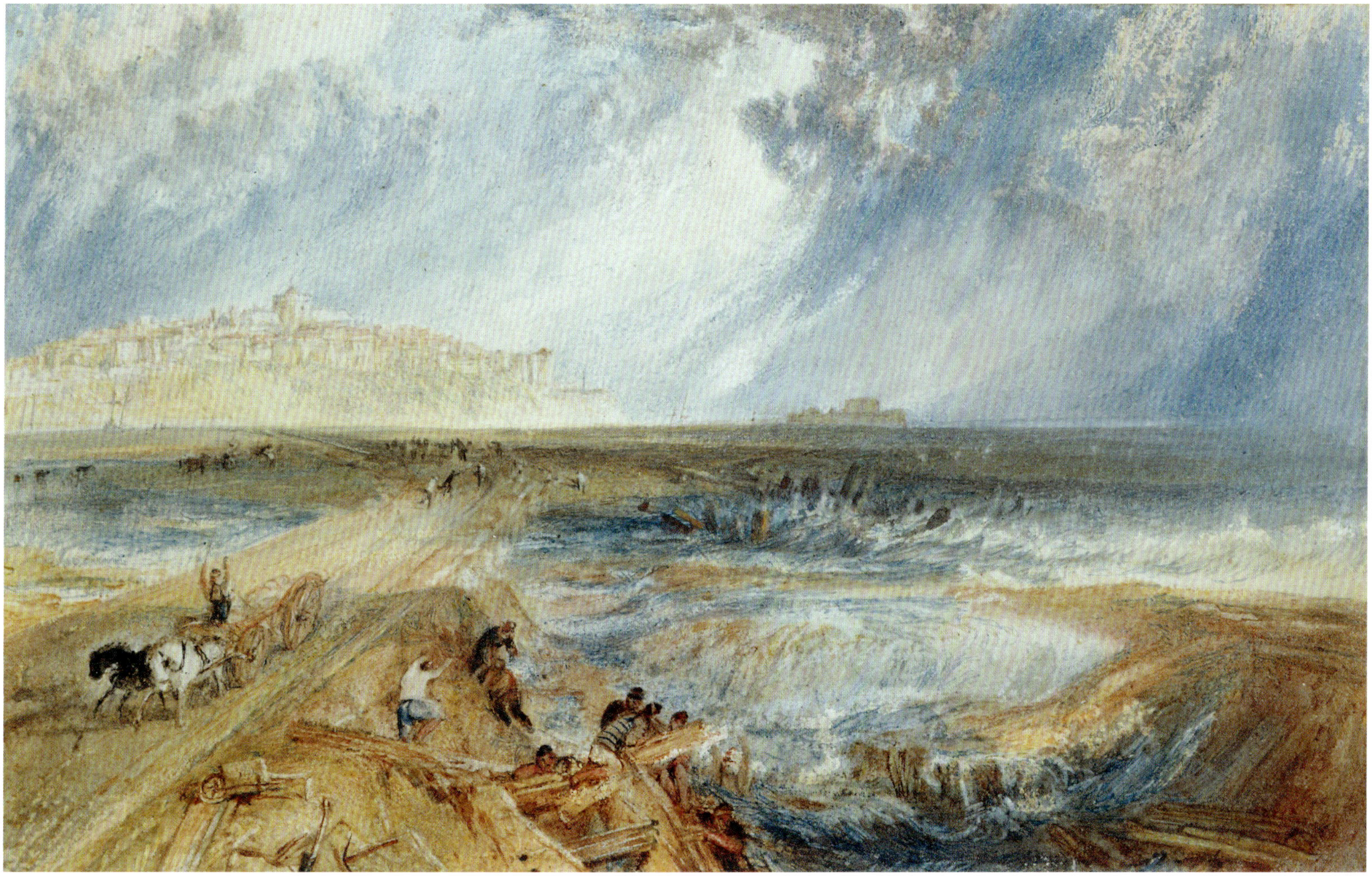

Turner The figures are merely suggested rather than painted in detail and in some ways merge with their surroundings.

48 Joseph Mallord William Turner (1775–1851)
Margate, ca. 1830s/40s
Gouache and pencil on blue-gray wove paper,
5 ½ x 7 ⅜ in. (14 x 18.9 cm)
Miss Gwendoline E. Davies Bequest, 1951 (NMWA 1745)

Turner exhibited numerous large, highly finished watercolors throughout his career, many of them at London's Royal Academy of Arts. These are commonly known as his "exhibition watercolors." However, all of the works by Turner purchased by the Davies sisters were either color studies or images produced for private sale or for engravings. This view is one of a whole series of works that Turner painted on colored paper. Here he has used blue paper, now rather faded, and incorporated the color into the composition and the overall color scheme. The work may have been intended to be made into an engraving; however, none is known.

This work is probably a view of Margate, a resort on the northern coast of Kent, which Turner had known since his childhood. Sent to Margate by his parents to stay with relatives at the age of eleven, he went to school there and obviously held the town in deep affection, as he painted it and the shoreline on many occasions throughout his life. He returned and lodged there with his mistress and landlady, Sophia Booth, between 1827 and 1847, and later in life he sometimes took the steamer there from London. Turner enjoyed the light in Margate and said the area had "the loveliest skies in Europe."[104]

Turner was a renowned and pioneering landscape painter; however, his works often incorporate a humanitarian aspect. People interacting with nature are frequently included. In this work, the foreground is dominated by a group of people on the beach, probably fishermen. The figures are merely suggested rather than painted in detail and in some ways merge with their surroundings. Turner is also famous for the majesty of his skies, and this work is no exception, with its low, bright white clouds and the higher cloud cover in the distance.

There are no records of the purchase of this work, although it is thought to have been purchased by Gwendoline Davies from Croal Thomson in 1919. At the time of purchase, the sisters already owned six oil paintings by Turner, all of which are views around the coast of Kent, England.

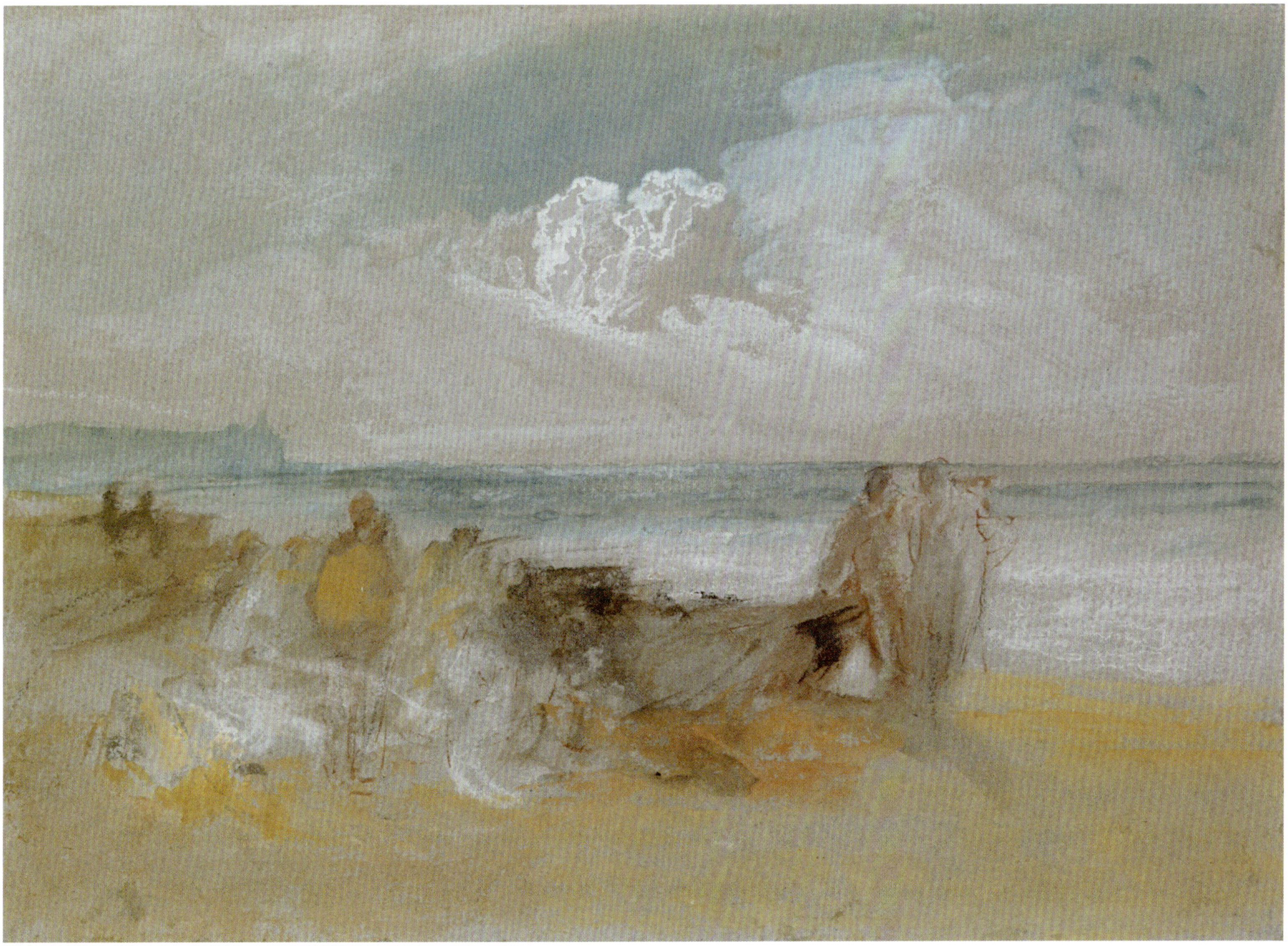

Turner He has employed numerous difficult techniques, including stippling and blotting-out in the sky to create depth and tonal gradations.

49 Joseph Mallord William Turner (1775–1851)
The Rainbow, ca. 1835
Watercolor and gouache with blotting out on wove paper, 9 ⅜ x 11 ⅞ in. (23.9 x 30 cm)
Miss Gwendoline E. Davies Bequest, 1951 (NMWA 1743)

The dynamism and luminosity of this work is typical of many of Turner's later colored sketches. He has brilliantly employed numerous difficult techniques, including stippling and blotting-out in the sky to create depth and tonal gradations. Along with watercolor, Turner has used red gouache, an opaque pigment, on the horizon of the work to suggest additional buildings, which adds warmth to the image.

Images of rainbows appear throughout Turner's work, as do depictions of churches. Here, the rainbow meets the land almost in the center of the page, silhouetting the spire of the church against the golden edge. The rainbow was commonly used in European art as a Christian symbol, recalling the rainbow that appears to Noah to signify the end of the flood. It can be assumed that Turner would have been aware of its symbolism, and other examples can be found in his oeuvre.

Like his contemporary John Constable, Turner was fascinated by the effects of weather and depicted it in his works. His sketchbooks and countless studies of different landscapes almost invariably reflect interest in weather conditions. The skies in many of his works depict accurately observed meteorological conditions, though the artist also used weather to add to the drama of a scene.

There is a pencil inscription on the back of this work that possibly reads *From Prague to/Frankfurt* and that has been identified as Turner's writing. Turner visited Prague in 1835, and the inscription could therefore relate to his return journey. As yet, however, there are no identified color works that derive from this journey.

In a letter of 1919, the London art dealer Croal Thomson wrote to Gwendoline Davies, "I felt sure you would like the Rainbow drawing by Turner."[105] She purchased it for £800 from Thomson and also bought *Würzburg* (cat. no. 53) at the same time.

For a number of years, this work was rejected as an authentic work by Turner and was omitted from some publications on the artist. However, current specialists, including Eric Shanes,[106] David Hill, and Ian Warrell, have identified it as a work by his hand that exemplifies Turner's skills and control of the watercolor medium.

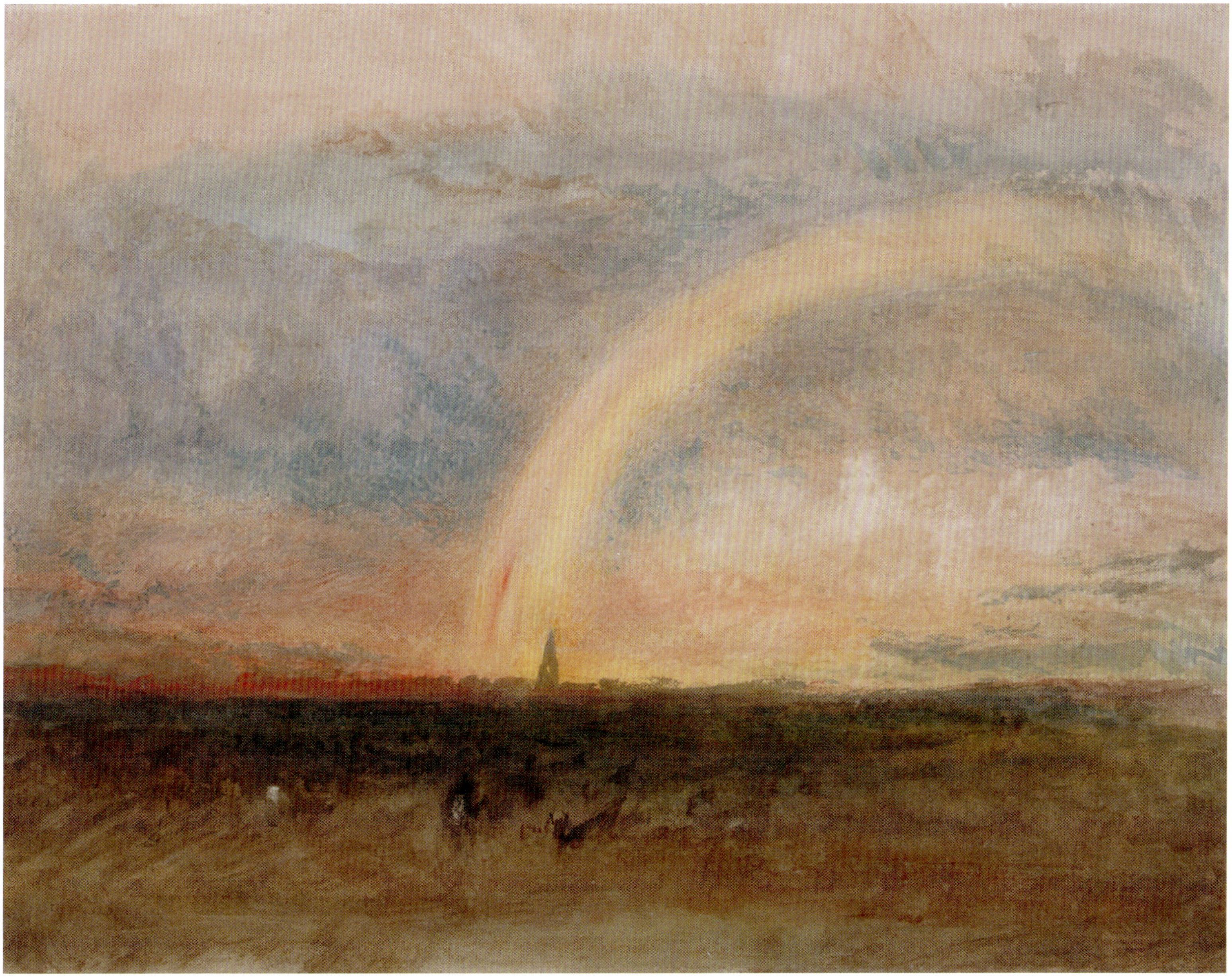

Turner He spent almost every summer touring with his sketchbooks, gathering information and ideas for future works.

50 Joseph Mallord William Turner (1775–1851)
Fort de l'Esseillon, Val de la Maurienne, 1836
Watercolor on wove paper, 9 ½ x 13 ¾ in. (24.2 x 34.8 cm)
Miss Gwendoline E. Davies Bequest, 1951 (NMWA 1744)

An avid traveler, Turner made numerous tours around Britain and Europe throughout his life. He spent almost every summer touring with his sketchbooks, gathering information and ideas for future works that he normally completed at home during the winter months. This watercolor was painted on Turner's 1836 tour of Mont Blanc and Val d'Aosta, where he traveled with Hugh Andrew Johnstone Munro, a wealthy Scottish landowner. He made more than five hundred pencil sketches in numerous sketchbooks on this tour alone, in addition to a number of larger sheets, with pencil and watercolor, such as this one.[107]

The work was drawn when Turner was on his way back home from Turin on a well-established route between Italy and France. The fort is described in 1827 by William Brockedon in his book *Passes of the Alps:*

> There is a savage character to the scene. It is barren, deep, and extensive on the one side, and there is a dark forest on the other; the road is terraced over a gulf of frightful depth; and on the opposite bank, overhanging the ravine, the fort rises in a formidable succession of ramparts, which command the passage: some defensive works are also constructed on the road-side; A little beyond, the fort communicates with the highroad by a bridge thrown across the gulf, at an alarming height above the torrent.[108]

There are three color studies of this fort (the other two are in the Metropolitan Museum of Art and Tate, London). Each shows a slightly different view. Here the viewpoint is from the west of the valley and shows the stepped fort to the right and mountains and a waterfall to the left. It was painted as Turner was descending the valley, looking back at the fort with Mont Cenis in the distance, painted in blue. The picture was previously known simply as *Swiss Mountains.* Its location was identified in 2000 by David Hill.

Gwendoline Davies purchased this work from the French Gallery, London, in 1913, along with other works by Matthijs Maris and Daumier and a book on Corot. The sisters purchased works by Turner intermittently between 1908 and the mid-1920s.

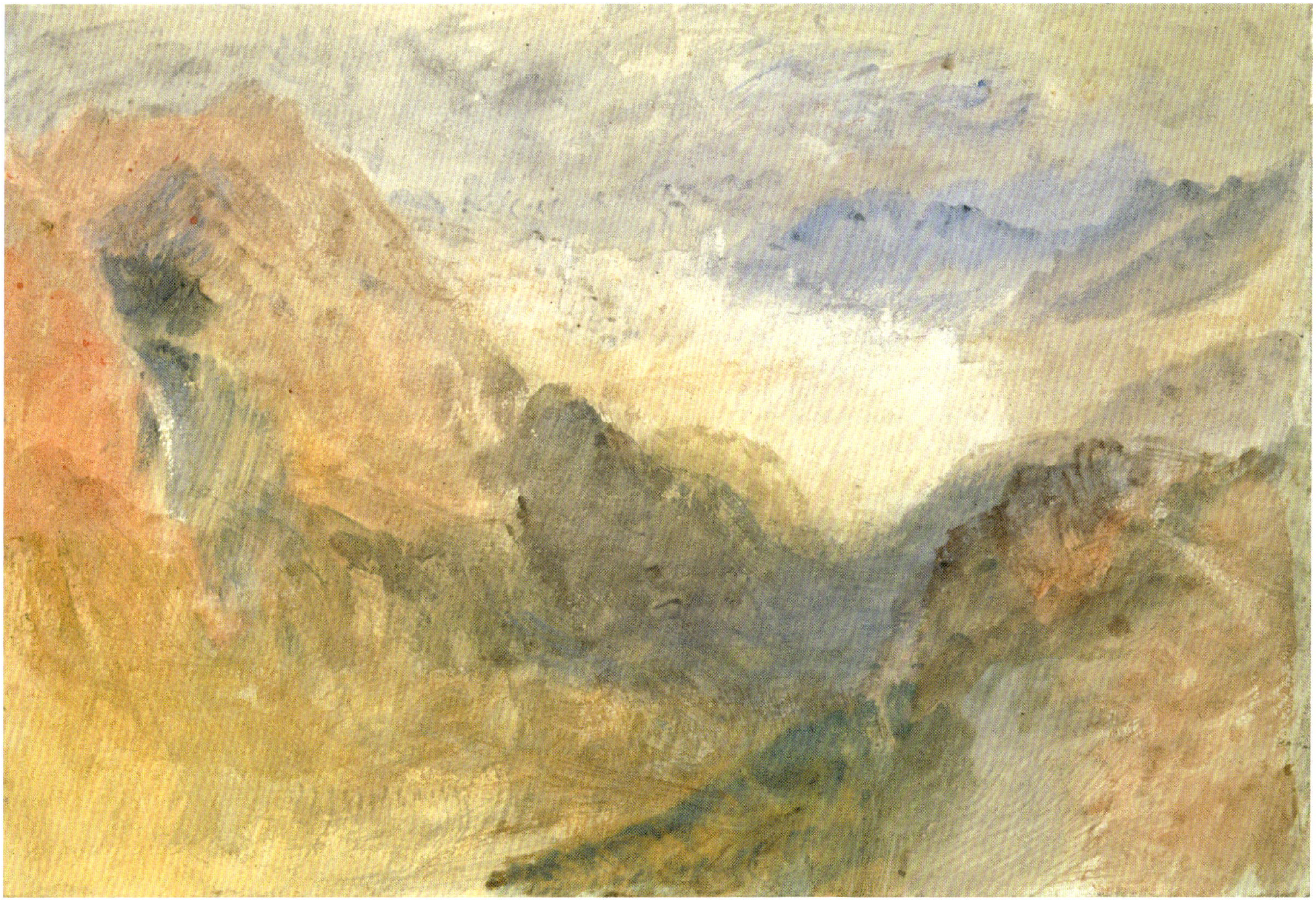

Turner Turner's watercolor-like treatment of oil paint is evident here in the fading suggestion of a harbor wall to the far left of the canvas and in the shadowy form of the central ship.

51 Joseph Mallord William Turner (1775–1851)
Morning after the Wreck, ca. 1840
Oil on canvas, 15 ¼ x 24 ⅜ in. (38.7 x 61.8 cm)
Miss Gwendoline E. Davies Bequest, 1951 (NMWA 436)

Beginning in the 1830s, Turner was a regular visitor to the seaside town of Margate in Kent, on the southern coast of England. While there, he made numerous depictions of the view outside the window of his lodgings, the scene on which this painting is most probably based. As with *The Storm* (cat. no. 54), the provenance of the picture is uncertain and the attribution has subsequently been doubted, though it is now accepted as genuine. It is possible that it went from Sophia Booth to Christie's, where it was sold as *Off Margate, a Hazy Morning*, which may have then led to the current titling. However, recent scholarship suggests that the light source to the west shows that this work is in fact an evening scene.[109]

It is highly likely that *Morning after the Wreck* depicts not an actual event but rather "an amalgam of Turner's lifetime's experience of seashore activity."[110] We see a foreshore view of the beach on which indistinct figures huddle together, picking over the debris that litters the sand. Turner's watercolor-like treatment of oil paint is particularly evident here in the fading suggestion of a harbor wall to the far left of the canvas and in the shadowy form of the central ship, which perhaps, like that in *The Fighting Temeraire*, signals the end of an era. The suggestion that this scene is in fact that of a sunset and an ending, rather than the traditionally assumed sunrise, does indeed fit more coherently with this inference.

While this painting chimes visually with other views of Margate, James Hamilton suggests that the location cannot be attributed exactly, observing that "there is a hint of the form of a harbour in *Morning after the Wreck*, in which a ghostly ship passes in full sail, haunting the foreshore as people pick over tangled wreckage. Though undoubtedly inspired by something Turner had seen from the Kent coast, we are nowhere in particular, just at the end of an era."[111] Ian Warrell has noted that although the size of canvas Turner used for this work was convenient for plein-air sketching, the image itself is more of an "evocative meditation," most likely developed in Turner's lodgings or in the studio.[112] *Morning after the Wreck* was purchased by Gwendoline Davies from the Dowdeswell Gallery, London, in November 1910.

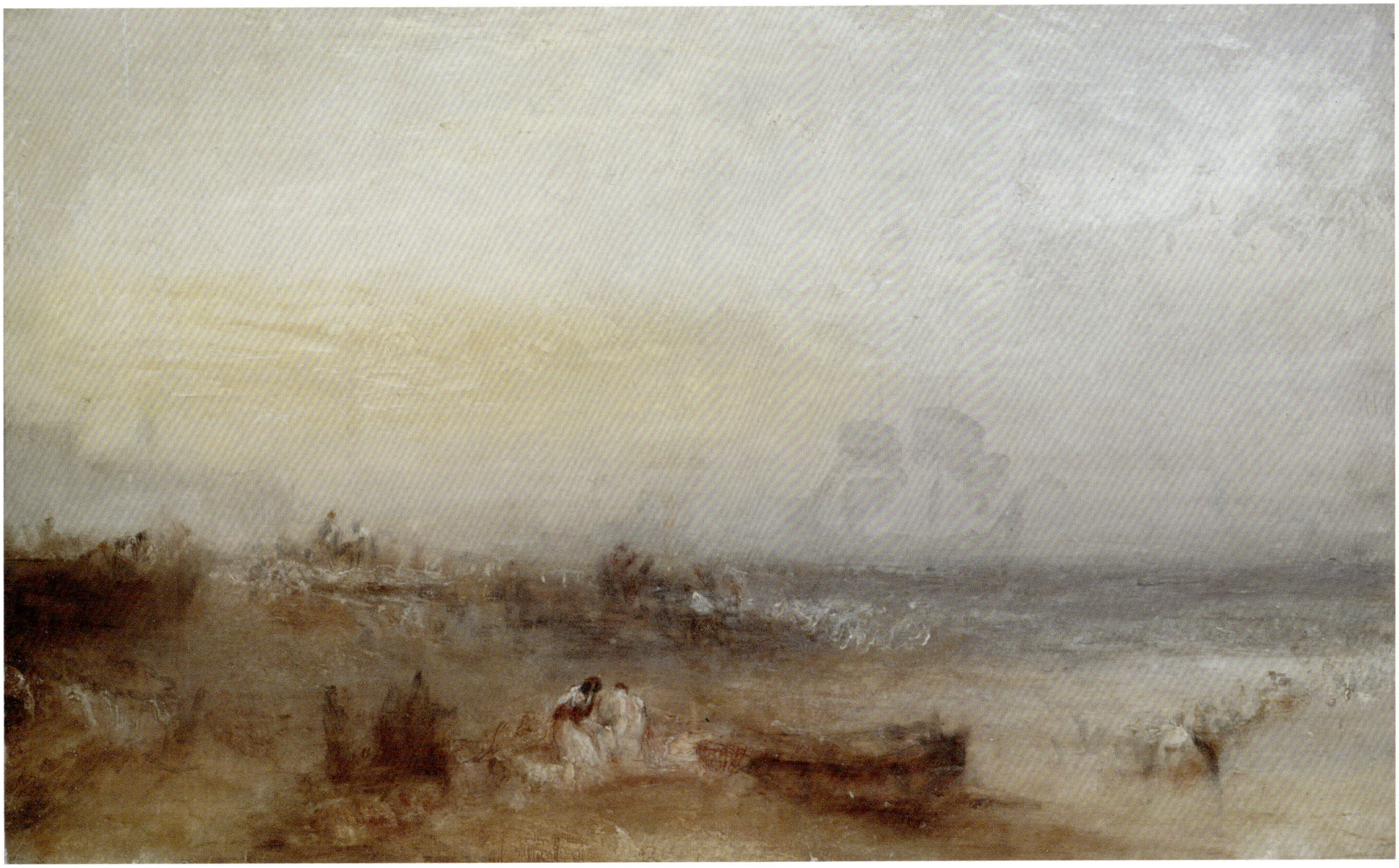

Turner The pencil work is vibrant and swiftly achieved, probably drawn from a boat on the river just north of Gondorf, with watercolor added later.

52 Joseph Mallord William Turner (1775–1851)
The Leyen Burg at Gondorf (recto and verso), 1840s
Watercolor over pencil on wove paper, 6 ⅝ x 9 ⅛ in. (15.7 x 23.3 cm)
Miss Gwendoline E. Davies Bequest, 1951 (NMWA 1740)

Located on the Mosel River in Germany, the Leyen Burg at Gondorf would have been a remarkable sight for a tourist such as Turner traveling on the river. Turner had made a number of pencil sketches of this castle from different angles, both from the river and from land, on earlier tours in 1824 and 1839, and had also made it the subject of a fine drawing in watercolor and gouache.[113]

Here he has applied watercolor over pencil. The pencil work is vibrant and swiftly achieved, probably drawn from a boat on the river just north of Gondorf, with watercolor added later. He merely suggests the main features of the castle and the hills behind and uses watercolor to make sense of his pencil markings. The verso of the paper shows the view from slightly further upstream. The Leyen Burg is now seen on the left, while the center is dominated by the village of Kobern. Beyond it, on the right, the river curves out of sight behind a shadowy blue hill. The subjects of both drawings were identified by Cecilia Powell in 1991. Until then, the scene on the recto was titled *The Mouse Tower*, referring to a stone tower on an island in the Rhine near Bingen.

As interest in the sublime and picturesque grew in Britain, inspired by the writings of the Reverend William Gilpin, so did an appreciation of the Rhineland. Travelers wrote admiringly of winding rivers, towering cliffs, and ruined castles. Turner first saw part of the Rhine in Switzerland in 1802, when he traveled to the Alps during a brief period of peace with France between the revolutionary and Napoleonic wars. It was not until 1815 that lasting peace was restored and Europe became safe for British travelers. Between 1817 and the 1840s, Turner made numerous tours throughout Europe, traveling frequently along the Rhine and visiting the Mosel, one of its most important tributaries, on at least four occasions.

Gwendoline Davies purchased this work sometime between 1908 and 1927. Together, the sisters purchased thirteen watercolors by Turner, eight of which came to the National Museum of Wales. The purchases were spread over a number of years from different sources. Their adviser, Hugh Blaker, wrote in 1910, "I am looking out for good Meissoniers, Israels and Turner watercolours as mentioned by my sister, but can hear of none of any consequence. Perhaps some of the latter may be offered at Christie's this Spring."[114] By this stage, Turner's works were highly sought after; their next recorded purchase was not until 1912.

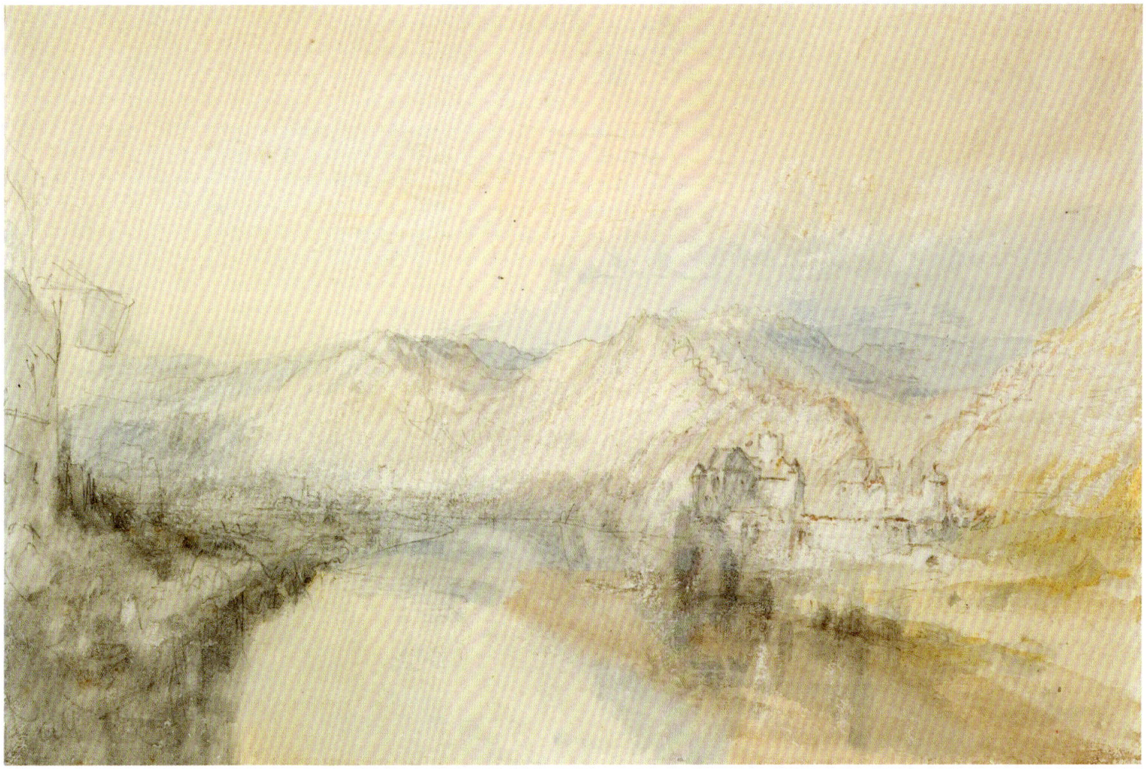

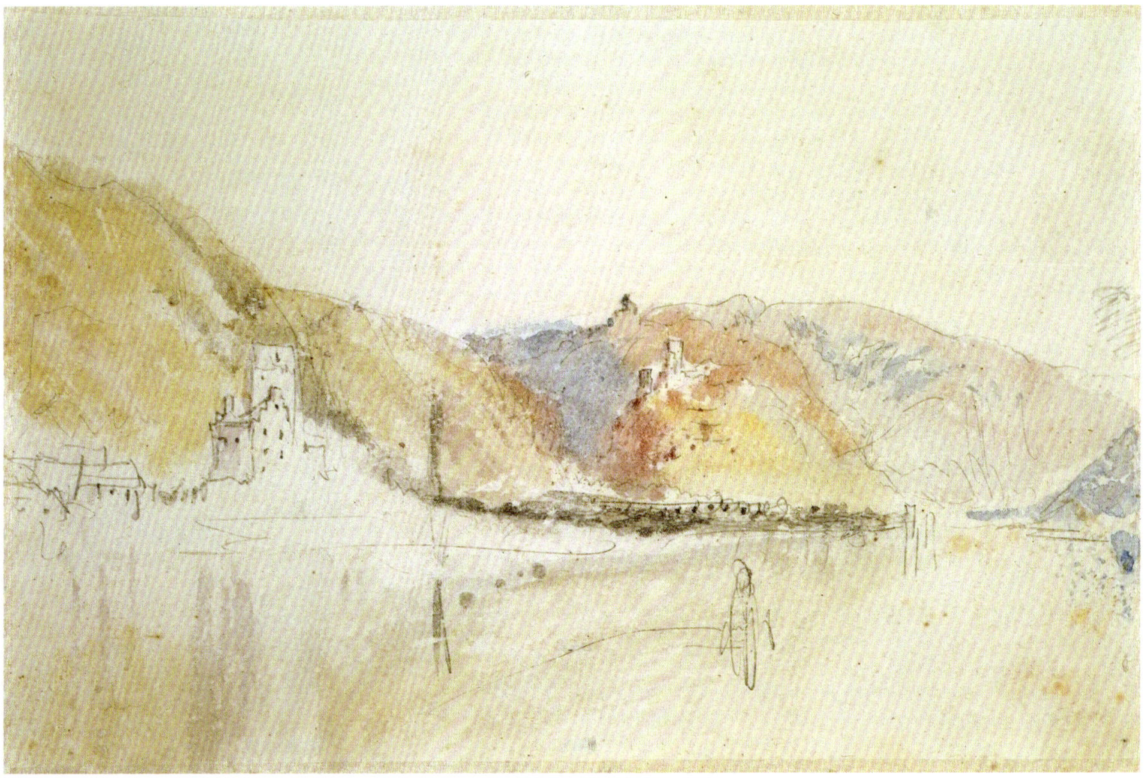

Turner This is one of two extensive studies of the city, which Turner probably worked up at a later date over on-the-spot pencil studies.

53 Joseph Mallord William Turner (1775–1851)
Würzburg, ca. 1840–41
Watercolor with blotting out on wove paper,
9 ⅛ x 11 ⅜ in. (23.1 x 28.8 cm)
Miss Gwendoline E. Davies Bequest, 1951 (NMWA 1753)

Returning home from Venice in 1840, Turner took a route through Austria and southern Germany, and he depicted Würzburg, a historic central German city on the Main River, on more than forty pages of a small sketchbook.[115] A Würzburg newspaper reporting the arrival of Turner, who was by then a well-known and established artist, recorded that he was staying in the Wittelsbacher Hof hotel in the town's marketplace.[116]

This is one of two extensive studies of the city, which Turner probably worked up at a later date over on-the-spot pencil studies. The city is shown from the south with its most prominent landmark, the Marienberg Fortress, dominating the work. The rooftops of the city are in the middle distance. The river, which runs below the fortress, is only just suggested, as is Würzburg's famous eighteenth-century stone bridge.

In 1919, David Croal Thomson, a London art dealer, wrote to Gwendoline Davies about two Turner watercolors he had available for purchase, *The Rainbow* and this work: "This morning I have been very happy to find one of the great drawings by Turner ... This splendid drawing is of the date 1841; the very highest point that Turner reached being expressed in or about that period. But the question of money value is very serious, and the *very lowest* price I can sell this for is Fifteen Hundred and Twenty Pounds."[117] Gwendoline purchased this and *The Rainbow* (cat. no. 49) at the prices Croal Thomson asked. He had acquired both works from the sale of the collector John Edward Taylor, who owned a number of important Turners.[118]

In total, the sisters purchased thirteen watercolors by Turner. Gwendoline bequeathed eight to the National Museum of Wales in 1952. Margaret sold five Turner watercolors at Sotheby's in 1960.[119] These were sold as part of a larger group of works, probably to raise money to spend on modern British paintings, which Margaret was collecting at the time. It is the only known instance of either sister selling works from their collection.

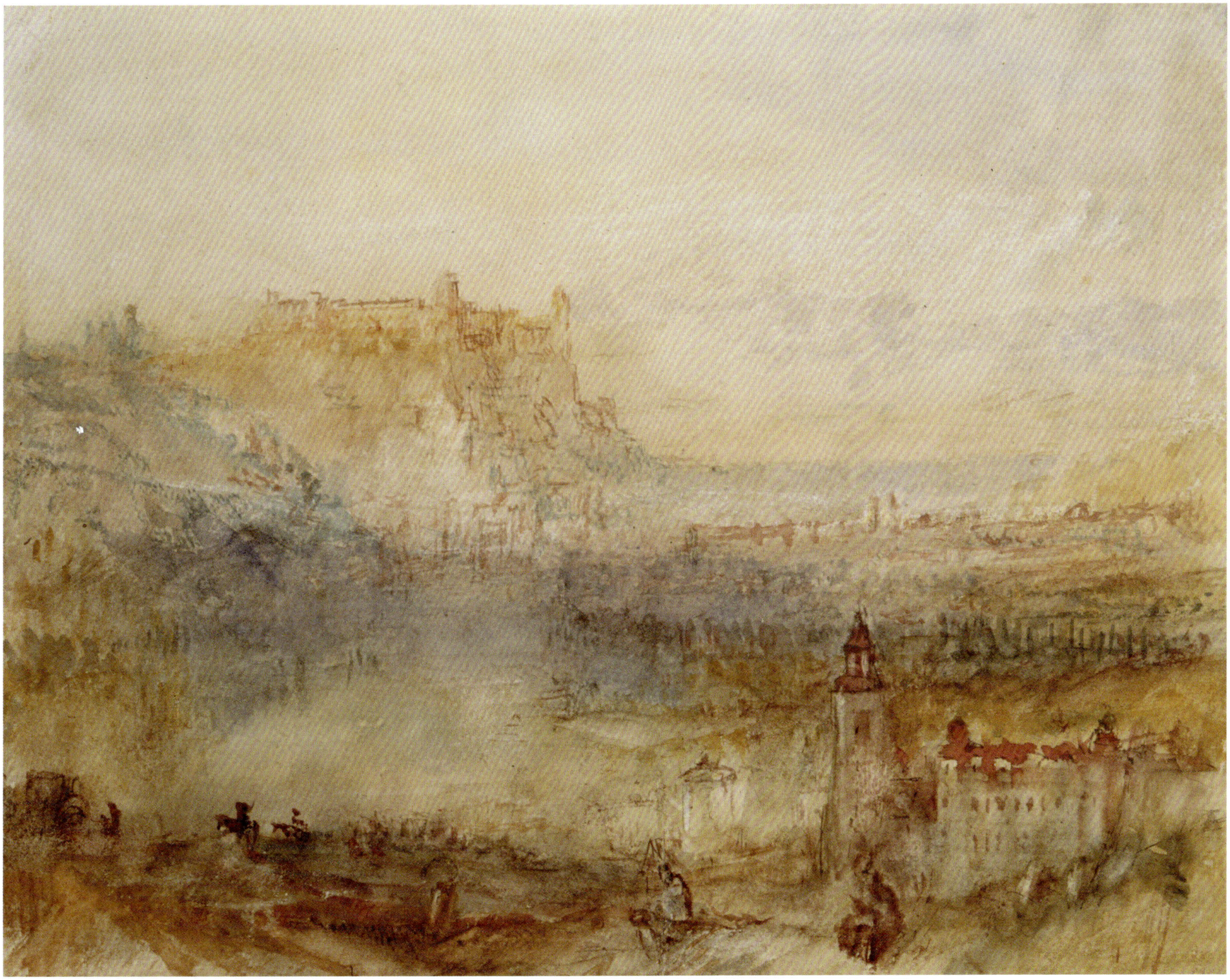

Turner The overwhelming sensation is of a combination of spray, mist, and wind through which only colors and vague forms are visible.

54 Joseph Mallord William Turner (1775–1851)
The Storm, ca. 1840–45
Oil on canvas, 12 ¾ x 21 ⅛ in. (32.5 x 53.8 cm)
Miss Margaret S. Davies Bequest, 1963 (NMWA 509)

The sea as subject matter spanned Turner's entire career, and in his later marine scenes, he produced some highly dramatic images that are the embodiment of the sublime. The present work depicts a storm-tossed sea, with the wreck of a boat in the foreground being engulfed by waves, its ropes flailing like tentacles. The sails, which have come adrift, can be seen to the left, while the masts and bow of a larger vessel are silhouetted against the skyline. A group of figures huddle together at the back of the stricken vessel, or possibly in a separate boat. The overwhelming sensation is of a combination of spray, mist, and wind through which only colors and vague forms are visible. The light source that emanates from the upper right of the canvas renders the sea in the lower left a deep, dark, terrifying green.

Turner depicted a number of anonymous storms, but the label on the back of the work reads, "Said to have been painted by Turner during the Storm which raged on the day in which the Princess Royal was born, Nov 21 1840." It is obviously impossible to attach any credence to this statement, though it has been observed that it would have been the sort of theme that would appeal to Turner, who may have heard of it from contemporary accounts.[120] A companion piece to *The Storm*, *The Day after the Storm* (not to be confused with *The Morning after the Wreck*, cat. no. 51), was purchased at the same time and shows figures trawling through debris on the beach, possibly at Margate. Full provenance for the work is difficult to establish, but a further label on the back states that this work was given by the artist to Mrs. Pounds [*sic*], who was Turner's landlady and mistress, Sophia Booth. The attribution of both *The Storm* and *The Day after the Storm* to Turner has been disputed by a number of sources. Martin Butlin and Evelyn Joll are divided on the point, with Joll accepting the attribution as genuine.[121] From an observation of certain areas of the handling, Joll suggests that the painting might have been reworked later in Turner's career.[122]

The Storm was purchased by Margaret Davies, while *The Day after the Storm* was bought by Gwendoline from the Chenil Gallery, London, in November 1908. They were the first oil paintings by Turner in the sisters' collection, two of twenty-one of the artist's works they acquired.

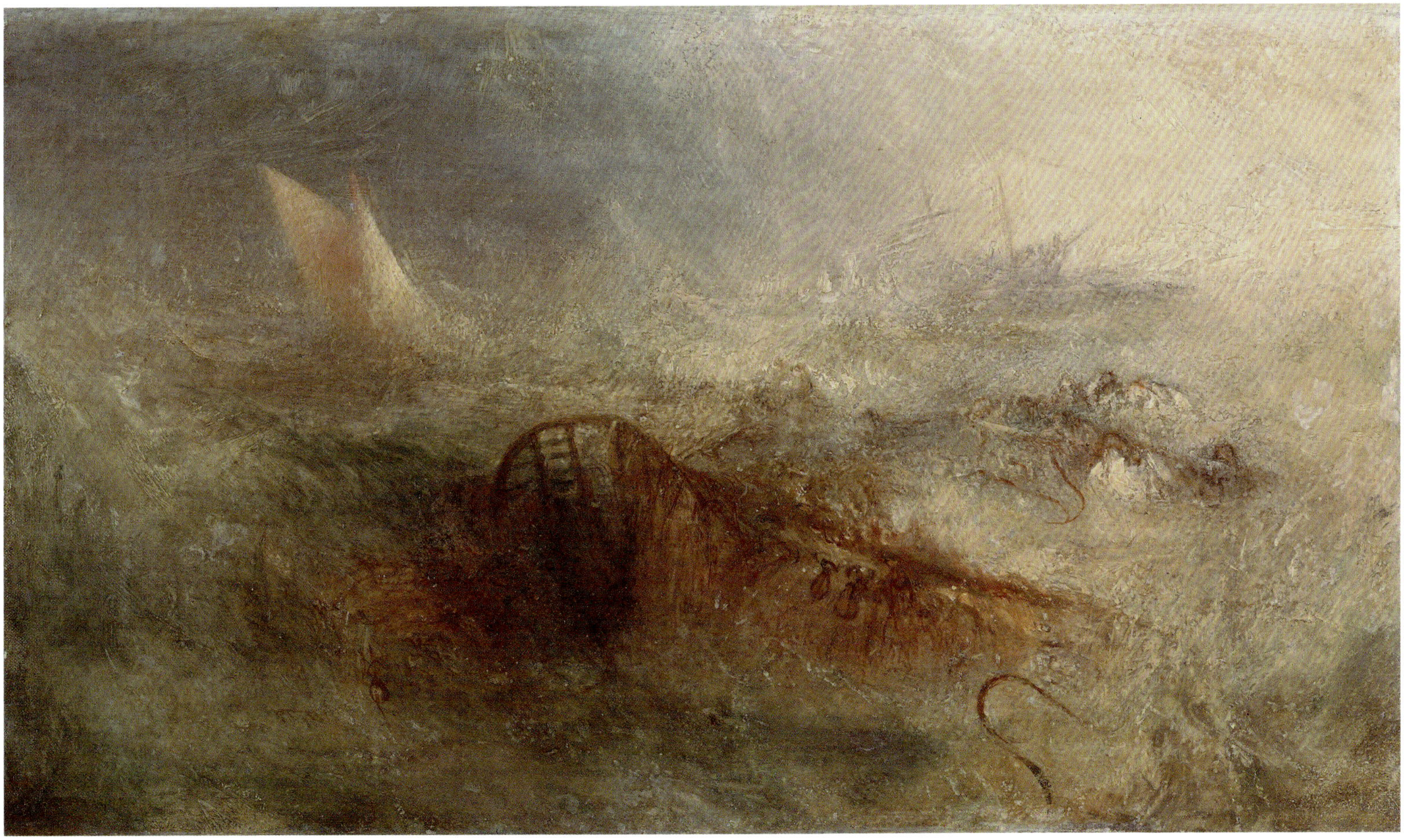

van Gogh The influence of Japanese prints can be seen in the division of the picture plane into blocks of color, demarcating the fields, village, and sky.

55 Vincent van Gogh (1853–1890)
Rain–Auvers, 1890
Oil on canvas, 19 ¾ x 39 ½ in. (50.2 x 100.3 cm)
Miss Gwendoline E. Davies Bequest, 1951 (NMWA 2463)

In May 1890, van Gogh moved north from the Saint-Rémy asylum in Provence to the town of Auvers-sur-Oise, north of Paris, where he lodged at the Café Ravoux. During the month of July, he painted thirteen double-square canvases of the countryside around Auvers. Letters to his brother Theo record him painting "vast fields of wheat beneath troubled skies,"[123] in which he had "not hesitated to express sadness, extreme solitude."[124]

Rain–Auvers dates from this period and is a particularly bleak scene. It has been suggested that the atmosphere recalls one of van Gogh's favorite poems, "The Rainy Day," by Henry Wadsworth Longfellow,[125] which begins, "My life is cold, and dark, and dreary/It rains and the wind is never weary," and ends:

Be still, sad heart! and cease repining;
Behind the clouds is the sun still shining;
Thy fate is the common fate of all,
Into each life some rain must fall,
Some days must be dark and dreary.

While the Longfellow poem is indeed gloomy, the final stanza is tinged with a certain optimism – something van Gogh himself was not. Fearing that he was a burden to his brother Theo, he shot himself on July 27, just weeks after completing this painting.

The work demonstrates van Gogh's interest in Japanese print techniques, which he had first encountered in Antwerp in 1885. Following his move to Paris in 1886, he began to collect Ukiyo-e prints and in 1887 made a copy of Hiroshige's *Ohashi Bridge in the Rain*, gaining some insight into how to describe the sensation of rain through the medium of paint. This was first incorporated into his oil painting in *Rain* (Philadelphia Museum of Art), which was made between November 1889 and early 1890, showing the landscape of Saint-Rémy.[126] In the present work, which is painted on a double canvas, van Gogh illustrates the driving, windblown rain through bold downward strokes that cut through the surface impasto. The influence of Japanese prints can be seen in the division of the picture plane into blocks of color, demarcating the fields, village, and sky. The distinctive row of poplars seen in the center of the canvas, surrounding the town, no longer exists.[127]

Purchased by Gwendoline Davies from Bernheim-Jeune for £2,020, *Rain–Auvers* had previously been exhibited in *Manet and the Post-Impressionists* at the Grafton Galleries, London, in December 1910. This landmark exhibition organized by the critic Roger Fry is frequently cited as a catalyst for modernism in Britain. Although this is the only example by van Gogh in the sisters' collection, it is highly significant as one of the first to enter a British collection.

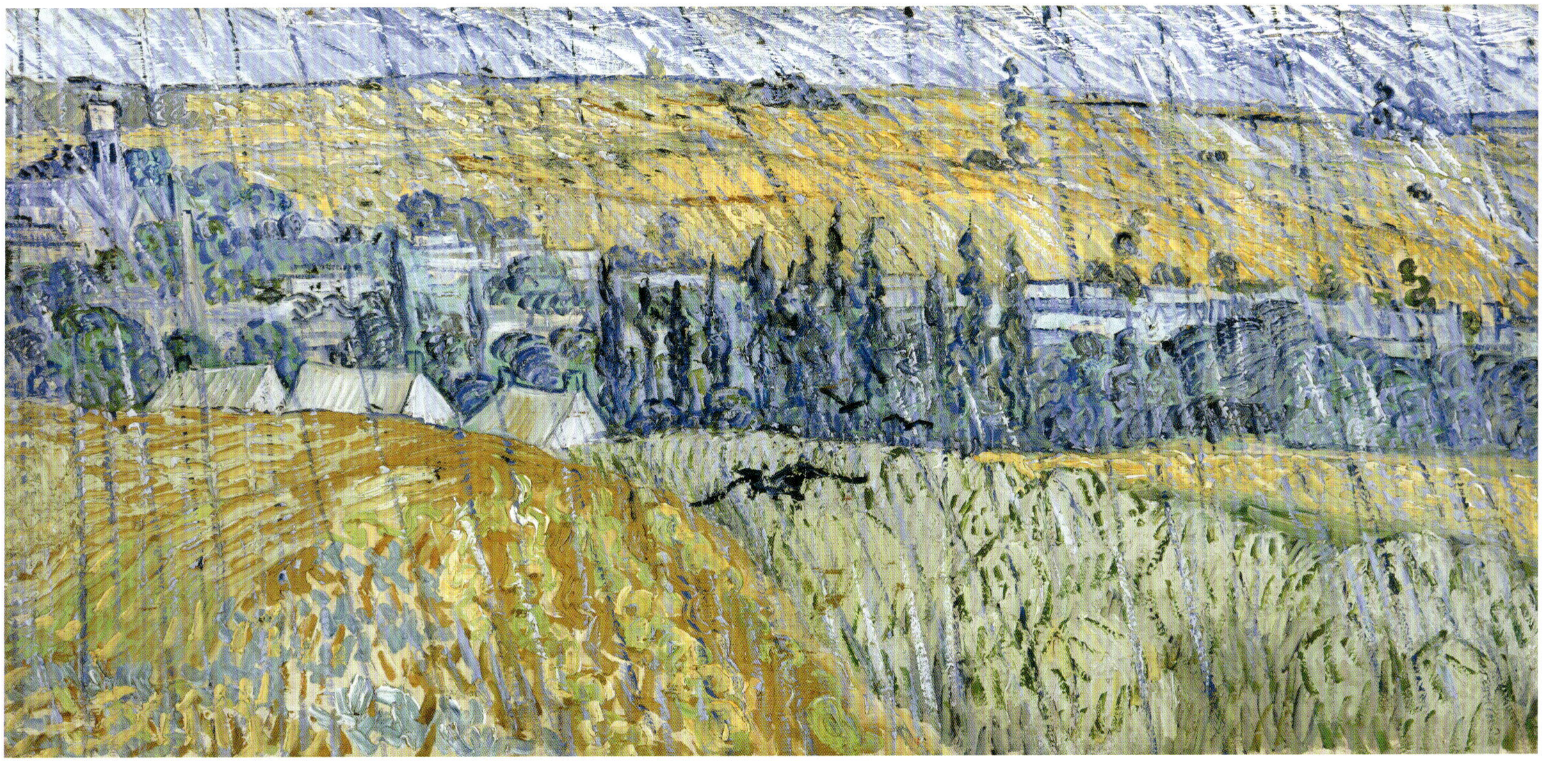

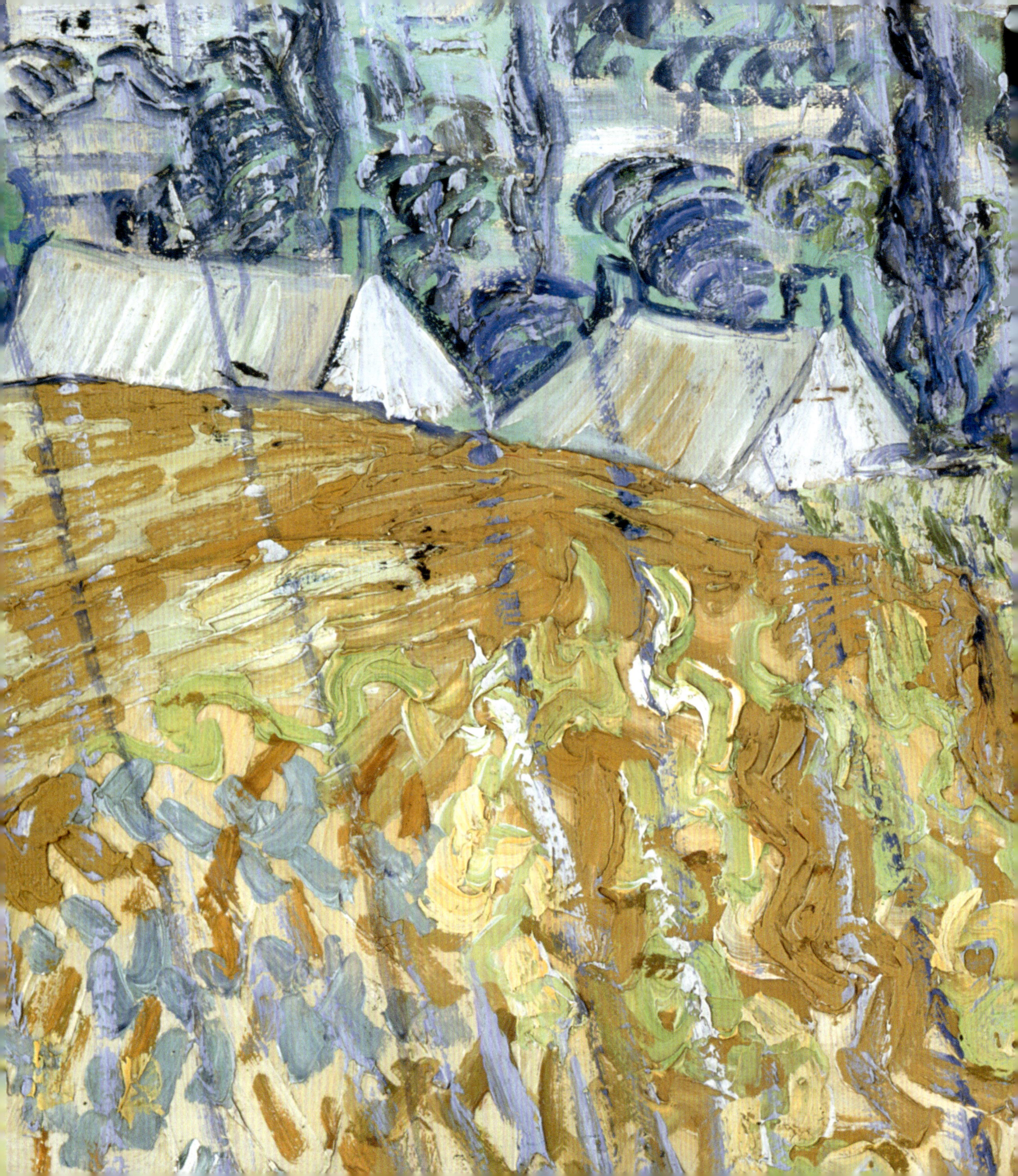

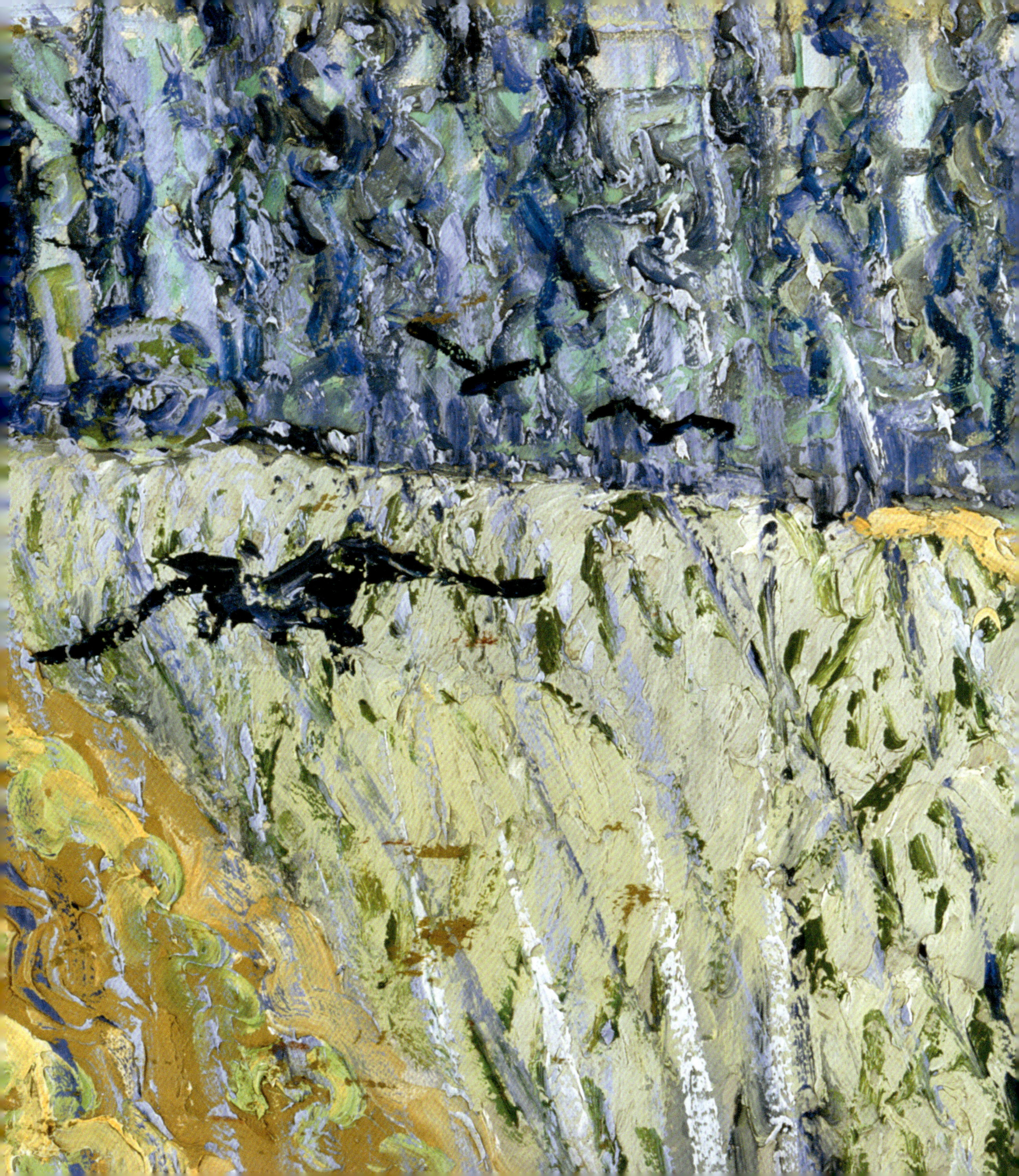

Vlaminck While *Village Street* is heavily influenced by the techniques of Cézanne, it also displays an awareness of the language of Cubism.

56 Maurice de Vlaminck (1876–1958)
Village Street, 1911–12
Oil on canvas, 22 ⅞ x 28 ⅞ in. (58.2 x 73.2 cm)
Miss Gwendoline E. Davies Bequest, 1951 (NMWA 2402)

A self-taught artist, Vlaminck was for a time a leading Fauve, yet like those of many of his contemporaries, his was a short-lived period of activity; beginning in 1907, he adopted a more subdued palette. This change of focus coincided with Vlaminck's first encounter with the work of Cézanne, at a retrospective at the Salon d'Automne the year after his death in 1906. Cézanne's painting had a profound effect on Vlaminck, leading him to develop a visual style heavily influenced by the technique of the older artist but also displaying, as in the present work, an awareness of the language of Cubism.

The location of *Village Street* is not known, but this particular type of visual construction was one clearly favored by Vlaminck. There are numerous other examples of a sharply recessing street, the road forming a base triangle whose apex tapers somewhere toward the center of the canvas, with houses crowding in on either side, giving the appearance of a high vantage point. In the present painting, the symmetry of the two houses directly at the end of the road, capped with the inverted triangle of a distant roof, demonstrates that Vlaminck had learned from Cézanne how to combine formal concerns with the existing landscape. Vlaminck also uses the classical framing device of trees to the foreground left of the painting, a tool much favored by Cézanne.

Village Street was purchased, along with *The Bridge* (cat. no. 57), by Gwendoline Davies from an exhibition organized by Léopold Zborowski, the dealer and poet. A year later, Margaret procured a portrait by André Derain of Zborowski's wife (see cat. no. 21). It was Hugh Blaker who advised Gwendoline to buy these two paintings by Vlaminck and secured them on her behalf. A certain reticence on the part of Gwendoline can be gleaned from Blaker's letters, and this was probably a case where she let professional advice override any personal preference. He wrote to convince her of their artistic merit and immediate collectability, saying, "I am sure you will get to like their strength and vigour."[128] Gwendoline had already purchased two works by Cézanne in 1918 (cat. nos. 7 and 8), and it is probable that Blaker saw the Vlamincks as a way of augmenting the purchase. Any reservations were clearly overcome a year later in 1920, when Margaret added to the group by purchasing six additional landscapes by Vlaminck. Margaret sold five of these in 1960 to facilitate acquisitions by different artists, and one, *Trees*, was given away shortly before her death in 1963, though it was reacquired for the National Museum of Wales in 1992. By selling off what she felt were duplicates, Margaret was freeing funds to include unrepresented artists in her collection, in this case, to buy Pierre Bonnard's *Sunlight at Vernon* (cat. no. 3).

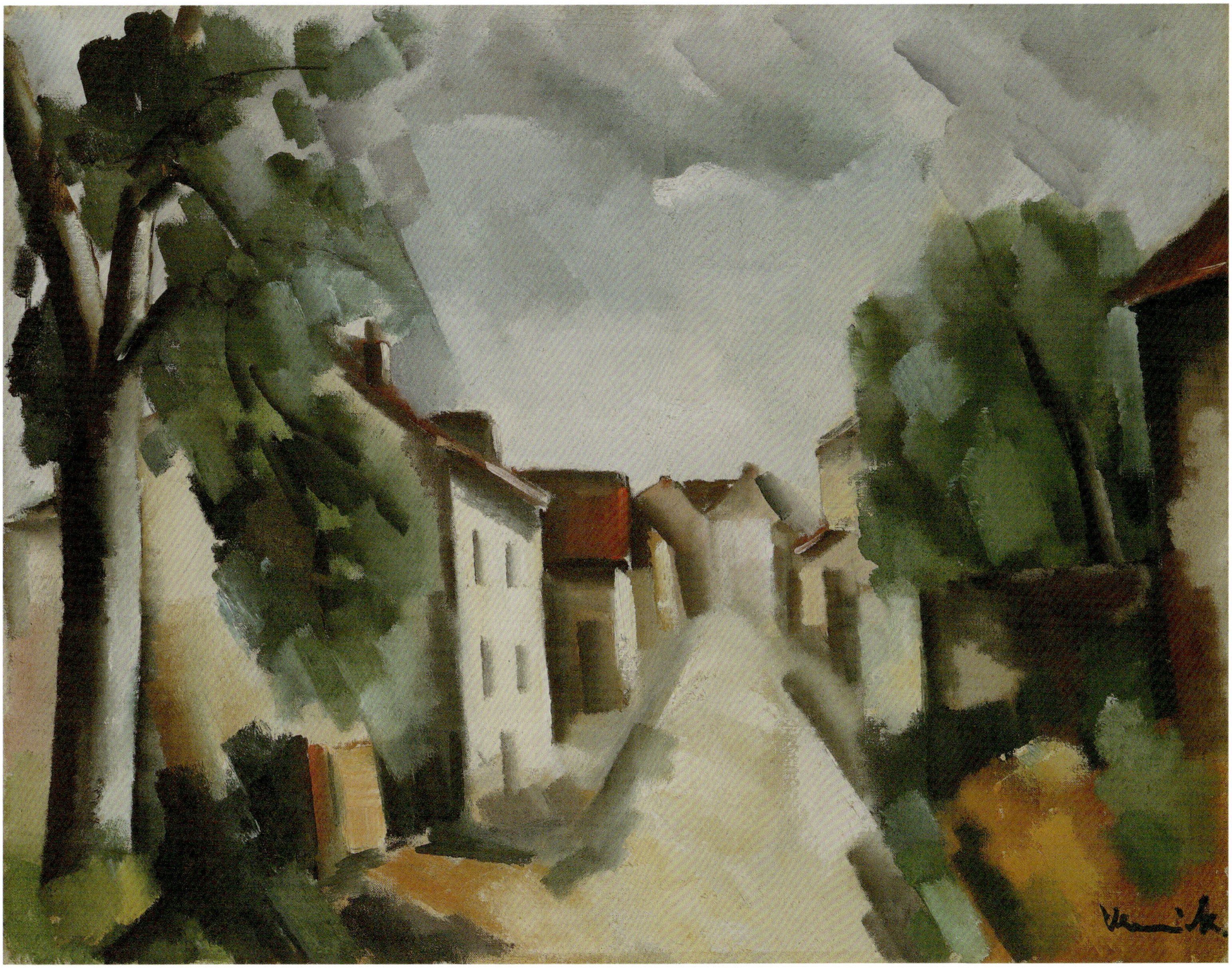

Vlaminck In *The Bridge*, Vlaminck uses a Cézanne painting as a model for exploring a personal motif – the railway bridge at Chatou, which appears in many of his canvases.

57 Maurice de Vlaminck (1876–1958)
The Bridge, 1912–13
Oil on canvas, 23 ½ x 28 ¾ in. (59.7 x 73 cm)
Miss Margaret S. Davies Bequest, 1963 (NMWA 2158)

Like *Village Street* (cat. no. 56), *The Bridge* demonstrates Vlaminck's debt to Cézanne, yet here his influence is more direct as this picture is almost certainly based on Cézanne's *Bridge over the Marne at Créteil* (Pushkin Museum, Moscow). Vlaminck has adopted the structure and compositional techniques of the Cézanne – the framing device of trees to the left mirrored by background detail to the right. In addition to the strong use of verticals, most striking is the way in which the picture plane is bisected by the bridge both vertically and horizontally in the two works, suggesting one definitely served as a template for the other.

Vlaminck's work is not, however, an image of the bridge at Créteil. In this painting, he uses the existing model of the Cézanne canvas to explore a personal motif. The bridge is identifiable as the Chatou railway bridge, which crosses the Seine on the outskirts of Paris. Vlaminck lived and worked in Chatou, and the bridge, which appears as a repeated motif in many of his canvases, is, in a way, his own version of Cézanne's *Mont Sainte-Victoire*. The buildings directly to the right of the bridge are featured in other depictions of this scene. Vlaminck was not the only artist to incorporate the bridge into his canvases. As the means to explore outlying areas of the city, this iron and concrete construction was for the Impressionists a demonstrable symbol of modernity. Renoir painted it in *The Railway Bridge at Chatou* (Musée d'Orsay, Paris), and it also appears in his *Luncheon of the Boating Party* (The Phillips Collection, Washington, D.C.), just visible through the trees at the back of the image.

Vlaminck uses Cézanne's device of mixing sharp verticals with diagonal strokes and curves, yet the blocked, smooth brushstrokes are more directly suggestive of Cubism than Cézanne's own broken brushwork. The dark color scheme is typical of Vlaminck's work of this period (referred to as his blue period) and also reflects Cézanne's frequent use of greens, blues, and terracotta. Of particular note is the way in which Vlaminck has omitted the cabling poles that flank the side of the bridge – these are visible in numerous other depictions he made and in contemporary photographs of the structure. It is possible that this omission is a direct homage to Cézanne, who regularly removed object detail to preserve the formal integrity of his compositions.

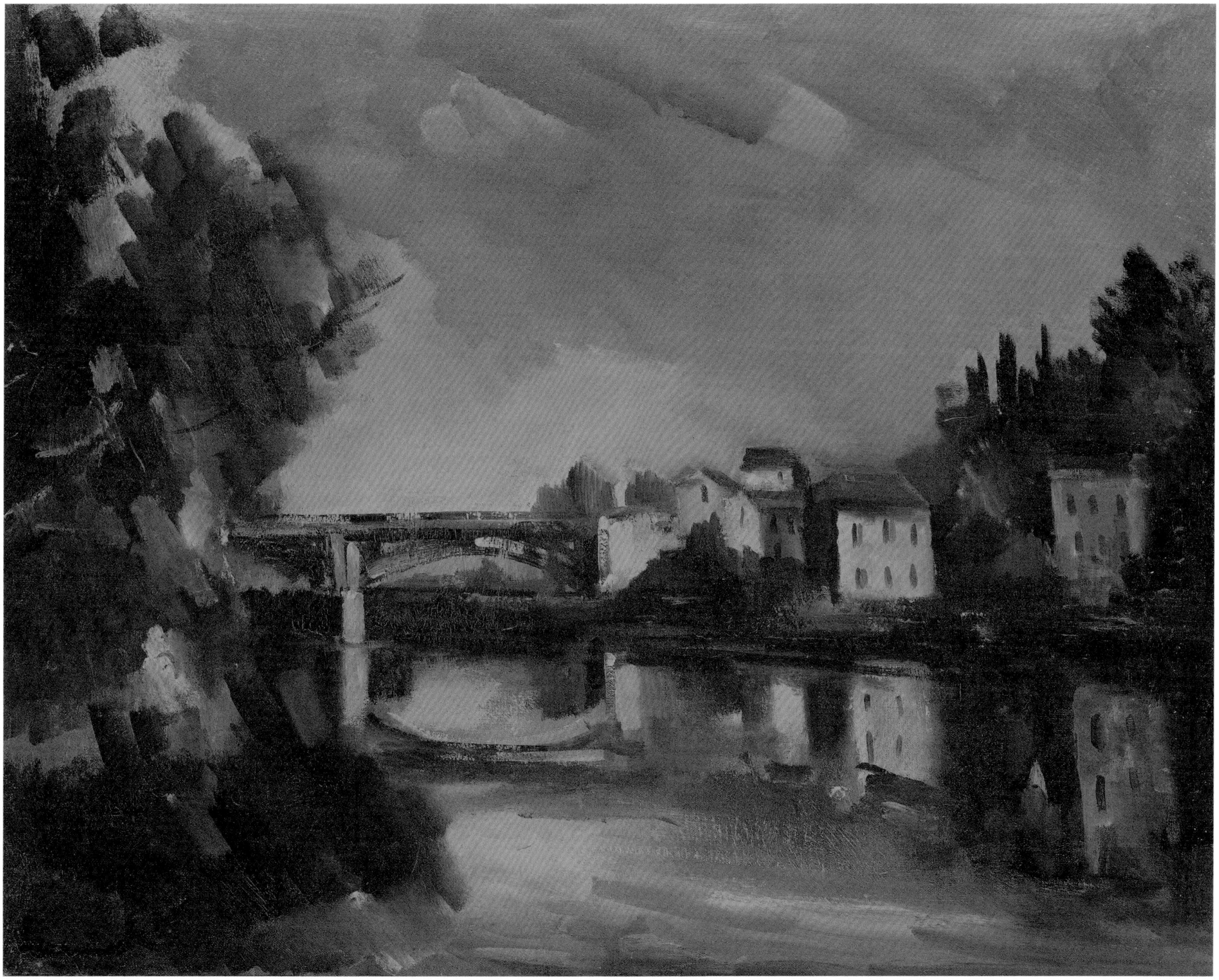

Whistler Whistler's brushwork is smooth and glassy, and the flecks of white to the left of the image show the newly installed gas light in the city, a truly modern subject.

58 James Abbott McNeill Whistler (1834–1903)
Nocturne: Blue and Gold, St. Mark's Venice, 1880
Oil on canvas, 17 ½ x 23 ½ in. (44.5 x 59.7 cm)
Miss Gwendoline E. Davies Bequest, 1951 (NMWA 210)

Whistler first visited Venice in 1879, following his infamous libel suit against the art critic John Ruskin, who had accused him of "flinging a pot of paint in the public's face," a comment on Whistler's *Nocturne in Black and Gold: The Falling Rocket*, which was exhibited at the Grosvenor Gallery in 1878. Although Whistler won his action, the symbolic yet derisory award of a farthing in damages with no costs rendered him bankrupt. This abrupt change in fortunes obliged him to accept a commission from the Fine Art Society to make a series of etchings of Venice. Although he meant to stay only a matter of months, Whistler was thoroughly seduced and remained in the city for a year.

Whistler produced many pastels and etchings of Venice and was one of the first artists to depict it as a living, working, contemporary city. This, however, is one of only three known existing oils he made there. Painted from the vantage point of the Café Florian under the arcades of the Procuratie Nuove on the south side of St. Mark's Square, the huge basilica, described by Mark Twain as like a "vast, warty bug taking a meditative walk,"[129] looms over the piazza. Only the essentials of the Byzantine architecture are represented, silhouetted against the deep blue of the night sky. Florian's was a popular meeting place for artists and a favorite haunt of the writer Henry James, who made an extended stay in Venice in 1881, the year after Whistler was there. In his novella *The Aspern Papers*, the narrator's description of St. Mark's by night chimes with Whistler's visuals: "The great basilica, with its low domes and bristling embroideries, the mystery of its mosaic and sculpture, looked ghostly in the tempered gloom ..."[130]

Whistler's brushwork is smooth and glassy, and the flecks of white to the left of the image show the newly installed gas light in the city, a truly modern subject. The light reveals, just to the left of the facade, the scaffolding that had been erected to carry out the restoration that so incensed Ruskin. The artist Otto Bacher described Whistler's nocturnal activity thus: "Night after night he watched ... without making a stroke ... Then he would return to his rooms and paint the scene ... going again and again to refresh some particular impression."[131] *Nocturne: Blue and Gold, St. Mark's Venice* was exhibited at the Society of British Artists in 1886–87, and Whistler declared it perhaps the best of his nocturnes.[132]

Bought by Gwendoline in 1912, this was the first of the paintings of Venice acquired by the Davies sisters. Margaret's diary gives some hint as to why this particular scene would have caught their eye. Describing nocturnal Venice on the evening before their departure from the city in 1909, she writes: "It is a lovely starlight night, many like ourselves take advantage of it to wander up and down in their gondolas. We pass by the Piazza, giving a last look at St. Mark's, the little lamps, on the facade which faces us, before the mosaic of the Madonna, are burning brightly, as they do each night."[133]

Notes

FAIRCLOUGH

In addition to the sources below, this essay draws heavily on insights into the sisters and their collection by my former colleagues Mark Evans and Ann Sumner. I am deeply grateful to them, and to Lord and Lady Davies, who generously allowed me access to papers and photographs.

1 Margaret Davies made her first purchase, a watercolor of an Algerian by Hercules Brabazon Brabazon, from the Goupil Gallery, London, on 1 December 1906. Both sisters bought regularly from 1908 to 1927. Gwendoline Davies's last purchase was made in 1926, but Margaret began buying again in 1934, mostly acquiring modern British art. She was to continue until 1962, the year before she died at the age of seventy-nine. For a chronology of the collection, see Mark Evans, "The Davies Sisters of Llandinam and Impressionism for Wales, 1908–1923," *Journal of the History of Collections*, 16, no. 2 (2004), pp. 219–53. Many receipts and some correspondence with agents, vendors, and others are in the archives of the Art Department, Amgueddfa Cymru–National Museum Wales.

2 See National Museum of Wales, Cardiff, *Catalogue of the Gwendoline E. Davies Bequest* (Cardiff: National Museum of Wales, 1953); and National Museum of Wales, Cardiff, *Catalogue of the Margaret S. Davies Bequest* (Cardiff: National Museum of Wales, 1963).

3 See John Ingamells, *The Davies Collection of French Art* (Cardiff: National Museum of Wales, 1967); Peter Hughes, *French Art from the Davies Bequest* (Cardiff: National Museum of Wales, 1982); Mark Evans and Oliver Fairclough, *A Companion Guide to the National Art Gallery* (Cardiff: National Museums & Galleries of Wales, 1993); Charlotte Gere and Marina Vaizey, *Great Women Collectors* (London: Philip Wilson, 1999), pp. 141–45; Bethany McIntyre, *Sisters Select: Works on Paper from the Davies Collection* (Cardiff: National Museum of Wales, 2000); Mark Evans, "The Davies Sisters of Llandinam and Impressionism for Wales 1908–1923"; and Ann Sumner, *Colour and Light: Fifty Impressionist and Post-Impressionist Works at the National Museum of Wales* (Cardiff: National Museum of Wales, 2005).

4 For the response to Impressionism from British public galleries, see Christopher Lloyd, "Britain and the Impressionists," in Ann Dumas and Michael E. Schapiro, eds., *Impressionism: Paintings Collected by European Museums*, exhib. cat. (High Museum of Art, Seattle Art Museum, and Denver Art Museum, 1999), pp. 65–76. In 1918, the Keeper of Art at the National Museum of Wales declined a major work by W.R. Sickert, describing it as "an example of the extreme impressionist school … this particular class of work is quite unsuitable for an important public collection as it only seems to excite the imagination of a very small number of people who mistake their unhappy affliction for genuine artistic perception."

5 For the characters and personal histories of the sisters, see Eirene White, *The Ladies of Gregynog* (Cardiff: University of Wales Press, 1985); Eric Rowan and Carolyn Stewart, *An Elusive Tradition: Art and Society in Wales 1870–1950* (Cardiff: University of Wales Press, 2002), pp. 125–53; and Oliver Fairclough, ed., *"Things of Beauty": What Two Sisters Did for Wales* (Cardiff: National Museum of Wales, 2007).

6 By 1914, they had traveled in France, Italy, Germany, Switzerland, Austria, Greece, and Egypt. After World War I, they continued to be adventurous travelers—Margaret's journal recording a visit to Palestine in 1924 survives, as does an itinerary for a tour that took them to Damascus, Baghdad, Petra, and the Holy Land again.

7 See Prys Morgan, "Introduction: The World of the Davies Family," in Fairclough, ed., *"Things of Beauty,"* pp. 16–22.

8 In Britain in 1913, a doctor could expect to earn around £400 a year, a male clerk about £100, and a female shorthand typist between £40 and £80. The £ sterling was then worth almost $5 US.

9 Beginning as a bridge builder and railway contractor, in the 1860s Davies became a pioneer of the south Wales coal industry and developed deep mines in the Rhondda, which became that industry's heartland. His company, the Ocean Coal Company Ltd., formed in 1887, was producing nearly two million tons of high-quality steam coal by 1890. It was then the largest company in the south Wales coalfield and was making gross profits of more than £470,000 a year. See David

Jenkins, "Whatsoever Thy Hand Findeth to Do: The 'Top Sawyer's' Legacy," in Fairclough, ed., "*Things of Beauty*," pp. 25–39. For David Davies, see also Ivor Thomas, *Top Sawyer: A Biography of David Davies of Llandinam* (London: Longmans, 1935); and Herbert Williams, *Davies the Ocean: Railway King and Coal Tycoon* (Cardiff: University of Wales Press, 1991). His nickname, "Top Sawyer," derives from his boast that as a skilled sawyer he always used a two-man saw on top of a log rather than in the sawpit beneath, getting covered in sawdust.

10 His wife, Margaret, shared a similar background. She was the sister of Evan Jones, who became an inspirational Calvinistic Methodist minister after being evicted from his Montgomeryshire farm for daring to vote against the wishes of his Conservative landlord.

11 As marriage to a deceased wife's sister was then illegal in Britain, the wedding took place in Canada, which may have added to the family's sense of isolation from conventional upper-class society. See White, *The Ladies of Gregynog*, p. 13.

12 Remembered by young relatives as a terrifying figure by the 1930s, she is said to have convinced her stepdaughters that any male admirer would be a fortune hunter. Although the sisters rode and played tennis and golf, they could not dance or drink alcohol. Gwendoline seems to have had an unhappy romantic episode in 1908, and World War I may have ended any other chance of marriage.

13 The school was founded in 1863 by Fanny and Annie Metcalfe and became one of the largest girls' schools in the country. *Hampton's Scholastic Directory* of 1902–03 records that "the education and culture of the individual girl is considered, rather than the requirements of high school or examination routine." It was within easy reach of London's West End so that the girls could benefit from regular visits to concerts and exhibitions.

14 The family had a London home, and the earliest of a number of surviving journals in a private collection (this one compiled by Margaret) records a visit at the time of Queen Victoria's Diamond Jubilee in 1897. In this she describes seeing the "old art, china and pictures and statues" at the South Kensington Museum and visiting the New Galleries and the British Museum. She also mentions that "Miss Blaker" is to take her and her sister to the Royal Academy of Arts.

15 For Blaker, see Robert Meyrick, "Hugh Blaker: Doing His Bit for the Moderns," *Journal of the History of Collections*, 16, no. 2 (2004), pp. 173–89. See also Murray Urquhart, "The Blaker Diary," *Apollo* 78 (1963), pp. 293–98; and Ingamells, *The Davies Collection of French Art*, pp. 19–22.

16 For Sir Hugh Lane, see Evans, "The Davies Sisters of Llandinam and Impressionism for Wales, 1908–1923," pp. 219–21. See also Thomas Bodkin, *Hugh Lane and His Pictures* (Dublin: Arts Council, 1956); and Robert O'Byrne, *Hugh Lane, 1875–1915* (Dublin: Lilliput Press, 2000).

17 Ingamells, *The Davies Collection of French Art*, p. 3. There is no trace of Margaret's attendance in the Slade archives, so this may have been brief and informal.

18 Private collection. Turner, for example, was one of the "most imaginative painters" who "wonderfully painted sky and water," and Whistler was "a romantic impressionist who painted night as no other artist painted it." Rodin was praised, and *The Kiss* (Gwendoline was to buy an over life-size bronze cast in 1912) was "the most beautiful of his works." Margaret's passport for the period survives in a private collection. Gwendoline may have been in Dresden as well, but there is no evidence of this, and at this date they often traveled with friends and other family members rather than together.

19 Both sisters' journals for the 1909 trip survive (private collection). They traveled in a small party that included Mr. and Mrs. William Jenkins (he was managing director of the family's Ocean Coal Company) but without either their stepmother or Jane Blaker. After visiting Pisa, they traveled to Florence, where Gwendoline admired Michelangelo's *David*, "just as strong, just as thoughtful, just as silent as when he left the master's workshop quite four hundred years ago," and the galleries of the Uffizzi, full of paintings "so arranged that you can trace the progress of Italian painting from its crude beginnings till it reached the zenith of its glory in the XVth century and after that the sad tale of decline." In Venice, they approached the Accademia in a similarly businesslike fashion. Margaret noted, "After watching the growth of painting in Florence, Siena and Perugia, we are going to study chiefly the School of the Venetians, the land of colour, the works of the Bellinis, of Carpaccio, the large works of Titian, of Paolo Veronese, of Tintoretto and of Palma Vecchio and many others."

20 A letter from Colnaghi and Co. records that "the two Turners have been most carefully packed according to instructions" and dispatched to Plas Dinam by passenger train (Archives, Art Department, Amgueddfa Cymru–National Museum Wales). Both pictures were apparently inspired by the great storm of 21 November 1840 and were originally among a number of works given by the artist to his housekeeper, Mrs. Booth. Two years later, the sisters were to purchase three more Turner oils from the same group.

21 Again via Hugh Blaker. She may also have warmed to the sitter—Mrs. Newbery—who was the sister of Robert Raikes, the promoter of English Sunday schools. The sisters always bought individually but sometimes on the same occasion, and in December 1910 Gwendoline acquired another late eighteenth-century British portrait of a woman, a work by Henry Raeburn of a Mrs. Robert Douglas, bought for £6,300.

22 Margaret's purchase of *Innocents and Card Sharpers* (cat. no. 27) the following year illustrates the role Hugh Blaker played in sourcing the sisters' early acquisitions and directing their interests. He reports, "I am looking for a good Meissonier, Israels and Turner watercolours, as mentioned by my sister." In March 1910, he found this costume piece at Wallis & Son's London gallery. Margaret then went to see it and decided to purchase it for the high price of £5,250. Blaker praised her decision ("you have done well!").

23 In April 1912, the sisters lent two of their Millets to an exhibition at the Grafton Galleries that included Manet's *The Rabbit*, subsequently acquired by Gwendoline in 1917. They also owned a copy of the 1906 edition of Duret's *Peintres Impressionistes*, although the date of acquisition is unknown.

24 Letter from Hugh Blaker to Gwendoline (?) Davies, 11 August 1912, Archives, Art Department, Amgueddfa Cymru–National Museum Wales). Additionally, "M. Monet complains a great deal about his eyes and his oculist fears he will have to operate on a cataract…" For the sisters' love of Venice, see Mark Evans, *Impressions of Venice from Turner to Monet*, exhib. cat. (Cardiff: National Museum of Wales, 1992), pp. 25–26.

25 Letter from Emile Bernheim to Hugh Blaker, 28 November 1912 (Archives, Art Department, Amgueddfa Cymru–National Museum Wales).

26 Sold 1960. Now Fine Arts Museum of San Francisco; gift of Osgood Hooker (1960.29).

27 Richard R. Brettell, *Impressionism, Painting Quickly in France, 1860–1890*, exhib. cat. (New Haven and London: Yale University Press in association with the Sterling and Francine Clark Art Institute, 2000), pp. 82–83.

28 For Rodin's British reputation and collectors, see Antoinette Le Normand-Romain, "When I consider the honours that have been bestowed on me in England," in *Auguste Rodin: Drawings and Watercolors*, exhib. cat. (London and New York: Thames & Hudson, 2006), pp. 119–54, and especially pp. 122–25 for the Davies sisters' acquisitions.

29 Gwendoline bought three oils by Maris from Wallis & Son in 1913. One of them, *He Is Coming*, was one of her most expensive purchases to date at £5,250 and actually cost more than Renoir's *La Parisienne*.

30 Wales today is one of the nations of the United Kingdom. Between the sixteenth and twentieth centuries, it was governed almost entirely as part of England but was distinguished by the survival of the Welsh language and later by a widespread rejection of the Anglican Church in favor of Nonconformism. The growth of representative

democracy in the late nineteenth century made it a stronghold of the Liberal Party. David Lloyd George (1863–1945), a radical chancellor of the exchequer (1908–15) and later wartime prime minister, is the best known of a new generation of Welsh-speaking middle-class politicians.

31 *Welsh Outlook*, November 1914.

32 Attitudes toward the visual arts in Wales during the "national revival" of the late nineteenth and early twentieth centuries are discussed at length in Peter Lord, *The Visual Culture of Wales: Industrial Society* (Cardiff: University of Wales Press, 1998); and *The Visual Culture of Wales: Imaging the Nation* (Cardiff: University of Wales Press, 2000).

33 For example, the Welsh symbolist artist Christopher Williams had called in 1908 for exhibitions of "great pictures … to let the people know what is going on in the world of Art today." See Jeremiah Williams, *Christopher Williams RBA* (Caernarfon, UK: The Delyn Press, 1954), p. 130.

34 In a letter to Thomas Jones of July 1924 (Aberystwyth, National Library of Wales, Thomas Jones Papers, Gregynog Collection, vol. 2), Gwendoline Davies would write (admittedly of the promotion of modern music), "we have led the Welsh horse to the clearest brook we could get, yet he has only tossed his head and walked straight through, throwing up all the mud and stones he could in doing so. He is so self-complacent, too self-sufficient—so ignorant—How are we ever to convince him he is thirsty?"

35 *A Loan Exhibition of Paintings*, exhib. cat. (Cardiff: National Museum of Wales, 1913). The sisters lent at least thirty-eight of the fifty-nine works (another six were the property of their stepmother).

36 Thomas Jones (1870–1955). Born in Rhymni, south Wales, Thomas Jones was a professor of economics at Belfast University when David Davies appointed him secretary of his King Edward VII Welsh National Memorial Association in 1910. Jones also was the first editor of *Welsh Outlook* and a close friend and confidant of Gwendoline Davies. He was deputy secretary to the cabinet from 1916 until 1930. Like the Davies sisters, he immersed himself in many charitable and philanthropic projects. He was one of the founders of the Gregynog Press in 1921–23, and from 1930 until 1945 he was the first secretary of the Pilgrim Trust. He published volumes of autobiography and diaries, and his papers are in the National Library of Wales, Aberystwyth.

37 Hugh Blaker declared it to be "a milestone in Welsh artistic development" and saw in its success the signs of a "long-awaited revival." Entry dated 4 February 1913 in Blaker's diary, quoted by Murray Urquhart in "The Blaker Diary," *Apollo* 78 (1963), pp. 293–98.

38 J. M. Staniforth in *Western Mail* (Cardiff, Wales), 6 February 1913. Manet's *Petit-Montrouge* "should never have been framed let alone exhibited," and the Impressionist painter [Monet] was one who conceals his ignorance by "a plenitude of gaudy colours."

39 Minne's daughter Marie later described how they received "this fantastic message from Mrs. Edward Davies of Llandinam and Miss Gwen and Miss Daisy Davies to invite Belgian artists to come to Wales, where they would not only be able to continue their work but also bring a specific talent to the Welsh people." Quoted in Moira Vincentelli, "The Davies Family and Belgian Refugee Artists and Musicians in Wales," *National Library of Wales Journal* 22 (1981), pp. 226–35. See also Oliver Fairclough, Robert Hoozee, and Caterina Verdickt, eds., *Art in Exile: Flanders, Wales and the First World War*, exhib. cat. (Antwerp: Pandora, 2002). The sisters had little interest in modern Belgian art per se. While two minor works by Pierre Paulus and Emile Fabry were included by Margaret Davies in her bequest to the National Museum, pictures by de Saedeleer and drawings and a bronze by Minne were not and remain at Gregynog.

40 Minne, a symbolist sculptor with a European reputation, had neither a studio nor access to a foundry, so he could only draw. De Saedeleer struggled to support himself painting landscape panoramas of the countryside around Aberystwyth, and van de Woestyne moved permanently to London in 1916.

41 For Augustus John, see Michael Holroyd, *Augustus John: The New Biography* (London: Chatto & Windus, 1996; New York: Farrar, Straus & Giroux, 1996); and David Fraser Jenkins and Chris Stephens, eds., *Gwen John and Augustus John*, exhib. cat. (London: Tate Britain, 2004). More purchases were to follow after the war, although John was by then past his prime. Gwendoline collected no other artist on this scale, and she was determined that his work be seen at the National Museum, persuading John to donate a set of his etchings and later placing several of her own purchases on loan. How much she knew of his notoriously bohemian lifestyle is unclear. The museum has since become the principal repository of John's work.

42 The Committee sent small groups of British women to operate canteens at railway stations, convalescent hospitals, and transit camps. The volunteers supplied French troops with free coffee, snacks, and cigarettes. They had to find their own accommodations and take care of all living expenses. Therefore, their ranks consisted of middle-class women, and some even took their maids with them. See Oliver Fairclough, "Knocked to Pieces: The Impact of the Great War," in "*Things of Beauty*." There are also two unpublished journals and a collection of essays by Margaret Davies, as well as two albums of photographs and other relevant materials (private collection). For background information, see Agnes M. Dixon, *The Cantineers* (London: John Murray, 1917).

43 Gwendoline was to remain in Troyes, with periods of home leave, until the end of the war. The *cantine des dames anglaises*, initially in a transit camp on the outskirts of the city, was transferred in August 1917 to the main railway station in Troyes. The *dames* had to buy food for the canteen (which was cooked by French military orderlies) and keep it clean, but their main task was to serve endless mugs of coffee or lemonade and give out a cigarette to each man. They provided writing paper and magazines, decorated the canteen with flowers and pictures, kept the gramophone going with a mix of patriotic songs and popular music, washed the dishes, talked to the soldiers, and coped when necessary with the amorous or drunk *poilu* and with the bureaucracy of the French army.

44 The Puvis de Chavannes was returned in partial payment of the two Cézannes (see note 45). Bernheim also bid on Gwendoline's behalf at Degas's sale in April 1918, securing Daumier's late *Don Quixote Reading* but losing a small Cézanne watercolor.

45 Blaker had been a great admirer of Cézanne since at least 1912, but he now had less influence on the sisters, and Gwendoline seems to have prepared herself methodically to make these purchases. The sisters' papers (private collection) include a manuscript translation (in Margaret's hand) of Ambroise Vollard's anecdotal account of Cézanne's life, which was not to be published in English until the 1930s. This was probably made after Roger Fry's review of the book appeared in *Burlington Magazine* in 1917.

46 See Ann Robbins, "Less a Luxury than a Necessity: Collecting Cézanne in Britain," in *Cézanne in Britain*, exhib. cat. (London: National Gallery, 2006), pp. 17–26. The educator Michael Sadler (1861–1943) acquired a Cézanne in 1911 and was apparently the first Briton to do so. He was followed by the Manchester businessman Herbert Coleman a year later.

47 In all, the Davies sisters lent eighteen paintings and three sculptures to this mixed loan exhibition at the Victoria Art Gallery, Bath (April 1918–September 1920). This was the first time that a coherent group of major Impressionist and Post-Impressionist paintings had been shown anywhere in Britain outside London. See also Robbins, "Less a Luxury Than a Necessity," p. 20.

48 For the impact of the war on the sisters, see Fairclough, "Knocked to Pieces."

49 Gwendoline and Margaret Davies moved out on this occasion and broke the habits of a lifetime by ordering a hamper of spirits from Harrod's—on a sale or return basis—for the benefit of the

prime minister's health. For information on Gregynog, see Eveline Holsappel, "The Beauty of Simplicity: Arts and Crafts Ideals for Wales"; and Robert Meyrick, "Wealth Wise and Culture Kind: Gregynog in the 1920s and 1930s," in Fairclough, ed., *Things of Beauty*. See also White, *The Ladies of Gregynog*; and Glyn Tegai Hughes, Prys Morgan, and Gareth J. Thomas, eds., *Gregynog* (Cardiff: University of Wales Press, 1977). Gregynog was also used as a venue for the meetings by organizations ranging from the BBC to the Montgomery County Nursing Association.

50 The aim of the press was to "help cultivate a love of beautiful things in the people of Wales by the means of the practice of such arts and crafts as printing, binding, [and] illustration," according to John R. Kenyon, "The Gaiety of These Books: The Gregynog Press," in Fairclough, ed., "*Things of Beauty*"; and Dorothy M. Harrop, *A History of the Gregynog Press* (Pinner: Private Libraries Association, 1980).

51 Martin Bailey, *Van Gogh and Britain: Pioneer Collectors*, exhib. cat. (Edinburgh: National Galleries of Scotland/Compton Verney, 2006), pp. 17–35, 70.

52 These were mostly supplied by Hugh Blaker, and, although costly (Margaret spent £9,000 on a portrait attributed to Frans Hals), few are now very well regarded. The group is of some interest as artists (Botticelli, El Greco, Hals, Velásquez, Van Dyck, and Gainsborough) admired as precursors by modernists.

53 Letter from Gwendoline Davies to Thomas Jones, November 1921, Aberystwyth, National Library of Wales, Thomas Jones Papers, R, Gregynog, vol. 2.

54 *A View in Windsor Great Park*, bought from Hugh Blaker for £460. Wilson, "the father of English landscape painting," had been born in the Davies sisters' native Montgomeryshire and was a source of patriotic pride in artistic circles in Wales.

55 Works by Renoir, Monet, and Cézanne went to the Tate Gallery. For the Tate's initial and controversial refusal of *The François Zola Dam*, see Ingamells, *The Davies Collection of French Art*, pp. 28–30; and Robbins, "Less a Luxury Than a Necessity," pp. 20–21.

56 Gwendoline's letters to Thomas Jones of the period 1920–23 (see note 53) express her hopes for Gregynog. "Any decoration or furniture must have this end in view: it must be beautiful but the beauty of simplicity and usefulness. … I don't mean to say that we won't have any cosy chairs or sofas but do let's keep them to their proper rooms. You can't do serious reading lolling in an armchair … If only Gregynog can become the home of honest, disinterested endeavor it will have been worthwhile."

57 They had a profound impression on the future Surrealist artist Ceri Richards (1903–1971), when he attended a workshop organized by Hugh Blaker in 1923. "I was staggered by the sight of the superb impressionist and post-impressionist paintings on the walls, and by the bronzes by Rodin. I was fascinated most of all by Monet. Imagine their effect on someone who had dreamed of great painting but had seen none at all" (quoted in Mel Gooding, *Ceri Richards* [Moffat, UK: Cameron & Hollis, 2002], p. 10). Writing in 1938, Mary Hackett, a visiting Australian, wrote, "Did I tell you of the Music Room with its wall hung with priceless pictures, the works of Turner, Monet, Manet and many others?" In the 1950s, another visitor writes, "the riot of colour in the music room … the house was an Aladdin's cave" (Archives, Art Department, Amgueddfa Cymru–National Museum Wales).

58 See Louisa Briggs, "'An All Consuming Drive': Margaret's Later Collecting," in Fairclough, ed., "*Things of Beauty*"; and Bryony Dawkes and Robert Meyrick, *Radical Visions: British Art, 1910–1950*, exhib. cat. (Newtown, UK: Oriel Davies Gallery, 2006).

59 Letter to Thomas Jones, 29 January 1925, National Library of Wales, Thomas Jones Papers, R, Gregynog, vol. 2. Their papers include many hundreds of photographs of works of art, some from dealers and including artists represented in the museum's collection.

60 Murray Urquhart, "The Blaker Diary," *Apollo* 78 (1963), p. 293; and John Ingamells, *The Davies Collection of French Art*, pp. 19–22. Other professional advisers included David Croal Thomson of Wallis and Son (and later Barbizon House) and Emile Bernheim, as well as Urquhart himself.

61 Writing to Thomas Jones in April 1920 about what would be needed at Gregynog, Gwendoline stated, "I have crossed out several of the art books as you see and I put a question here beside some others, so many of these big volumes are just written by people who want to make a name for themselves as an authority on the subject. Often, they have no literary value and very little artistic beyond being a collection of minute information which it would take years (almost!) to wade through and one would not be (artistically) much wiser at the end! … Their chief value is often the illustrations they contain but these we can always get separately. We will have portfolios containing photographs and prints of works of art etc." National Library of Wales, Thomas Jones Papers, R, Gregynog, vol. 2.

62 Ibid.; 4 December 1918: "We are going to the Chenil Gallery tomorrow … to see Augustus John's great design for the Canadian war memorial picture – also his portrait of W.H. Davies, the Welsh poet, of which I enclose a photograph. I have already seen this. It is a wonderful thing and was exhibited in the Grosvenor Gallery last March. I hear it is for sale at quite a reasonable price and I am hoping to get it for Cardiff this time!! I don't think they would refuse … p.s. Have you and Mr Greenslade even seen my Rodin marble at the South Kensington Museum. It is waiting there till I decide where to put it finally …"; 5 March 1920: "Got a lovely little Carrière called the 'Dawn' which just fits with things at the moment."

63 They were spending an average of £19,000 a year on art prior to World War I. This sum was to fall somewhat in the postwar period, when they had the additional burden of running Gregynog, which cost them about £10,000 a year.

GREENHALGH

1 Ann Sumner, *Colour and Light: Fifty Impressionist and Post-Impressionist Works at the National Museum of Wales* (Cardiff: National Museum of Wales, 2005), pp. 21–29.

2 Ibid.

3 Eric J. Hobsbawm, *The Age of Capital, 1848–1875* (London: Weidenfeld and Nicolson 1975), pp. 2–6.

4 See Paul Greenhalgh, "A Brief History of Progress," in *The Modern Ideal: The Rise and Collapse of Idealism in the Visual Arts from the Enlightenment to the Present Day* (London: Victoria and Albert Museum, 2005), chap. 3.

5 See Raymond Williams, *The Country and the City* (London: Oxford University Press, 1973 and 1975).

6 National Museum of Wales Art Collections Online, entry for Jean-François Millet, *The Gust of Wind*.

7 John House, *Monet: Nature into Art* (London: Guild Publishing, 1986), p. 15.

8 Charles Dickens, *Hard Times*, 1854 (London: Penguin, 1978).

9 Emile Zola, *Germinal* (Paris: Gaillard, 1885).

10 See Martin Wiener, *English Culture and the Decline of the Industrial Spirit: 1850–1980* (London: Cambridge University Press, 1981).

11 See Joseph Maudaunt-Crook, ed., *The Strange Genius of William Burges* (Cardiff: National Museum Wales, 1981).

12 See Mark Girouard, The *Return to Camelot: Chivalry and the English Gentleman* (New Haven: Yale University Press, 1981).

13 The collection and a new wing were dedicated at the Corcoran in 1927.

14 Roger Fry, introduction, in *Manet and the Post-Impressionists*, exhib. cat. (London: Grafton Galleries, 1910).

15 Ibid.

16 The catalogue published by the Sackville Gallery to accompany the exhibition was *The Italian Futurist Painters* (London, 1912).

17 Interestingly, the chosen style of much of the site's architecture was a heavy, exotic Neo-Baroque and was remarkably similar in feel to the civic buildings being erected at the same time in Cardiff. One of these buildings, the National

Museum of Wales, would eventually house the Davies sisters' collection. See Paul Greenhalgh, "The Franco-British Exhibition of 1908," *Art History* (December 1985).

18 Sir Walter Armstrong, "Art at the Exhibition," *The Guardian* (London), 3 June 1908.

19 See Paul Greenhalgh, "Problems in French Furniture," in Paul Greenhalgh, ed., *Modernism in Design* (London: Reaktion, 1990).

20 See Theodore Zeldin, "Taste and Corruption," in *France, 1848–1945* (Oxford and New York: Oxford University Press, 1980), pp. 95–134.

BAILEY

1 "Et c'est simple, et c'est beau, et c'est frais," John Rewald, "Extraits du journal inédit de Paul Signac, II, 1897–1898," *Gazette des Beaux-Arts* (April 1952), p. 276, Signac's entry for 16 February 1898.

2 See the chronology in Anne Distel and John House, *Renoir*, exhib. cat. (Hayward Gallery, London; Grand Palais, Paris; Museum of Fine Arts, Boston, 1985), pp. 294–300.

3 For excellent summaries of *La Parisienne*, see Distel and House, *Renoir*, p. 204; and Ann Sumner, *Colour and Light: Fifty Impressionist and Post-Impressionist Works at the National Museum of Wales* (Cardiff: National Museum of Wales, 2005), pp. 120–23. Interesting observations on the context for such modernist figure painting can be found in Tamar Garb, *Bodies of Modernity: Figure and Flesh in Fin-de-Siècle France* (London: Thames and Hudson, 1998), pp. 145–55; and Ruth E. Iskin, *Modern Women and Parisian Consumer Culture in Impressionist Painting* (New York: Cambridge University Press, 2007), pp. 198–204.

4 Charles S. Moffett, ed., *The New Painting: Impressionism 1874–1886*, exhib. cat. (Fine Arts Museums of San Francisco, National Gallery of Art, Washington, D.C., 1986), p. 122.

5 Anne Distel, *Renoir: "Il faut embellir"* (Paris: Gallimard, 1993), p. 40, reproducing the page from the annotated catalogue of the first Impressionist exhibition, formerly in the possession of Claude Roger-Marx, with the prices for which Renoir offered his paintings for sale.

6 See, most recently, John House, "Modernity in Microcosm: *Loges* in Context," in Ernst Vegelin van Claerbergen and Barnaby Wright, *Renoir at the Theatre: Looking at* La Loge, exhib. cat. (London: The Courtauld Gallery, 2008), pp. 27–43.

7 For the sale of Renoir's *Harvesters* to the music publisher Georges Hartmann, see Colin B. Bailey and Christopher Riopelle, eds., *Renoir Landscapes, 1865–1883*, exhib. cat. (London: National Gallery, 2007), pp. 124–27. In 1875, Renoir would sell *La Loge* to the dealer Pierre-Firmin Martin for 425 francs; *The Dancer* was acquired in 1878 by Charles Deudon, heir to a mining fortune, for 950 francs; see Colin B. Bailey, "Portrait of the Artist as a Portrait Painter," in Colin B. Bailey, ed., *Renoir's Portraits: Impressions of an Age*, exhib. cat. (New Haven and London: Yale University Press, 1997), p. 17.

8 Bailey et al., *Renoir Landscapes*, p. 55.

9 Bailey, ed., *Renoir's Portraits*, pp. 118–21.

10 Bailey et al., *Renoir Landscapes*, p. 55.

11 These documents are published in full in John Rewald, *Histoire de l'Impressionisme* (Paris: Albin Michel, 1955), pp. 358–69, and are incorporated into the later English editions of Rewald's fundamental survey.

12 Françoise Heilbrun, Maria Morris Hambourg, and Philippe Néagu, *Nadar*, exhib. cat. (New York: Metropolitan Museum of Art, 1995), pp. 33, 331. Nadar's vast atelier, which opened in September 1861, had operated for barely a decade; in 1871, he transferred his premises to 51 rue d'Anjou.

13 John Rewald, *The History of Impressionism*, 4th ed. (New York: Museum of Modern Art, 1973), p. 313. For the various exhibition expenses, see the balance sheet drawn up in May 1874, published in Rewald, *Histoire de l'Impressionisme*, p. 365.

14 See the documents in Anne Distel, *Centennaire de l'Impressionisme*, exhib. cat. (Paris: Grand Palais, 1974), pp. 223–24; and Martha Ward, "Impressionist Installations and Private Exhibitions," *Art Bulletin* (December 1991), pp. 602–03.

15 Philippe Burty, "The Paris Exhibitions: *Les Impressionistes*," *The Academy* (30 May 1874), in Ruth Berson, ed., *The New Painting: Impressionism 1874–1886, Documentation*, 2 vols. (San Francisco: Fine Arts Museum of San Francisco, 1996), vol. 1, p. 10.

16 Philippe Burty, "Exposition de la société anonyme des artistes," *La République française* (25 April 1874), in Berson, *The New Painting*, vol. 1, p. 37.

17 For a recent analysis of *La Loge*, see John House's entry in van Claerbergen and Wright, *Renoir at the Theatre*, pp. 72–74; on Renoir's technique in *La Parisienne*, see Anthea Callen, *The Art of Impressionism: Painting Technique and the Making of Modernity* (New Haven and London: Yale University Press, 2000), p. 77 (in which the ground tone is mistakenly described as yellow).

18 See article 22 of the Société Anonyme's draft regulations, in Rewald, *Histoire de l'Impressionisme*, p. 363.

19 Edmond d'Hervilly, "L'exposition du boulevard des Capucines," *Le Rappel* (17 April 1874), in Berson, *The New Painting*, vol. 1, p. 24.

20 Degas had criticized the official system of stacking works on three levels in a strongly worded letter published in *Paris Journal* on 12 April 1870, reproduced in Theodore Reff, "Some Unpublished Letters of Degas," *Art Bulletin* (March 1968), p. 87; Pissarro had insisted on casting lots to determine the order in which works would be hung; see Rewald, *History of Impressionism*, p. 312.

21 "Complètement débrouillé avec cet accrochage compliqué." See Renoir's undated letter to Philippe Burty, which must date from early April 1874, in Musée du Louvre, Fonds Hernraux, Ms 310 (3). Georges Rivière (*Renoir et ses amis*, [Paris: H. Floury, 1921], p. 46) noted that "after two days, [Renoir] accomplished this delicate task more or less on his own."

22 Louis Leroy in *Le Charivari* (25 April 1874) noted that Renoir's *Dancer* could be seen "upon entering the first room"; Marc de Montifaud in *L'Artiste* (1 May 1874) confirms that it was visible from the third room: "Looked at from far away, for example, from the back of the third room on the ground floor, *The Dancer* can be considered an original production," in Berson, *The New Painting*, vol. 1, pp. 25, 29.

23 Jean Prouvaire [pseud.] in *Le Rappel* (20 April 1874), in Berson, *The New Painting*, vol. 1, p. 34.

24 My description of the costume is greatly indebted to discussions with Aileen Ribeiro and David J. Burke. Ribeiro speculates that Renoir's *Parisienne* "wears a costume for shopping on foot"; see her essay "The Art of Dress: Fashion in Renoir's *La Loge*," in van Claerbergen and Wright, *Renoir at the Theatre*, p. 52.

25 See, for example, the plates in the *Journal des Demoiselles* (March–November 1873); I am grateful to Rii Nie of the Kyoto Costume Institute for bringing this material to my attention.

26 Cited in Iskin, *Modern Women and Parisian Consumer Culture*, pp. 193–94, emphasis mine.

27 See *Modachrome: el color en la historia de la moda* (Madrid: Museo del Traje, 2007), p. 134. I am grateful to Aileen Ribeiro for bringing this catalogue to my attention and to Rii Nie for information about the dress's materials and construction.

28 W. H. Perkins, "On the Aniline or Coal-tar Colours," *Chemical News* (August 1870), p. 65.

29 For Perkins's pioneering role in the manufacture of synthetic dyes, see Simon Garfield, *Mauve: How One Man Invented a Colour that Changed the World* (New York: W.W. Norton, 2001).

30 David Bomford, ed., *Art in the Making: Impressionism*, exhib. cat. (London: National Gallery, 1991), pp. 56, 157.

31 Renoir may have used a standard 120 landscape-format canvas (1.62 x 1.14 cm); see the charts in Bomford, ed., *Art in the Making*, pp. 45–46. My thanks to Kate Lowry, Chief Conservator at the National Museum of Wales, for information about the structure and paint handling of *La Parisienne*.

32 Arsène Alexandre, in *Exposition A. Renoir* (Paris: Galeries Durand-Ruel, 1892), p. 16.

33 Garb, *Bodies of Modernity*, p. 84.

34 Jean Prouvaire [pseud.], *Le Rappel* (20 April 1874),

quoted in Berson, *The New Painting*, vol. 1, p. 34.

35 F. de Gantès, "Courrier artistique: L'Exposition du boulevard," *La Semaine Parisienne* (25 April 1874); Leon L. de Lora, "Petites nouvelles artistiques: Exposition libre des peintres," *Le Gaulois* (18 April 1874), quoted in Berson, *The New Painting*, vol. 1, pp. 23, 27.

36 Armand Silvestre, "Chronique des beaux-arts: Physiologie du refusé-L'Exposition des révoltés," *L'Opinion nationale* (22 April 1874), quoted in Berson, *The New Painting*, vol. 1, p. 40.

37 Ernest Chesnau, "A côté du Salon: II. Le Plein Air: Exposition du boulevard des Capucines," *Paris-Journal* (7 May 1874), quoted in Berson, *The New Painting*, vol. 1, p. 18.

38 For an introduction to the vast literature on *La Parisienne*, see Novelene Ross, *Manet's* Bar at the Folies-Bergères *and the Myths of Popular Illustration* (Ann Arbor, UMI Research Press: 1982), chap. 3 ("La Parisienne"); Garb, *Bodies of Modernity*, chap. 3 ("James Tissot's 'Parisienne' and the Making of the Modern Woman"); and Iskin, *Modern Women and Parisian Consumer Culture*, chap. 6 ("The Chic Parisienne: A National Brand of French Fashion and Femininity").

39 Jean Prouvaire [pseud.] in *Le Rappel* (20 April 1874), quoted in Berson, *The New Painting*, vol. 1, p. 34.

40 Bailey, ed., *Renoir's Portraits*, p. 134.

41 Marc Le Coeur, "Le Peintre, son première modèle et ses premiers amateurs," in *Renoir o Pintor da Vida*, exhib. cat. (São Paulo: Museo de Arte de São Paulo, 2002), pp. 214–15.

42 Bailey, ed., *Renoir's Portraits*, pp. 136–37; the sketchiness of handling in the National Gallery of Art's *Madame Henriot* leads me to revise the dating to 1875, slightly earlier than published in the 1997 catalogue.

43 Marcel Guérin, ed., *Lettres de Degas* (Paris B. Grasset, 1945), p. 36; "It's going very well…We are bringing in 200 francs a day and by November 1 we will be all set," Degas to Bracquemond, undated letter (April 1874); see Distel, *Centennaire de l'Impressionisme*, p. 224, for the fullest listing of the painters' asking prices, from the annotated exhibition catalogue formerly in Claude Roger-Marx's possession.

44 Bailey, ed., *Renoir's Portraits*, p. 17. Renoir's receipt to Rouart for 1,200 francs, dated 1 October 1874, "prix d'un tableau intitulé Parisienne que je lui ai vendu," appeared most recently in *The Collection of Georges Cosmatos*, Sotheby's, London, 31 March 1998, no. 369; the sum is mistakenly given as 1,500 francs in Sumner, *Colour and Light*, p. 123.

45 Bailey, ed., *Renoir's Portraits*, pp. 118, 277.

46 Théodore Duret, *Renoir* (Paris, 1924), pp. 13, 15.

47 Janine Bailly-Herzberg, ed., *Correspondance de Camille Pissarro*, 5 vols. (Paris: P.U.F., 1980), vol. 1, p. 94, citing Duret's letter to Pissarro of 2 June 1874.

48 *Au Coeur de l'Impressionisme: La Famille Rouart*, exhib. cat. (Paris: Musée de la Vie Romantique, 2004), pp. 17–48.

49 Moffett, ed., *The New Painting: Impressionism 1874–1886*, p. 7. Rouart exhibited six landscapes, three watercolors, and two etchings. In one of the drafts of the Société Anonyme's bylaws, Rouart and Renoir are listed together as the two *commissaires* for the exhibition (Rewald, *Histoire de l'Impressionisme*, p. 363).

50 Anne Distel, *Impressionism: The First Collectors* (New York: Abrams, 1990), pp. 177–93. Among the outstanding works in Rouart's collection were Millet's *Winter: The Faggot Gatherers* (cat. no. 31) and Degas's *Rehearsal* (The Frick Collection, New York). The third Renoir that Rouart owned was *Woman in a Garden* (*La femme à la mouette*) (ca. 1868; private collection, on loan to the Kunstmuseum, Basel), which had entered his collection in 1872.

51 *Exposition A. Renoir*, Galeries Durand-Ruel, Paris, 1892, no. 110, "La Dame en bleu." The exhibition lasted two weeks only, between 7 and 21 May.

52 Julie Manet, *Journal (1893–1899)* (Paris: C. Klincksieck, 1979), p. 150. Among Rouart's figure paintings by Corot was *La Dame en blue* (Musée d'Orsay, Paris), which was painted the same year as *La Parisienne*, and entered his collection in 1889, see Gary Tinterow, ed., *Corot, 1796–1875*, exhib. cat. (Grand Palais, Paris; National Gallery of Canada, Ottawa; The Metropolitan Museum of Art, New York, 1996–97), pp. 436–38.

53 Manet, *Journal*, p. 151: "puis une femme en bleu et autre chose."

54 Rewald, "Extraits du journal inédit de Paul Signac," p. 276. Whether Vuillard reacted similarly to *La Parisienne* is not recorded, and his visit to Rouart's collection in Signac's company has escaped the notice of historians of the Nabis.

55 Information from Knoedler's Stock Books (London), which lists the purchase price as "61,600 francs; our half 30,800"; my thanks to Edye Weissler for her assistance.

56 Alice C. Frelinghuysen, ed., *Splendid Legacy: The Havemeyer Collection*, exhib. cat. (New York: Metropolitan Museum of Art, 1993), pp. 260–61.

57 Renoir to Paule Gobillard, Berthe Morisot's niece, undated letter (December 1912) in Jeanne Baudot, *Renoir, ses amis, ses modèles* (Paris: Editions littéraires de France, 1949), p. 105.

58 Caroline Durand-Ruel Godfroy, ed., *Correspondance de Renoir et Durand-Ruel*, 2 vols. (1995), vol. 2, p. 121: "As you know, up to now, la maison Knoedler had always been opposed to paintings from the new school."

59 Quoted in Sumner, *Colour and Light*, p. 19.

CATALOGUE

1 See Gerald Ackerman, *Charles Bargue: Drawing Course with the Collaboration of Jean-Léon Gérôme* (Paris: ACR Edition International, 2003).

2 Ibid., p. 294.

3 Quoted in Sarah Whitfield, "Fragments of an Identical World," in Sarah Whitfield, ed., *Bonnard*, exhib. cat. (London: Tate Publishing, 1998), p. 9.

4 Letter, 9 June 1895, Davies archives, National Museum Wales.

5 Mark L. Evans, *Impressions of Venice from Turner to Monet* (Cardiff: National Museum of Wales; London: Lund Humphries, 1992), p. 54.

6 See Jane R. Becker, "Carrière, Bergson le durée et l'élan vital," in *Eugène Carrière, 1849–1906* (Strasbourg: Musée de Strasbourg, 1997), pp. 27–33.

7 John House and Mary Anne Stevens, *Post Impressionism – Cross Currents in European Painting*, exhib. cat. (London: Royal Academy of Arts, 1979), p. 51.

8 Claude Roger-Marx, *Eugène Carrière*, exhib. cat. (London: Marlborough Galleries, 1970), p. 35.

9 Edward Lucie-Smith, *Symbolist Art* (London: Thames and Hudson, 1972), p. 88.

10 See, for example, Joseph J. Rishel, *Cézanne*, exhib. cat. (Philadelphia: Philadelphia Museum of Art, 1996), p. 190; Ann Robbins, *Cézanne in Britain* (London: National Gallery, 2006), p. 78; and Ann Sumner, *Colour and Light: Fifty Impressionist and Post-Impressionist Works at the National Museum of Wales* (Cardiff: National Museum of Wales, 2005), p. 47.

11 Roger Fry, "The Burlington Fine Arts Club: Cézanne Once More," *The New Statesman* (27 May 1922), pp. 210–11.

12 Rishel, *Cézanne*, p. 189. See also Merete Bodelsen, "Gauguin's Cézannes," *Burlington Magazine* (May 1962), pp. 204–11.

13 See Oliver Fairclough, "The Great Joy of Collecting," this publication.

14 Ann Robbins, *Cézanne in Britain* (London: National Gallery, 2006), p. 21.

15 Roger Fry, "Cézanne and the Nation," *Burlington Magazine* (May 1921), pp. 209–14.

16 Fry, "The Burlington Fine Arts Club: Cézanne Once More," p. 210.

17 Richard Verdi, *Cézanne and Poussin: The Classical Vision of Landscape*, exhib. cat. (London: Lund Humphries/National Gallery of Scotland, 1990), p. 131.

18 Lorenz Eitner, *19th-Century European Painting: David to Cézanne* (Boulder, Colorado: Westview Press, 2002), p. 218.

19 Denys Sutton and Peter Cannon-Brookes, *Paintings from the Davies Collection*, exhib. cat. (London: Wildenstein, 1979), no. 13.

20 Margaret Davies, diary, 1909 (private collection).
21 Charles Harrison and Paul Wood, eds., *Art in Theory, 1815–1900: An Anthology of Changing Ideas*, trans. Peter Collier (Oxford: Blackwell, 1998), p. 535.
22 Eitner, *19th-Century European Painting*, p. 222.
23 John Ingamells, *The Davies Collection of French Art* (Cardiff: National Museum of Wales, 1967), p. 45.
24 See, for example, Paul Spencer-Longhurst, *Moonrise over Europe: J. C. Dahl and Romantic Landscape*, exhib. cat. (Birmingham, England: Barber Institute of Fine Arts; London: Philip Wilson, 2006).
25 Michael Pantazzi in Henri Loyrette, Michael Pantazzi, Ségolène le Men, Edouard Papet, and Michel Melot, *Daumier: 1808–1879*, exhib. cat. (Ottawa: National Gallery of Canada, 1999), p. 228.
26 Bruce Laughton, *Honoré Daumier* (New Haven and London: Yale University Press, 1996), p. 21.
27 They also collected prints, which were bequeathed to the National Library of Wales.
28 For further information on their watercolors and drawings, see Bethany McIntyre, *Sisters Select: Works on Paper from the Davies Collection* (Cardiff: National Museums & Galleries of Wales, 2000).
29 See K. E. Maison, *Honoré Daumier: Catalogue Raisonné of the Paintings, Watercolours and Drawings* (London: Thames and Hudson, 1968).
30 See, for example, *The Laundress*, now in the Musée d'Orsay.
31 Quoted in Laughton, *Honoré Daumier*, p. 74.
32 K. E. Maison, "Daumier Studies—III," *Burlington Magazine* (April 1954), p. 106.
33 Aviva Burnstock and Mark Evans, "Three Daumiers in Cardiff Reassessed," *Burlington Magazine* (May 2000), pp. 282–84.
34 Pantazzi in Loyrette et al., *Daumier: 1808–1879*, p. 343.
35 John Ingamells, "The Gwendoline and Margaret Davies Bequest to the National Museum of Wales," *The Connoisseur* 156 (May–Aug. 1964), p. 113.
36 Pantazzi in Loyrette et al., *Daumier: 1808–1879*, p. 306.
37 Laughton, *Honoré Daumier*, p. 306.
38 Pantazzi in Loyrette et al., *Daumier: 1808–1879*, p. 306.
39 Quoted in Pantazzi in Loyrette et al., *Daumier: 1808–1879*, p. 363.
40 McIntyre, *Sisters Select*, plate 4 text.
41 Pantazzi in Loyrette et al., *Daumier: 1808–1879*, pp. 339–41.
42 Ibid., pp. 422–31.
43 Maison, *Honoré Daumier, Catalogue Raisonné of the Paintings, Watercolours and Drawings*, pp. 149–50.
44 Burnstock and Evans, "Three Daumiers in Cardiff Reassessed," pp. 281–87.
45 Simonetta Fraquelli, Norman Rosenthal, and Emily Braun, *Modigliani and His Models*, exhib. cat. (London: Royal Academy of Arts, 2006), p. 153.
46 See Michael Holroyd, *Augustus John: The New Biography* (New York: Farrar, Straus & Giroux, 1996).
47 Other images of Dorelia from around this period, for example, *Portrait of a Woman* of 1911 (Tate Gallery, London), show her with a blunt bob.
48 Quoted in Holroyd, *Augustus John*, p. 92.
49 Mark L. Evans, *Portraits by Augustus John: Family, Friends, and the Famous* (Cardiff: National Museum of Wales, 1988), p. 40.
50 "Saint Pierre du Petit Montrouge," *Journal Chrétien d'Information du XIVe, no Special 194 bis* (October 1984).
51 See, for example, Manet's lithograph *The Barricade*, of 1871 (Prints Division, New York Public Library).
52 See Edward Lilley, "Manet's 'Modernity' and *Effet de Neige à Petit Montrouge*," *Gazette des Beaux-Arts* (September 1991), p. 107.
53 Ibid., p. 108.
54 At this date, Sceaux was behind Prussian lines and would therefore have been inaccessible to Manet.
55 Paul Hayes Tucker, *The Impressionists at Argenteuil*, exhib. cat. (Washington, D.C.: National Gallery of Art; London and New Haven: Yale University Press, 2000), p. 129.
56 Ibid., p. 130.
57 John Sillevis, "Mauve's Watercolours," *Burlington Magazine* (July 1988), p. 556.
58 Frank Rutter, "A Consideration of the Work of Anton Mauve," *The Studio* 42, no. 175 (October 1907), p. 3.
59 Ronald de Leeuw, John Sillevis, and Charles Dumas, eds., *The Hague School: Dutch Masters of the 19th Century*, exhib. cat. (London: Royal Academy of Arts, 1983), p. 255.
60 Constance Cain Hungerford, "Meissonier and the Founding of the Société Nationale des Beaux-Arts," *The Art Journal* 48, no. 1 (Spring 1989), p. 76.
61 Constance Cain Hungerford, *Ernest Meissonier: Master in His Genre* (Cambridge: Cambridge University Press, 1999), p. 80.
62 Margaret Davies, diary, 1909 (private collection).
63 Timothy Stevens, "Bergère Assise: The Davies Sisters and French Painting in Cardiff," *National Collections Fund Review* (1992), p. 83.
64 Robert Herbert et al., *Jean-François Millet*, exhib. cat. (London: Hayward Gallery, 1976), p. 104.
65 Letter from Millet to Alfred Sensier, 27 January 1867, quoted in Arthur Tomson, "Art Collecting as an Investment," *The Art Journal*, no. 853 (July 1909), p. 208.
66 Stevens, *"Bergère Assise,"* p. 82.
67 Letter from Millet to Alfred Sensier, 1 February 1851, quoted in Alfred Sensier, *La vie et l'oeuvre de Jean-François Millet* (Paris: A. Quantin, 1881), p. 130.
68 *Spring, Summer*, and *Autumn* are now in the Musée d'Orsay, the Museum of Fine Arts, Boston, and the Metropolitan Museum of Art, respectively.
69 Stéphanie Constantin, "Millet's 'Four Seasons' and the Cardiff 'Faggot Gatherers,'" *Burlington Magazine* (April 1997), pp. 257–61.
70 Ibid., p. 259. Millet's portraits date mainly from the 1840s, and Constantin asserts that the nature of the fusion of overpainting to underpainting shows that the present work cannot have been painted more than twenty years after the original portrait, casting doubt on the received dating and inclusion therefore as part of a set depicting the four seasons.
71 John Ingamells, "The Margaret Davies Bequest to the National Museum of Wales," *The Connoisseur* 156 (May–August 1964), p. 116.
72 Walter Richard Sickert, *A Free House* (London: Macmillan, 1947), pp. 134–36.
73 Herbert et al., *Jean-François Millet*, p. 212.
74 See Katherine Lochnan, ed., *Turner Whistler Monet*, exhib. cat. (London: Tate Publishing in association with the Art Gallery of Ontario, 2004), pp. 179–83.
75 John House, *Monet: Nature into Art* (New Haven and London: Yale University Press 1986), p. 61.
76 Letter to René Gimpel, quoted in Grace Seiberling, *Monet in London*, exhib. cat. (Atlanta: High Museum of Art, 1988), p. 55.
77 Sumner, *Colour and Light*, p. 91.
78 Vivian Russell, *Monet's Garden: Through the Seasons at Giverny* (London: Frances Lincoln, Ltd., 1995), p. 42.
79 Sylvie Patin, "The Last Act: Turner, Whistler and Monet in Venice," in Lochnan, ed., *Turner Whistler Monet*, p. 204.
80 Quoted in Gustave Geffroy, *Claude Monet: Sa vie, son temps, son oeuvre* (Paris: Cres, 1922) ch. 52, pages unnumbered.
81 Evans, *Impressions of Venice from Turner to Monet*, p. 69.
82 Margaret Davies, diary, 1909 (private collection).
83 Claire Sauvage, *"Henri Moret,"* in *Henry Moret: Aquarelles et Peintures*, exhib. cat. (Pont-Aven, France: Musée de Pont-Aven, 1988), p. 12.
84 Sumner, *Colour and Light*, p. 104.
85 Both the Sisley and Bonnard works were purchased in 1960.
86 Richard R. Brettell and Joachim Pissarro, *The Impressionist and the City: Pissarro's Series Paintings* (New Haven and London: Yale University Press, 1992), p. 147.
87 For more information on Henriot, see Colin B. Bailey, ed., *Renoir's Portraits: Impressions of an Age*, exhib. cat. (New Haven and London: Yale University Press, 1997), pp. 134–36.
88 It is first referred to as *La Dame en Bleu* at the gallery Durand-Ruel, when lent by Rouart.

89 Ingamells, *The Davies Collection of French Art*, p. 71.
90 Robert Rosenblum, *19th-Century Art* (Upper Saddle River, New Jersey: Pearson Prentice Hall, 2005), p. 402.
91 See Colin B. Bailey and Christopher Riopelle, eds., *Renoir Landscapes, 1865–1883*, exhib. cat. (London: National Gallery, 2007).
92 Denys Sutton, "Armand Séguin, peintre maudit," in *Une vie de bohème: Lettres du Peintre Armand Séguin à Roderic O'Conor, 1895–1903* (Pont-Aven, France: Musée du Pont-Aven, 1989), p. 289.
93 Quoted in Russell T. Clement, Annick Houzé, and Christiane Erbolato-Ramsey, *A Sourcebook of Gauguin's Symbolist Followers: Les Nabis, Pont-Aven, Rose + Croix* (Westport, Connecticut: Greenwood Publishing; London: Praeger, 2004), p. 221.
94 Evans, *Impressions of Venice from Turner to Monet*, p. 60.
95 Ibid.
96 Alessandro Bettagno, *Venezia da stato a mito* (Venice: Fondazione Giorgio Cini/Marsilio, 1997), p. 382.
97 Matthew Sturgis, *Walter Sickert: A Life* (London: HarperCollins, 2005), p. 223.
98 Richard Shone, *Sisley* (London: Phaidon, 1992), p. 184.
99 Ann Dumas, "Alfred Sisley: The True Impressionist," in Ann Dumas and Mary Anne Stevens, *Alfred Sisley: Poète de l'Impressionisme* (Lyon: Musée des Beaux-Arts, 2002), p. 329.
100 Sumner, *Colour and Light*, p. 142.
101 Letter from Hugh Blaker, Davies Archives, National Museum Wales.
102 Malcolm Yorke, *Matthew Smith: His Life and Reputation* (London: Faber and Faber, 1997), p. 92.
103 Quoted in Fernand Khnopff, "Alfred Stevens, Belgian Painter," *The Studio* 39 (1907), p. 219.
104 J.M.W. Turner to John Ruskin, in John Ruskin, *The Complete Works of John Ruskin* (1891), p. 128.
105 Davies Archives, National Museum Wales.
106 Eric Shanes, "A Turner Reclaimed," *Apollo* (March 2007), pp. 64–68.
107 David Hill, *Joseph Mallord William Turner: Le Mont-Blanc et la Vallée d'Aoste*, exhib. cat. (Aosta, Italy: Museo Archeologico Regionale, 2000), p. 257.
108 Quoted in ibid., p. 293.
109 Ian Warrell, ed., *J.M.W. Turner*, exhib. cat. (London: Tate Publishing, 2007), p. 191.
110 James Hamilton, *Turner's Britain* (Birmingham, England: Birmingham Museums & Art Gallery, 2003), p. 183.
111 Ibid.
112 Warrell, ed., *J.M.W. Turner*, p. 190.
113 See works in Turner Bequest, Tate, London: TB CCXVI 130v; CCXCI 24v-27r; TB CCLIX 23.
114 Letter from Hugh Blaker to Miss [Gwendoline] Davies, 12 January 1910, Davies Archives, National Museum Wales.
115 See Turner Bequest, Tate, London, TB CCCIII.
116 It was conventional for newspapers of the time to record new arrivals in town and also where they were staying.
117 Letter from David Croal Thomson to Miss Gwendoline Davies, 11 July 1919. Davies Archives, National Museum Wales.
118 For a discussion of John Edward Taylor, see Charles Nugent and Melva Croal, *Turner Watercolors from Manchester* (Washington, D.C.: The Trust for Museum Exhibitions, 1996).
119 These works were titled *St. Goar* (now identified as *Bernkastel and the Landshut*, ca. 1839, Wilton 1979, no. 1030; private collection); *Forest Road* (unidentified); *Falls on the Rhine* (Wilton 1979, no. 1461; Indianapolis Museum of Art); *Landscape with Cattle* (unidentified); and *A Yorkshire River* (Wilton 1979, no. 891; National Gallery of Art, Washington, D.C.).
120 Martin Butlin and Evelyn Joll, *The Paintings of J.M.W. Turner* (New Haven and London: Yale University Press, 1984), p. 292
121 Ibid.
122 Ibid.
123 Quoted in Ronald Pickvance, *Van Gogh in Saint-Rémy and Auvers*, exhib. cat. (New York: Metropolitan Museum of Art, 1986), p. 271.
124 Quoted in Jan Hulsker, *New Complete Van Gogh: Paintings, Drawings, Sketches, Revised and Enlarged Edition of the Catalogue Raisonné of the Works of Vincent van Gogh* (Philadelphia: John Benjamins Co., 1996), p. 476.
125 Evert van Uitert, Louis van Tilborgh, and Sjraar van Heugten et al., *Vincent van Gogh: Paintings*, exhib. cat. (Milan: Mondadori Arte, 1990), addendum.
126 Pickvance, *Van Gogh in Saint-Rémy and Auvers*, p. 139.
127 Alain Mothe, *Vincent van Gogh à Auvers-sur-Oise* (Paris: Editions du Valhermeil, 1987), p. 117.
128 Letter from Hugh Blaker to Gwendoline Davies, Davies Archives, National Museum Wales.
129 Mark Twain, *A Tramp Abroad*, 1880 (London: Penguin Classics edition, 1997), p. 363.
130 Henry James, *The Aspern Papers*, 1888 (London: Penguin Modern Classics, 2003), p. 79.
131 Margaret MacDonald, *Palaces in the Night: Whistler in Venice* (London: Lund Humphries, 2001), p. 30.
132 Evans, *Impressions of Venice from Turner to Monet*, p. 34.
133 Margaret Davies, diary, 1909 (private collection).

Bibliography

Ackerman, Gerald. *Charles Bargue: Drawing Course with the Collaboration of Jean-Léon Gérôme*. Paris: ACR Edition International, 2003.

Adhémar, Jean. *Honoré Daumier*. Paris: P. Tisné, 1954.

Adler, Kathleen, and Tamar Garb. *Berthe Morisot*. Oxford: Phaidon, 1987.

Bacher, Otto. *With Whistler in Venice*. New York: The Century Co., 1908.

Bailey, Colin B., ed. *Renoir's Portraits: Impressions of an Age*. Exhib. cat. New Haven and London: Yale University Press, 1997.

Bailey, Colin B., and Christopher Riopelle, eds. *Renoir Landscapes, 1865–1883*. Exhib. cat. London: National Gallery, 2007.

Bailey, Martin. *Van Gogh and Britain: Pioneer Collectors*. Exhib. cat. Edinburgh: National Galleries of Scotland/Compton Verney, 2006.

Bantens, Robert James. *Eugène Carrière: The Symbol of Creation*. New York: Kent Fine Art, 1990.

Bataille, Marie-Louise, and Georges Wildenstein. *Berthe Morisot: Catalogue des peintures, pastels, et aquarelles*. Paris: Beaux-Arts, 1961.

Berthier, François. *Van Gogh et le Japon*. Paris, 1981.

Bettagno, Alessandro, ed. *Venezia da stato a mito*. Venice: Fondazio Giorgio Cini/Marsilio, 1997.

Bevan, Robert A. *Robert Bevan, 1865–1925: A Memoir by His Son*. London: Studio Vista, 1965.

Blaker, Hugh. "Cézanne" [letter]. *Saturday Review* (17 December 1921).

Blanton, Catherine W. "An Unpublished Daumier Panel in the Fogg Art Museum: Scapin and Géronte." *Burlington Magazine* (October 1966), pp. 511–18.

Bodelsen, Merete. "Gauguin's Cézannes." *Burlington Magazine* (May 1962), pp. 204–11.

Bomford, David, ed. *Art in the Making: Impressionism*. Exhib. cat. London: National Gallery, 1991.

Bowness, Alan, and K. E. Maison. *Daumier: Paintings and Drawings*. Exhib. cat. London: Arts Council of Great Britain, 1961.

Bowness, Alan, and Philippe Julian. *French Symbolist Painters: Moreau, Puvis de Chavannes, Redon and Their Followers*. Exhib. cat. London: Arts Council of Great Britain, 1972.

Brettell, Richard. *Impression: Painting Quickly in France, 1860–1890*. Exhib. cat. New Haven and London: Yale University Press, in association with the Sterling and Francine Clark Art Institute, 2000.

Brettell, Richard, and Anne-Birgitte Fonsmark. *Gauguin and Impressionism*. Exhib. cat. New Haven and London: Yale University Press, 2005.

Brettell, Richard, and Joachim Pissarro. *The Impressionist and the City: Pissarro's Series Paintings*. Exhib. cat. New Haven and London: Yale University Press, 1992.

Buley-Uribe, Christina, et al. *Auguste Rodin – Eugène Carrière*. Exhib. cat. Paris: Flammarion and Musée d'Orsay, 2006.

Burnstock, Aviva, and Mark Evans. "Three Daumiers in Cardiff Reassessed." *Burlington Magazine* (May 2000), pp. 281–87.

Butlin, Martin, and Evelyn Joll. *The Paintings of J.M.W. Turner*. New Haven and London: Yale University Press, 1977; rev. ed., 1984.

Cachin, Françoise, et al. *Cézanne*. Exhib. cat. Philadelphia: Philadelphia Museum of Art, 1996.

Callen, Anthea. *The Art of Impressionism: Painting Technique and the Making of Modernity*. New Haven and London: Yale University Press, 2000.

Claerbergen, Ernst Vegelin van, and Barnaby Wright. *Renoir at the Theatre: Looking at* La Loge. Exhib. cat. London: The Courtauld Gallery, 2008.

Clarke, Michael. *Corot and the Art of Landscape*. London: British Museum Press, 1991.

Clement, Russell T., Annick Houzé, and Christiane Erbolato-Ramsey. *A Sourcebook of Gauguin's Symbolist Followers: Les Nabis, Pont-Aven, Rose + Croix*. Westport, Connecticut: Greenwood Publishing; London: Praeger, 2004.

Coles, William A. *Alfred Stevens*. Ann Arbor: University of Michigan Museum of Art, 1977.

Conisbee, Phillip, and Denis Coutagne. *Cézanne in Provence*. New Haven and London: Yale University Press, 2006.

Constable, W. G. "Modern Art at the Victoria Art Gallery, Bath." *Burlington Magazine* (February 1920), pp. 88–93.

Constantin, Stéphanie. "Millet's 'Four Seasons' and the Cardiff 'Faggot Gatherers.'" *Burlington Magazine* (April 1997), pp. 257–61.

Dauberville, Jean, and Henry Dauberville. *Bonnard: Catalogue raisonné de l'oeuvre peint, 1920–1939*. Paris: J. et H. Bernheim, 1973.

Daulte, François. *Alfred Sisley: Catalogue raisonné*. Lausanne: Editions Durand-Ruel, 1959.

——. *Auguste Renoir: Catalogue raisonné de l'oeuvre peint*. Vol. 1: Figures, 1860–1890. Lausanne: Editions Durand-Ruel, 1971.

Dawkes, Bryony, and Robert Meyrick. *Radical Visions: British Art, 1910–1950*. Exhib. cat. Newtown: Oriel

Davies Gallery, 2006.

Distel, Anne, and John House. *Renoir*. Exhib. cat. Hayward Gallery, London; Grand Palais, Paris; Museum of Fine Arts, Boston, 1985.

Dorment, Richard, and Margaret F. MacDonald. *James McNeill Whistler*. Exhib. cat. London: Tate Gallery, 1994.

Dumas, Ann, and Mary Anne Stevens. *Alfred Sisley: Poète de l'Impressionisme*. Exhib. cat. Lyon: Musée des Beaux-Arts, 2002.

Dumas, Ann, and John Collins. *Renoir's Women*. London: Merrell, 2005.

Dumas, Ann, Colta Ives, and Susan Alyson Stein. *The Private Collection of Edgar Degas*. New York: Metropolitan Museum of Art, 1997.

Eisenman, Stephen F. *Nineteenth-Century Art: A Critical History*. London: Thames and Hudson, 1994.

Eitner, Lorenz. *19th-Century Painting: David to Cézanne*. Boulder, Colorado: Westview Press, 2002.

Evans, Mark L. *Portraits by Augustus John: Family, Friends and the Famous*. National Museum of Wales. Exhib. cat. Cardiff: National Museum of Wales, 1988.

——. *Impressions of Venice from Turner to Monet*. Exhib. cat. Cardiff: National Museum of Wales; London: Lund Humphries, 1992.

Evans, Mark L., and Oliver Fairclough. *The National Museum of Wales: A Companion Guide to the National Art Gallery*. Cardiff: National Museum of Wales, 1983.

Fairclough, Oliver, ed. *"Things of Beauty": What Two Sisters Did for Wales*. Cardiff: National Museum of Wales, 2007.

Fairclough, Oliver, Robert Hoozee, and Caterina Verdickt, eds. *Art in Exile: Flanders, Wales and the First World War*. Exhib. cat. Ghent: Museum of Fine Arts; Heino: Hannema de Stuers Foundation; Cardiff: National Museum of Wales, 2002.

Frantz, H. "The Rouart Collection III – The Works of Millet." *The Studio* 59 (July 1913), pp. 97–107.

Fraquelli, Simonetta, Norman Rosenthal, and Emily Braun. *Modigliani and His Models*. Exhib. cat. London: Royal Academy of Arts, 2006.

Fry, Roger. "Cézanne and the Nation." *Burlington Magazine* (May 1921), pp. 209–14.

——. "The Burlington Fine Arts Club: Cézanne Once More." *The New Statesman* (27 May 1922), pp. 210–11.

Frèches-Thory, Claire, and Antoine Terrasse. *The Nabis: Bonnard, Vuillard and Their Circle*. Paris: Flammarion, 1990.

Gaches-Patin, Sylvie, Sylvie Patry, and Hugues Wilhelm. *Berthe Morisot, 1841–1895*. Exhib. cat. Lille: Palais des Beaux-Arts de Lille, 2002.

Gaunt, William. *Renoir*. Oxford: Phaidon, 1982.

Geffroy, Gustave. *Claude Monet: Sa vie, son temps, son oeuvre*. Paris: Cres, 1922.

Gere, Charlotte, and Marina Vaizey. *Great Women Collectors*. London: Phillip Wilson Publishers, 1999.

Greenhalgh, Paul. *Modern Ideal: The Rise and Collapse of Idealism in the Visual Arts from the Englightenment to Postmodernism*. London: Victoria & Albert Publications, 2005.

Greenhalgh, Paul, ed. *Art Nouveau, 1890–1914*. London: Victoria & Albert Publications, 2000.

Halton, E. G. "The Collection of Mr Alexander Young, I – The Corots." *The Studio* 39 (October 1906).

Hamilton, James. *Turner's Britain*. Birmingham, UK: Birmingham Museums & Art Gallery, 2003.

Herbert, Robert, et al. *Jean François-Millet*. Exhib. cat. London: Hayward Gallery, 1976.

Hill, David. *Joseph Mallord William Turner: Le Mont-Blanc et la Vallée d'Aoste*. Aosta, Italy: Aosta Museo Archeologico Regionale, 2000.

Holmes, C. J. "Three Pictures by Turner." *Burlington Magazine* (October 1908), pp. 17–25.

Holroyd, Michael. *Augustus John: A Biography. Vol. 1, The Years of Innocence*. London: Heinemann, 1974.

——. *Augustus John: The New Biography*. London: Chatto & Windus, 1996; New York: Farrar, Straus & Giroux, 1996.

Honour, Hugh, and John Fleming. *The Venetian Hours of Henry James, Whistler, and Sargent*. London: Walter Books, 1991.

House, John. "The Impressionists in London." *Burlington Magazine* (March 1973), pp. 194–97.

——. *Monet: Nature into Art*. New Haven and London: Yale University Press, 1986.

——. "Modernity in Microcosm: Loges in Context." In Ernst Vegelin van Claerbergen and Barnaby Wright, *Renoir at the Theatre: Looking at* La Loge. Exhib. cat. London: The Courtauld Gallery, 2008, pp. 27–43.

House, John, and Mary Anne Stevens. *Post-Impressionism – Cross-Currents in European Painting*. Exhib. cat. London: Royal Academy of Arts, 1979.

Hughes, Peter. *French Art from the Davies Bequest*. Cardiff: National Museum of Wales, 1982.

Hulsker, Jan. *New Complete Van Gogh: Paintings, Drawings, Sketches, Revised and Enlarged Edition of the Catalogue Raisonné of the Works of Vincent van Gogh*. Philadelphia: John Benjamins Co., 1996.

Hungerford, Constance Cain. "Meissonier and the Founding of the Société National des Beaux-Arts." *Art Journal* 48, no. 1 (Spring 1989), pp. 71–77.

——. *Ernest Meissonier: Master in His Genre*. Cambridge: Cambridge University Press, 1999.

——. *Ernest Meissonier: Retrospective*. Exhib. cat. Lyon: Musée des Beaux-Arts de Lyon, 1993.

Ingamells, John. "The Margaret Davies Bequest to the National Museum of Wales." *The Connoisseur* 156 (May–August 1964).

——. *The Davies Collection of French Art*. Cardiff: National Museum of Wales, 1967.

Jamot, Paul, "Les Salons de 1906." *Gazette des Beaux-Arts* 35 (1906), pp. 353–60.

Jenkins, David Fraser. *Gwen John and Augustus John*. Exhib. cat. London: Tate Publishing, 2004.

Joyes, Claire. *Monet at Giverny*. London: Matthews Millar Dunbar, 1975.

Khnopff, Fernand. "Alfred Stevens, Belgian Painter." *The Studio* 39 (1907), pp. 211–23.

Kosinski, Dorothy. *Van Gogh's Sheaves of Wheat*. London: Yale University Press, 2006.

Larkin, Oliver W. *Daumier: Man of His Time*. London: Weidenfeld & Nicholson, 1967.

Laughton, Bruce. *Honoré Daumier*. New Haven and London: Yale University Press, 1996.

Lee, Jane. *Derain*. Oxford: Phaidon, 1990.

Leeuw, Ronald de, John Sillevis, and Charles Dumas, eds. *The Hague School: Dutch Masters of the 19th Century*. Exhib. cat. London: Royal Academy of Fine Arts, 1983.

Lilley, Edward. "Manet's 'Modernity' and Effet de Neige à Petit-Montrouge." *Gazette des Beaux-Arts* (September 1991), pp. 107–10.

Lilly, Marjorie. *Sickert: The Painter and His Circle*. London: Elek, 1972.

Lloyd, Christopher, and Richard Thomson. *Impressionist Drawings from British Public and Private Collections*. Exhib. cat. London: The Arts Council of Great Britain, 1986.

Lochnan, Katherine, ed. *Turner Whistler Monet*. Exhib. cat. London: Tate Publishing in association with the Art Gallery of Ontario, 2004.

Loyrette, Henri, Michael Pantazzi, Ségolène le Men, Edouard Papet, and Michel Melot. *Daumier: 1808–1879*. Exhib. cat. Ottawa: National Gallery of Canada, 1999.

Lucie-Smith, Edward. *Symbolist Art*. London: Thames and Hudson, 1972.

MacDonald, Margaret. *Palaces in the Night: Whistler in Venice*. London: Lund Humphries, 2001.

McIntyre, Bethany. *Sisters Select: Works on Paper from the Davies Collection*. Cardiff: National Museum of Wales, 2000.

Mainards, Patricia. *The End of the Salon: Art and State in the Early Third Republic*. Cambridge: Cambridge University Press, 1993.

Maison, K. E. "French Paintings in the Gwendoline Davies Bequest, Part 1." *Apollo* (July 1952).

——. "Daumier Studies – III." *Burlington Magazine* (April 1954), pp. 105–09.

——. *Honoré Daumier: Catalogue Raisonné of the Paintings, Watercolours and Drawings*. London: Thames and Hudson, 1968.

——. *Daumier Drawings*. New York and London: Thomas Yoseloff, 1960.

Masson, Henry. *Armand Séguin: La vie errante, l'oeuvre insolite*. 1995.

Mitchell, Peter. *Alfred Emile Leopold Stevens*. London: John Mitchell & Sons, 1973.

Moffett, Charles, Eliza Rathbone, Katherine Rothkopf, and Joel Isaacson. *Impressionists in Winter: Effets de Neige*. London: Philip Wilson, 1998.

Moreau-Nélaton, Etienne. *Millet: Raconté par lui-même*. Paris: H. Laurens, 1921.

Mothe, Alain. *Vincent van Gogh à Auvers-Sur-Oise*. Paris: Editions du Valhermeil, 1987.

Murphy, Alexandra. *Jean-François Millet*. Boston: Museum of Fine Arts, 1984.
Nugent, Charles, and Melva Croal. *Turner Watercolors from Manchester*. Exhib. cat. The Trust for Museum Exhibitions, 1996.
Pennec, Jos, and Catherine Puget. *Armand Séguin, 1869–1903*. Exhib. cat. Pont-Aven: Musée de Pont-Aven, 1989.
Pickvance, Ronald. "Daumier in Scotland." *Scottish Art Review* 12, no. 1 (1968).
——. *Van Gogh in Saint-Rémy and Auvers*. Exhib. cat. New York: Metropolitan Museum of Art, 1986.
Piguet, Philippe. *Monet et Venise*. Paris: Herscher, 1986.
Pissarro, Ludovic Rodo, and Lionello Venturi. *Camille Pissarro: son art – son oeuvre – catalogue raisonné*. 2 vols. San Francisco: Alan Wolfsy Fine Arts, 1989.
Pollock, Griselda. *Millet*. London: Oresko Books, 1977.
Powell, Cecilia. *Turner's Rivers of Europe, The Rhine, Meuse and Mosel*. London: Tate Gallery, 1991.
——. *Turner in Germany*. London: Tate Gallery, 1995.
Rapetti, Rodolphe, et al. *Eugène Carrière*. Exhib. cat. Strasbourg: Musées de Strasbourg, 1996.
Robaut, A. *L'oeuvre de Corot*. Vol. 2. Paris, 1905.
Robbins, Ann. *Cézanne in Britain*. Exhib. cat. London: National Gallery, 2006.
Roger-Marx, Claude. *Eugène Carrière*. Exhib. cat. London: Marlborough Galleries, 1970.
Rosenblum, Robert. *19th-Century Art*. Upper Saddle River, New Jersey: Pearson Prentice Hall, 2005.
Rosenblum, Robert, Mary Anne Stevens, and Ann Dumas. *1900: Art at the Crossroads*. Exhib. cat. New York: Harry N. Abrams, 2000.
Russell, Vivian. *Monet's Garden: Through the Seasons at Giverny*. London: Frances Lincoln Ltd., 1995.
Rutter, Frank. "A Consideration of the Work of Anton Mauve." *The Studio* 42, no. 175 (October 1907), pp. 3–18.
Sauvage, Claire. "Henri Moret." In *Henry Moret: Aquarelles et Peintures*. Exhib. cat. Pont-Aven, France: Musée de Pont-Aven, 1988.
Séguin, Armand, Denys Sutton, and Catherine Puget. *Une vie de bohème: Lettres du peintre Armand Séguin à Roderic O'Conor,* 1895–1903. Pont-Aven: Musée de Pont-Aven, 1989.
Seiberling, Grace. *Monet in London*. Exhib. cat. Atlanta: High Museum of Art, 1988.
Selz, Jean. *Vlaminck*. Milan: Uffici Press, 1970.
Sensier, Alfred. *La vie et l'oeuvre de Jean-François Millet*. Paris: A. Quantin, 1881.
Shanes, Eric. *Turner: The Great Watercolours*. London: Royal Academy of Arts, 2000.
Shanes, Eric. "A Turner Reclaimed." *Apollo* (March 2007), pp. 64–68.
Shennan, Margaret. *Berthe Morisot: The First Lady of Impressionism*. Stroud: Sutton Publishing, 1996.
Shone, Richard. *Sisley*. London: Phaidon, 1992.
Sickert, Walter Richard. *A Free House*. London: Macmillan, 1947.
Sillevis, John. "Mauve's Watercolours." *Burlington Magazine* (July 1988), pp. 556–57.
Spencer-Longhurst, Paul. *Moonrise over Europe: J. C. Dahl and Romantic Landscape*. Exhib. cat. London: Phillip Wilson, 2006.
Steegman, John. "National Museum of Wales – The Gwendoline Davies Bequest." *The Connoisseur* 129 (January–June 1952).
Stenlake, Frances. *From Cuckfield to Camden Town – The Story of Artist Robert Bevan*. Cuckfield, UK: The Trustees of Cuckfield Museum, 1999.
Stevens, Timothy. "Bergère Assise: The Davies Sisters and French Painting in Cardiff." *National Collections Fund Review* (1992), pp. 80–85.
Sturgis, Matthew. *Walter Sickert: A Life*. London: HarperCollins, 2005.
Sumner, Ann. *Colour and Light: Fifty Impressionist and Post-Impressionist Works at the National Museum of Wales*. Cardiff: National Museum of Wales, 2005.
Sutton, Denys, and Peter Cannon-Brookes. Exhib. cat. *Paintings from the Davies Collection*. London: Wildenstein, 1979.
Tilborgh, Louis van. *Millet: Van Gogh*. Exhib. cat. Paris: Musée d'Orsay, 1998.
Tomson, Arthur. *Jean-François Millet and the Barbizon School*. London: G. Bell & Sons, 1905.
——. "Art Collecting as an Investment." *The Art Journal*, no. 853 (July 1909), pp. 207–08.
Thompson, Belinda. *Gauguin's Vision*. Exhib. cat. Edinburgh: National Galleries of Scotland, 2005.
Tucker, Paul Hayes. *The Impressionists at Argenteuil*. Exhib. cat. Washington D. C.: National Gallery of Art; London and New Haven: Yale University Press, 2000.
Uitert, Evert van, et al. *Vincent Van Gogh: Paintings*. Exhib. cat. Milan: Mondadori Arte, 1990.
Venturi, Lionello. *Cézanne, son art, son oeuvre: catalogue raisonné*. Paris: Rosenberg, 1936, reprinted San Francisco: Alan Wofsy Fine Arts, 1989.
Verdi, Richard. *Cézanne and Poussin: The Classical Vision of Landscape*. Exhib. cat. London: Lund Humphries/National Gallery of Scotland, 1990.
Wallraf-Richarz Museum. *J. M. William Turner: Köln und der Rhein*. Cologne: Wallraf-Richarz Museum, 1980.
Warrell, Ian, ed. *J.M.W. Turner*. Exhib. cat. London: Tate Publishing, 2007.
White, Barbara Ehrlich. *Renoir: His Life, Art, and Letters*. New York: Abrams, 1984.
Whitfield, Sarah, ed. *Bonnard*. Exhib. cat. London: Tate Publishing, 1998.
Wildenstein, Daniel. *Claude Monet – biographie et catalogue raisonné*. Lausanne/Paris: Bibliothèque des Arts, 1985.
Wilton, Andrew. *The Life and Work of J.M.W. Turner*. London: Academy Editions, 1979.
Yetton, Christopher. *Monet in the 20th Century: An Introduction*. Exhib. cat. London: Royal Academy of Arts, 1999.
Yorke, Malcolm. *Matthew Smith: His Life and Reputation*. London: Faber and Faber, 1997.
Young, Andrew McLaren, Margaret MacDonald, Robin Spencer, and Hamish Miles. *The Paintings of James McNeill Whistler*. 2 vols. New Haven and London: Yale University Press, 1980.
Ziff, J. "Butlin/Joll: The Paintings of J.M.W. Turner" [review]. *Art Bulletin* (March 1980), pp. 166–71.

Index

Page numbers in italics refer to illustrations.

Alexandre, Arsène 33
Alexis, Paul 30
Amgueddfa Cymru–National Museum Wales
  building design 17, *17*, 165–166(n17)
  Davies sisters' gifts, to 21, 164(n41)
  founding of 16
  A Loan Exhibition of Paintings (1913) 17, *17*
Apples on a Wicker Chair (Smith) 132, *133*
Argenteuil–Boats (Manet) 88, *89*
Armstrong, Sir Walter 29
Artist's Model, The (Bargue) 14, 40, *41*, 92, 134
Artôt, Paul
  Thomas Jones (1870–1955) 17, 18, *18*
At Bougival (Morisot) 25, 114, *115*, 120

Bacher, Otto 160
Baldwin, Prime Minister Stanley 20, 164–165(n49)
Barbizon school 36, 58, 90, 94, 104
Bargue, Charles 40, *41*
  The Artist's Model 14, 40, *41*, 92, 134
Bell, Vanessa 124
Bernard, Emile 112, 122
Bernheim, Emile 15
Bernheim-Jeune gallery (Paris)
  Claude Monet: Venise exhibition (1912) 15, 110
  Davies sisters' purchases, from 18, 19, 20, 52, 54, 88, 108, 152
Bevan, Robert Polhill 42, *43*
  Maples at Cuckfield, Sussex 42, *43*
Blaker, Hugh
  as Davies sisters' art adviser 15, 21, 163(n22), 164(n45)
  described 13, *14*, 15
  on *A Loan Exhibition of Paintings* (1913) 17, 164(n37)
Blaker, Jane 13
Boldini, Giovanni *35*
Bonnard, Pierre 48, 122
  Sunlight at Vernon 20, 44, *45*, 112, 130, 156, 168(n85)
Booth, Sophia 138, 144, 150
Boudin, Eugène 46, *47*
  Venice, The Molo 16, 46, *47*
Breton Peasant Women at Mass (Seguin) 20, 112, 122, *123*
Bridge, The (Vlaminck) 80, 156, 158, *159*
Bridge over the Marne at Créteil (Cézanne) 158
Brown, Ford Maddox
  David Davies *13*
Burdon-Evans, Major 17
Burges, William 27
Burrell Collection (Glasgow) 66
Burty, Philippe 31, 32
Butlin, Martin 150

Camden Town Group 42
Cardiff City Hall, exhibition at (1913) 17, *17*
Carrière, Eugène 18, 72, 165(n62)
  Maternity 16, 48, *49*, 50
  Maternity (Suffering) 16, 50, *51*
Castel Gandolfo, Dancing Tyrolean Shepherds by Lake Albano (Corot) 56, *57*, 58, 60
Cézanne, Paul 28, 29
  artistic style of 21, 26, 156, 158
  and British collectors 18, 164(n46)
  The François Zola Dam 18–19, 26, 52, *53*, 54, 156, 164(n45), 164(n44)
  Provençal Landscape 18–19, 54, *55*, 156, 164(nn44, 45)
  Still Life with Teapot 20, 21, *21*
Charing Cross Bridge (Monet) 16, 23–24, 106, *107*, 108, 110
Chase, William Merritt
  William Andrews Clark *26*, *27*
Chenil Gallery (London) 84, 150
Christie's 13, 58, 96, 136, 144, 146
Clark, William A. *26*, *27*, 28
Claude Monet: Venise exhibition (1912) 15, 110
Cloisonnism 112, 122
Colnaghi (London dealer) 14, 70, 163(n20)
Constable, John 14, 90, 130, 140
Conversation (Renoir) 18, 120, *121*
Corcoran Gallery of Art (Washington, D.C.) 28, 165(n13)
Corot, Camille
  artistic style of 24, 36, 94
  Castel Gandolfo, Dancing Tyrolean Shepherds by Lake Albano 56, *57*, 58, 60
  Distant View of Corbeil 14, 60, *61*
  Fishermen Moored at a Bank 15, *15*
  The Pond 14, 24, 58, *59*, 60
Courbet, Gustave 24, 84
  Ornans 24, *24*, *25*
Courtauld, Samuel 20, 52, 88
Cox, David 14, 90
Crossing the Street (Boldini) *35*
Cubism 28, 29, 64, 156, 158

Dancer, The (Renoir) 30, 31, *31*, 32, 33–34
Dancers Practicing at the Bar (Degas) 37
Daumier, Honoré
  Head of a Man (ca. 1850) 16, 64, *65*, 68, 74
  Head of a Man (ca. 1852–56) 64, 68, *69*
  The Heavy Burden 16, 66, *67*, 70
  The Lawyer and His Client 72, *73*
  A Lawyer, Walking 64, 74, 78, 79
  The Night Walkers 14, 16, 62, 63, 66, 70, 102
  A Third Class Carriage 76, *77*
  Three Sketches of Heads in Chalk 74, *75*
  Two Studies for the Return of the Prodigal Son 64, 74, 75
  The Watering Place 70, *71*
David Davies (Brown) *13*
Davies, David (grandfather) 12–13, 13, 26–27, 162(n9)
Davies, David (Lord Davies of Llandinam) 12, 16, 18, 164(n36)
Davies, Edward 13
Davies, Elizabeth 13, 16, 163(nn11, 12)
Davies, Gwendoline ("Gwen")
  and art collecting 16, 20–21, 23, 28–29, 82, 104, 162(n1), 163(n21), 165(n63)
  and Blaker, as art adviser 21
  charitable works 12, 16–20, *18*, 164(nn42, 43)
  childhood 12–13
  described 12, 13, *13*, 16, 163(n12), 164(n36)
  exhibition lending 16–17, 164(nn35, 47)
  gifts and bequests, to National Museum of Wales 21
  at Gregynog Hall *19*, 19–20, 21, *21*
  at Plas Dinam 12–13, *14*, 15, 16
Davies, Margaret ("Daisy")
  and art collecting 16, 20–21, 23, 28–29, 132, 162(n1), 163(n21), 165(n63)
  and Blaker, as art adviser 21
  charitable works 12, 16–20, *18*, 164(nn42, 43)
  childhood 12–13
  described 12, 13, *13*, *18*

exhibition lending 16–17, 164(nn35, 47)
gifts and bequests, to National Museum of Wales 21
at Gregynog Hall *19*, 19–20, 21, *21*
at Plas Dinam 12–13, *14*, 15, 16
Plas Dinam (woodcut) *14*, 15
works sold from collection 148, 156, 169(n119)
Davies, Mary (Jones) 13
Day, Sir John Charles 100
Day Dress (fashion, ca. 1874) 33, *34*, 35
Degas, Edgar 20, 37, 124
in Sociéte Anonyme exhibition (1874) 32, 166(n20)
Delacroix, Eugène 120, 126
Delance, Paul 134
Denis, Maurice 122
Derain, André 20, 26
Madame Zborowska 80, *81*, 156
Díaz de la Peña, Narcisse-Virgile 60, 104
Distant View of Corbeil (Corot) 14, 60, *61*
Divisionism 126
Dowdeswell Gallery (London) 144
Durand-Ruel, Paul 106
Durand-Ruel gallery (Paris) 16, 46, 110, 112
and Renoir 36, 37

Ecole des Beaux-Arts 48, 94
Effect of Snow at Petit-Montrouge (Manet) 16, 86, *87*, 164(n38)
Eldar Gallery (London) 126
Engraver, The (Seiler) 92

Fauvism 28, 42, 80, 132
and Davies sisters' collecting 22, 26, 29, 80
Fine Arts Museum (San Francisco) 44, 76
Fishermen Moored at a Bank (Corot) 14, *15*
Fitzwilliam Museum (Cambridge, England) 82
Fort de l'Esseillon, Val de la Maurienne (Turner) 142, *143*
Fragonard, Jean-Honoré 40, 120
Franco-British Exhibition (1908) *28*, 28–29, *29*, 165–166(n17)
François Zola Dam, The (Cézanne) 18–19, 26, 52, *53*, 54, 156, 164(nn44, 45)
French Gallery (London) 106, 142
Friesz, Othon 80
Fry, Roger
on Cézanne's work 52, 164(n45)
on formalism 42
and *Manet and the Post-Impressionists* exhibition (1910) 14, 28, 152
Futurism 28, 29

Gauguin, Paul 48, 52
artistic influence of 42, 112, 122
and Post-Impressionism 26, 28
Gérôme, Jean-Léon 40, 112
Gilman, Harold 20, 42, 124
Gogh, Vincent van 26, 90, 126, 130
Rain 152
Rain–Auvers 20, 26, 88, 152, *153*, *154–155*
Good Samaritan, The (Millet) 96, *97*, *98–99*
Goose Girl at Gruchy, The (Millet) 14, 94, 100, *101*, 102, 104
Gore, Spencer 132
Gothic Revivalism 27
Goupil & Sons (Hague) 90
Grafton Galleries (London)
Manet and the Post-Impressionists exhibition (1910) 14, 27, *27*, 28, 29, 152
Second Post-Impressionist Exhibition (1912) 27, *27*, 29, 163(n23)
Gregynog Hall (Wales) *19*, 19–20, 21, *21*
Gregynog Press 20, 164(n36), 165(n50)
La Grenouillère (Monet) 25, *25*
Grosvenor Gallery (London) 37, 66, 118, 160
Gust of Wind, The (Millet) 24–25, 104, *105*

Hague school 90
Hamburg Kunsthalle 92
Hamilton, James 144
Hartmann, Frederic 102
Harvesters (Renoir) 30, 166(n7)
Head of a Man (Daumier) (ca. 1850) 16, 64, *65*, 68, 74
Head of a Man (Daumier) (ca. 1852–56) 64, 68, *69*
Head of Dorelia (John) 18, 82, *83*, 84
Heavy Burden, The (Daumier) 16, 66, *67*, 70
He Is Coming (Maris) 134, 163(n29)
Henriot, Henriette 34, *37*
and *La Parisienne* (Renoir) 22, 34–35, 118
Portrait of Madame Henriot (Renoir) 35, *37*, 118
Highfield School (Hendon) 13, 163(n13)
Hill, David 140, 142
Hiroshige, Ando 152
Hobsbawm, Eric 23
House, John 25, 106
Hunterian Museum & Art Gallery (Glasgow) 60

Impressionism
British collectors, and demand 18, 164(n46)
Davies sisters' interest, in 14–16, 114
early critics, on 12, 162(n4)
Fry, on 28
and landscape painting 25–26, 30
Société Anonyme exhibition (1874) 25, 30–32, 34, 35, 36, 118, 166(n20), 167(n49)
See also specific artist
Industry to Impressionism exhibition (2007) 8
Innes, J. D. 82
Innocents and Card Sharpers (Meissonier) 14, 17, 40, 92, *93*, 163(n22)
Israels, Jozef 14, 60, 90

Japonaiserie 118, 134, 152
John, Augustus 18, 165(n62)
Head of Dorelia 18, 82, *83*, 84
Self-Portrait 18, 82, 84, *85*
John, Gwen 82
Joll, Evelyn 150
Jones, Mary. *See* Davies, Mary (Jones)
Jones, Thomas 17, 18, *18*, 19, 20, 164(n36)
Journal des Demoiselles 32, *33*

Kiss, The (Rodin) 16, *16*, 17, 163(n18)
Knoedler & Co. (London) 37, 167(n58)
Kyoto Costume Institute, The 32–33, 35

landscape painting 23, 24, 52, 54, 58, 138
and Impressionism 25–26, 30
Lane, Sir Hugh 13, 15, 37
Lawyer, Walking, A (Daumier) 64, 74, 78, *79*
Lawyer and His Client, The (Daumier) 72, *73*
Lefevre Gallery (London) 64, 74, 78
Leicester Galleries (London) 116
Lemonnier, Camille 134
Leyen Burg at Gondorf, The (Turner) 146, *147*
Loan Exhibition of Paintings, A (1913 exhibition) 17, *17*, 164(nn35, 37, 38)
Loge, La (Renoir) 30, 31, *31*, 166(n7)
London Group 132
Longfellow, Henry Wadsworth 152
Lorrain, Claude 56
Louvre (Paris) 14, 56, 92, 104
Luncheon of the Boating Party (Renoir) 158

Madame Zborowska (Derain) 80, *81*, 156
Maison, K. E. 64, 66, 76
Mancini, Antonio
Portrait of a Girl 16, *16*, 17
Manet, Edouard 88, 114
Argenteuil–Boats 88, *89*
artistic influence of 30, 118, 134
Effect of Snow at Petit-Montrouge 16, 86, *87*, 164(n38)
Manet and the Post-Impressionists exhibition (1910) 14, 27, *27*, 28, 29, 152
The Rabbit *21*, 163(n23)
Manet, Julie 36
Manet and the Post-Impressionists exhibition (1910) 14, 27, *27*, 28, 29, 152
Mannerism 26
Maples at Cuckfield, Sussex (Bevan) 42, *43*
Margate (Turner) 14, 138, *139*
Maris, Matthijs 16, 134, 142, 163(n29)
Marquet, Albert 26, 80
Maternity (Carrière) 16, 48, *49*, 50
Maternity (Suffering) (Carrière) 16, 50, *51*
Matisse, Henri 28, 126
Mauve, Anton 14
The Shepherdess 66, 90, *91*, 102
McNeill, Dorelia 82, *83*, 168(n47)
Meissonier, Jean-Louis-Ernest
Innocents and Card Sharpers 14, 17, 92, *93*, 163(n22)
Metropolitan Museum of Art, The (New York) 37, 50, 56, 142
Millet, Jean-François 14, 24, 90
The Good Samaritan 96, *97*, *98–99*
The Goose Girl at Gruchy 14, 94, 100, *101*, 102, 104
The Gust of Wind 24–25, 104, *105*
The Seated Shepherdess 66, 94, *95*, 102
Winter: The Faggot Gatherers 14, 94, 102, *103*
Minne, George 17, 164(nn39, 40)
modernism (Britain) 13, 42, 132, 152
Monet, Claude, 25–26, 88
artistic influence of 44, 112, 126, 130
Charing Cross Bridge 16, 23–24, 106, *107*, 108
La Grenouillère 25, *25*
The Palazzo Dario 16, 46, 106, 108, 110, *111*, 124
Rouen Cathedral: Setting Sun 18, 19, *19*
San Giorgio Maggiore by Twilight 15, *15*
in Sociéte Anonyme exhibition (1874) 30–31
Waterlilies 16, 25, 106, 108, *109*
Monticelli, Adolphe 16
Moret, Henry
Village in Clohars 20, 112, *113*
Moret-sur-Loing (Rue de Fosses) (Sisley) 20, 25, 112, 130, *131*, 168(n85)
Morisot, Berthe
At Bougival 25, 114, *115*, 120
Morning after the Wreck (Turner) 144, *145*
Morris, William 16, 27
Musée Bonnat (Bayonne) 100
Musée de Pont-Aven 112

Musée des Beaux-Arts (Tournai) 88
Musée d'Orsay (Paris) 114, 158
Musée Marmottan (Paris) 110
Museum of Fine Arts (Boston) 102

Nabis 42, 44, 112, 122, 167(n54)
Nadar (photographer) *32*, 33, 166(n12)
Nash, Paul 132
National Gallery (London) 52
National Gallery of Art (Washington, D.C.) 74
Naturalism 22, 25, 28, 42, 48, 60
Neoclassicism 26, 56, 134
Neo-Impressionism (Pointillism) 26, 126, 130
New Painting 34, 37
Night Walkers, The (Daumier) 14, 16, 62, *63*, 66, 70, 102
Nocturne: Blue and Gold, St. Mark's Venice (Whistler) 15, 46, 160, *161*

Obach Gallery (London) 14
Ornans (Courbet) 24, *24*, 25

Palazzo Dario, The (Monet) 16, 46, 106, 108, 110, *111*, 124
Palazzo Eleanora Duse, Venice (Sickert) 20, 124, *125*
Pantazzi, Michael 68, 76
Parisienne, La (Renoir) 30–37, *31*, 118, *119*
  acquired by Gwendoline Davies 16, 118
  acquired by Rouart 35, 36
  artistic style of 31, 114
  and composition 33–34
  critics, on 34, 35
  described 32–33
  detail *33*, *35*
  in Durand-Ruel exhibition (1892) 36
  model for 22, 34–35, 118 (see also Henriot, Henriette)
  modernity reflected in 22–23
  and painting size 33, 166(n31)
  pricing of 30, 35, 118
  in Société Anonyme exhibition (1874) 30–32, 34
  and women's fashion 32–33, *33*, *34*, *35*
Paris Salon 14, 126
  artists' boycott of 30
Philadelphia Museum of Art 102, 152
Phillips Collection, The (Washington, D.C.) 46, 158
Pissarro, Camille 25, 26, 116, 126
  Pont Neuf, Snow Effect, 2nd Series 21, 23–24, 116, 117
  in Société Anonyme exhibition (1874) 32, 166(n20)
Plas Dinam (Wales) 12–13, *14*, 15, 19
plein-air painting 44, 46, 58, 88, 90, 126, 130

Pointillism. *See* Neo-Impressionism (Pointillism)
Pond, The (Corot) 14, 24, 58, *59*, 60
Pont Neuf, Snow Effect, 2nd Series (Pissarro) 21, 23–24, 116, *117*
Porte aux Vaches by the Snow: Solitude, La (Millet) 102
Portrait of a Girl (Mancini) 16, *16*, 17
Post-Impressionism 26
  Manet and the Post-Impressionists exhibition (1910) 14, 27, *27*, 28, 29
  Second Post-Impressionist Exhibition (1912) 27, *27*, 29
  See also specific artist
Poussin, Nicolas *56*
Powell, Cecilia 146
Pre-Raphaelites 13, 27
Primitivism 18
Prouvaire, Jean 34, 35
Provençal Landscape (Cézanne) 18–19, 54, *55*, 156, 164(nn44, 45)
Pushkin Museum (Moscow) 158
Puvis de Chavannes 18, 164(n44)

Rabbit, The (Manet) *21*, 88, 163(n23)
Railway Bridge at Chatou, The (Renoir) 158
Rain–Auvers (van Gogh) 20, 26, 88, 152, *153*, *154–155*
Rainbow, The (Turner) 140, *141*, 148
"Rainy Day, The" (Longfellow) 152
Realism 24, 25
Redon, Odilon 50
Renoir, Pierre-Auguste 25, 88, 120
  artistic style of 26, 33–34
  Conversation 18, 120, *121*
  The Dancer 30, 31, *31*, 32, 33–34
  La Loge 30, 31, *31*, 166(n7)
  La Parisienne (*See Parisienne, La* (Renoir))
  Portrait of Madame Henriot 35, *37*, 118
  Riding in the Bois de Boulogne 30, *32*, 33, 35, 36, 37
  in Société Anonyme exhibition (1874) 30–32, 166(n21)
Riding in the Bois de Boulogne (Renoir) 30, 32, 33, 35, 36, 37
Rodin, Auguste 48
  The Kiss 16, *16*, 17, 163(n18)
Romanticism 62, 104
Romney, George 14, 90
Rothenstein, William 84
Rouart, Stanislas-Henri 35–37, 62, 94, 102, 104, 167(nn49, 50)
Rouen Cathedral: Setting Sun (Monet) 18, 19, *19*
Rousseau, Théodore 94, 104
Royal Academy of Arts (London) 138

Royal Museum of Fine Arts (Copenhagen) 104
Rudier, Alexis 17
Ruskin, John 110, 160
Rye, Sussex (Turner) 136, *137*

Sackville Gallery (London) 28
Saedeleer, Valerius de 17, 164(n40)
St. Tropez (Signac) 26, 126, *127*, *128–129*
Salon. *See* Paris Salon
San Giorgio Maggiore by Twilight (Monet) 15, *15*
Seated Girl (Stevens) 134, *135*
Seated Shepherdess, The (Millet) 66, 94, *95*, 102
Second Post-Impressionist Exhibition (1912) 27, *27*, 29
Seguin, Armand
  Breton Peasant Women at Mass 20, 112, 122, *123*
Seiler, Carl 92
Self-Portrait (John) 18, 82, 84, *85*
Sérusier, Paul 122
Seurat, Georges 26, 126
Shanes, Eric 140
Shepherdess, The (Mauve) 66, 90, *91*, 102
Sickert, Walter Richard 42, 132, 162(n4)
  on Millet 25, 104
  Palazzo Eleanora Duse, Venice 20, 124, *125*
Signac, Paul 26
  on Renoir's *La Parisienne* 30, 36, 167(n54)
  St. Tropez 26, 126, *127*, *128–129*
Silvestre, Armand 34
Sisley, Alfred 25, 130
  Moret-sur-Loing (Rue de Fosses) 20, 25, 112, 130, *131*, 168(n85)
Slade School of Fine Art (London) 13, 82, 84, 132
Smith, Matthew
  Apples on a Wicker Chair 132, *133*
Société Anonyme exhibition (1874) 30–32, 34, 35, 36, 166(n20), 167(n49)
Société des Artistes Indépendants 126
Sotheby's 148
Spencer, Stanley 132
Stevens, Alfred (Emile Léopold)
  Seated Girl 134, *135*
Still Life with Teapot (Cézanne) 20, 21, *21*
Storm, The (Turner) 14, 144, 150, *151*, 163(n20)
Sunlight at Vernon (Bonnard) 20, 44, *45*, 112, 130, 156, 168(n85)
Symbolism 22, 44, 48, 164(n40)

Tate Gallery (London) 52, 132, 142
Third Class Carriage, A (Daumier) 76, *77*
Thomas Jones (1870–1955) (Artôt) 17, 18, *18*
Thomson, David Croal 16, 138, 140, 148
Three Sketches of Heads in Chalk (Daumier) 74, *75*
Tucker, Paul Hayes 88
Turner, Joseph Mallord William
  artistic influence of 48, 106, 130
  Fort de l'Esseillon, Val de la Maurienne 142, *143*
  The Leyen Burg at Gondorf 146, *147*
  Margate 14, 138, *139*
  Morning after the Wreck 144, *145*
  The Rainbow 140, *141*, 148
  Rye, Sussex 136, *137*
  The Storm 14, 144, 150, *151*, 163(n20)
  Würzburg 140, 148, *149*
Two Studies for the Return of the Prodigal Son (Daumier) 64, 74, *75*

University College of Wales, Aberystwyth 12, 16, 21
Urquhart, Murray 16, 17, 21

Van de Woestyne, Gustave 17, 164(n40)
Venice, The Molo (Boudin) 16, 46, *47*
Victoria Art Gallery (Bath) 19, 122, 164(n47)
Village in Clohars (Moret) 20, 112, *113*
Village Street (Vlaminck) 80, 156, *157*, 158
Vlaminck, Maurice de 26, 156
  The Bridge 80, 156, 158, *159*
  Village Street 80, 156, *157*, 158
Vorticism 28, 29, 42
Vuillard, Edouard 36, 122, 167(n54)

Wallis & Son gallery (London) 14, 16, 68, 94, 96, 102, 134, 163(nn22, 29)
Warrell, Ian 140, 144
Watering Place, The (Daumier) 70, *71*
Waterlilies (Monet) 16, 25, 106, 108, *109*
Welsh Outlook (journal) 16, 18, 164(n36)
Whistler, James Abbott McNeill 134
  artistic influence of 106, 124
  Nocturne: Blue and Gold, St. Mark's Venice 15, 46, 160, *161*
William Andrews Clark (Chase) *26*, *27*
Wilson, Richard 20, 165(n54)
Winter: The Faggot Gatherers (Millet) 14, 94, 102, *103*
Würzburg (Turner) 140, 148, *149*

Young, Alexander 40, 96

Zborowska, Hanka (Anna) 80, *81*
Zborowski, Léopold 80, 156
Zola, Emile 27, 32, 34